For my grandchildren
Robert, Mary, Emma and Jacob

....

Acknowledgements

Fifth edition

The reception of the four previous editions of this book has been gratifying and I am glad to report an alternative edition – in Russian. It is clear that a wide-ranging exploration of Christianity, in a paperback of reasonable size, is attractive to many people. I welcome the opportunity this new edition gives me of adding to the text, updating some information and contributing to the website (www.teachyourself.com). I'm glad, too, to thank my editor Helen Rogers – and to have this further opportunity of recording my gratitude and indebtedness to Harry Scoble of Hodder, and my colleague, Carrie Geddes. I am delighted that Archbishops Rowan Williams and John Sentamu have commended the book, and gladly record my thanks to them both.

John Young, York, UK

Fourth edition

I am very grateful to Hodder Education – especially Lisa Grey and Harry Scoble – for their encouragement and practical help. Dr Peter Brierley responded promptly to a stream of requests for up-to-date statistical information, for which I am also extremely grateful. Above all, my thanks go to Carrie Geddes for her total commitment in typing drafts and helping to research information, check facts and correct proofs.

Previous editions

On reflection, I am surprised at just how many people have been involved in producing one book of modest size. I am extremely grateful to them for reading drafts of the proofs and for making many valuable suggestions, and I hope they will not be embarrassed at being publicly associated with the finished work:

Dr David Barrett, Dr Peter Brierley of *Christian Research*, Fr Cyril Brooks OSB, Pastor Iain Collins, Fr Bill East, Nicky Enticknap, Nigel Forde, Revd Dr Michael Frost, Carrie Geddes, Christopher Idle, Jacquie Lawless, Duncan McInnes, Brother Patrick Moore FSC, Revd David Mullins, Revd Dr John Polkinghorne KBE FRS, Bishop Stephen Robson, David and Sheana Steels, Dr Alison Wray and Chris Woodcock.

My special thanks are due to three friends who agreed to write specific chapters and then bravely submitted themselves to my editorial control:

- ▶ *The Revd Canon John Cockerton, Chapter 7*
- ▶ *The Revd Canon Dr John Toy, Chapters 12 and 19*
- ▶ *The Revd Canon Dr Peter Williams, Chapters 15, 16, 17 and 18*

I wish to record my gratitude to Catherine Coe, my editor, for her patience, expertise and wise judgement. Needless to say I am also indebted to the many Christian leaders who have commended this book (see pages v and vi). Above all, to Yolande Clarke, Linda Norman, Carolyn Prestwick, Barbara Thompson and Sharon Winfield, upon whom I came to depend for endless drafts and carefully researched information – one immense THANK YOU.

The author and publishers would like to thank the following for their kind permission to reproduce extracts from copyright material:

The Central Board of Finance of the Church of England for *The Mystery of Salvation*, Church House Publishing, 1995; HarperCollins Publishers Ltd for *Surprised by Joy* by C S Lewis; Darton, Longman and Todd for *School for Prayer* by Metropolitan Anthony of Sourozh (Archbishop Anthony Bloom); Hodder & Stoughton Ltd for *With Hope In Our Hearts* by David Sheppard and Derek Warlock;

Newspaper Publishing plc for an article by William Rees-Mogg, *The Independent*, 21 December 1992; Oxford University Press for *The Oxford Dictionary of Saints* edited by David Hugh Farmer, 3rd edition, 1992; SCM Press Ltd for *Our Faith* by Emil Brunner, 1936, and *Introducing the Christian Faith* by A M Ramsey, revised edn 1970; SPCK for *The Way the World Is* by John Polkinghorne, *The Resurrection of Jesus* by Pinchas Lapide, *Who Was Jesus?* by N T Wright, *The Lantern and the Looking-Glass* by Nigel Forde, and *To Be a Pilgrim* by Basil Hume; Times Newspapers Limited for 'Odds on God's fine tuning' by Clifford Longley, *The Times*, 13 April 1991 © Times Newspapers Limited, 1991; the *Church Times* for the use of a letter by P K M M'Pherson, © *Church Times*, 12 April 2002.

What they said about previous editions

An exciting, engaging and intellectually serious book that gives a really comprehensive picture of how Christians behave, what they think and how they believe their faith makes a difference in today's world. John Young offers us a first-class survey of doctrine and history along with a sympathetic account of prayer and ethics as Christians understand them.

The Archbishop of Canterbury, Dr Rowan Williams

This is a well-researched, accessible guide to the central themes of the Christian faith. It is not only a useful resource to those exploring Christianity for the first time, but I'm sure experienced believers will find it a most invaluable point of reference.

The Archbishop of York, Dr John Sentamu

I am very happy to commend this comprehensive work, which provides a wealth of information for people who seek to know more about the Christian faith.

Former Cardinal Archbishop of Westminster, Cormac Murphy-O'Connor

John Young has written an invaluable guide to the history of Christianity and the story of its founder and I warmly commend it.

Former Archbishop of Canterbury, Dr George Carey

John Young's Teach Yourself Christianity *not only informs, it excites, and in so doing invites the reader on a journey of discovery.*

Former Archbishop of York, Dr David Hope

You could find no better guide than John Young to teach yourself the Christian faith. This important book is highly readable and gives the reader access to the heart of the Christian story.

Bishop James Jones

A tour de force!

Bishop John Finney

Excellent material ... timely and right on target. There is a crying need for such a book.

Bishop Michael Marshall

John Young has that happy knack of explaining complicated things simply ... Teach Yourself Christianity will inform and stimulate any reader and could also usefully form the basis of a group study course on the Christian faith.

Revd Brian Hoare, former President of the Methodist Conference

An amazing compilation succinctly put together with examples and stories at regular intervals to make the whole thing come alive. Brilliant!

Dr Peter Brierley, Executive Director of Christian Research

Teach Yourself Christianity ... *should find its place on every pastor's and lay person's shelf!*
Alan Palmer, Director of Open Learning

Oak Hill College

John Young's excellent book deserves a place on every reader's shelves ... Nearly all of us will be able to learn from it more about the difficult art of expressing theological truths with profundity and accuracy, yet with a simplicity of language which reflects the wonder and mystery of God.

Archdeacon Emeritus, the Venerable Leslie Stanbridge

Excellently produced at a most reasonable price.

Canon Michael Howard

I think it's brilliant! Whether you are a preacher, pastor, student or enquirer this exceptionally useful book will often be your first port of call.

Bishop Stephen Cottrell

Contents

Meet the author   ix
Only got a minute?   x
Only got five minutes?   xii
Preface   xv

Part one: The central figure
1   **Jesus Christ**   3
2   **Crucified Saviour**   26
3   **Risen Lord**   43
4   **The Bible: contents**   61
5   **The Bible: questions**   78

Part two: Christian belief and practice
6   **Christian experience of God**   101
7   **Prayer and worship**   117
8   **The Sacraments**   135
9   **Facing death: the four last things**   155
10 **Christian faith in a scientific age**   172

Part three: The Christian Church
11 **Saints, martyrs, sins and virtues**   193
12 **One Church, many churches**   212
13 **Modern movements**   237
14 **Church and society**   259

Part four: Key events in Church history
15 **The first five centuries**   283
16 **One thousand turbulent years: AD 500–1500**   299
17 **The Reformation**   317
18 **To the present day**   330

Part five: A great inheritance

19	Holy places, art and architecture	351
20	Music and literature	367
21	Modern lives	383
	Glossary	388
	Taking it further	394
	Index	398

Meet the author

Welcome to *Christianity – An Introduction*.

I've had a variety of jobs – paperboy, hospital porter, farmhand, soldier (National Service), teacher, lecturer, occasional broadcaster and journalist, author, Anglican minister. My early ambition to be a professional footballer remains unfulfilled thus far ...

I have a love-hate relationship with writing (it's hard work!) but to my surprise I've written over 30 books/booklets and around half a million copies of these are in circulation. My work has been translated into several languages, including Chinese and Russian.

I worked for two Archbishops of York, and was a member of the General Synod of the Church of England for many years. Today I'm a Canon Emeritus of York Minster. I've travelled fairly widely, and so have first-hand experience of Christianity in countries other than Britain, where I live. I've preached in some of Britain's great cathedrals – including St Paul's, where the entire back row got up and walked out. (I like to think they were tourists who had a bus to catch, but ...)

It's been a huge privilege to broadcast occasionally on BBC Radio 2, Radio 4 and the World Service. A personal highlight was when Radio 4 selected a modern 'parable' which I'd written and presented on local radio, for its prestigious programme *Pick of the Week*.

Arising from my work as a broadcaster and co-founder of *York Courses*, I've interviewed a number of eminent Christians including the Archbishop of Canterbury, Professor Sir John Houghton (climatologist) and Revd Dr John Polkinghorne (former Professor of Mathematical Physics at Cambridge University). These conversations are available on CD from www.yorkcourses.co.uk.

(Revd Canon) John Young, 2010

Only got a minute?

Christianity is the world religion which is based on the life and ministry of Jesus, who is also called Jesus Christ ('Christ' means *Messiah*).

At the heart of Christianity there is a profound puzzle. For this huge and influential movement is based upon an apparent failure.

Jesus died young. He suffered a terrible, shameful death. He left no writings. The only record of his life and teaching was in the memories of his followers. When the pressure was on, they drifted away. One betrayed him; another denied all knowledge of him.

The movement he founded had never been very large, even after three years in the public eye. By the time of his death it had crumbled to nothing – apart from a few demoralized, frightened friends. It looked like just one more heroic – but futile – attempt to stand against authority.

Yet the stubborn fact remains. From that hopeless beginning, the movement grew. And grew. And grew. It became the largest, most influential movement of all time. The world dates its calendar from its Founder's birth.

These are facts that cry out for adequate explanation. The explanation given in the Bible is the only one that gets near to solving this immense puzzle. Three days after Roman soldiers nailed Jesus to the cross, God raised him from the dead. Jesus defeated death. This glorious event has huge implications for all of us. It is celebrated at Easter – the Church's greatest festival. A few weeks later (at Pentecost) God sent the Holy Spirit – the Spirit of Jesus himself – into the hearts and lives of his followers.

No longer afraid and dismayed, they told the world about God's love revealed in Jesus. The long – and fascinating – story of Christianity had begun ...

5 Only got five minutes?

The great scientist Albert Einstein said this about Jesus of Nazareth : 'I am a Jew, but I am enthralled by the luminous figure of the Nazarene ... No one can read the Gospels without feeling the actual presence of Jesus. His personality pulsates in every word. No myth is filled with such life.'

Over the centuries, Christianity has encountered many problems – practical, pastoral, intellectual, ethical. The movement has grown. And it has divided.

From the earliest days, the most important factor leading to growth has been the attractive lifestyle of believers. The Roman Empire was characterized by harshness and indifference. Christians were 'counter cultural'. They were tough – sometimes dying for their faith. But they showed love and forgiveness, which proved stronger than brutality and revenge. Early in its history the Church showed practical care – sharing possessions and organizing food programmes.

Christianity continues to grow today. While the Church struggles to maintain its membership and influence in Western Europe, the worldwide Church is growing fast – especially in Africa, the Americas and Asia (notably China).

The Church has divided for a variety of reasons – cultural, doctrinal, political ... Today's Church is divided into Roman Catholic, Orthodox, Protestant, Anglican, Pentecostal and Independent. The World Council of Churches, as well as numerous local initiatives, ensures that Christians talk, relate and work together across these divisions.

Christianity has survived severe persecution, whether by Roman emperors or under Nazism and Marxism. Above all, it has *adapted* – adapted to every culture, making it clear that ALL are welcome. In its earliest days, St Paul insisted that Christianity was for *everyone* regardless of nationality, gender or social class: *'There is neither Jew nor Greek, slave nor free, male nor female, for you are all one in Christ Jesus.'* (Galatians 3:28.)

Alongside these great truths, Christians have to face other, harsher, facts. For the Church has also been associated with terrible episodes such as the Crusades and Inquisition. At times, men with no regard for the teaching of Christ, whose lives were untouched by the Spirit of Christ, have nevertheless held high office in the Church of Christ.

The Bible has been read, studied and discussed. Its teaching has been applied to the many 'hot' issues thrown up in every generation and by every culture. Sometimes the Church has taken a wrong turning. It has also achieved great things in the name of Christ.

Christianity laid the foundations for modern science and modern democracy. It has transformed lives. It has founded hospitals and monasteries, schools and universities. Its members have started great movements – Save the Children, Amnesty International, the modern hospice movement … Inspired by their faith, great Christians such as William Wilberforce, Lord Shaftesbury and Elizabeth Fry fought slavery, established factory Acts and transformed prisons.

It is the largest movement in all history. The Christian Church is found on every continent. Over two million people – about one third of the world's population – call themselves 'Christian'. The Christian faith has inspired – and continues to inspire – heroic and holy lives, great art, amazing buildings and wonderful music.

Great composers such as J.S. Bach have written music to the glory of God. The greatest poets and authors have embraced Christian themes. Renowned architects, fine craftsmen and heroic labourers have built in praise of the Creator and Sustainer of all things.

World politicians (such as Barack Obama) and civil rights leaders (of the calibre of Martin Luther King) have gained courage and conviction from Jesus Christ. Ordinary people have done ordinary – and extraordinary – things in the name of the One whom they acknowledge as their Lord and Saviour.

Christianity has inspired worship in many styles. It has nurtured reflection and prayer. It has helped millions to die in faith, with fortitude – and with the hope of Heaven in their hearts.

This book is about this extraordinary and far-reaching movement. It is a 'warts and all' account of the most influential phenomenon of all time.

Preface

To the surprise of many observers, in the twenty-first century religion is front page news. However, interest in the world's great Faiths is not matched by knowledge. So a survey of the Christian faith is timely. But is it possible?

Anyone who attempts to write about 2000 years of Christianity in one volume is open to the charge of arrogance, ignorance or folly. Is he not aware that the Christian faith has generated thousands of books, because it has influenced almost every aspect of life over two millennia?

That was my first response on being invited to write this book for the *Teach Yourself* series. But I was pleased to accept, because I am aware that there are certain crucial facts and key events which deserve to be more widely known. My judgement as to what these are (see the topics included or omitted) is certainly open to question. Another author would have tackled the task differently.

Throughout this volume I am as concerned with 'feel' as with fact. What is it about the Christian faith that attracts people? Why do so many, more today than ever before, respond to the invitation of Jesus of Nazareth to 'Come, follow me'?

There has been, and is, much that is shameful in the life of the Church. It is not surprising that many turn away. But I hope that by the end of this book, readers will have a clearer idea as to why millions continue to embrace the Christian way of being human.

How to use this book

To some, this will be obvious. They will start at Chapter 1 and read one chapter each day for three weeks. Others, however, may choose to tackle the book differently.

For example, some readers may be particularly interested in a survey of Church History and will begin at Chapter 15. Others might omit the historical chapters (15–18) altogether. Whatever their particular interests, it is my hope that *all* readers will tackle Chapters 1, 2, 3, 6 and 21, together with pages 342–7. These passages attempt to give some idea of the significance for Christians of Jesus Christ, and to provide a glimpse of what it means to be a Christian today.

Throughout the book I have given Bible references. Those who wish to look these up are advised to use a good modern translation. I would recommend the *New Revised Standard Version*, the *New Jerusalem Bible* (an official Roman Catholic translation) or *The New International Version* (NIV). Most Bible quotations in this book are taken from the NIV and NRSV.

An attempt has been made to explain technical terms in the text itself. Reference has also been made to other chapters which refer to related issues. There is a short **Glossary** at the end of the book, as well as an **Index**.

I have used a wide range of books and I am grateful for permission to quote from several. At the end of this book is a **Taking it further** section for those who wish to find out more. On some topics in this book I have written elsewhere (especially in *The Case Against Christ*).

Part one
The central figure

1

Jesus Christ

In this chapter you will learn:

- *about the immense impact and significance of Jesus*
- *about the puzzle presented by Jesus' life and teaching*
- *about the wide testimony to his greatness.*

> *For me, no other subject can rival its scale and drama. For 2000 years Christianity has been one of the great players in world history, inspiring faith, but also squalid politics. It is an epic story, starring a cast of extraordinary people, from Jesus himself and the first apostles, to empresses, kings and popes; to reformers and champions of human conscience; to crusaders and sadists. Religious belief can transform us for good or ill. It has brought human beings to acts of criminal folly as well as the highest achievements of goodness and creativity … Today there are two billion Christians – a third of humanity … In modern Europe Christianity seems threatened by the apathy of a secular society. Will it survive? Can it?*
>
> Professor Diarmaid MacCulloch, *A History of Christianity*
> (broadcast on BBC television in 2009)

The impact of Jesus

Professor Hans Küng, a leading Christian scholar, makes the following points about Jesus Christ and the faith which bears his name:

> *None of the great founders of religions lived in so restricted an area. None lived for such a terribly short time. None died so*

young. And yet how great his influence has been ... Numerically,
Christianity is well ahead of all world religions.

(*On Being a Christian*, Collins)

This is not quoted in a spirit of competitive superiority; it is
nothing more nor less than a statement of significant fact. In
considering the Christian faith, we are studying the largest
movement in history. Christianity has exercised tremendous
influence (for good and ill) upon our world.

Jesus has been the focus of more study, more controversy and more
art than any other figure. He is the one who has 'chopped history
in half': BC *before Christ*; AD *Anno Domini* – in the year of Our
Lord (sometimes called CE or *Common Era*). In today's world,
millions of people – from every continent and nearly every country –
claim some allegiance to him. Christians make up about one-third
of the world's population.

Ralph Waldo Emerson, the American essayist, summed up the
significance of Jesus when he said that his impact is not so much
written on, as *ploughed into*, the history of the world. All this is
remarkable enough. But when we consider the short and rather
obscure life of Jesus, it becomes extraordinary. However, according
to the Bible, there were clear indications of his greatness even
before his birth.

Insight

Many famous individuals outside the Church have found
inspiration and moral direction in Jesus. For example,
H.G. Wells, Mahatma Gandhi and Albert Einstein. They
honour him as a great teacher whose name has been
'ploughed into' the history of the world.

The life of Jesus

According to St Luke's Gospel, the story began in the district of
Galilee in Israel. A young woman, betrothed but not yet married

to a man called Joseph, was visited by the angel Gabriel. He announced (hence 'the Annunciation' – beloved by medieval artists) that she had been chosen by God to give birth to a son who was to be called Jesus. Troubled as Mary was by this news ('How will this be, since I am a virgin?') she declared herself ready to do God's will: 'I am the Lord's Servant' (Luke 1:38).

The child was due to be born at the time of a Roman census. For Mary and Joseph this entailed a journey of about 70 miles from Nazareth to Bethlehem near Jerusalem. The baby was born in Bethlehem and he was visited by local shepherds and wise men from eastern lands; a choir from heaven celebrated the birth. King Herod, on hearing from the eastern travellers of the birth of 'a king', tried to kill the infant Jesus. But Mary, Joseph and Jesus ('the holy family') escaped to Egypt and so fulfilled a prophecy (Matthew 2:15). Eventually they returned to Nazareth, where Joseph earned his living as a carpenter – a craft which he taught his son.

The Birth Narratives raise questions

Why do only two of the four Gospels (see Chapters 4 and 5) carry these narratives?

And why are these two accounts so different: one focusing on Mary, the other on Joseph?

Are we intended to read these accounts of the birth of Jesus as history?

Or are they a particular kind of story, alerting readers to the fact that this child is very special indeed?

We are told little about the early years of Jesus, apart from one visit to Jerusalem when he was 12 years old. On that occasion Jesus went to the Temple, where he listened to the teachers and asked and answered questions: 'Everyone who heard him was amazed at his understanding and his answers' (Luke 2:47).

We learn nothing more for nearly 20 years, when Jesus was baptized by his cousin John ('the Baptist') in the river Jordan. At his baptism, a voice from heaven declared, 'This is my Son, whom I love; with him I am well pleased' (Matthew 3:17). Then Jesus was led by God's Spirit into the desert where he fasted and wrestled with the devil for 40 days. This time of temptation was to fashion the shape of his ministry. Now he was ready.

After spending a night in prayer, Jesus called 12 disciples and set out on his travels around his small country. He began his ministry in his home area in the north, in the towns, villages and countryside around the Lake of Galilee. The four Gospels record some of his deeds and words. Jesus healed people with a wide range of diseases: a paralysed man, a man with leprosy, a woman who suffered from excessive bleeding, a man possessed by a demon. He even raised the dead (Luke 7:15; John 11:43).

He also showed power over nature: he turned water into wine, stilled a storm, and fed a huge crowd from five loaves and two fish. Jesus became known as a powerful and controversial teacher, who was willing to challenge established traditions. All this made him famous and popular. Time for rest, solitude and prayer was limited, but he 'often withdrew to lonely places and prayed' (Luke 5:16).

The teaching of Jesus

Insight

Jesus is renowned as a great teacher. He brings comfort to the oppressed and sorrowful. But his words carry a sharp moral challenge for the way we live and relate to other people. Jesus makes it clear that his teaching is for *everyone* – not just pious and devout people.

Christianity is based not only on ideas, but on events. At its centre we do not find a theory, but a person: Jesus Christ. Many people have a sentimental picture of Jesus. They view him as a rather anaemic character, more interested in flowers, birds and children than in the harsh world of adult reality. How different is the towering figure of the New Testament. We see there:

▶ *a man marked out as a dangerous rebel by the authorities*
▶ *a man who drew large crowds*
▶ *a man who inspired others*
▶ *a man who took the uncompromising road to martyrdom*
▶ *a man of deep passion and decisive action.*

The Gospels assure us that Jesus *was* interested in children and in nature. And with the down-trodden he was very gentle. But the world he inhabited was a harsh world of hatred, intrigue, brutality and revenge. The Gospels portray a dynamic figure who waged war against evil with the weapons of love, openness, honesty and forgiveness. His honesty was fearless. Against those greatest sins of pride, hypocrisy and indifference, his attack was blistering and devastating.

Jesus did not set out to be an 'original' teacher. As a Jew he stood in a tradition which was steeped in the Hebrew Scriptures (known to Christians as the Old Testament). He drew on those Scriptures and his central demands – that we should love God with all our heart and our neighbour as ourselves – link two separate Old Testament texts (Deuteronomy 6:5; Leviticus 19:18). This was his genius: to make new connections, to bring fresh emphases, to take old ideas and give them new content, to reveal the deeper meaning which was latent within them.

The Sermon on the Mount

Jesus' Sermon on the Mount (Matthew 5–7: page 14) starts with a series of Beatitudes:

(Contd)

Blessed are the poor in spirit for theirs is the kingdom of heaven.

Blessed are those who mourn for they shall be comforted.

Blessed are the meek for they will inherit the earth...

The Sermon also contains:

- a breathtaking call to love and forgiveness: 'But I tell you: Love your enemies and pray for those who persecute you ... For if you forgive those who sin against you, your heavenly Father will also forgive you' (Matthew 5:44; 6:14)
- an encouragement to faith in God: 'So do not worry, saying, "What shall we eat?" or "What shall we wear?" ... your heavenly Father knows that you need them' (Matthew 6:31)
- an encouragement to pray: 'Ask and it will be given to you; seek and you will find; knock and the door will be opened to you' (Matthew 7:7)
- an uncompromising call to accept Jesus' teaching: 'But everyone who hears these words of mine and does not put them into practice is like a foolish man who built his house on sand' (Matthew 7:26).

The Kingdom of God

Jesus spoke frequently about 'the Kingdom of God' or 'the Kingdom of heaven'. This idea is certainly found in the Jewish Scriptures. But Jesus put it at the *centre* of his teaching and illustrated (but never defined) its meaning with a series of brilliant, yet often puzzling, pictures and parables. In this way he made his hearers, and now his readers, think very hard.

The kingdom of heaven is like treasure hidden in a field. When a man found it, he hid it again, and then in his joy went and sold all he had and bought that field. Again, the kingdom of heaven is like a merchant looking for fine pearls. When he found one of great value, he went away and sold everything he had and bought it.

(Matthew 13:44–46)

Jesus made it clear that his notion of God's kingly rule was very different from the popular views of his time. His country was under enemy occupation. The hated Romans were in charge and there were many Jews who looked for armed revolt. Their nation had a famous history of success on the battlefield; perhaps this teacher would be the new military leader? To those who wanted to go down that road, Jesus was a great disappointment: 'My kingdom is not of this world' (John 18:36). In *his* Kingdom, disciples would turn the other cheek and leadership must be characterized by humble service.

MIRACLES OF THE KINGDOM

Many miracles are recorded in the Gospels, demonstrating Jesus' power over sickness, sin, nature, demons and death. When his enemies accused him of healing by Satan's power he replied, 'But if I drive out demons by the finger of God, then the kingdom of God has come to you' (Luke 11:20).

God's kingly rule was present because Jesus was present. But his ministry was also the sign of a future in which God's kingly rule would be fulfilled and consummated. One day the 'Son of Man' (see Glossary) will come 'in his Father's glory with the holy angels' (Mark 8:38). *Now* and *not yet* are held in balance.

PARABLES OF THE KINGDOM

Jesus became famous for his stories or parables. A parable is a story which works on two levels. It is 'an earthly story with a heavenly meaning'. At one level it is an interesting tale with strong human interest. But the story has a deeper meaning and a personal application. Jesus' hearers are usually left to work this out for themselves. Some parables convey the notion of *growth*. Others convey a sense of *crisis*: decisions must be made, sides must be taken. Jesus' stories are usually about people:

- ▶ *a woman who lost a coin (Luke 15:8)*
- ▶ *a woman who badgered a judge for justice (Luke 18:1)*
- ▶ *a man who built a tower (Luke 14:28)*

- ▶ a farmer who scattered seed (Mark 4:3)
- ▶ a Samaritan traveller who cared for a man who was mugged and robbed (Luke 10:25)
- ▶ a young man who left home and squandered his money ('the Prodigal Son') before returning to a father who forgave him and a brother who resented him (Luke 15:11).

The best known parables are The Good Samaritan and The Prodigal Son. The former is not just an exhortation to compassion and kindness (though it is that). It is a strong attack upon racism and bigotry. Samaritans were widely despised by Jews and vice versa. Jesus was taking a huge risk in making a *Samaritan* the hero, in contrast to the establishment figures of his own race and religion. Here were the seeds of conflict with the authorities which would end in his death by crucifixion.

'The teaching of Jesus stands on an Everest alone. No other teaching has had the same impact and influence, in countless lives and diverse cultures. No other teaching has provoked so much change, or stirred so much debate.'   (Professor Sir Norman Anderson)

'With every sceptical faculty alive and kicking I do believe that nearly 2000 years ago, in the land we today call Israel, the "word"… was made flesh and dwelt in a Galilean Jew called Jesus … for a brief moment in history there was magic in the air. The sick were healed, men and women caught a glimpse of heaven, all too good of course to last.'   (Ian Wilson)

Alec McCowen, the British actor, set out to memorize St Mark's account of the ministry and death of Jesus – as a hobby! To his surprise, large audiences around the world wanted to hear his recitation of the life of Jesus, taken straight from the Bible. When asked what he made of the story he replied: 'Something absolutely marvellous happened in Palestine 2000 years ago.'

The anguish of the Prodigal Son is captured powerfully by the sculptor Rodin, whose bronze figure of the Prodigal is in the Tate Collection. Archbishop Desmond Tutu describes the significance of this story with typical vigour and enthusiasm:

> *What a tremendous relief ... to discover that we don't need to prove ourselves to God. That is what Jesus came to say, and for that he got killed ... The Good News is that God loves me long before I could have done anything to deserve it. He is like the father of the prodigal son, waiting anxiously for the return of his wayward son ... That is tremendous stuff – that is the Good News. Whilst we were yet sinners, says St Paul, Christ died for us. God did not wait until we were die-able for He could have waited until the cows come home.*
>
> (*Hope and Suffering*, Desmond Tutu, Collins)

The parable of the Prodigal Son could equally well be entitled *The Forgiving Father*. Again, the notion of God as Father was familiar to Jesus' contemporaries. But Jesus underlined its importance, stressing both the *rule* and the *love* of God.

He emphasized his own close relationship with God and taught that discipleship cannot be reduced to a set of rules. At its centre is a relationship with the living God, who is 'your Heavenly Father' – to be loved and trusted. But a loving father is not a doting uncle.

Insight

In his parables, Jesus focuses on the possibility of forgiveness and a fresh start. No one is beyond the love and grace of God. The key is not 'keeping the rules' but building a relationship with God our 'Heavenly Father' and adopting the radical values of the Kingdom of God.

Much of Jesus' teaching is uncompromising in its moral and spiritual demands:

▶ *turn the other cheek (Matthew 5:39)*
▶ *go the extra mile (Matthew 5:41)*
▶ *judge not or you will be judged (Matthew 7:1)*
▶ *forgive seventy times seven (Matthew 18:22)*
▶ *sell your possessions and give to the poor (Mark 10:21).*

His teaching makes intellectual demands too. Jesus did not spoonfeed his largely uneducated audience; he respected their intelligence. He often said things that he did not mean! By exaggeration and paradox Jesus left, and leaves, his hearers thinking furiously, 'He can't really mean *that*. So just what does he mean ...':

- ▶ *let the dead bury their dead (Matthew 8:22)*
- ▶ *become like a little child (Matthew 18:3)*
- ▶ *cut off a foot rather than allow it to lead to sin (Mark 9:45)*
- ▶ *hate your father and mother (Luke 14:26)*
- ▶ *you must be born again (John 3:3).*

A father's love includes discipline as well as encouragement. Hence Jesus taught us to *trust* God, to *love* God and to *fear* God – to hold him in respect and awe, for God *is* GOD. He emphasized that prayer, forgiveness, honesty, humility and generosity are all involved in accepting God's kingly rule in our lives. All this is summed up in the world's most famous prayer, given by Jesus in response to his disciples' request, 'Lord teach us to pray':

**Father, hallowed be your name,
your kingdom come.
Give us each day our daily bread.
Forgive us our sins, for we also
forgive everyone who sins against us.
And lead us not into temptation.** (Luke 11:2; see Matthew 6:9–13)

Early Christian testimony to Jesus

Inevitably, it fell to the followers of Jesus to write about his life, his death, and his remarkable impact. This need not detract from the reliability of these accounts. Many of the finest, most detailed studies of great people have come from their friends or followers (Boswell on Dr Johnson, for example). Of course we make allowances for bias. But we also recognize that close friends have detailed, accurate information.

The four Gospel writers are called 'Evangelists' because that word means 'bringer of good news'. They do not claim to be objective reporters. They are convinced of the immense significance of Jesus and want to convince others. St John makes this quite clear when he disarmingly admits that 'these [signs] are written that you may believe that Jesus is the Christ, the Son of God, and that by believing you may have life in his name' (John 20:31).

At the same time, they insist that they are recording the truth about Jesus. There was no need to exaggerate, because Jesus was big enough already! Of course, they did not have recording equipment. They were dependent upon memories, stories and records. But Middle Eastern memories were good (and still are: many Muslims today can recite the entire *Qur'an* from memory). And there were enough eyewitnesses to act as a check on wild exaggeration.

There is lively debate among scholars concerning the way in which the first Christians regarded Jesus of Nazareth. To cite one celebrated theological question: is the 'Jesus of history' the same as the 'Christ of faith'? Some scholars believe that the early Christians used Jesus' teaching freely, adapting it to their own purposes; even inventing sayings of their own. Others are convinced that the first believers treated his teaching with great reverence and took trouble to remember and record it accurately (page 85). They also point out that it would take someone of the stature of Jesus to invent the teaching of Jesus.

The gospels (we are told) are faith-documents: therefore, they are not about history. The gospels are the product of long theological reflection: therefore, they are not biographies. The first thing to be said to this is that these are false alternatives ... the theological reflection which they offer is emphatically Jewish. Like Jesus himself, they wear their Jewish ancestry on page after page. And the great thing about first-century Judaism ... was its concentration on history.

(*Who Was Jesus?* N T Wright, SPCK)

The authority of Jesus

'... the crowds were amazed at his teaching, because he taught as one who had authority, and not as their teachers of the law'

(Matthew 7:28–29). Jesus quickly established himself as a popular, unconventional and controversial teacher. The established leadership felt threatened. No doubt his striking authority had its roots in his dynamic personality. But it was emphasized by the content of his teaching.

THE TEMPLE AND THE SABBATH

These were two of the foundation stones of Jewish society at the time of Jesus. He challenged the traditions which had grown up around them. It was Jesus' dramatic action in overturning the tables of the money-changers in the Temple precincts that led to his crucifixion, according to the influential American scholar E P Sanders. Jesus claimed to be greater than the Temple itself (Matthew 12:6), and greater than some important Old Testament characters, such as the prophet Jonah and King Solomon (Matthew 12:41–42). And he caused controversy by healing on the Sabbath. This drew the accusation that he disregarded the religious laws, because the Sabbath was a day of rest and healing the sick was regarded as work. In response, Jesus reminded his hearers that he was 'Lord even of the Sabbath' (Mark 2:28).

THE SERMON ON THE MOUNT

At the beginning of this famous discourse (page 7), Jesus declares a blessing on anyone who is persecuted 'for my sake'. In the middle he considers some important moral issues: murder, adultery, divorce, honesty, revenge and love. He refers to the established interpretation of the Jewish law ('you have heard that it was said to the people long ago') before giving his own interpretation ('... but I tell you': with the stress on the 'I'). In this way Jesus claims to be *the* authoritative interpreter of the sacred Law. Even more startling, on the final Day of Judgement people will address Jesus as 'Lord, Lord' and he will judge the nations. The sermon ends with a vivid picture of two men: one wise, the other foolish. What is the difference between them? The wise man 'hears these words of mine and puts them into practice' (Matthew 7:26).

THE LAST SUPPER

The supper which Jesus ate with his disciples (page 27) just before
his arrest and crucifixion, has been painted by countless artists –
most famously by Leonardo da Vinci. At this meal Jesus instituted
a new covenant 'in my blood'. 'Covenant' is an important biblical
term. It describes an 'agreement' between unequals: God and his
people. God was faithful to them; he required faithfulness from
them. But the nation had failed and a new covenant was needed.
Six hundred years before Jesus sat down to eat the Last Supper
with his disciples, the prophet Jeremiah had promised that God
would make a new, more glorious covenant. By his words and
actions, Jesus indicated that the great day had arrived at last – and
that he, Jesus, was the central figure.

RELATIONSHIP WITH GOD

In a beautiful and gentle passage, Jesus asserts that he alone knows
God and that he alone can reveal God (Matthew 11:25–29). He
frequently speaks of the Kingdom of God; occasionally he refers
to it as 'my kingdom' (Luke 22:30; John 18:36).

A PUZZLE

Here is a puzzle indeed! Jesus taught humility. He associated
with and served ordinary people. He chose fishermen for his close
companions. He lived a simple, rough life, and befriended outcasts
such as prostitutes and tax-collectors who collaborated with the
hated Romans. Yet in an unassuming way, he made explosive
claims. The New Testament scholar Bishop John Robinson
summed up:

> *He steps in the eyes of his contemporaries into the space reserved
> for God ... It is impossible to escape the conclusion that he went
> around not just talking about God (that would not have provoked
> the reaction he did) but standing in God's place, acting and
> speaking for him.* (Can We Trust the New Testament?, Mowbray)

To find such a humble man saying the sort of things which Jesus claimed for himself is puzzling, even shocking. It is to this puzzle that we turn next.

Jesus: more than a man?

> The New Testament emphasizes that Jesus experienced deep emotions – and that he was tempted, just like us. It emphasizes that Jesus is a real human being who understands the human condition 'from the inside'. Yet he resisted temptation at every point – demonstrating that temptation and sin are not the same (Luke 4:1–13 and Hebrews 4:14–16).
>
> Scholars have long debated whether the Gospels were written by people who saw and met Jesus. In 2009, Professor Richard Bauckham won the Michael Ramsay prize for his book *Jesus and the Eyewitnesses: The Gospels as eyewitness testimony*, which explores this question. He asks, 'When we read the Gospels, are we in touch with the real Jesus?' In contrast to many older scholars, he produces evidence and arguments which enable him to conclude with an emphatic 'Yes'.

All the New Testament writers assert the human nature of Jesus. Like us he got hungry, thirsty and tired. He experienced the full range of human emotions, including joy, sorrow and desolation. But attend a church service which includes the Nicene Creed and you will hear the congregation recite or sing these astonishing words:

> *We believe in one Lord, Jesus Christ,*
> *the only Son of God,*
> *eternally begotten of the Father,*
> *God from God, Light from Light,*
> *true God from true God,*
> *begotten, not made,*
> *of one Being with the Father;*
> *through him all things were made.*
> *For us and for our salvation*

> *he came down from heaven,*
> *was incarnate of the*
> *Holy Spirit and the Virgin Mary*
> *and was made man.*
> *For our sake he was crucified …*

This Jesus, a real human being, is the focus of Christian worship. Such worship contrasts sharply with all other great world religions. In speaking about Sikh attitudes to their Gurus in *Sikhism – An Introduction* (Hodder Education) Owen Cole writes: 'This can be summed up in one brief statement; profound respect falling well short of worship.' The same is true for the Muslim attitude to Muhammad. He is a great prophet, a key figure. But he is not to be worshipped. So Muslims dislike being called 'Muhammadans'. In contrast, Christians rejoice at the fact that their title links them so closely with Jesus Christ, whom they honour as 'my Lord and my God!' (John 20:28).

Insight

The impact of Jesus raises an immense puzzle. He lived a short life, taught in a small country, wrote nothing (except a few words in the sand) and died an apparent failure. Yet he is the best-known figure in history, followed – and worshipped – by billions. These are facts which cry out for adequate explanation.

The language of worship and praise is found throughout the New Testament. Even great words like Prophet and Messiah are not big enough for Jesus. The writers stretch language to its limits with terms like Son of God, Light of the World, Saviour, Emmanuel, Word made Flesh, Lord and God. All this raises three immense questions.

1 *WHERE DID THESE IDEAS COME FROM?*

The first disciples of Jesus were God-fearing Jews; strict monotheists. Frequently they recited the *Shema*: 'Hear, O Israel: the Lord our God is one Lord' (Deuteronomy 6:4). Notice: *one* Lord. Most Jews refused to embrace the Roman gods or to acknowledge the Roman emperor as divine, for that would mean denying their belief in *one* God. So we can sympathize with those Jews who objected to the exalted view of Jesus which came to be held by his followers. The notion that a man could be divine held no great problems for most Gentiles. But for Jews it was unthinkable. *Yet some of them came to think the unthinkable.* At the same time they insisted that they were monotheists, who continued to be loyal to the one true God.

In a remarkably short space of time, the early Christians came to the startling conclusion that Jesus was *divine* as well as human. This resulted partly from their belief in his resurrection (see Chapter 3). But their conclusion finds its seeds in the teaching of Jesus himself: in his teaching about authority and the Temple and the New Covenant which we noted earlier. Of course Jesus did not go around saying, 'I am God.' Indeed, he joyfully acknowledged his dependence upon God his 'heavenly Father'. He was no usurper. *But he did claim a unique relationship with God; he did claim a unique mission from God; and he did claim that he, and only he, was able to do things which it was proper only for God to do.*

In this way Jesus himself laid the foundations for the kind of language used about him in the New Testament and (later) in the Nicene and other Creeds. As the New Testament scholar Professor C H Dodd put it: *'His words carried divine authority and his actions were instinctive with divine power.'* Over the years the distinctive Christian view of God emerged. He is three 'Persons' in one God: Father, Son and Holy Spirit. This doctrine of the Trinity (page 114) was not invented by the early Christians; it has its seeds in the teaching of Jesus himself. Those seeds can be seen in bloom on other pages in the New Testament.

> ▸ *He is the image of the invisible God, the firstborn over all creation ... all things were created by him and for him.*
>
> (Colossians 1:15–16)

> ▸ *May the grace of the Lord Jesus Christ, and the love of God, and the fellowship of the Holy Spirit be with you all.* (2 Corinthians 13:14)

> ▸ *Your attitude should be the same as that of Christ Jesus:*
> *Who, being in very nature God,*
> *did not consider equality with God*
> *something to be grasped ...* (Philippians 2:5, 6)

> ▸ *Thomas said to him [Jesus], 'My Lord and my God!'* (John 20:28)

At the same time, the New Testament writers held that Jesus *was a real human being*. Their concern was to declare that God reveals himself through Jesus Christ – not to speculate on the innermost nature of God. Such speculation came later, as Christians pondered the relationship between Father, Son and Holy Spirit. The result of this mature consideration can be seen in the Nicene and other Creeds (pages 16, 293 and 388).

Insight

The New Testament was largely written by Jews – monotheists who drew a sharp distinction between God and human beings. It is therefore extraordinary that they speak of Jesus both as a real man *and* as the Lord who is to be worshipped and obeyed.

2 HOW CAN CHRISTIANITY RELATE TO OTHER FAITHS?

We live in a multifaith world. Tragically, this sometimes leads to strife, even war. For religious faith is a passionate business. It *matters* to those who practise it; it matters a lot. And, of course, over the centuries the world's religions have become linked to particular cultures and nations. So people fighting over territory or language or history or other issues sometimes seem to be fighting about religion – and sometimes are, of course.

One of the most important questions facing the modern world is: how can adherents of the great religions live together in harmony? Christians are called by Jesus to be *peacemakers* (Matthew 5:9) and many wish to contribute actively to establishing good interfaith relationships. This does not mean surrendering or 'fudging' distinctive beliefs. Dialogue is at its healthiest when the differences between faiths, as well as the similarities, are openly recognized.

At the theological (as distinct from social) level, interfaith dialogue raises sharp issues for Christians. For if Jesus Christ is the Son of God, the Light of the world and the Word made flesh, what are they to make of other faiths? Can other religions be regarded as equally valid vehicles of God's revelation? We shall consider this key question later (Chapter 14).

3 'WHO DO YOU SAY THAT I AM?' (MARK 8:29)

Any study of Christianity is bound to focus on Jesus Christ. And any study of Jesus leaves each of us with a personal challenge. It is impossible to understand Christianity from a Christian perspective, without experiencing this challenge.

Jesus continues to issue his gentle invitation, which is also a tough command: 'Come, follow me.' Michael Ramsey, 100th Archbishop of Canterbury, expressed this challenge with powerful simplicity as he described some of the claims of Christ which we have considered, and drew out their implications.

> *Perhaps you are trying the line that you welcome Christ's moral teaching and admire it: but reject his own claims. It seems to me a most unconvincing line. The moral teaching and the claims are woven in one, for both concern the reign of God. I see no escape from the dilemma: either Jesus is fraudulent, or his claim is true: either we judge him for being terribly amiss, or we let him judge us. That was, in fact, the dilemma that cut through the consciences of his contemporaries.* (Introducing the Christian Faith, SCM Press)

Jesus in our image

It is moving to find African artists painting an African Jesus, Indian artists painting an Indian Jesus, and English artists painting an English Jesus. Some artists have painted a female Christ. They are claiming that Jesus is one of them. He speaks to all people; he transcends cultures, nations and centuries. Jesus came not primarily as a first-century Jew but as a human being. He is able to cut through cultural differences; he shows us what it means to be truly human.

But Incarnation – the belief that in Jesus Christ, God became a human being – carries with it the necessity of particularity. In one sense, no one man can be universal. He must belong to one period in history, to one nation, to one culture, to one family. Jesus, in his particularity, was a first-century Palestinian Jew. In this sense he is, for most modern Western people, an uncomfortable figure, not easy to fathom. Perhaps too often, however, he is all too easy to understand. So we feel the force of Mark Twain's quip: 'It's not the parts of the Bible which I can't understand that bother me, it's the parts that I can understand!'

Conclusion: Jesus our contemporary

'Christianity is Christ.' That statement sums up the Christian view of Jesus of Nazareth. Hans Küng expresses the challenge of Jesus for his disciples like this:

A real Christian is not only a good and well-intentioned person but a man or woman for whom Jesus Christ is ultimately decisive; for whom Jesus – not Caesar, not another god, not money, sex, power, or pleasure – is Lord.

David L Edwards, a former Speaker's Chaplain in the House of Commons, made the same point:

There are many ways of defining what a Christian is. The best one is this: a Christian is one who takes orders from Jesus Christ as Lord.

But this figure who challenges us at every turn is also the source of all comfort. The Lutheran pastor Dietrich Bonhoeffer spoke strongly against 'cheap grace'; he insisted that Christian discipleship is costly and challenging. He demonstrated this during his years in a Nazi concentration camp, and by his execution just before the end of the Second World War. Throughout those long difficult months, he felt the comfort and encouragement of Jesus. In a letter from prison he wrote:

All we may rightly expect from God and ask him for is to be found in Jesus Christ ... If we are to learn what God promises ... we must persevere in quiet meditation on the life, saying, deeds, sufferings, and death of Jesus ... it is certain that in all this we are in a fellowship that sustains us ...

This then is the Jesus of the New Testament, the Jesus of history and the Jesus for today – whenever *our* 'today' might be. He comes to us with tough demands – calling us to serve a troubled and divided world in his name and with his strength. He comes, too, with unutterable comfort.

To a world beset by problems he comes as guide. In a world where many are lonely, he comes as friend. To a world which often seems to lack meaning, he brings understanding. For a world tempted to despair, he provides the ground for hope. Over a world where dying is the single certainty, he sits enthroned as the conqueror of death.

The words of Jesus as recorded in St John's Gospel have been tested and proved in countless lives: *'I am the light of the world. Whoever follows me will never walk in darkness, but will have the light of life'* (John 8:12).

With the help of the Dead Sea Scrolls and Jewish literature, in particular the major work of the Jewish historian Fabius Josephus, you can reconstruct Jewish life of that age, and you put Jesus into this, and he emerges as a living figure, not someone who fell down from heaven.

Professor Geza Vermes, Jewish Biblical scholar

*

On a spring morning in about the year 30 CE three men were executed by the Roman authorities in Judaea. Two were 'brigands'... the third was convicted of having claimed to be 'King of the Jews' – a political title. It turned out that the third man, Jesus of Nazareth, would become one of the most important figures in human history.

E P Sanders in The Historical Figure of Jesus (Penguin)

Early non-Christian references to Jesus

As far as the Roman authorities were concerned, Jesus was a small-time trouble maker. They were forced to revise their opinion when the movement which bore his name grew rapidly – after his death. His followers were accused of many things: cannibalism because they spoke of feeding on the body and blood of Christ in Holy Communion (see Chapter 8); atheism because they did not accept the Roman gods.

▶ TACITUS, a Roman historian born in AD 55, describes (in his *Annals*) how the Emperor Nero blamed Christians for the burning of Rome. 'Therefore, to scotch the rumours, Nero substituted as culprits, and punished with the utmost cruelty, a class of men, loathed for their vices, whom the crowd styled Christians. Christus, the founder of the name, had undergone the death penalty in the reign of Tiberius, by sentence of the procurator Pontius Pilate.'

▶ PLINY THE YOUNGER (Roman Governor of Bithynia, AD 0–113) complained of the problems caused by Christians who sang 'a hymn to Christ as to a god'.

▶ JOSEPHUS was a Jewish historian who defected to the Romans in the Jewish-Roman war which began in AD 66. He affirmed that Jesus was 'the Christ' who rose from the dead. There is no textual evidence against Josephus' remarkable testimony to Jesus. But many scholars assume that some key words were inserted later, because they cannot believe that Josephus would have written so positively about him.

▶ The Jewish TALMUD (an ancient commentary on Jewish teaching) acknowledges Jesus as a Jew. His miracles, his teaching and his disciples are referred to, and he is described as a false teacher who was executed.

Twentieth-century non-Christian testimony to Jesus

▶ MAHATMA GANDHI, the great Hindu: 'I believe that Jesus belongs not only to Christianity but to the entire world, to all races and people.'

▶ MILAN MACHOVEC, a Czech Marxist, wrote a book entitled *A Marxist Looks at Jesus*. He acknowledged that Jesus 'set the world on fire', and he explains why: '... he himself was the attraction. They saw in him a man who already belonged to this coming Kingdom of God; they saw what it meant to be "full of grace" ...'

▶ MARTIN BUBER, the influential Jewish teacher: 'From my youth onwards I have found in Jesus my great brother ... I am more than ever certain that a great place belongs to him in Israel's history of faith and that this place cannot be described by any of the usual categories.'

▶ GEZA VERMES, another Jewish scholar, warmly acknowledges Jesus as a fellow Jew who was 'an unsurpassed master of the art of laying bare the inmost core of spiritual truth'.

▶ H G WELLS, the early science fiction writer, was not a Christian; nor was he a natural ally of the Christian Church. But his admiration for Jesus was boundless. In his *Outline of History* he wrote several fine pages on the impact of Jesus, including these sentences: 'He was too great for his disciples ... He was like some terrible moral huntsman digging mankind out of the snug burrows in which they had lived hitherto ... Is it any wonder that men were dazzled and blinded and cried out against him? Is it any wonder that to this day this Galilean is too much for our small hearts?'

▶ ALBERT EINSTEIN, Nobel Prize winning physicist: 'I am a Jew, but I am enthralled by the luminous figure of the Nazarene ... No one can read the Gospels without feeling the actual presence of Jesus. His personality pulsates in every word. No myth is filled with such life.'

10 THINGS TO REMEMBER

1   Jesus led a short life, wrote no books and did not travel beyond his own small country.

2   Despite this, Jesus' impact is immense and Christianity is the largest movement in history.

3   The birth of Jesus forms the basis of our calendar (BC and AD).

4   Jesus is widely acknowledged as a great teacher.

5   He taught in parables and stressed that God is 'our Heavenly Father'.

6   Central to Jesus' teaching was 'the Kingdom (or rule) of God' with its stress on love and forgiveness.

7   The values of this Kingdom include humility, generosity and service – especially to the poor and marginalized.

8   Many in the Roman Empire, both Jews and Gentiles, testified to Jesus as a radical teacher and troublemaker.

9   Jesus continues to be regarded as an inspiring figure by many influential, modern non-Christians.

10 Most early Christians were also Jews. As Jews, they risked being accused of blasphemy for worshipping Jesus as the Son of God.

2

Crucified Saviour

In this chapter you will learn:
- *about the challenge of the cross*
- *about the importance of verbal images*
- *about questions raised by the crucifixion of Jesus.*

The final week

Insight

Jesus suffered a cruel death by crucifixion – a form of execution favoured by the Romans. For Jews like Jesus this was a most degrading death, for the Old Testament declares that 'anyone hung on a tree is under God's curse' (Deuteronomy 21:23).

Towards the end of his three years in the public eye, Jesus faced a crucial decision. Should he return home to the safety of Galilee? Or should he go on to Jerusalem and to conflict? In his Gospel, Luke tells us that 'Jesus resolutely set out for Jerusalem.' That decision led to his death.

In Mark's Gospel we find a refrain on Jesus' lips: 'The Son of Man must suffer.' And in John's Gospel, Jesus refers to his death as his 'hour'. Everything he taught and did led up to his climactic death. This is seen most clearly in the dramatic events of the last week of his life.

The week began with his entry into Jerusalem. Jesus timed this to coincide with the great Jewish festival of Passover, when Jerusalem was teeming with pilgrims. His reputation ensured a large crowd. He rode on a humble donkey, fulfilling the prophecy of Zechariah 9:9.

> *Rejoice greatly, O Daughter of Zion!*
> *Shout, Daughter of Jerusalem!*
> *See, your king comes to you,*
> *righteous and having salvation,*
> *gentle and riding a donkey...*

Here was no worldly king, coming in glittering style to impress and command. Here was the Prince of Peace, riding in great humility. The crowds greeted him with shouts: 'Hosanna', which means *'Save Now'*. They scattered coats and palm branches on the road (hence *Palm Sunday*). As he approached Jerusalem, Jesus wept bitterly over the city. For some days, he taught in the precincts of the Temple – a fabulous building erected by King Herod 'the Great', who had tried to kill him as a baby. Jesus made a direct attack on the attitudes and practices of many of the leaders of his people. He even drove out those who were trading in the Temple precincts. *'It is written'*, he said to them, *'My house shall be a house of prayer, but you have made it a den of robbers'* (Luke 19:46).

The central Christian belief is that Christ's death has somehow put us right with God and given us a fresh start. Theories as to how it did this are another matter. A good many different theories have been held as to how it works; what all Christians are agreed on is that it does work.

(C S Lewis)

To mark the annual Passover festival, Jewish people gathered in their homes to eat a celebration supper – a practice which continues to this day. This was the last supper which Jesus ate with his disciples; it was to become the most celebrated meal in history. After they had eaten, Judas – one of the 12 disciples – left the room and betrayed Jesus to the Jewish authorities. He was rewarded with 30 silver coins. They plotted to arrest Jesus by night, away from the crowds. Although the other disciples swore undying allegiance, Jesus warned that they too would abandon him. His prophecy was tragically fulfilled.

After their meal, they sang a hymn and walked to a garden called Gethsemane on the Mount of Olives. Jesus knew what was coming. He prayed with deep emotion, asking that he might be spared the dreadful suffering which the next few hours would bring. But his prayer ended with these famous words, '... *yet not my will, but yours be done*' (Luke 22:42). Shortly after this, Jesus was arrested and interrogated through the night by hastily convened Jewish and Roman courts.

Rabble-rousers stirred up the people. No longer did the crowds cry 'Hosanna!' and 'Welcome!' Now they shouted 'Crucify!' Pontius Pilate, the Roman Procurator of Judaea (AD 26–36) wanted to release Jesus but gave way to the popular outcry. To distance himself from this decision he washed his hands in public (Matthew 27:24).

Jesus was stripped. Nails were driven through his hands and feet. The cross was raised, and he was left hanging between two criminals. Soldiers gambled for his single worldly possession: a seamless robe. Later, his side was pierced with a spear to ensure that he was dead. As he was dying, Jesus uttered seven sentences which are recorded in the four Gospels. Among these is his astonishing prayer: '*Father, forgive them, for they know not what they are doing.*'

Jesus' words from the Cross

- 'Eloi, Eloi, lama sabachthani? – My God, my God, why have you forsaken me?' (Matthew 27:46; Mark 15:34, from Psalm 22:1)
- 'Father, forgive them, for they know not what they are doing' (Luke 23:34).
- 'I tell you the truth, today you will be with me in paradise' (Luke 23:43).
- 'Father, into your hands I commit my spirit' (Luke 23:46 from Psalm 31:5).
- 'Dear woman, here is your son ... Here is your mother' (John 19:26–27).
- 'I am thirsty' (John 19:28).
- 'It is accomplished' (John 19:30).

A startling contrast

Blandina was a Christian who had the misfortune to live in Lyons in Gaul (modern France) in AD 77. The authorities wished to stamp out the Church. The job was straightforward: they had to persuade the Christians to disown their God and swear by the pagan gods.

Eusebius, an early historian (*c.*260–*c.*340), recorded these events. Blandina, he reported, wore out her tormentors with her endurance. So they put her back in prison. Later, they brought her into the arena, together with a 15-year-old boy called Ponticus. After he had been killed, they put Blandina in a net and presented her to a bull. 'And so', wrote Eusebius, 'she travelled herself along the same path of conflicts as they (her fellow martyrs) did, and hastened to them rejoicing and exulting in her departure.'

The peace and serenity, and the sense of the presence of God displayed by Blandina, is characteristic of the Christian martyrs since the time of Stephen (Chapters 9, 11 and 15). *It is in sharp contrast to the death of Jesus himself.*

In the Passion Narratives in the Gospels (e.g. Mark 14:32–15:47):

▶ *We find a lack of serenity: 'He began to be deeply distressed and troubled.'*
▶ *We find a lack of peace: 'My soul is overwhelmed with sorrow.'*
▶ *We find a desire for escape: 'Abba, Father, everything is possible for you, take this cup from me.'*
▶ *We even find a sense of abandonment by God, as Jesus quotes the opening line of Psalm 22: 'My God, my God, why have you forsaken me?'*

Jesus was no less courageous than the martyrs who followed him. He could have escaped to safe obscurity. Instead, he pressed on to Jerusalem, to his fatal confrontation with the authorities. But the striking contrast remains. *For those who died for Jesus Christ – a constant sense of the presence of God. For Jesus as he died – a sense of abandonment by God and of utter loneliness.* The martyrs faced death willingly; Jesus shrank from it.

Add to this the fact that those who followed Jesus to martyrdom drew their inspiration from his death, and we have a remarkable puzzle. It is a puzzle to which the New Testament gives a solution. The answer given there is that, for Jesus, there was an *extra factor*. The martyrs suffered physically; Jesus suffered *physically and spiritually*, as he experienced separation from God the Father for the first time in his life.

The martyrs bore *pain* for him; he bore *sin* for them: not only their own sin but the sin of the whole world. And it is sin which separates from God – hence the cry of abandonment from the cross. All this was summed up by John the Baptist when he referred to Jesus as 'the Lamb of God, who takes away the sin of the world' (John 1:29).

Insight

The death of Jesus is central to the Christian understanding of salvation. According to the Bible, his death broke down the barriers of rebellion and indifference which separate us from God and one another.

The Mediator

> *For there is one God, and one mediator between God and men, the man Christ Jesus ...* (1 Timothy 2:5)

We cut ourselves off from other people when we turn our backs on them, or when we relate to them only at a superficial level. The Bible teaches that we human beings have cut ourselves off from God through disobedience and indifference. To bring two separated parties together, a mediator or trouble-shooter is sometimes required. To be a mediator can be dangerous, for it might mean getting involved in the dispute. This is what Jesus did. According to the New Testament, he became the Mediator between God and humanity – at the cost of his life. The apostle Peter conveys this with great power. Echoing the prophet Isaiah, he wrote: 'He himself bore our sins in his body on the cross ... by his wounds you have been healed' (1 Peter 2:24).

Many people know what it is to experience a sense of alienation, 'lostness', guilt and meaninglessness. The New Testament writers see the death of Jesus Christ as *the* solution to this dilemma. It is for this reason that they place such emphasis on this event and devote so much space to exploring its significance. This same emphasis has been maintained within the Christian community over the centuries. The cross has become *the* central symbol of Christianity.

Not only do we find a cross or crucifix within most churches, but many church buildings are designed in cruciform shape (Chapter 19). The two great sacraments of the Church focus on the cross (Chapter 8). *Baptism* is 'into Christ', and especially into his death and resurrection. In *Holy Communion*, the bread and wine refer to the broken body and shed blood of Jesus.

Light from a dark place

The death of Jesus Christ takes us to the heart of the Christian understanding of salvation. It is, according to St Paul, of 'first importance' (1 Corinthians 15:3). John Polkinghorne, former Professor of Mathematical Physics at Cambridge University, sums it up:

> *In that lonely figure in the dark, in the spent force of a deserted man dying on a cross, they see not the ultimate triumph of evil or futility but the only source of hope for mankind. 'God was in Christ reconciling the world to himself' (2 Corinthians 5:19) ... The crucifixion was not something which got out of hand, a tragic mistake which marred an otherwise wonderful life. On the contrary, it was the inevitable fulfilment of the life, purposed by God.*
>
> (*The Way the World Is*, SPCK)

Why was it necessary for Jesus to die to gain our salvation? This is a deep mystery. Indeed, St Paul admits that the notion of a man dying on a cross to save the world, appears very foolish (1 Corinthians 1:18–25). It cannot be fully understood; it can only be proclaimed – and believed or denied. But this mystery sheds light upon, and brings meaning to, countless lives. The New Testament probes the significance of the death of Christ at many points: we may attempt to sum up its significance under four headings.

THE CROSS REVEALS THE DEPTH OF HUMAN SIN

It was pride which opposed Jesus; it was greed which betrayed Jesus; it was jealousy which condemned Jesus. Cruel men flogged and mocked him. Then they led him out to die a shameful death in a public place called Golgotha, which means 'The Place of the Skull'.

As Jesus died, the land was covered in daytime darkness. '*At the birth of the Son of God there was brightness at midnight, at the death of the Son of God there was darkness at noon*' (Douglas Webster). It was as though heaven itself was saying: this is the most dreadful day of all. But Christians believe that God took those evil actions and attitudes and used them as the raw materials from which to quarry our salvation.

THE CROSS REVEALS THE DEPTH OF GOD'S LOVE

Rather than using his power to dominate, Jesus chose to submit himself to human wickedness. So the power of God is seen in symbols of weakness: a borrowed manger for his birth and a wooden cross at his death. Here is power kept in check; power handed over; power utterly controlled by love. Jesus' body was broken like bread and his life was poured out like wine, for the forgiveness of sins. One of the most famous of Bible verses begins: 'For God so loved the world that he gave his only begotten Son ...' (John 3:16).

THE CROSS REVEALS THE WAY BACK TO GOD

In the Temple in Jerusalem, a large curtain hung between the Most Holy Place and the rest of the building. It was a symbol of the separation between the Holy God and the human race, resulting from our sin. As Jesus died, that curtain was torn in two from top to bottom. It was a dramatic sign of new access into the presence of God.

On the cross Jesus cried out: 'It is finished.' The Greek word ('*tetelestai*') carries a triumphant ring. Not 'It's all over' but 'It is *accomplished*.' According to the Bible, only his death, the death of the Son of God, could break down the barriers of rebellion and indifference which separate us from God and from one another. So we call that terrible day Good Friday. The day was terrible, but the fruit of the day is beautiful.

THE CROSS REVEALS THE DEMANDS OF CHRISTIAN DISCIPLESHIP

> *'We all have to choose between two ways of being crazy; the foolishness of the gospel and the nonsense of the values of this world.'*
>
> Jean Vanier

'Follow me', said Jesus. Then he took the road to crucifixion. As baptism indicates (Chapter 8), following Christ always involves a sort of death. It means trying to hold Christian standards in a world which often rejects those standards. It means following Jesus in a world which is often indifferent towards him. Jesus summed up like this: 'If any want to become my followers, let them deny themselves and take up their cross and follow me' (Mark 8:34).

Paradoxically, Jesus insists that the cross is also about *life*. He goes on to say, 'For those who want to save their life will lose it, and those who lose their life for my sake, and for the sake of the gospel, will save it.'

George McLeod founded the modern Iona Community in Scotland. His words remind us that the crucifixion of Jesus is not just a terrible but fascinating incident in history, nor a puzzle in theology, nor simply an object for adoration and art. It is a constant challenge to all who seek to follow the crucified Christ.

> *I simply argue that the cross be raised again at the centre of the marketplace as well as on the steeple of the church. I am recovering the claim that Jesus was not crucified in a cathedral between two candles, but on a cross between two thieves; on the town garbage heap; at a crossroads so cosmopolitan that they had to write his title in Hebrew and Latin and in Greek ... at the kind of place where cynics*

talk smut, and thieves curse, and soldiers gamble. Because this is
where he died. And this is what he died about. And that is where
churchmen ought to be and what churchmen should be about.

> **Insight**
>
> The cross of Jesus Christ sets the pattern for Christian living.
> Believers are called to 'die to self' and are reminded of this at
> Baptism and Holy Communion. However, the emphasis is on
> *life*. Because God raised Jesus from the grave, his death and
> resurrection create the gateway for our new life.

Painting pictures with words

The second of the Ten Commandments tells us that the early
Israelites were forbidden to make graven images (Exodus 20).
It was an essential instruction for a people surrounded by nations
that fashioned images and worshipped idols. As a result of this
prohibition, painting was an art form which did not flourish
in ancient Israel. But other art forms did, especially music,
architecture and literature – including poetry.

Much of the Bible is rich in pictorial language and many of the
great Bible themes paint pictures on the mind. For example, in the
Psalms, God is seen as a shepherd, king, judge, rock, fortress, etc.
To make good sense of this we need to be aware of the way in
which such verbal images 'work'. Calling God a rock does not
mean that he is lifeless; it does mean that he is utterly dependable.
One image needs to be balanced by another.

Bible language about salvation is highly pictorial too: from death
to life; from darkness to light. The word 'salvation' is dramatic,
suggesting rescue from danger. So is the word 'atonement', which
means 'at-one-ment' or reconciliation with God.

So it is no surprise to find that language concerning the death of
Jesus – of which there is a great deal in the Bible – is full of verbal
images or pictures. Dr Colin Morris put it like this:

The writers of the New Testament ransacked language to find some way of conveying the sense of what had happened to Jesus on Calvary. They used the jargon of the law courts and the slave galleys and the slaughter house to get across the meaning of his death ...

Consideration of some of these great images helps us to understand the significance afforded to the crucifixion in the Bible, as follows:

Ransom St Mark records these words of Jesus: 'The Son of Man came not to be served, but to serve, and to give his life as a ransom for many' (Mark 10:45). A slave in the ancient world could be redeemed (set free) by a ransom price paid on his behalf. The Bible teaches that every person, regardless of culture, background, virtue or vice, can be set free ('redeemed') from sin, fear, guilt and death, by the death and resurrection of Jesus.

Reconciliation The Christian gospel is about reconciliation (2 Corinthians 5:19, 20). The death of Jesus built bridges across apparently unbridgeable gaps. To change the image, it knocked down two dividing walls (Ephesians 2:14):

▶ *between the Holy God and sinful human beings*
▶ *between Jews and Gentiles (non-Jews).*

Elsewhere, the New Testament is even bolder. Christ's death brings together *all things* previously fragmented. Nature itself will be redeemed (Colossians 1:20; Romans 8:20–22).

The idea of atonement for sin runs throughout the Bible. In the Old Testament we find an elaborate set of rituals based on the tabernacle and the temple. These found their focus in animal sacrifices. Those ancient practices have no practical significance for Christians today. They were the shadow; the death of Jesus was the substance – the fulfilment and summation of the entire sacrificial system. For on the cross, Jesus became the *one perfect sacrifice* and the *one true High Priest*. This is spelt out in detail in the New Testament Letter to the Hebrews. The way back to God is open; through Jesus we may come to God the Father with confidence (Hebrews 10:19; Ephesians 3:12).

Suffering Servant The prophet Isaiah wrote about the *Servant of the Lord*. He was the *suffering* Servant. The earliest Christians made the connection: *Jesus was that Servant*. Indeed, Jesus saw his own ministry like that: '... the Son of Man... came to serve' (Mark 10:45). This servant identified himself with the poor, the powerless, the stranger, and the marginalized: 'Whatever you did for one of the least of these brothers of mine, you did for me' (Matthew 25:40).

This emphasis is particularly important for our times, for more people have suffered in wars during the last century than in all previous centuries put together. The image of the suffering servant provides a vital clue as we face the sharpest of all questions for those who believe in a loving God. Where is God when we suffer? Where was he in the Nazi concentration camps and the Soviet labour camps? Where is he in the sweatshops of our world? Where is he when people suffer illness, torture, drought and famine?

This profound and difficult question was addressed powerfully by the German theologian Jürgen Moltmann. His answer was that *God in Christ is there in the anguish*, sharing the bitter pains of a suffering world. The crucifixion assures us that God does not sit on the side-lines; he gets involved. The Son of God did not only suffer *for* us; he suffers *with* us. In this way, he brings redemption and shows his love. The Bible does not offer us a theoretical solution to the question, 'Why does God allow suffering?' Instead, it offers us a *God who suffers with us, and who redeems us through the cross.*

'God was in Christ reconciling the world to himself' (2 Corinthians 5:19). It was God in Christ who died a degrading death. It was God in Christ who hung naked, exposed and helpless. That is the message of the cross. All this leads to a gospel of hope. Christians are confident that we human beings are not on our own in a cold, heartless universe. At the centre of all things is the crucified God – who brings life out of death, as the resurrection shows. Indeed, the most anguished and problematic words in the whole Bible point to this conclusion. 'My God, My God why have you forsaken me?' cried Jesus from the cross, quoting Psalm 22:1. Rabbi Hugo Gryn pointed out that the opening line of a Psalm represents the whole Psalm to a devout Jew. And Psalm 22 ends in confidence and faith. Even the desolation, though desperately real, is shot through with light and hope.

Insight

Rather than using his power to dominate, Jesus chose to submit himself to human wickedness. So the power of God is seen in symbols of weakness: a borrowed manger for his birth and a wooden cross at his death. Here is power kept in check; power handed over; power utterly controlled by love.

A theory of the atonement?

None of this amounts to one definitive 'theory of the atonement'. Just *how* the death of Jesus on the cross saves us is not spelt out in detail in the Bible. Ultimately it is a deep mystery – a mystery of love which conveys life and light. Throughout Christian history, theologians have tried to explain this mystery. They have set several ideas before us, based upon Bible images. Jesus is seen as:

▶ *the perfect Penitent*
▶ *the Victor over the powers of darkness*
▶ *the One who paid the ransom to set us free*
▶ *the Substitute who died in my place*
▶ *the Representative who died for all humanity*
▶ *the perfect Sacrifice for sin*
▶ *the One whose death satisfies the demands of holy justice*
▶ *the One who delivers us from a guilty verdict in a law court*
▶ *the supreme Example of self-giving love*
▶ *the One whose death moves and inspires us to acts of loving service.*

Each of these helps us to understand; none contains the whole truth. So it is not surprising that no single account has been adopted by the Church as *the* 'official theory' of the atonement. Indeed, the term 'theory' is often criticized as being inappropriate for this great act of passion, love and sacrifice. Perhaps, in the end, the significance of the death of Jesus can be understood only through pictures, parables and stories.

> One such story is *The Long Silence* (author unknown). It is set on Judgement Day, when people who have suffered terribly complain that 'God leads a pretty sheltered life'. To qualify as Judge, they say, God should be sentenced to live on earth as a man.
>
> 'Let him be born a Jew and let the legitimacy of his birth be questioned. Let him be doubted by his family and betrayed by his friends. Let him face false charges and be tried by a prejudiced jury in front of a hostile crowd. Let him be tortured to death – and as he dies, let him feel abandoned and alone.'
>
> When this judgement was pronounced, there was a long silence. Nobody moved. For suddenly all knew that God had already served his sentence.

The Cross through the centuries

He who did not spare his own Son, but gave him up for us all – how will he not also, along with him, graciously give us all things?

(St Paul: Romans 8:32)

Like a sheep to the slaughter he humbled himself, and by his death delivered us from the peril into which our sins had put us.

(Origen: c. 185–254)

Then the young Hero – it was God Almighty – strong and steadfast, stripped himself for the battle; he climbed up on high gallows, constant in his purpose.

(Anglo-Saxon: Anon)

Where is the strength of Christ? ... Surely his strength is in his hands, for his hands were nailed to the arms of the cross ...

O hidden strength! A man hanging on a cross lifts the weight of eternal death; a man fixed on wood frees the world from everlasting death. O hidden power!

(Anselm: c. 1033–1109)

Thus naked am I nailed? O man, for thy sake
I love thee, then love me. Why sleepest thou? Awake!

(Medieval: Anonymous)

... his most dreadful cry, which at once moved all the powers in heaven and earth, 'My God, my God, why hast thou forsaken me?' Weigh well that cry, consider it well, and tell me if ever there were cry like to that of his. Never the like cry, and therefore never the like sorrow.

(Lancelot Andrewes 1555–1626)

And where pride and envy and hatred ... are suffered to live, there the same thing is done as when Christ was killed and Barabbas was saved alive.

(William Law 1686–1761)

Thomas, be not faithless, but believing. Christ shall show you his hands and his feet. He is the same now as He was yesterday, full of love and graciousness to self-condemned sinners. That you may experience the full power and efficacy of the Redeemer's blood is the ardent prayer of, dear Thomas, your sincere friend, George Whitefield.

(1714–1770)

– 1 –

Am I a stone, and not a sheep,
    That I can stand, O Christ, beneath Thy cross,
    To number drop by drop Thy blood's slow loss,
And yet not weep?

– 2 –

Not so those women loved
    Who with exceeding grief lamented Thee;
    Not so fallen Peter weeping bitterly;
Not so the thief was moved;

– 3 –

Not so the Sun and Moon
    Which hid their faces in a starless sky,
    A horror of great darkness at broad noon –
I, only I.

– 4 –

Yet give not o'er,
    But seek Thy sheep, true Shepherd of the flock;
    Greater than Moses, turn and look once more
And smite a rock.

(Christina Rossetti 1830–1894)

On June 7th, 1917, I was running to our lines half mad with fright ... being heavily shelled. As I ran I stumbled and fell over something. It was an undersized, underfed German boy, with a wound in his stomach and a hole in his head ... Then there came light ... It seemed to me that the boy disappeared and in his place

*there lay the Christ upon his cross, and cried, 'Inasmuch as ye
have done it unto the least of these my little ones ye have done
it unto me.' From that moment on I never saw a battlefield as
anything but a crucifix. From that moment on I have never seen the
world as anything but a crucifix.* (G A Studdert Kennedy: 1883–1929)

*The Cross of Christ is the reality to which we must continually
return. For this is the light in which all our values are to be seen. Our
understanding of the good and the true and the beautiful is to be
jarred and rejigged by the divine humility.* (Bishop Richard Harries)

*I could never myself believe in God, if it were not for the cross ...
In the real world of pain, how could one worship a God who was
immune from it?* (Dr John Stott)

I recall speaking with a woman whose child had died. One saying of
Jesus had helped her more than any other. It was not his affirmation
of victory over death ('I am the resurrection and the life'). It was not
his promise of strength ('I am with you always'). It was his cry of
dereliction: 'My God, my God, why have you forsaken me?' She felt that
Jesus understood her desolation. She saw his cry as an affirmation – not
a denial of faith.

The power of the Cross

*Jews demand miraculous signs and Greeks look for wisdom,
but we preach Christ crucified: a stumbling-block to Jews and
foolishness to Gentiles ... For the foolishness of God is wiser than
man's wisdom, and the weakness of God is stronger than man's
strength.* (1 Corinthians 1:22–25)

The apostle Paul wrote these words after his conversion to Jesus
Christ. As Saul had persecuted the Church of Christ. In those days
he *knew* that the Christians were wrong, because he knew the
Hebrew Scriptures. Deuteronomy 21:22–23 is clear: 'anyone who
is hung upon a tree is under God's curse'. Jesus had been crucified –
hung upon a tree – therefore he was accursed. So he could not be
the Messiah, as his followers claimed. This was the logic which had
motivated Saul's persecution of the church.

Later, the apostle came to see that the cross was indeed the place of a curse. But the curse which Jesus bore was *ours*, not his. For he took upon himself the curse of human sin. So, with immense daring, Paul could write: 'Christ delivered us from the curse of the law, having become a curse for us' (Galatians 3:13).

So it was that Paul discovered and described the power of the cross in this vivid, perhaps shocking, way. Throughout the next 20 centuries, countless individuals would come to find its power by one route or another. This is captured by the historian G Kitson Clark, who ends his book *The Kingdom of Free Men* (Cambridge University Press) with these moving words:

> **So we have reached the end of our journey, and we have arrived at no pleasant place. It is in fact a place of public execution. Yet all human roads lead here in the end. This is the capital of the kingdom of free men and there, ruling from the gallows, is the King.**

Beyond imagination

Some features of the Christian story are so surprising that they appear to be thrust upon us – given rather than created. When we consider the situation in which they arose, they appear to be beyond the power of imagination or invention.

- ▶ The worship of Jesus by monotheistic Jews (pages 17–19).
- ▶ The rise of the Christian movement from the ashes of disaster (Chapter 3).
- ▶ The centrality of the Cross.

'The Christian doctrine of the incarnation, and the gospel story, argue for an intervention rather than an emergence. It is difficult to posit that humans, on their own, would invent a crucified corpse as a role-model. The gospel story (part history, part mystery) is too strange and beautiful.'

Professor P K M M'Pherson

10 THINGS TO REMEMBER

1   *The death of Jesus is central to the entire New Testament.*

2   *Christians believe that, through his death, Jesus accomplished something of eternal significance.*

3   *This achievement is caught in the cry of Jesus from the cross, 'It is accomplished' (John 19:30).*

4   *In Greek, this cry is a single, triumphant word: tetelestai.*

5   *Christians do not claim to fully understand how Christ's death achieved our salvation.*

6   *This is a profound mystery – but it casts light upon the lives of millions in the modern world.*

7   *The New Testament helps us unravel this mystery by using a wide range of word pictures – redemption, salvation, victory, reconciliation …*

8   *In the Bible, the death of Jesus is always linked with his resurrection.*

9   *Christianity does not revel in gloom; it glories in the promise of new and abundant life.*

10 *There is no official 'theory of the Atonement'. A range of ideas has been developed over the centuries, based on the rich language of the New Testament.*

3

Risen Lord

In this chapter you will learn:
- *about the centrality of the resurrection*
- *ten facts that need explaining*
- *the implications for today.*

The Acts of the Apostles describes a visit made by the apostle Paul to Athens. As he spoke, some local philosophers asked, 'What is this babbler trying to say?' They were told that he seemed to be speaking about foreign gods, 'because Paul was preaching the good news about Jesus and the resurrection' (Acts 17:18). As they half-listened, Paul's hearers thought that he was talking about two deities (*Jesus* and *Anastasis* – the Greek word for resurrection), because they heard these two words so frequently linked together.

This stress on Jesus and his resurrection is found throughout the New Testament. The Letters were written in the conviction that Jesus is alive. The Acts of the Apostles contains sermons which declare that God raised Jesus from the dead. The Gospels end, not with the death and burial of Jesus, but with stories about the way in which he appeared to his disciples.

Post-resurrection appearances of Jesus

▶ Two Marys encounter the risen Lord (Matthew 28:1–10)
▶ The risen Christ commissions the 11 disciples (Matthew 28:16–20)
(Contd)

- ▶ Three women are bewildered and afraid at the empty tomb (Mark 16:1–8)
- ▶ Jesus appears to two disciples on the road to Emmaus (Luke 24:13–35)
- ▶ Jesus eats with his disciples (Luke 24: 36–39)
- ▶ Mary Magdalene encounters Jesus at the tomb (John 20: 10–18)
- ▶ Thomas doubts until he meets Jesus (John 20:24–29)
- ▶ A miraculous catch of fish followed by breakfast (John 21:1–14)
- ▶ Jesus encourages and commissions Peter (John 21:15–23)
- ▶ Jesus appears for 40 days before ascending to heaven (Acts 1:3–11)
- ▶ Saul has a vision of the risen Lord on the Damascus Road (Acts 9:1–9)
- ▶ Jesus appears to more than 500 people (1 Corinthians 15:3–8)

The different situations in which Jesus appeared, and the different people to whom he appeared, is striking. This can be viewed as a problem: can these appearances be harmonized into one coherent narrative of events? Or it can be seen as a strength: if the first disciples had invented the resurrection, surely they would have made a tidier presentation?

We will consider just one of these stories: the appearance of Jesus to Mary Magdalene. St John tells us (John 20:1) that Mary went to the garden tomb very early on the first day of the week, only to find the stone removed from the entrance. She alerted two disciples, Peter and John, who inspected the empty tomb and then returned home.

Mary remained and encountered an angel and a man. Thinking that the man was the gardener, Mary asked if he had moved the body. But according to the fourth Gospel, Mary was not talking to a gardener – she was talking to a carpenter. It was Jesus himself, risen from the dead. Jesus addressed Mary by name and she recognized him. He instructed her to tell his followers ('my brothers') about their meeting. Mary went to the disciples with her exciting news: 'I have seen the Lord.'

This story focuses on two important features which occur frequently in the Gospels:

- ▶ *the tomb was empty*
- ▶ *the risen Lord appeared to one (sometimes more than one) of his followers.*

Insight

The Gospels do not end with Jesus' death, but with extraordinary tales about his many appearances – alive and well – to his disciples. The New Testament describes this as resurrection to new life, not mere survival.

The centrality of the resurrection

The resurrection of Jesus Christ is not just one aspect of Christianity. We cannot remove a portion of the Christian jigsaw labelled 'resurrection' and leave anything which is recognizable as Christian faith. Subtract the resurrection and you destroy the entire picture. Indeed, without the resurrection of Jesus from the dead, it is unlikely that we would have a trace of his teaching, or anything else in the New Testament.

In the early Church there was no preaching about Jesus except as risen Lord. Nor could there be. For without the Apostles' conviction that they had seen Jesus alive again after his crucifixion, there would have been no preaching at all. There would have been deep mourning for a lost friend and great admiration for a dead hero. No doubt his profound teaching would have been remembered and cherished by his small, loyal circle of followers. But when they died, he would have been forgotten. Significantly, the early Christian preachers were less concerned to expound his teaching than to declare his death and resurrection.

The central Christian claim that God raised Jesus from the dead has been carefully examined and vigorously debated. Nobody disputes

(Contd)

that the first Christians made this extraordinary claim but various alternative explanations have been put forward – and vigorously dismissed by others. The scholar-bishop John Austin Baker summed up the Christian position like this:

'It is still very important, in a sceptical and often hostile culture, that the Easter story should stand up to attack – no easy matter at a distance of almost 2000 years. But stand up it does.'

Some have gone even further. Lord Darling, a former Lord Chief Justice of England, asserted that: 'There exists such overwhelming evidence, positive and negative, factual and circumstantial, that no intelligent jury in the world could fail to bring in the verdict that the resurrection story is true.'

Approaching the evidence

Christian scholars vary in their approach to the resurrection. Some, observes Pinchas Lapide (a *Jewish* scholar), appear to be embarrassed by the physical nature (the 'facticity') of the resurrection. So they make assertions such as:

- ▶ *'Easter means: the cause of Jesus goes on' (Willi Marxsen)*
- ▶ *'Jesus has risen into the Kerygma, i.e. the preaching of the Church (Rudolf Bultmann)*
- ▶ *'To believe in the resurrection of Jesus means to undertake the surprising risk to reckon with Jesus Christ as a present reality' (Meinrad Limbeck).*

Other scholars, such as Lapide, feel that this is far too cautious. It is, he says:

all too abstract and scholarly to explain the fact that the solid hillbillies from Galilee who, for the very real reason of the crucifixion of their master, were saddened to death, were changed within a short period of time into a jubilant community of believers. Such a post-Easter change, which was no less real than sudden and unexpected, certainly needed a concrete foundation which can by no means exclude the possibility of any physical resurrection.

(The Resurrection of Jesus, SPCK)

The assertion that a man who was dead and buried has been raised up from the grave is breathtaking: those who make such a claim must give their reasons. In this chapter, some important facts will be set out and their possible implications discussed. Readers may consider the evidence to be strong or weak. Certainly it is not overwhelming. There will always be some who will assert that something as extraordinary as resurrection simply could not have happened, however strong the evidence might appear to be.

The Gospel accounts of the post-resurrection appearances of Jesus are striking in this regard. They provide readers with space in which to doubt, to question and to explore. For they freely admit that the disciples themselves found the whole thing very difficult to accept. St Matthew tells us that at the end of the 40 days during which Jesus appeared, 'some doubted' (Matthew 28:17). St Luke tells us that even with the risen Lord present, the disciples 'disbelieved for joy' (Luke 24:41). It was simply too good to be true! The burning conviction which runs throughout the New Testament did not come easily.

In any case, evidence can take us only so far. We may sympathize with 'doubting Thomas' who reserved his judgement until he received convincing proof. But when he received the evidence which he requested, he did not simply say, 'So it is true.' Rather, he acknowledged the risen Christ as 'My Lord and my God!' (John 20:28). For Thomas, fact and evidence were followed by faith and commitment. With this in mind, we turn to ten significant facts which cry out for adequate explanation.

Insight

After his crucifixion, God raised Jesus from death to new life. This extraordinary affirmation is central to the Christian faith. We are wise to approach it with scepticism. But as we examine the facts surrounding this claim, the evidence seems surprisingly strong – strong enough to convince many brilliant and questioning minds.

FACT 1 NO ONE PRODUCED THE BODY

The Church began, not primarily by the spreading of ideas, but by the proclamation of a *fact*. Something has *happened*, said the apostles: God has raised Jesus from the dead. Those who wanted to discredit the apostles – and the Jewish leaders wanted to do that very much indeed – had only to produce one piece of evidence. *All they had to do was produce the body of Jesus. If they had done so, we would never have heard of him or his followers. There would be no New Testament and no Church.*

It is very significant that they did not do this. If the authorities had taken the body, or discovered it still in the tomb – because the disciples had lied, or gone to the wrong grave – they would have produced the corpse. This would have silenced all talk of resurrection. Instead, the authorities imprisoned, threatened, and beat the disciples. And they circulated the report that the disciples had stolen the body. It is clear that the Jewish and Roman leaders had no idea what had happened to Jesus. Yet the stubborn fact remains: his body had gone.

FACT 2 THE TOMB WAS NOT VENERATED

The empty tomb is strongly supported by the fact that the grave of Jesus did not become a place of pilgrimage. Tomb veneration was common at the time of Jesus; people would often gather at the grave of a prophet – as they do today. In surprising contrast, the earliest Jewish Christians did no such thing. '*No practice of tomb veneration, or even of meeting for worship at Jesus' tomb is attested for the first Christians*', writes Professor James Dunn in *The Evidence for Jesus* (SCM Press). (The practice of venerating Jesus' tomb did start 200–300 years later, and it persists today. But it is the *risen* Lord who is worshipped there.)

That the tomb of Jesus did not become a place of pilgrimage for the first Christians, has only one satisfactory explanation. As Professor Dunn puts it: '*The tomb was not venerated, it did not become a place of pilgrimage, because the tomb was empty!*'

The focus of attention was not on the tomb but on Jesus, who was gloriously alive according to the growing band of believers.

FACT 3 THE MOVEMENT ALMOST DIED

The Christian faith shares some common features with other great world religions. In particular, it looks back to a charismatic founder whose teaching is central for all his followers. In this it is like Buddhism, which traces back to Gautama the Buddha; and Islam, which owes so much to the energy, vision and inspiration of Muhammad, the Prophet of Allah. But when all the similarities have been noted, the *differences* between Jesus and other great religious leaders are startling and puzzling. Three in particular are relevant to this chapter, as follows:

- ▶ *Jesus died very young:*
  - ▷ *Gautama the Buddha died c. 483 BC, aged 80;*
  - ▷ *Muhammad died in AD 632, aged 62;*
  - ▷ *Jesus died c. AD 33, while only in his 30s*
- ▶ *Jesus spent no more than three years in the public eye*
- ▶ *when Jesus died, the movement which he founded was in rapid decline.*

Movements do grow and develop after the founder's death; we have ample evidence of this. It happens when the founder leaves a growing movement. And it happens when the founder's followers are in a buoyant frame of mind, because everything depends on their 'get-up-and-go'. When Jesus died, these two factors were conspicuously absent. His followers were dwindling in number; those who remained were dispirited and afraid.

Yet somehow this demoralized group experienced a remarkable turn-around. Within a few weeks they were full of creative energy. They launched the biggest movement the world has ever seen, and one of the eventual fruits of this remarkable turn-around was the New Testament. *In other words, it was the resurrection of Jesus which gave the teaching of Jesus to the world.*

No resurrection; no record of his teaching.

Jesus' disciples gave two reasons for their own remarkable transformation, and these reasons have been celebrated ever since, in two great Christian festivals, as follows.

Easter The first disciples claimed that God had raised Jesus from the dead. Because this happened on a Sunday, they transferred their 'special' day from the traditional Jewish Sabbath (the last day of the week) to the first day. This change is in itself a remarkable fact, requiring adequate explanation. For Christians, every Sunday is a 'mini-Easter'.

Pentecost (sometimes called Whitsun) The first disciples claimed that God had given them the gift of his Holy Spirit. They affirmed that it was God's Spirit within them who gave them boldness, joy and insight.

It is clear that Christians face a problem as they seek to convince an unbelieving world. But those who deny the resurrection of Jesus Christ also face a problem. They must find a satisfactory alternative explanation for the start and rapid rise of the Church in such unlikely circumstances.

FACT 4 THE DISCIPLES SUFFERED FOR THEIR PREACHING

'Then all the disciples deserted him and fled.' In this short sentence, Matthew describes the behaviour of the disciples of Jesus following his arrest. He goes on to tell of the way in which Peter, for all his earlier boasting, denied all knowledge of Jesus. In the circumstances, such behaviour was completely understandable. However, a few weeks later those men were out in the streets, preaching that God had raised Jesus from the dead. These were the same men who had deserted him. They were the same men who had been shattered by his crucifixion. But as the Acts of the Apostles makes very clear, they were very different same men!

In place of bitter disappointment there was joyful confidence; in place of fear there was boldness. Instead of thinking gloomily that their leader was dead, they proclaimed that he had conquered death. In other words, they were transformed. The question is:

what transformed them? They claimed that it was their experience of the risen Lord. Were they right? Were they mistaken? Or were they guilty of the most successful fraud in history?

An invention?

From time to time during his ministry, Jesus spoke about his future death and resurrection. Perhaps his disciples embellished this idea into stories about a sequence of appearances by Jesus after his death? This possibility is undermined by one significant fact: history and human psychology teach us that people will suffer for deeply held convictions. However, nobody is prepared to suffer for an invention. We tell lies to get *out* of trouble, not to get *into* it. The whip and the sword soon uncover fraud. Besides, liars do not usually write high-calibre moral literature like the New Testament.

In any case, if they *were* inventions they were not all that good. A shared, deep conviction about Jesus' resurrection is clear from the Bible. But the details of his appearances vary considerably from Gospel to Gospel. It is unlikely that a conspiracy would have given rise to so many puzzles. It is even less likely that inventors would have given so much prominence to the testimony of women, for in ancient Jewish culture such evidence carried little weight.

We note too that the Bible gives no description of the resurrection itself. Nobody witnessed that holy moment when God raised Jesus from the dead. Perhaps no human being could have withstood such an awesome outpouring of love and power. Whatever the reason, the records freely admit that nobody was there: the accounts start with the empty tomb and the appearances of the risen Lord. It is quite likely that inventors would have attempted a description of the resurrection itself. And it is unlikely that inventors would have given such emphasis to the fear, bewilderment and doubt (page 47) which were such a central feature of the experience of the first disciples. Christians believe that the Gospel accounts carry 'the ring of truth.'

Did Jesus really die?

The willing suffering of the disciples also rules out the 'swoon' theory. On this view, Jesus did not die on the cross. Despite terrible wounds, he recovered in the tomb and escaped. The disciples nursed him back to health, or tried to and failed.

This theory bristles with problems. Roman soldiers knew when a man was dead; and there was a guard on the tomb. But if we allow that somehow the disciples overcame these problems, the events which follow simply do not fit. Jesus would have cheated death; he would not have *conquered* it. No doubt the disciples would have been delighted, but they would have kept the whole thing very quiet. *Publicity and preaching would have been fatal*, for these would have resulted in a search. The authorities would not have made a second mistake.

Besides, to preach that God had raised Jesus from the dead – which is exactly what they *did* preach – would have been a lie. We are back where we started. The lash, the dungeon and the sword would soon have loosened their tongues. People will suffer and die for their *convictions*, but not for their inventions. A handful of frightened men would not preach boldly about the resurrection to the very people who had killed their leader – especially if they knew it was not true. This would be far too risky. People do not behave like that *unless something tremendous happens to drive away the fear and disappointment.*

FACT 5 HALLUCINATIONS NEED CERTAIN CONDITIONS

One thing is certain. The first disciples passionately *believed* that God had raised Jesus and that Jesus had appeared to them. Were they mistaken? Perhaps they saw a ghost, or suffered from hallucinations?

If it was a vision or ghost which appeared to them, it spent a lot of time and energy trying to persuade them otherwise! The risen Lord had extraordinary powers of appearance and disappearance. But he convinced the disciples that it was *in his body*, albeit remarkably transformed, that he came and went. He ate with them and encouraged Thomas to touch him: they concluded that God had raised Jesus from the dead.

Perhaps the disciples were suffering from hallucinations? At first sight this is a stronger possibility. However, when we compare the factors involved in hallucinations with the appearances recorded in the Gospels, they do not fit either. For one thing, hallucinations happen to individuals. Several people in a group – under the influence of drugs, for example – might hallucinate together, but they will experience *different* hallucinations, arising from the unconscious mind. And every individual's subconscious is as personal as his or her fingerprints.

In his book *Jesus Christ: the Witness of History*, Professor Sir Norman Anderson examined this possibility. He discussed five factors which count against the likelihood of hallucinations:

▶ *people from a wide range of personality types claimed to see Jesus*
▶ *1, 2, 7, 10, 11 and 500 people are unlikely to experience the same fantasy*
▶ *there was deep mourning at Jesus' death, but no strong sense of wishful thinking or expectancy about his resurrection*
▶ *the outward circumstances (timing and setting) varied*
▶ *hallucinations, if repeated, usually continue for a considerable period; the appearances of Jesus all occurred within 40 days, then stopped abruptly – apart from occasional subsequent visions of Christ which were of a different order, e.g. to Saul on the road to Damascus (pages 285–6).*

We are forced to consider another possibility: perhaps the disciples were telling the truth. In the words of Cambridge scholar John Robinson: 'HE *came to them … Jesus was not a dead memory but a living presence, making new men of them.*'

FACT 6 THEY PREACHED RESURRECTION, NOT RESUSCITATION OR SURVIVAL

Professor James Dunn underlines this point. Throughout history, including Jewish history, extraordinary happenings have convinced some people about life after death. For example, ancient Jewish literature speaks of people seeing visions of their dead heroes, such as Abel and Jeremiah. But as Professor Dunn says, 'In no other case did the ones seeing the vision conclude: "This man has been raised from the dead."'

It is true that many Jews believed in resurrection. But this belief was about the resurrection of *all people* on the 'last day' – not of *one man* in the middle of history. Nothing in the thought-forms of the day led the disciples to expect the resurrection appearances of Jesus to occur in the way in which the New Testament describes them. Like so many other factors surrounding Jesus, the events are unique and unexpected.

FACT 7 EYEWITNESSES WERE AVAILABLE

Around AD 55, the apostle Paul wrote what has become a classic passage about resurrection (1 Corinthians 15). In this he states: '*For what I received I passed on to you as of first importance: that Christ died for our sins according to the Scriptures, that he was buried, that he was raised on the third day according to the Scriptures, and that he appeared...*' Scholars have detected an early Christian creed attesting faith in the resurrection, embedded in this passage (hence the word 'received'). Some date this creed to within three to eight years of the crucifixion.

Paul goes on to list various eyewitnesses – people who had seen the risen Lord, who were still alive when he wrote and who could be questioned. This list includes a crowd of 'more than 500'. Free invention for purposes of propaganda could have been checked and contradicted.

FACT 8 JESUS IS CALLED LORD

As we noted in Chapter 1, the early disciples were Jews – devout monotheists who frequently recited the *Shema*: 'The Lord our God, the Lord is one' (Deuteronomy 6:4). Then they met Jesus or heard about him in sermons and conversations.

At no point did they abandon their belief in One God. It would have been unthinkable for them to become 'bi-theists' (believers in two gods). Yet their concept of God was greatly enlarged as a result of their contact with Jesus. So, while continuing to assert that God is One, they began to speak of God the Father and God the Son. Indeed, shortly after his death they had firmly placed Jesus, the man from Nazareth, on the *Godward* side of that line which divides humanity from divinity. They did not doubt that he was truly human, but they offered him their worship (page 16).

How can this amazing shift in attitude be explained? How can we account for the fact that those Jewish men and women (some of whom knew Jesus personally, and all of whom knew that he was a man who sweated and wept) addressed him as *Lord*?

Jewish men and women would have been incapable of *deciding* to use the word 'Lord' in that way. Their entire upbringing was against it, because it carried a huge risk of being blasphemous. No, it was forced upon them – partly by the teaching of Jesus but mainly by their conviction that God had raised Jesus from the dead. They quickly came to realize that if Jesus was Lord over death, he was quite simply... 'LORD'.

FACT 9 CHRIST'S CONTINUING PRESENCE

One surprising feature of the reported resurrection appearances is that they were confined to a period of six weeks. After that they stopped abruptly. Yet the first disciples continued to speak and behave as though Jesus were still with them – not physically, but by his Spirit. Even more remarkable is the fact that this conviction came to be shared by others – at first by hundreds, then thousands, then millions – who had never seen Jesus, before or after his crucifixion.

This evidence is not confined to the past. Thousands of men and women continue to experience a new power, and a continuing 'Presence' in their lives. Although of differing backgrounds, cultures, ages and temperaments, they put it down to the same cause: the risen Lord is with them – alive and at work in our world and in our lives.

FACT 10 SIGNIFICANT WITNESSES ENDORSE IT

In a court of law, expert and surprising witnesses are sometimes called: those with special expertise in the subject under consideration, or people whose background and insights might lead the jury to expect them to come down on the opposite side. One such witness is the mathematical physicist Professor John Polkinghorne. As a physicist he might be expected to disbelieve in such an extraordinary miracle as resurrection, which appears to contravene the laws of nature. In fact he understands this in terms of 'regime change' – a scientific concept which he applies to the resurrection of Jesus. (Fuller details are on the CD *Science and Christian Faith* www.yorkcourses.co.uk). Two other surprising and significant witnesses in this investigation are *Jewish* scholars with no Christian axe to grind. We might expect them to reject the Christian claim, but Professor Geza Vermes of Oxford University wrote this about that first Easter morning:

> **First, the women belonging to the entourage of Jesus discovered an empty tomb and were definite that it was the tomb. Second, the rumour that the apostles stole that body is most improbable. From the psychological point of view, it is likely that they would have been too depressed and shaken to be capable of such a dangerous undertaking. But above all, since neither they nor anyone else expected a resurrection, there would have been no purpose in faking one.**
>
> (*Jesus the Jew*, Collins)

Rabbi Pinchas Lapide, another Jewish scholar (page 46), goes even further: '*I accept the resurrection of Jesus not as an invention of the community of disciples, but as an historical event.*'

But perhaps the weightiest witnesses of all are those who have experienced the transforming power of the resurrection in a profound way. Many people whose lives were in a mess (such as drug addicts and criminals) are now living stable, honest lives. They deny that it was a question of turning over a new leaf or pulling up their socks, because they say that they lacked the moral vision and spiritual strength to put their own lives in order. Rather, they claim to have 'met' the risen Lord. They talk of finding a new sense of direction and a new source of energy (Chapter 6). Such testimony is not easily discounted.

> After reviewing the cumulative evidence for the resurrection of Jesus from the dead, Professor C F D Moule of Cambridge put this searching question:
>
> 'If the coming into existence of the Nazarenes [i.e. the Christian Church] ... rips a great hole in history, a hole of the size and shape of Resurrection, what does the secular historian propose to stop it up with?'

Implications

Christians believe that the resurrection of Jesus from the dead has enormous implications. The New Testament sees it as a great new act of creation by God. It is 'a primal act of God, unimaginable and indescribable, like the creation, with which it is sometimes compared' (C F Evans). At least two implications are clear, and extremely practical.

Death is dead

We shall consider this more fully in Chapter 9. At this point we simply note the fact that our mortality exercises a profound influence upon our lives – producing a range of responses from fear to curiosity. Most reflective people occasionally feel the need to consider the fact that they will die, and the related need to attempt to make sense of life in the light of this inevitable but awesome fact.

The words of Jesus, as recorded in the fourth Gospel, are breathtaking in their sweep:

> **I am the resurrection and the life. He who believes in me will live, even though he dies; and whoever lives and believes in me will never die. Do you believe this?** (John 11:25, 26)

Here is the highest arrogance and folly, or the most profound wisdom. Which of these alternatives is true, depends upon the truth or otherwise of the resurrection of Jesus himself.

In a moving passage, the Venerable Bede (c. 673–735) reports that Edwin, King of Northumbria, gathered his warriors to listen to the missionary Bishop Paulinus. As Paulinus urged them to accept his teaching, a bird flew through the hall and out into the darkness. One of the nobles commented:

> **The life of man is as if a sparrow should come to the house and very swiftly flit through. So the life of man here appears for a little season, but what follows or what has gone before, that surely we know not. Wherefore, if this new learning has brought us any better tidings, surely methinks it is worthy to be followed.**

Insight

The New Testament claims that the resurrection of Jesus from the dead is not simply an *extraordinary* event. It is a highly *significant* event - nothing less than the death of death itself (1 Corinthians 15).

Jesus is alive

As we have noted, countless believers from all cultures and personality types testify to a sense of being 'accompanied' through life by a 'presence' which, though unseen, is very real (see Chapter 6). This presence, they affirm, is a Person – the risen Christ. They claim that he challenges, guides, encourages, inspires and renews them. Their experience is captured by the great (and controversial) Albert Schweitzer (1875–1965), a radical theologian and brilliant musicologist. He abandoned his outstanding academic career to train as a doctor, in order to go to West Africa as a missionary. Albert Schweitzer wrote:

> *He comes to us as one unknown, without a name, as of old by the lakeside. He came to those men who knew Him not. He speaks to us the same word: 'Follow thou me!' and sets us to the tasks which He has to fulfil for our time. He commands. And to those who obey Him, whether they be wise or simple, He will reveal himself in the toils, the conflicts, the suffering which they shall pass through in His fellowship, and, as an ineffable mystery, they shall learn in their own experience Who He is.*

(*The Quest of the Historical Jesus*, SCM Press)

Insight

The second implication of the great Easter message that 'Christ is risen', is that Jesus is alive and active in our world – and in our lives – by his Spirit (Matthew 28:20).

10 THINGS TO REMEMBER

1 *The resurrection of Jesus from the dead is central to the Christian faith.*

2 *Close examination of the facts makes it difficult to explain them in other than Christian terms.*

3 *The resurrection of Jesus is not just one part of 'the jigsaw'. Without it, there would be no jigsaw at all – no Church, no New Testament, no Christianity.*

4 *It was belief in Jesus' resurrection which gave rise to the huge explosion of energy that kick-started the Christian movement.*

5 *The resurrection of Jesus is not only about ancient history; it has huge implications for our lives today.*

6 *If true, the resurrection points to another life beyond the grave – a richer, fuller life.*

7 *The resurrection of Jesus brings strength – reassuring us that, by his Spirit, Christ is alive and active in our world and in our individual lives.*

8 *By his Spirit, the risen Christ accompanies us through life (Matthew 28:20), offering guidance, comfort – and challenge.*

9 *The resurrection narratives were not inventions. The first Christians suffered for their beliefs, and people will suffer for their convictions – but not for their inventions.*

10 *The resurrection of Jesus has support from surprising authorities, including scientists, Jews, keen legal minds and reformed criminals …*

The Bible: contents

In this chapter you will learn:
- *about the Bible's significance in today's world*
- *an overview of the Scriptures*
- *about the impact of the Gospels.*

The Bible in the modern world

Insight

For millions of people in the modern world the Bible brings direction, encouragement, challenge and comfort – a word from God for all seasons.

Rowan Williams is the 104th Archbishop of Canterbury. At his first press conference he said:

> *My first task is that of any ordained teacher, to point to the source without which none of our activity would make sense, the gift of God as it is set before us in the Bible and Christian belief.*

Martin Niemöller was a Christian Pastor imprisoned under the Nazis. For his opposition to Hitler he suffered solitary confinement and spent four years in Dachau concentration camp. Afterwards, he reflected on the importance of the Bible to him during those long years:

> **The Word of God was simply everything to me – comfort and strength, guidance and hope, master of my days and companion of my nights, the bread which kept me from starvation, and the water of life which refreshed my soul.**

Brian Redhead was a popular British broadcaster. To prepare for a BBC series entitled *The Good Book* he read the Bible from cover to cover and commented:

> **It's really a journey through life. It makes sense of the universe we find ourselves in. The story line is tremendous. It just is the greatest document of the lot, and once you've read it, your life is never the same.**

Howard Marshall is Emeritus Professor of New Testament Exegesis at Aberdeen University. He immerses himself in the Greek and Hebrew Scriptures and is aware of keen debate about all aspects of the Bible. He ended one of his books with this moving testimony:

> **So the Christian is faced by the authority of Scripture as the Word of God in its written form... It is through the Bible that I know of the God who has declared his salvation in the life, death and resurrection of Jesus, and with deepest thankfulness I embrace that saving truth and stake my life on it:**

We turn now to consider this all-time best-seller, written by numerous people (many of them unknown) over a time span of more than 1000 years. As we do so, we recognize the immense impact it has had, and continues to have, on nations and on individuals. For many people in the modern world this ancient book is also a living book, providing direction and encouragement, correction and challenge, puzzlement and mystery, inspiration and joy. To use word pictures from the Bible itself, the Word of God is:

- ▶ *sweeter than honey (Psalm 19:10)*
- ▶ *a lamp which gives light to our path (Psalm 119:105)*
- ▶ *a fire burning in our hearts (Jeremiah 20:9)*
- ▶ *a hammer which breaks rocks in pieces (Jeremiah 23:29)*
- ▶ *sharper than a two-edged sword (Hebrews 4:12).*

Before Christ: the Hebrew Scriptures

The Hebrew (Jewish) Scriptures are called the Old Testament by Christians. These writings describe God's dealing with the Jewish people over the centuries before Christ. But they begin with an account of Creation through the command and will of God. Running through the first chapter of the first book of the Bible (Genesis) are two refrains:

▸ 'And God said …'
▸ 'And God saw that it was good.'

> 'In the beginning God created the heavens and the earth. Now the earth was formless and empty, darkness was over the surface of the deep, and the Spirit of God was hovering over the waters. And God said, 'Let there be light', and there was light. God saw that the light was good, and he separated the light from the darkness.'
>
> (Genesis 1:1–4)

Genesis does not attempt to give a scientific account of the creation of the universe, for it was written in a pre-scientific age. The focus of attention is not upon the 'mechanics' (the how) of creation, but upon the central fact that our universe was made, and is sustained, by the creative power of God (see also Chapter 10). *We are not here by chance.* Further, these early chapters of the Bible underline our responsibility as God's stewards of the natural world.

In Chapter 3 of Genesis we read of the temptation of Adam and Eve, their disobedience and the entry of disharmony, pain and toil ('the Fall'). Thus we find a recognition by the biblical writers of a world which is both beautiful and unpredictable, exciting and terrifying. In Genesis Chapter 4 we find an account of the murder of Abel by his brother Cain. This story of jealousy and violence would be at home in our newspapers. These chapters hold up a mirror to our own times. History as we know it had begun.

This is typical of the Bible. *It is consistently realistic, reflecting real life with all its glory and its degradation.* It refuses to whitewash even its heroes. This realism is one factor which gives the Bible its enduring validity. In some ways the gulf in outlook and experience between ourselves and those men and women is immense. But the Scriptures deal with the 'constants' in human life – with anguish and joy, with personal relationships, with our need to make sense of life.

These ancient writings tell us about men and women who worked, worried, fell in love, laughed, suffered, married, betrayed, forgave, grew old and died. They are about people like us. The Bible considers the great and abiding issues of life and death, sensitively and profoundly. It illuminates the human condition with deep insight and enduring wisdom. As the late Queen Elizabeth the Queen Mother put it:

> **Men turn this way and that in their search for new sources of comfort and inspiration, but the enduring truths are to be found in the Word of God.**

Myths – Good and Bad

In everyday speech the word 'myth' denotes an untrue story, designed to mislead. In contrast, when academics describe an ancient story as myth, they are heaping praise upon it! Myths are enduring stories which carry profound and abiding truths, which cannot be portrayed in any other way. Hence the 'Creation Myths' or the 'Myth of Noah's Flood' are stories conveying powerful – and true – messages about God's love and constancy, the inevitability of judgement, and the glory of nature. To take these tales literally – whether to dismiss them as childish nonsense or to build an anti-scientific view of the world – is to make a fundamental 'category mistake'.

JUDGEMENT AND EXODUS

In Chapter 6 of Genesis, we encounter God's judgement on human sin and arrogance. Only Noah and his family, together with a multitude of animals, escape a great flood. At the end of this famous story, God points to the rainbow as a sign of his covenant of faithfulness (Genesis 9:16). In their pride, men seek to build a tower to heaven (the tower of Babel) and God scatters them throughout the earth. He 'confused the language of the whole world' (Genesis 11:9).

The small group which escaped the flood became numerous and the history of the nation of Israel began with Abraham, Isaac and Jacob (the Patriarchs). Following a widespread famine, the Hebrews were enslaved and oppressed in Egypt. After many years, they escaped from the Egyptian Pharaoh under the leadership of Moses. This escape became known as the *Exodus* and it is celebrated today by Jews everywhere, in the *Passover* meal (pages 141–42).

Moses insisted that this escape was due to the Lord (Yahweh or Jehovah), who is not a local god but the Creator of heaven and earth. God chose this relatively small nation, but not because it had intrinsic merit. Rather, because it was small and vulnerable compared with the surrounding super-powers, Israel was an ideal vehicle to demonstrate God's power and love. Throughout the Bible there runs a reminder that God is saving them – but not simply for their own sake; they are to be a blessing to all the nations. This idea was often resisted by the people and their leaders. Prophets made themselves unpopular by reminding them of this challenging truth.

Insight

The Jewish (Hebrew) Scriptures are called the 'Old Testament' by Christians. They see God's interaction with his people in these 39 books as preparation for the coming of Jesus Christ, who is God's Messiah.

CONQUEST AND EXILE

Following their escape from Egypt, the people grumbled against their leaders and spent 40 years as nomads in the desert. Eventually they conquered Canaan and settled in the land which we know today as Israel/Palestine. The Bible gives an action-packed account of the fortunes of the nation: its rise to power under Kings David and Solomon (c. 1000 BC) and its conquest by mighty empires such as Assyria and Babylon. Often the nation seemed doomed but God remembered his covenant of faithfulness. Despite disobedience by kings, leaders and people, the authentic voice of faith was kept alive by a series of prophets and poets, and by ordinary people with extraordinary vision and courage.

The prophets preached and wrote powerful condemnations of the way in which their nation was served by its leaders. They spoke out against injustice and foreign treaties made in desperation, which showed a lack of faith. They warned of God's judgement but spoke words of hope too. The prophet Jeremiah bought a field at the very moment his nation was conquered and many were exiled to Babylon. It was Jeremiah's way of expressing his God-given conviction that, in course of time, God would restore the nation.

Over the centuries, key institutions developed. These included:

▸ *the Sabbath as a day without work, because God rested after creating the world*
▸ *circumcision of male children on the eighth day*
▸ *the Temple in Jerusalem, the city also known as Zion*
▸ *synagogues in every town.*

Gifted poets expressed the anguish and joy of the nation in a series of Psalms or songs. The Bible contains 150 of these, varying considerably in length and style.

The Hebrew Scriptures contain three major sections: the Law, the Prophets and the Writings. The Psalms fall within the Writings. So does the book of Job, a profound exploration of suffering, and the much pithier book of Proverbs. We also find there a tender celebration of erotic love entitled The Song of Solomon (or Song of Songs).

During times of oppression and disappointment, the people looked for – longed for – a great leader who would rescue and redeem his people. He would be anointed by God. In the Hebrew language the *anointed one* is the *Messiah*. In Greek, it becomes *Christ*. So when we refer to Jesus of Nazareth as Jesus Christ we are acknowledging that, for some of his fellow Jews, Jesus fulfilled that longing and that prophecy – even though others did not recognize him. The New Testament is written by those who joyfully accepted Jesus as the Son of God (Mark 1:1).

> 'Whoever made this book made me; it knows all that is in my heart' (a Chinese reader of the Bible).
>
> 'The Bible is the cradle in which Christ is laid' (Martin Luther).
>
> 'For Christians, the Bible centres on Christ – the New Testament being explicitly about him, the Old foretelling him' (Professor Ninian Smart).

One Bible, two Testaments

The Christian Bible is divided into two unequal parts. The New Testament (or Covenant) contains 27 'books'; the Old Testament contains 39 books and is far longer. It is highly significant that on accepting Jesus as the great new act of God, the early Christians did not feel that the Hebrew Scriptures were redundant. They had been *fulfilled*, not replaced.

The Old Testament contains a rich variety of styles: story, history, law, poetry, lament, reflection ... The New Testament writers frequently drew from these older writings, especially the prophets and the psalms. Among Old Testament passages which are especially loved by Christian believers are Psalm 23 and Isaiah 53. The first Christians viewed the latter as a highly significant passage, pointing to – even describing in detail – the crucifixion of Jesus (Acts 8:26–35).

The Old Testament prophets spoke about a *New Covenant* yet to come (Jeremiah 31:31). At the Last Supper which Jesus ate with his disciples, he made it clear that this New Covenant was about to be sealed in the terrible events to follow. Thus, for Christians, the two sections are held together: the Old pointing forward to the New; the New fulfilling the Old. It is also true that the New Testament marks a radical new beginning. There is *contrast* as well as *continuity*. Christians believe that the centre and fulcrum of it all is Jesus Christ – the light and hope of the world.

'The Lord is my shepherd, I shall not want...
Surely goodness and love will follow me all the days of my life, and I will dwell in the house of the Lord for ever.' (Psalm 23:1,6)

'But he was pierced for our transgressions, he was crushed for our iniquities; the punishment that brought us peace was upon him, and by his wounds we are healed. We all, like sheep, have gone astray, each of us has turned to his own way; and the Lord has laid on him the iniquity of us all' (Isaiah 53:5,6).

'The time is coming,' declares the Lord, 'when I will make a new covenant with the house of Israel and with the house of Judah. It will not be like the covenant I made with their forefathers when I took them by the hand to lead them out of Egypt, because they broke my covenant, though I was a husband to them,' declares the Lord (Jeremiah 31:31,32).

The Apocrypha

Pick up a modern Bible translation, e.g. New RSV (page xvi), and it might contain a section between the Old and New Testaments called the Apocrypha. This term refers to later texts, which were included in the ancient Greek translation of the Hebrew (i.e. Jewish) Scriptures known as *The Septuagint* or LXX – even though they were not in the original Hebrew Scriptures. These texts (sometimes referred to as deutero-canonical) are accepted by the Roman Catholic and Eastern Orthodox Churches as Holy Scripture.

Protestant Churches regard them as helpful, in that they cast further light upon Bible times, but not on a level with the 39 Old Testament and 27 New Testament books.

The four Gospels

The New Testament contains not one, but four, summaries of the life, teaching, death and resurrection of Jesus. The first three Gospels are often referred to as the Synoptic Gospels, which literally means 'with one viewpoint'.

This draws attention to:

▶ *the many similarities to be found between Matthew, Mark and Luke*
▶ *the different approach taken by John as he paints his pen-portrait of Jesus.*

Mark is widely regarded as the earliest Gospel, although it is placed after Matthew in the Bible. It was probably completed around AD 65, some 30 years after the death of Jesus. Written in fairly rough Greek, it breathes dynamic action: 'immediately' is one of Mark's favourite words. He includes some Aramaic words (Chapter 5) and takes care to explain Jewish customs for Gentile readers. Jesus is seen as the One who has authority over sickness, sin and chaos.

A quarter of Mark's 16 chapters focus on the death of Jesus. He also describes the beheading of John the Baptist, whose work of preparation for Jesus is recorded in all four Gospels. This Gospel ends on an enigmatic note, with the women visiting the tomb in which Jesus was laid. The tomb is empty and they are overawed by forces and events which are beyond their understanding. Mark's account ends abruptly and there is debate about a possible lost ending. A 'longer ending' was written later and is included in most Bibles as Mark 16:9–20.

Because Mark's account is probably the first, and as Christianity is the largest movement in all history, Lord Blanch (a former Archbishop of York) described this short Gospel as 'the most important document in the history of the world'.

Matthew This is a longer account than Mark's, written from a Jewish perspective. The writer gathers the teaching of Jesus into five sections, consciously echoing the *Pentateuch* – the five books of 'the law of Moses' at the beginning of the Bible.

The first of these blocks of teaching is the *Sermon on the Mount*, which begins with the *Beatitudes* (page 7). Matthew records other beautiful, gentle words of Jesus: '*Come to me, all you who are weary and burdened, and I will give you rest …* ' (11:28–30). Yet from the same pen we read words of fierce judgement and the refrain: 'Woe to you… ', spoken against hypocrites (Matthew 23).

Jesus is seen as a new and greater Moses. But despite his Jewish background and emphasis, Matthew records the visit of the Gentile Wise Men from the East to the infant Christ. In this way he makes it clear that Jesus is the Saviour of the *whole world*, not just the Jewish people. This Gospel ends on a universal note with 'the great commission' in which Jesus commands his followers to make disciples from 'all nations'. The final sentence contains an inspiring promise by Jesus, which sustains and encourages Christian believers in every generation: 'I will be with you always, to the end of the age (Matthew 28:20).'

If the Gospels are more hymn-sheets than history books, then we should not be looking for the harmony we insist on in, say, the testimony of witnesses to a road accident. All four Gospels agree that to encounter Jesus is to be drawn to him. The Evangelists, each from his own perspective, explore the nature of the extraordinary authority Jesus exercises. Their accounts of what happened may differ, but there is nothing discordant in their understanding of what it means to meet Jesus for the first time.   (Dr John Pridmore)

Luke, probably a Gentile (non-Jewish) doctor, picks up this theme of the universal significance of Christ. In a song often used in Christian worship (the Nunc Dimittis), Luke records the response of an old man (Simeon) to the infant Jesus in the temple in Jerusalem. Simeon describes him as *'a light to lighten the Gentiles and the glory of [God's] people Israel'* (Luke 2:32). Luke underlines the concern of Jesus for women, for the poor, and for the marginalized – his Gospel carries the parables of the Good Samaritan and the Prodigal Son. He stresses the importance of prayer and the activity of the Holy Spirit. Luke's Gospel is the first of a two-part work; the Acts of the Apostles (page 74) is also from his pen. The scholar Ernest Renan described St Luke's account as 'the most beautiful book ever written'.

John It is widely agreed that the fourth Gospel was written last. A reflective account of the impact and importance of Jesus, this Gospel revolves around certain miracles of Jesus, described by John as *signs*. These are linked with *discourses* which highlight the significance of Jesus through a sequence of 'I am' sayings. Thus the healing of a blind man is linked with, 'I am the light of the world'. The raising of Lazarus from the dead is linked with Jesus' breathtaking statement, 'I am the resurrection and the life'. In the same way, Jesus is seen as 'the door', 'the way, the truth and the life', 'the vine' and 'the bread of life'. *Eternal life* is a frequent 'Johannine' phrase. This term means everlasting life; it also carries the meaning of a new quality of life in this world, given to all who put their trust in Jesus Christ.

In the fourth Gospel the enormous significance of Jesus is underlined. John makes it clear that Jesus breaks through and transcends all the usual categories. Even great words like teacher, prophet and Messiah are not significant enough to capture him. He is Lord, God and the Word made flesh. Yet John shows Jesus as a real human being. He thirsts, grows tired and experiences deep emotions, including sorrow and joy. 'Jesus wept' (John 11:35) is the shortest, and perhaps the most poignant, verse in the Bible.

Here in the Gospel narratives we find the foundation stones for key Christian doctrines, especially the *Incarnation*, the *Trinity*, and the *Atonement*, which would develop over the centuries. Modern scholarship understands the Gospels as 'the Christian faith put in narrative form'.

> E V Rieu was invited to translate the Gospels for *The Penguin Classics*. After doing so, he wrote:
> 'They are full of quiet humour. The crowds must often have laughed. Superimposed on all my previous impressions is one of power, tremendous power, utterly controlled.
> It was his (Jesus') eyes that seem to have impressed his followers most deeply. Of the other features of his face they have left no record.
> Of what I have learnt from these documents in the course of my long task, I will say nothing now. Only this, that they bear the seal of the Son of Man and God, they are the Magna Charta of the human spirit.'

Other New Testament writings

Well before these four celebrated Gospels were completed, other Christian pens had been at work. After their completion, many more Christian documents were written, few of which were accepted as belonging to the Canon of Holy Scripture.

Insight

The New Testament is directly about Jesus – his life and ministry, his death and resurrection. It also charts the rise of the early Church, which has grown into the largest movement in all history.

LETTERS

There are 21 letters (epistles) in the New Testament, written by a range of authors. Although they stand after the four Gospels in the Bible, many of them were written before the Gospels were completed. Some are very brief; others are more comprehensive.

Several bear the names of, or are linked to, apostles: Peter (two letters); John (three letters); James (one letter); Jude (one letter). One lengthy letter is anonymous (the letter to the Hebrews).

Paul wrote most of the letters in the New Testament (13 carry his name). Following his conversion on the Damascus road (Chapter 15), he poured his vision and energy into planting churches in the countries surrounding the Mediterranean. He regarded the preaching of the good news of Jesus Christ and the formation of Christian communities as events of enormous, cosmic significance. Paul believed that God was creating nothing less than a new humanity.

Yet he was well aware of the fragility of the whole enterprise. Professor David Ford has calculated that the number of Christians in Corinth in New Testament times was probably less than 50. They were surrounded by powerful pagan influences which many converts continued to find attractive.

Paul knew that the enterprise was secure; ultimately it was God's work and Paul had unshakeable faith in 'the God and Father of our Lord Jesus Christ' (2 Corinthians 1:3). But on another level, he realized that these churches and individual Christians were very vulnerable. So he wrote letters to these small communities in which he challenged, encouraged and argued, displaying intense passion and great tenderness.

He dealt with *doctrinal questions* such as the importance of 'justification by faith' (Chapter 17), and the cosmic significance of Christ. He dealt with *ethical questions*, seeking to strengthen ties of faith, love, family life and Christian fellowship. Paul was a trained Jewish scholar who employed the Hebrew Scriptures in the service of Christ, boldly and creatively.

Frequently he focused on the significance of the death of Jesus, the implications of the resurrection of Jesus and the power of the Spirit of Jesus. His thought is complex, but if there is a single key it is this: '*God was in Christ reconciling the world to himself*'

(2 Corinthians 5:19). This theme of reconciliation is vital for an understanding of the Christian faith. According to Paul, through Jesus, God knocked down all the barriers which divide:

▶ *the barriers which sin erects between disobedient humanity and the holy God*
▶ *the barriers between races, social classes and the sexes ('There is neither Jew nor Greek, slave nor free, male nor female, for you are all one in Christ Jesus', Galatians 3:38).*

THE ACTS OF THE APOSTLES

Following the four Gospels there is a fast-moving 'book' of 28 chapters, which describes the expansion of the Christian Church, following the death and resurrection of Jesus. This account is written as a sequel to his Gospel by Luke, who focuses on certain key individuals: Peter, Stephen, Philip, Barnabas, Silas, Lydia, Priscilla and Aquila, Timothy and Paul ...

Acts is dedicated to 'Theophilus' (which means 'lover of God') and seeks to give an orderly account of recent extraordinary events. The key event occurs in Acts chapter 2 when, at the Jewish Festival of Pentecost in Jerusalem, God's Holy Spirit comes in power upon the disciples (Chapter 15).

Peter is centre-stage for the first few chapters but after Paul's conversion (pages 285–86), Luke focuses on him. His three great missionary journeys – full of action and incident – are described in detail. As he seeks to take the gospel to Jews and Gentiles, Paul is knocked about, imprisoned and opposed, but nothing is able to suppress him. At certain points Luke writes in the first person plural (the 'we' passages), for he was one of Paul's travelling companions. Friendship and mutual support were key factors in the spread of the gospel.

In a telling phrase in Acts, Luke informs us that in his Gospel he outlined 'all that Jesus began to do and teach' (Acts 1:1). In this way, Luke affirms his faith that Jesus continues to be active in and through his followers, by his Spirit. They do not worship a dead hero; they are inspired, guided and empowered by a living Presence.

REVELATION

The Bible ends with a remarkable book, cast in the form of a series of visions or revelations experienced by John (Revelation 1:1) in exile on the Isle of Patmos. (This 'John' is probably not the author of the fourth Gospel. John, like Mary, is a very common name in the New Testament.)

Written when the Church was being persecuted, it belongs to a genre of writing called 'apocalyptic'. '*Revelation belongs to the literature of protest and religious revolt*' (John Court). This book encourages embattled Christians by:

▶ *pointing to Jesus, the Lamb upon the Throne*
▶ *assuring them that God will ultimately judge and overthrow the persecuting powers*
▶ *reassuring them that perseverance will result in victory and glory.*

Written in a kind of code, its meaning is not always transparent to the modern reader. This book has become a key text for some sects and cults, who claim to be able to work out from its pages the precise date and programme for the end of the world. Jesus himself pointed out the futility of this exercise (Mark 13:32–33).

The Book of Revelation and, therefore, the entire Bible, ends with John's vision of 'a new heaven and a new earth.' A moving passage, often read at Christian funeral services, contains these beautiful words:

> *And I heard a loud voice from the throne saying, 'Now the dwelling of God is with men, and he will live with them. They will be his people, and God himself will be with them and be their God. He will wipe every tear from their eyes. There will be no more death or mourning or crying or pain, for the old order of things has passed away.'* (Revelation 21:3–4)

The Bible is a great love story. It describes how, despite our disobedience and indifference, God persevered with the human race. Indeed, 'God loved the world so much that he gave his only Son' (John 3:16). The Bible is also a book about a battle: it describes a cosmic struggle between good and evil. That great struggle finds its focus in Jesus Christ. We read that light and darkness, love and hatred, compassion and indifference have contended and that he – Jesus – is Victor, Lord and Saviour.

We find, too, that at a more modest level we are all caught up in that same struggle. The Bible assures us that eternal issues are at stake, as it challenges us with this central question: will we follow 'the true light' (John 1:9) or do we 'love darkness rather than light' (John 3:19)?

10 THINGS TO REMEMBER

1 The Bible throws light upon the deep questions and complexities of life in every age.

2 The Bible is an ancient book which deals with the 'constants' in human life – relationships, love, hate, war, forgiveness, the created world …

3 To take the Bible seriously does not involve taking all of it literally.

4 The Bible has sustained people in the toughest of circumstances (e.g. concentration camps).

5 The Hebrew (Jewish) scriptures are called the 'Old Testament' by Christians.

6 Christians believe that the Old Testament points forward to the coming of Jesus Christ.

7 The New Testament is directly about Jesus Christ and the life of the early Church.

8 The Bible refuses to whitewash its heroes and heroines. It is consistently realistic – the saints are also sinners, saved by God's grace.

9 The Bible contains various kinds of literature – law, history, parable, poetry. Overall, it is the story of God's love and faithfulness.

10 The Bible is regarded by Christians as a 'living' text through which we can hear the word of God. It is 'God breathed' (2 Timothy 3:16).

5

The Bible: questions

In this chapter you will learn:

* *how the Bible was formed*
* *about the significance of biblical criticism*
* *about translations and the Dead Sea Scrolls.*

Remembering and recording

> **Insight**
> The original 'books' of the Bible were first written, and
> then copied, on parchment scrolls. They were owned by
> communities and read aloud. The codex – a book with a
> spine – was developed by the fourth century AD.

Jesus of Nazareth and his first disciples (all Jews) were conscious of
standing in a long and noble tradition. It was a tradition in which
the Scriptures had a central place. In his Gospel Luke tells us that
Jesus went into the synagogue in his home town of Nazareth, where
the people had gathered for worship on the Sabbath. He took a
scroll of Hebrew Scripture and read from the prophet Isaiah:

> *The Spirit of the Lord is upon me, because he has anointed me
> to preach good news to the poor. He has sent me to proclaim
> freedom for the prisoners and recovery of sight for the blind, to
> release the oppressed, to proclaim the year of the Lord's favour.*

(Luke 4:18,19)

Jesus returned the scroll to the official and declared: '*Today has this prophecy been fulfilled in your hearing.*'

Jesus constantly drew on the Hebrew Scriptures, bringing out deeper meanings, making new connections and – astonishing to his hearers – claiming to be the One to whom the Hebrew prophets pointed. This notion of Jesus fulfilling the rich promises and prophecies scattered throughout the Old Testament, became a key theme for the writers of the New Testament.

Scrolls represented weeks of careful work by authors or scribes. The development of the *codex* (a book with a spine) by the fourth century AD would bring a minor revolution, but scrolls carried the first written accounts of the good news about Jesus Christ.

Many scrolls were communal property which were read out to the assembled company. In addition, unrecorded stories were passed on by word of mouth. This is how the stories about Jesus, and accounts of his teaching, circulated in the days of his ministry and in the months and years following his death. Teaching, preaching, storytelling; hearing, remembering, repeating: these were crucial elements in the spread of the message of Jesus and his early followers. The oral and the written accounts intermingled at an early stage.

Which languages?

Eventually the first disciples grew old, or their lives were in danger from persecution. The need for a written record of the actions and teaching of Jesus became urgent. In a remarkably short time, the four Gospels which stand at the beginning of the New Testament came into being – written in Greek.

Jesus and his first disciples were almost certainly tri-lingual. They spoke Aramaic and a few Aramaic words are scattered throughout the New Testament. They understood Hebrew, the language of their own Jewish Scriptures. But to communicate widely they also needed Greek, the language spoken and written throughout the Roman Empire. This is the language of the New Testament.

From God or men?

These Greek accounts of the activity and teaching of Jesus have been studied more closely than any other documents in history. Scholars continue to be fascinated by the relationship of one Gospel record to another.

▶ *Which came first?*
▶ *Were sections from one copied into another?*
▶ *If so, why are there so many puzzling differences?*
▶ *Do they give a reliable account of events and teaching?*
▶ *How many years elapsed between the events which they record and the written accounts?*

The Christian Church has, by and large, welcomed this scholarly scrutiny.

The Church accepts and rejoices in the authority of the New Testament as sacred Scripture, inspired by God's Spirit and authoritative for Christian living. But its inspiration by God's Spirit (or more accurately its 'expiration': the Greek word is *God-breathed* – 2 Timothy: 3:16) subtly works through the personalities and outlook of the human authors (2 Peter 1:20, 21 – page 91).

The *Catechism of the Catholic Church* sums up like this:

> **God inspired the human authors of the sacred books. To compose the sacred books, God chose certain men who, all the while he employed them in this task, made full use of their own faculties and powers so that, though he acted in them and by them, it**

was as true authors that they consigned to writing whatever he wanted written, and no more.

In this regard the Christian view of the Bible is different from the Muslim view of the *Qur'an* or the Mormon view of *The Book of Mormon*. These sacred texts are believed by the adherents of those faith communities to have been dictated by the angel Gabriel, and sent from heaven on golden tablets, respectively. Human involvement in the production of their sacred books is minimal, according to Muslims and Mormons. In contrast, the strong human involvement in the production of the Christian Scriptures is to be expected and welcomed in a faith which centres on Incarnation – God becoming a human being.

Why these books?

Insight

Some recent popular books have claimed to reveal a conspiracy by the Church to suppress the truth about Jesus – citing the authority of one or more of the 'Apocryphal Gospels'. In fact, the four Gospels in the New Testament have their roots in real history and were written earlier than Apocryphal Gospels such as 'Thomas' or 'Judas', which circulated among Gnostic groups.

The first few Christian centuries gave rise to a considerable volume of literature. So two questions arise: why and how did these particular 27 books come to comprise the New Testament?

In the early Church, the term 'Scripture' originally referred to writings from the Old Testament. But the second letter of Peter refers to Paul's letters as Scripture and very soon Christian writers, such as Justin Martyr (*c.* 100–165), were referring to 'the New Testament'. For some time there was debate about whether certain books should be included (for example, hesitations were expressed about Hebrews, 2 Peter and Jude). In the Armenian Church, the inclusion of Revelation was resisted until the twelfth century.

Some other early writings, such as the *Didache* and the *First Letter of Clement*, were serious contenders for inclusion. There was also some disagreement about the *order* of the books. The four Gospels and Paul's letters were accepted as authoritative by the end of the second century. In AD 367, Bishop Athanasius wrote a letter in which he listed the 27 books of the New Testament as being canonical, i.e. official Scripture.

What criteria were used for deciding which books should be included in the 'canon' of the New Testament? Presumed authorship by an apostle was one strong reason for including some books; but not, for example, the Gospels of Mark and Luke (although the early Bishop Papias [*c.* 60–130] asserts that Mark received his material from St Peter. It has also been suggested that Mark was the young man who fled naked – Mark 14:51–52). Apostolic authorship of some of these documents would be questioned by some biblical critics, several centuries later. Dr Alister McGrath helpfully sums up:

The basic principle appears to have been that of the recognition rather than the imposition of authority.

In other words, the works in question were recognized as already possessing authority, rather than having an arbitrary authority imposed upon them.

Apocryphal Gospels

'At the age of five, Jesus fashioned 12 sparrows from clay on the Sabbath day. This was reported to Joseph who asked, "Why are you doing these things which ought not to be done on the Sabbath?" Jesus clapped his hands and called out to the sparrows, "Be off!" At this the birds flew away chirping.'

This charming story comes from the **Infancy Gospel of Thomas**. It reminds us that the four Gospels in the Bible were not the only early documents about Jesus. Other non-biblical writings include the **Gospel of Nicodemus**, the **Acts of Pilate**, the **Gospel of Peter**, the **Gospel of Judas** and the **Gospel of Thomas**.

The last named is the best known. The brief extract below gives a flavour of this document which was used by a Gnostic community (Chapter 15).

'These are the secret words which Jesus, the living one, spoke and Didymus Judas Thomas wrote down …

▶ And he said: "Whoever finds the interpretation of these words will never face death.
▶ Love your brother as your own soul; guard him like the apple of your eye.
▶ Split the wood; I am there. Lift up the stone and you will find me there." '

Publishers love conspiracy theories! Theories about the Church and the origins of Christianity sell books, as is evidenced by the Dan Brown phenomenon. For this reason, the Apocryphal Gospels are a happy hunting ground for writers looking for a sensation. On closer examination, the 'sensations' are usually found to have flimsy foundations (see, for example, the section on the Dead Sea Scrolls: page 88). The Apocryphal Gospel of Thomas is a Coptic document which was discovered near Nag Hammadi in Upper Egypt in 1945. It is a short work, containing 114 sayings attributed to Jesus, with no narrative setting and few roots in history. Some of these sayings resemble Jesus' words in the New Testament Gospels; many do not. The material does not pre-date the Gospels in the Bible (the 'canonical' Gospels) and was not originally called a 'Gospel'. Nothing in this 'Gospel' threatens to shake long-accepted views of the origins of Christianity.

Biblical criticism

We turn now to examine some of the tools and approaches which scholars employ in their study of the Christian Scriptures.

The word 'criticism' has two meanings. In everyday speech, to criticize is to say something negative (however constructive the outcome may be). In the Arts, however, it is a neutral term. Film critics are not always critical. They may say that a film is poor or superb, and go on to give their reasons: such critics are simply using their critical faculties. Whether they praise or condemn, they are seeking to make a careful analysis leading to an informed judgement.

Biblical 'critics' do not stand in judgement on the Scriptures. Rather, they seek to deepen understanding by bringing knowledge and discernment. Indeed, *all* who read the Bible seriously find themselves involved in this enterprise. Sooner or later we are bound to ask such questions as:

▶ *Why does Luke include the shepherds in his birth narratives but not the visit of the wise men (included only in Matthew)?*
▶ *Why does Matthew have a Sermon on the Mount and Luke a Sermon on the Plain?*
▶ *Why do different evangelists record different post-resurrection appearances of the risen Lord?*

We are intrigued by the possible reasons for these and other differences, which engage our critical faculties. In pursuing such questions, scholars have developed many tools and we shall look briefly at six different kinds of biblical criticism.

Textual criticism
This activity is designed to establish, as closely as possible, what those who wrote the biblical texts actually recorded on their scrolls. Textual critics work with the numerous early copies available to them. They note and seek to resolve differences, and attempt to provide translators with accurate Hebrew and Greek texts. This is sometimes called *Lower Criticism*, not because it is an inferior form of activity, but because it lays the foundation for all Bible study and translation. All other kinds of biblical criticism taken together are called *Higher Criticism*.

Source criticism
This was first applied to the Pentateuch (the first five books in the Old Testament) in the eighteenth century. Later it was applied to

the New Testament, especially the Gospels. The things which Jesus said and did were remembered and passed on by word of mouth: some material was written down. In the course of time, the Gospel writers (Evangelists) drew on a variety of oral and written sources, none of which has survived in its own right. Many scholars have tried to unravel this process in an attempt to discern the various sources which fed into the completed Gospels. Two questions are of particular interest:

▶ *Was there a document (now lost) containing collected sayings of Jesus? (Scholars refer to this as Q, probably from 'Quelle', the German word for 'source' – although even this is debated!)*
▶ *What is the relationship between the three Synoptic Gospels? For centuries it was thought that Mark abbreviated Matthew's Gospel, but most modern scholars believe that Matthew and Luke drew on Mark's Gospel, which was written first.*

Form criticism

Form critics are concerned with the various forms of material in the Bible: miracle stories and sayings of Jesus, for example. They are also concerned with the '*Sitz im Leben*' (situation in life) of the various units.

In the fourth Gospel, we read that Jesus said and did far more than could be recorded. Why then was *this* episode recorded but not *that*? And why does Luke (for example) include material omitted by Mark? Possibly because one writer had access to different information about Jesus from the others. Possibly because they had different interests. Possibly too, because the communities for which the different authors originally wrote, had particular concerns (hence '*Sitz im Leben*': a consideration of the circumstances of the early Christian communities for which the Gospels were first written). If Jesus addressed issues of importance to these churches, it would be natural for the Evangelists to record those particular words and deeds.

Form criticism flourished in Germany in the mid-twentieth century. Some form critics were very radical – assuming that the early church would readily invent sayings which they attributed to Jesus.

Other scholars disputed this. John Robinson spoke for these in *Can We Trust the New Testament?* (Mowbray):

> *There seems to have been a reverence for the remembered speech and acts of Jesus which provided an inbuilt resistance to the temptation to make him merely their mouthpiece or puppet.*

Redaction criticism

This was a reaction against methods based on analysis and dissection. True, the Evangelists used a range of sources, but they did not 'cut and paste'. *Selection is interpretation* and they were skilful editors (i.e. *redactors*) and purposeful theologians. The four Evangelists were highly creative – weaving their sources into genuine works of art. Redaction criticism considers the complete text, the particular concerns of each writer and the different emphases which he wished to make.

Narrative criticism

This is concerned with the Bible as a sequence of stories within an overall story. It takes seriously the universal appeal of story, in its various forms. *Why Narrative?* edited by S Hauerwas and L G Jones (Wipf and Stock), and *Telling the Story* by Andrew Walker (SPCK) develop this.

Canonical criticism

This emphasizes the final form of the biblical text. It is less concerned with stages in the development of the text; more interested in asking what it means to honour a text as sacred Scripture. The Church has received this text as canonical. What are the implications of this? The next question is but a short step away: just what is the Bible saying to the living community of believers *today*?

> 'However much Christianity has to update itself and adapt to circumstances, it can never cut adrift from the spirit of Jesus, whether he suits us or whether he does not. And the New Testament, honestly read and studied, is the one place you can face that bit of reality.'
>
> (Professor Leslie Houlden)

Reliable manuscripts?

Insight

The world's libraries and museums have far more old copies of the Scriptures (part or whole) than of any other ancient book. The Bible, and especially its four Gospels (Matthew, Mark, Luke and John), has been subjected to closer and more intense scrutiny than any other book in history.

Existing ancient documents have survived a hazardous journey down the centuries. They were written and copied by hand (a slow and laborious process) and were liable to damage or destruction by fire, water, rough usage or simple neglect. So it comes as no surprise to learn that the world's museums and libraries contain only:

- *eight ancient copies of* Thucydides' History
- *ten ancient copies of* Caesar's Gallic War
- *two ancient copies of the* Histories of Tacitus.

By ancient copies we mean that there is a gap of about 1300, 900 and 700 years respectively, between the originals of these famous historical documents and the copies which have survived. In contrast, hundreds of ancient copies of the Gospels can be found in the world's museums and libraries. So it is evident that there is a rich harvest of ancient biblical texts for scholars to work with.

> *The wealth of manuscripts, and above all the narrow interval of time between the writing and the earliest extant copies, make it by far the best-attested text of any ancient writing in the world.*
>
> (John Robinson)

> *The New Testament manuscripts in our possession are much closer in time to the original writings, more numerous and in closer agreement with each other than any other ancient book.*
>
> (Professor Hans Küng)

In the end, of course, we weigh all the available evidence and decide to trust the records – or not, as the case may be.

Professor David Ford puts the Christian position with great clarity:

> **The Gospels are testimony. Because we cannot re-run historical events, you either have to trust or not trust some of the people who were there. It is important that we as Christians are part of a community that did decide early on to trust certain testimonies. That does not rule them out from cross-examination. But we can be absolutely confident that in terms of the testimony of Jesus, there is no disproof of the main thrust of that testimony.**

Hundreds of early copies of parts of the New Testament are available to scholars. Two complete copies of the New Testament are dated around AD 350 – less than 300 years after the original. One is in the Vatican Library; the other in the British Museum. The latter was bought from the Soviet Government on Christmas Day 1933 for £100,000. The earliest undisputed find, a fragment from St John's Gospel, is dated around AD 130 and is held in the John Rylands Library in Manchester.

The Dead Sea Scrolls

From time to time an archaeological find, or a new theory, makes headlines because it gives rise to sensational claims which appear to disprove established ideas. One famous example is the Dead Sea Scrolls. These scrolls were from the library of a Jewish community based at Qumran on the north-western shore of the Dead Sea, between 150 BC and AD 68. Their discovery in 1947 was described by Professor W F Albright as 'the greatest manuscript discovery of modern times'.

Wild claims were made for the Scrolls. In particular, a few writers suggested that there were strong similarities between Jesus and the original leader (*The Teacher of Righteousness*) of the community which wrote and preserved the scrolls. It was argued that Christianity had its roots in the teaching of this Jewish sect, which flourished before Jesus was born. A group of scholars working on the Scrolls denied this. They issued a statement asserting that: '*Nothing that appears in the scrolls hitherto discovered throws any doubts on the originality of Christianity.'* There is a marked contrast between:

▶ *the Community at Qumran (where the scrolls were found) and the early Christians*
▶ *the Teacher of Righteousness and Jesus.*

This contrast was later confirmed by two Jewish scholars: Geza Vermes and Yigael Yadin. The position is summed up by the British archaeologist, Professor Alan Millard: *'The differences between the Teacher of Righteousness and Jesus are huge.'*

This does not detach Jesus from his culture. There *are* similarities between Jesus and other Jewish teachers of his day. As we have seen (Chapter 1), Jesus was unique in approach and stature but he did not set out to be 'original'. He gladly accepted many of the rich traditions of his nation and was aware of standing within the flow of its history.

Pursuing links between Jesus and the Teacher of Righteousness may have ended in a cul-de-sac, but the Dead Sea Scrolls do have some bearing upon the Bible: both Old and New Testaments.

The Scrolls increase our confidence in the text of the Old Testament. At least part of every Old Testament book (except Esther) has been found in the Scrolls. They are about 1000 years older than any other text of the Hebrew Scriptures so far discovered. Careful comparison shows just how successful Jewish scribes were, over the centuries, in their desire to pass on faithful and accurate copies of the Scriptures. Magnus Magnusson rightly spoke of 'the essential integrity of the scribal tradition'.

Insight

When the Dead Sea Scrolls were discovered in 1947, extravagant allegations were made for their destructive impact on the Bible. In fact, further study of the Scrolls has shown that scribes over the centuries were remarkably careful and faithful when copying the Jewish Scriptures (the Christian 'Old Testament').

The Scrolls illuminate the world of the New Testament, for they were written between 150 BC and AD 68. Before the Scrolls were discovered, some scholars believed that John's Gospel was a free composition, written in the second century under Greek influence. If so, it had no strong roots in history. But when we put the Dead Sea Scrolls alongside the fourth Gospel, we see how very Jewish St John's work is. Contrasts like 'light and dark' and 'life and death', which abound in John's Gospel, were thought to be Greek in origin. The Dead Sea Scrolls show that these contrasts are at home in first-century Jewish thought. So the fourth Gospel fits well into the Jewish background which it describes; it has a secure basis in the history of that period.

In 2007 Professor Michael Jursa of the British Museum deciphered an ancient cuneiform inscription on a clay tablet dating from 595 BC, confirming a payment by Nabu-sharrussu-ukin, 'chief eunuch' at the court of King Nebuchadnezzar. He commented, 'A throwaway detail in the Old Testament turns out to be accurate and true. I think that means that the whole of the narrative [of the prophet Jeremiah] takes on a new kind of power.'

The Word of God?

For centuries, belief in the inspiration of Scripture by God was uncontroversial and widespread. Just what was meant by such phrases as the *Word of God* and *inspired Scripture* was not a real issue, until Enlightenment thinking (Chapter 18) gave rise to biblical criticism. In today's Church, various views are held concerning the precise nature of divine inspiration. Debate centres around questions such as:

- ▶ *What does the Bible teach about itself?*
- ▶ *How did Jesus view and use the Hebrew Scriptures?*
- ▶ *How did the New Testament writers use the Old Testament?*
- ▶ *Does 'inspired' necessarily mean 'infallible'?*
- ▶ *Must 'inspired' always mean 'inspiring'?*
- ▶ *Did God inspire the writers and/or the text itself? Does his Holy Spirit also inspire the reader to understand the true meaning?*
- ▶ *Should we refer to the Bible as 'the Word of God'? Or does it contain the Word of God?*

In this regard, there are two important Bible verses:

▶ All Scripture is inspired [literally 'breathed'] by God and profitable for teaching, for reproof, for correction, and for training in righteousness *(2 Timothy 3:16–17). This indicates the practical nature of the Bible. It is recorded for our guidance and obedience. God's word speaks to our condition: it shines in a dark world which desperately needs light. The concept of* revelation *(self disclosure by God) is vital to Christianity. Christians believe that the Bible reveals otherwise hidden truths about God, about life, and about the way of salvation. '"Revelation" does not mean merely the transmission of a body of knowledge, but the personal disclosure of God within history' (Alister McGrath).*

▶ No prophecy ever came by the impulse of man, but men moved by the Holy Spirit spoke from God *(2 Peter 1:20–21). This shows that inspiration by God does not rule out full human participation in the communication of his message. Debate about the precise nature of inspiration continues. But all churches believe that they are called to live under the Bible's authority. Interpretation and application can and do vary, but the Bible is – or should be – decisive for Christian belief and behaviour.*

Blessed Lord,
who caused all holy Scriptures
to be written for our learning:
help us so to hear them,
to read, mark, learn, and inwardly digest them
that, through patience, and the comfort
of your holy word,
we may embrace and for ever hold fast
the hope of everlasting life,
which you have given us in our Saviour Jesus Christ.

(Collect for Bible Sunday)

Inspiring?

'Inspired' does not always mean *inspiring*. Some of the Bible is intrinsically boring. Tables of family names, and detailed rules and regulations for sacrifices to be offered in tabernacle and temple do not make exciting reading! Nor is every part of equal importance. Some of the rules for worship in the Old Testament have no authority over Christians, because those rules have been fulfilled and superseded by Jesus Christ.

However, these passages are necessary if we are to understand the overall message. And of course some passages are wonderfully inspiring. Who cannot be stirred by the storm scenes in the book of Acts? Who can fail to be moved by the suffering servant in Isaiah 53, the passion narratives, and the great hymn about love in 1 Corinthians 13? Who is not comforted by Psalm 23? Whose heart is not lifted on hearing the Sermon on the Mount? Whose will is not challenged by the call to forgiveness in the Lord's Prayer?

Some passages which seem at first sight to be of little direct relevance, contain underlying principles with universal application. Few Western Christians face the question of 'meat offered to idols' discussed by the apostle Paul (Romans 14; 1 Corinthians 8). But the need for empathy, mutual support and consideration of the effects of our behaviour on others, is never out of date. These issues are at the heart of that debate.

It is because the Bible 'speaks' to us that it is read at the bedsides of the sick and dying and on occasions of great joy such as weddings. And many Christians meditate upon a Scripture passage daily and find with the psalmist that it is 'sweeter than honey'. To use another image from the Bible itself, it is a lamp which gives light to their path through life – encouraging, inspiring and challenging by turns.

Insight

The Bible is consistently realistic, refusing to whitewash even its heroes. It deals with the 'constants' in human life – with anguish and joy, love and hatred, anger and reconciliation, and with the need to make sense of our lives ...

Why so much sex and violence?

The Bible takes the form of a history, not a treatise. This is why it contains so much sex and violence, for all real history does! We learn from this that God is concerned with the world as it *really* is. The ancient world was certainly very violent. Fighting between nations was widespread, and Israel was no exception. Many battles are described in the Bible, and the Jewish people prayed for God's help as they fought.

But the Israelites were different from their neighbours in various significant ways. They knew that certain forms of violence were forbidden by God – human sacrifice for example. And their teachers and prophets emphasized the importance of offering care and hospitality – especially to orphans, widows, and foreigners within their borders.

Two further points are relevant. First, the Bible is an honest book. It tells the truth about its heroes – even when this is painful. Peter's cowardice in denying Jesus just before his crucifixion is not hushed up (Matthew 26:70). Nor are King David's murder of Uriah and seduction of Bathsheba (2 Samuel 11), Abraham's deception (Genesis 12) or the psalmist's desire for revenge (Psalm 137).

These things are recorded, not because they are uplifting but because they happened. They show us real human beings with all their glory and shame – not plaster saints. Their deception, cowardice and violence are condemned by the very Scriptures which describe these human failings with such honesty. In this way, they help us to understand our own motives and actions. *Above all, they illuminate God's grace, mercy and transforming power. And they challenge us to repentance, faith and obedience, as they invite us to become part of the ongoing story.*

We note too that the Bible shows moral and spiritual development. We do not find a smooth progression over the centuries, from violence to love. The upward path was very uneven, and some Old Testament characters were streets ahead of many in the New Testament, or in the modern world. But development there is. Slowly, through many years and even more hard lessons, God taught the people of Israel more and more about love and forgiveness. The climax came when Jesus told his astonished hearers, 'Love your enemies.' He put his own teaching into practice. On the cross he prayed for his torturers: 'Father, forgive them, for they do not know what they are doing.'

Abraham and Isaac – A 'Dream' Sequence?

Many pens have addressed the story of Abraham's (very reluctant) willingness to sacrifice his son, Isaac. It has been addressed from a psychological viewpoint (what did it do to their relationship?) and a historical viewpoint (did it really happen?). Another approach is to think of it as a kind of 'dream sequence', familiar to us from films.

The story arose from the oral tradition. We can imagine a semi-nomadic group gathered around the late night fire after a good supper. Time for an exciting story! These stories addressed the big issues of the day, and the most important of these was how to ensure a plentiful harvest. A poor harvest meant suffering – starvation. All around the Hebrews were people who thought they could ensure abundance by fertility rites ('sacred prostitution') and human sacrifice to their gods. Abraham and his people believed that the Lord (Yahweh) hated these practices. But the possibility that their neighbours might be right after all was in the back of many minds. Empty stomachs needed powerful stories to keep them from wielding the knife. So in this 'dream sequence', Abraham struggles with this hot issue of human sacrifice in a dramatic way. In the end he turns his back on it – and prospers. He concluded that this is not Yahweh's will or way – and so influenced for good the future behaviour of an entire nation. This powerful story linked religion and morality – an unusual combination in the ancient world – and 'ethical monotheism' was born.

Active today?

As we draw to the end of a chapter of thorny issues, we need to ask the question: so what? A study of the Bible raises questions which send us to scholars and source books. Yet it continues to speak to ordinary people, with no great learning. Numbers of people testify to the power of the Bible to alter the course of their lives.

For the Olympic medal winning athlete **Kriss Akabusi**, the Bible was the way into the Christian faith. During the Commonwealth Games in Edinburgh, he found a modern New Testament translation in his hotel room. He read it from cover to cover. 'There was a guy in there', he said, referring to Jesus. 'I'd used his name before, but I never realized he actually lived. I thought he was like the Tooth Fairy or Father Christmas.' That Bible pointed that athlete to Jesus Christ, whom he accepted as Teacher, Lord and Saviour.

Jon Jeffery found himself in hospital following a bad 'fix'. It looked as though he would lose his arm. The doctor who treated him gave him a Bible, although Jon would have preferred a cigarette! But he flicked through the New Testament and two sentences registered:

- ▶ *Fear not, for I am with you.*
- ▶ *If the Son shall set you free, you shall be free indeed.*

In the event the surgeon was able to save his arm, although two fingers had to be amputated. Jon was sent to prison for drug offences and he linked up with the Prison Christian Fellowship. As a Jew he knew the Old Testament well and 'made a nuisance' of himself by asking difficult questions. But eventually, in his prison cell on Christmas Day, Jon put his faith in Jesus Christ. Today he is off drugs and happily married with two sons. He has a fulfilling job with the Bible Society – very fitting for a man who probably owes his life to the power of the ancient Scriptures to speak in the modern world.

> More than 50 million Bibles have been printed in the People's Republic of China by the Amity Foundation, a Chinese Christian agency, in a joint venture with the United Bible Societies. The 50 millionth Bible was printed on 11 September 2007.
>
> Sales of the Bible through the Amazon website increased by 120 per cent in 2006.

Translations

One verse in the Bible (John 3:16) has been translated into approaching 3,000 languages. Here are eight of them:

ENGLISH
For God so loved the world that He gave His only begotten Son, that whoever believes in Him should not perish, but have everlasting life.

RUSSIAN
Ибо так возлюбил Бог мир, что отдал Сына Своего единородного, дабы всякий, верующий в Него, не погиб, но имел жизнь вечную.

SINHALESE
මක්නියාද දෙවියන්වහන්සේ සව කීය ඒකජාතක පුතුයාණන් දෙන තරම ලෝකයාට පේම කළ සේක. එසේ කළේ උන්වහන්සේ කෙරෙහි අදහා ගන්න සෑමදෙනම විනාය නොවී සදා කාල ජීවතය ලබත පිණීසය.

SPANISH
Porque de tal manera amó Dios al mundo, que ha dado a su Hijo unigénito, para que todo aquel que en él cree, no se pierda, mas tenga vida eterna.

SWAHILI
Kwa maana jinsi hii Mungu aliupenda ulimwengu, hata akamtoa Mwanawe pekee, ili kila mtu amwaminiye asipotee; bali awe na uzima wa milele.

SWEDISH
Ty så älskade Gud världen, att han utgav sin enfödde Son, på det att var och en som tror på honom skall icke förgås, utan hava evigt liv.

TAMIL
தேவன், தம்முடைய ஒரேபேறான குமாரனை விசுவாசிக்கிறவன் எவனோ அவன் கெட்டுப்போகாமல் நித்தியஜீவனை அடையும்படிக்கு, அவரைத் தந்தருளி, இவ்வளவாய் உலகத்தில் அன்புகூர்ந்தார்.

WELSH
Canys felly y carodd Duw y byd fel y rhoddodd efe ei unig-anedig Fab, fel na choller pwy bynnag a gredo ynddo ef, ond caffael ohono fywyd tragwyddol.

Figure 5.1 John 3:16 in eight languages.

Source: Reproduced by kind permission of Gideons International

An estimated 6,900 languages and major dialects are spoken around the world. But many of these are spoken by minority groups who are often competent in at least one other mainstream language. At the beginning of 2008, the number of languages with a translation of some or all of the Bible reached 2,426. In 2006 the complete Bible was available in 429 languages and the New Testament had been translated into a further 1,144. This means that at least part of the Bible is available to the vast majority of nations, tribes and clans.

The first book to be printed using moveable type was the *Gutenberg Bible* in 1456. This was the Old Latin version by Jerome (342–420) called the *Vulgate*. The world's presses continue to print hundreds of thousands of copies of the Bible, which remains the world's best-seller (even though copies are often given away free of charge). English translations abound; among the most famous are:

▶ Tyndale's Translation, *which was based on Hebrew and Greek manuscripts. It is incomplete, because William Tyndale was executed in 1536 (page 200) before he finished his great work. It formed the basis for the Authorized Version. Tyndale's work is 'probably the most influential book that's ever been in the history of language – English or any other' (Melvyn Bragg).*
▶ The Geneva Bible, *which was dedicated to Queen Elizabeth I who came to the throne in 1558. This Bible introduced the verse numbers that are now in universal use. Before this, only chapter divisions had been available.*
▶ The Authorized Version *(or King James Version) of 1611, which established itself as the English edition for 300 years. It is still in use but many regular Bible readers use modern editions. These are easier to understand and based on more numerous and accurate sources (see Preface).*

Moving stories are told of churches where Bibles are scarce. The Scriptures are treasured, memorized, copied and circulated with great care and love. By their commitment these believers declare with the Psalmist that:

The ordinances of the Lord are sure
and altogether righteous.
They are more precious than gold,
than much pure gold.

(Psalm 19:9, 10)

10 THINGS TO REMEMBER

1   *The Scriptures were originally written on scrolls.*

2   *The 66 books in the Bible were written over a period of more than one thousand years.*

3   *The Old Testament was written in Hebrew; the New Testament in Greek, with some Aramaic words.*

4   *Christians believe that God's Spirit guided the human authors, whose backgrounds, personalities and formal education (or lack of it!) shine through.*

5   *The Bible has been subject to more careful scrutiny than any other book in history.*

6   *The copies of the Bible we have are more numerous, and much closer in time to the originals, than all other famous ancient documents.*

7   *Discovered in 1947, the Dead Sea Scrolls increase our confidence in the reliability of the text of the Old Testament.*

8   *The Dead Sea Scrolls also illuminate the world of the New Testament.*

9   *The Bible continues to be the world's best-selling book. Over 50 million copies have been printed in modern China.*

10 *The Bible has been translated into all the world's major languages – and (in whole or part) into hundreds of minority languages.*

Part two
Christian belief and practice

6

Christian experience of God

In this chapter you will learn:

- **about experience of God in the Bible**
- **about experience of God in history**
- **about experience of God in today's world.**

Author's note: *We shall return to the subject of Christian experience of God throughout this book e.g. faith and doubt (page 206), love and hope (page 207), conversion (pages 249, 259 and 385).*

Starting with the Bible

The Bible is full of people who claim to have had an experience of God. Celebrated examples in the Old Testament are:

▶ *Abraham, who heeded a call from God to leave his home in order to 'go to a land which I will show you' (Genesis 12:1). This is frequently recalled throughout the Bible as a key example of obedience and trust.*

▶ *Moses, who encountered God in a burning bush, where God revealed himself as 'I am who I am' (Exodus 3:14).*

▶ *Isaiah, who received a vision of the blazing holiness of God in the Temple in Jerusalem. He had a deep sense of his own unworthiness, and received a call from God to be a prophet to his people (Isaiah 6).*

As with the Old Testament, so with the New. Its pages describe numerous examples of people encountering God – sometimes with joy, often with awe and fear.

▶ *At the first Christian Pentecost, the Holy Spirit came in power upon 120 followers of Jesus (Acts 2). They became bold and were able to communicate with those who had gathered in Jerusalem for the Festival, even though the visitors spoke a wide range of languages.*

▶ *The apostle Peter, a devout Jew, was wrestling with the question of Gentiles (non-Jews) and the gospel. Was it possible that they could be welcomed as full members of the Church without first becoming Jews? As he prayed, Peter had a vision in which he was commanded by God to eat food which was 'impure' according to the Jewish law. He protested but a voice replied, 'Do not call anything impure that God has made clean' (Acts 10:15). Peter came to realize that he had the answer to his question: the gospel is for everyone, regardless of race. That realization by one praying man was a defining moment for the history of the world.*

▶ *John, the author of Revelation, was in exile on the Isle of Patmos when he had a vision of the risen and ascended Christ. So awesome was the sight that he 'fell at his feet as though dead'. Jesus encouraged him with words of gentleness and an instruction to 'write what you have seen' (Revelation 1:17–19).*

Somewhat similar experiences have been recorded throughout Christian history. Some have become famous; others are known to only a few. In this chapter we shall consider a tiny sample, to illustrate the breadth of the Christian experience of God.

Conversion

The human heart is heavy and hardened. God must give a man a new heart. Conversion is first of all a work of the grace of God who makes our hearts turn to him... God gives us the strength to begin anew. (Catechism of the Catholic Church)

St Augustine of Hippo (modern Annaba in Algeria) was born in north Africa to a pagan father and Christian mother. He wrestled with the Christian faith for many years. In AD 386 he was in his garden when he heard a child singing the words, 'Take up and read.' He picked up the Scriptures and read these words from Paul's letter to the Romans:

> *... not in sexual immorality and debauchery, not in dissension and jealously. Rather, clothe yourselves with the Lord Jesus Christ, and do not think about how to gratify the desires of the sinful nature.* (Romans 13:13–14)

That moment was a turning point for Augustine, and for the Church. From then on, he employed his formidable intellect in the service of Christ.

Much more recently, the British politician **Jonathan Aitken** had a somewhat similar experience. A former cabinet minister, he was convicted of perjury in 1999 and sent to jail. In prison he encountered the living Christ who gave him fresh values and a new direction. He has written about this in two autobiographical books entitled *Pride and Perjury* and *Porridge and Passion* (Continuum). In November 2007 Jonathan Aitken was asked by the British Conservative Party to make practical proposals for prison reform.

Malcolm Worsley was a thief. On the day of yet another release from prison, a prison officer remarked, 'You'll be back, Worsley.' That officer was right; Malcolm did return, but as a member of staff! For in prison, Malcolm had been converted to Christ. He trained to be a probation officer, and worked with people who are dependent on drugs. In July 1996, Malcolm was ordained as a minister in the Church of England.

Metropolitan **Anthony Bloom** was different from Malcolm Worsley in almost every way: education, personality, upbringing and culture. In turn he became a surgeon, a member of the resistance movement in the Second World War and leader of the Russian Orthodox Church in Britain. He too had a remarkable experience which gave shape and direction to his future life.

As a teenager he wanted to prove to himself that Christianity was untrue, so he read St Mark's Gospel. (He chose St Mark because it is the shortest, and he didn't want to waste time on the exercise!) He wrote:

> *Before I reached the third chapter, I suddenly became aware that on the other side of my desk there was a presence. And the certainty was so strong that it was Christ standing there that it has never left me. This was the real turning point. Because Christ was alive and I had been in his presence I could say with certainty that what the Gospel said about the crucifixion of the prophet of Galilee was true, and the centurion was right when he said, 'truly he is the Son of God'.*
> (*School for Prayer*, DLT)

Hugh Montefiore, Anglican Bishop of Birmingham from 1978 to 1987, had a somewhat similar experience. He grew up in a Jewish family and went to Rugby School. One wintry afternoon, as a teenager alone in his room, he became aware of a figure in white. In his autobiography he wrote:

> *I heard the words 'Follow Me.' Interestingly, I knew that this was Jesus, heaven knows how: I knew nothing about him.' He goes on to say that this was 'an indescribably rich event that filled me afterwards with overpowering joy. I could do no other than follow those instructions… it shaped the whole of my future life'.*
> (*Oh God, What Next?* Hodder & Stoughton)

Sir Alec Guinness told an engaging story in his autobiography *Blessings in Disguise* (Penguin). This incident suggests that the Holy Spirit can use a range of experiences to nudge us towards Christian faith. Sir Alec describes how he gradually moved from hostility towards the Roman Catholic Church, to membership of it. A whole cluster of events led up to this, including one brief encounter with an unknown child. Alec was filming *Father Brown* in France. At dusk he walked back to his hotel, dressed as a Catholic priest. Suddenly a boy of seven or eight appeared, clutched his hand and walked with him. Sir Alec commented:

> *He was full of excitement, hops, skips and jumps, but he never let go of me. Although I was a total stranger he obviously took me for a priest and so to be trusted … I was left with an odd calm sense of elation. Continuing my walk, I reflected that a Church*

> *that could inspire such confidence in a child, making its priests,*
> *even when unknown, so easily approachable, could not be as*
> *scheming and creepy as so often made out. I began to shake off*
> *my long-taught, long-absorbed prejudices.*

There are two further points to note about conversion. First, the phrase 'conversion of life'. Many writers on spirituality insist that conversion is a process. Every day we need to do battle with temptation and turn to Christ. Second, Christian discipleship does not depend upon dramatic experiences. From the New Testament we learn that Timothy (a younger colleague of the apostle Paul) came to faith gradually through the influence of a Christian home (2 Timothy 1:5; 2 Timothy 3:15). Research suggests that a minority of Christians have a dramatic conversion experience. The way into faith is less important than the outcome.

David L Edwards (page 21) makes this point clearly and helpfully:

> *That is why everyone is challenged to respond to God through Jesus Christ in a personal turning (which is what the word 'conversion' means). You have to meet Jesus yourself, and to accept him as your friend and as your Lord ... In many Christian lives, this turning or conversion reaches a climax which can be dated. People can remember the exact time when they accepted Jesus Christ as Lord and Liberator, often after intense struggles to escape from the pressure of his love. But it is not necessary to be able to date your conversion like that.*
>
> *What is essential is that everyone should have his or her personal reasons for being a Christian. You cannot inherit Christian faith as you can inherit red hair or a peculiar nose. You cannot copy Christian faith as you can copy hairstyle or an accent. And you cannot get it completely out of books, as you can get a knowledge of history.*
>
> *Your faith, to be authentic, to guide your life, must be your own. Your very own experience, whether it is dramatic or quiet, long or short, must lead you to know Jesus Christ as your personal liberator.* (What Anglicans Believe, Mowbray)

If David Edwards is right, then the phrase 'born-again Christian' must be used with care. It is true that Jesus told Nicodemus, a Pharisee, that 'no-one can see the kingdom of God unless he is born again' (John 3:3). And, of course, conversion experiences do give a dramatic sense of new beginnings: people like St Augustine and Malcolm Worsley have indeed been 'born again'.

The danger is that those who come to faith more slowly and less dramatically can feel themselves to be spiritually inferior. Another translation of that phrase is 'born from above' (i.e. by the Holy Spirit). In this sense, all who put their trust in Jesus Christ are 'born-again Christians', whether they turn to him in an instant or gradually over a period of time. But, however it starts, this turning to Christ must continue throughout life.

Insight

Conversion to Christ, whether sudden or gradual, has had an enormous impact on world history. Best known is Saul the persecutor, who became St Paul the Apostle. 'A road to Damascus experience' is widely used to describe any dramatic change of direction in life.

Guidance

When I look back at those days, I have no doubt that Providence guided us, not only across those snowfields, but across the storm-white sea that separated Elephant Island from our landing-place on South Georgia. I know that during that long and racking march of thirty-six hours over the unnamed mountains and glaciers of South Georgia, it seemed to me often that we were four, not three. I said nothing to my companions on the point, but afterwards Worsley said to me, 'Boss, I had a curious feeling on the march that there was another person with us.'

(*South*, Ernest Shackleton, 1919)

Michael Bourdeaux is an Anglican clergyman who speaks fluent Russian. He is founder of the Keston Institute, a research unit which, during the years of the Cold War, devoted its resources to helping believers in Communist lands. The way in which he was 'directed' into this work is striking.

In 1963 he received a letter, via Paris, in semi-literate Russian. The letter was not addressed to him personally, but it described the fierce persecutions under Nikita Khruschev, including the confinement of active Christians in psychiatric asylums.

The following year Michael went to Moscow. He set out to visit the church of St Peter and St Paul, only to find that it had been destroyed by order of the authorities. As he looked at the rubble, two elderly women were doing the same. They talked, and to his astonishment he found that these two strangers had written that all-important letter. Those women had travelled 700 miles to Moscow and its recipient had flown from Britain. They would not have met if either of them had arrived at the site of the demolished church an hour earlier or later. The women spoke for Michael as well as themselves when they said, 'God sent you to meet us.'

We begin to see what Archbishop William Temple meant when he commented that when he stopped praying, coincidences stopped happening! Following the women's plea for help, Michael Bourdeaux launched his life's work: careful research into the facts concerning the situation of believers (Jewish, Muslim, Christian, Buddhist and others) in Communist lands.

Frances Young is a university professor and a mother. She teaches theology, and returns home to a severely disabled son. Frances is a radical, probing theologian, who knows that there are no knock-down arguments for the existence of God. Yet she speaks with deep conviction of her own faith, and about certain experiences which convince her of the reality of a personal God.

One day she was sitting in a chair when she had a 'loud thought'. It was as though a voice said to her, 'It doesn't make any difference to Me whether you believe in Me or not!' Later, when driving her car, she had another 'loud thought' telling her to be ordained. She cannot remember the journey itself ('I must have been on automatic pilot or something!') but she remembers the experience very clearly.

I had the whole of my life laid out in front of me; and all its peculiar twists and turns which hadn't seemed to make very much sense suddenly fell into a pattern, as though this was all leading up to that moment and that conclusion. It was quite dramatic in its way.

Frances was ordained as a minister in the Methodist Church on 3 July 1984.

Alexander Solzhenitsyn, the Russian novelist, also believed that he received a commission from God for his life's work. As a young dissident he was imprisoned by the Soviet authorities. In his memoir *The Oak and the Calf* he described his despair at being told that, because of cancer, he had only three weeks to live. He had so much to tell the world and he feared that the Soviet authorities would discover and destroy his writings. Desperately he hid his work (in champagne bottles!). That was in 1953. In 1970 he won the Nobel Prize for literature. He commented:

> **With a hopelessly neglected and acutely malignant tumour, this was a divine miracle; I could see no other explanation. Since then all the life that had been given back to me has not been mine in the full sense: it is built around a purpose.**

Prayer, protection and reassurance

A remarkable example of God apparently answering prayer, has been recounted by the Russian poet **Irina Ratushinskaya.** Irina spent four years in Soviet prisons and labour camps for her literary and human rights activities, before being released in 1986. In a poem, Irina describes herself as 'a huddle by an icy wall'. This gives a sense of the biting cold, the inadequate clothing and the poor diet. But she testifies to two kinds of warmth which she sometimes experienced: the inner emotional warmth of joy and a physical warmth throughout her body, despite the freezing conditions. It is her conviction that these phenomena (experienced by other prisoners, too) were a direct answer to prayer, as this extract from one of her poems shows.

> **Believe me, it was often thus**
> **In solitary cells, on winter nights**

A sudden sense of joy and warmth
And a resounding note of love.
And then, unsleeping, I would know
A huddle by an icy wall:
Someone is thinking of me now,
Petitioning the Lord for me.   from: *Pencil Letter* (Hutchinson)

Gerald Priestland was a distinguished BBC Foreign Affairs correspondent. Following a breakdown, he underwent psychoanalysis and moved from atheism to belief in God. He became a Quaker. Gerald once said, 'I hope I believe. I know that I trust.' His faith, his doubts and his questions were essential tools for his next job as BBC Religious Affairs correspondent.

In 1991 Gerald suffered a stroke. In one of his last broadcasts, his voice marked by a slur resulting from the stroke, he spoke these moving words:

> *I have had the feeling of being crushed under a rock till I could see only one crack of light, and that was the love of God, the absolute certainty, when everything else had been taken from me, that God loved me.*

Mysticism

Can the above experiences properly be described as 'mystical'? Professor Owen Chadwick defines mysticism as 'an experience of direct communication with God. It is not, for example, reading about Jesus and saying that is what God must be like: but kneeling down to say a prayer and suddenly feeling God there, facing you or beside you or in you'. He goes on to say that while people often attempt to describe such experiences, they all acknowledge the inadequacy of words to capture them. Other writers point out that while such experiences can be accompanied by a sense of ecstasy, this is not always the case. It is clear, therefore, that most of the experiences described above could be called 'mystical' – although the people involved might not wish to use that term. Such phenomena have been experienced by Christians throughout the centuries and some have become famous. Three examples are given below:

Mother Julian of Norwich (c. 1342–1414)
Julian was an anchoress who chose to live in a sealed cell in Norwich, where she gave herself to prayer and meditation. In May 1373 she received a series of 16 revelations or 'shewings'. Her book *Revelations of Divine Love* has become a classic and is still widely read today. The revelations were centred on the Holy Trinity and the suffering (the Passion) of Jesus. She held a hazelnut in her hand and took it to represent the whole world. '*In this little thing I saw three properties. The first is that God made it, the second that God loves it, the third that God keeps it.*'

Despite confining herself to a cell, she was visited by many people, for she became famous as a spiritual counsellor. Her direct experiences of God gave Mother Julian a deep sense of peace and assurance, as her most famous utterance shows: '*all shall be well, and all shall be well, and all manner of thing shall be well*'.

Blaise Pascal (1623–1662)
A mathematician and scientist of great stature, he is as famous for his theological writing as for his scientific work. In particular, his *Pensées* (*Thoughts on Religion and Some Other Subjects*) are still read today. On a 'Night of Fire' he experienced the reality of 'the God of Isaac, of Abraham and Jacob' (as opposed to the 'First Cause' God of the philosophers). He describes this in a series of vivid words: '*Fire … Certainty … Peace … Joy, tears of joy.*' He wrote, '*the heart has its reasons, of which reason knows nothing*'.

John Wesley (1703–1791)
As a student at Oxford he engaged vigorously in religious activities and was a member of the 'Holy Club', whose members came to be called Methodists (because of their methodical approach to life). He was ordained as an Anglican priest and travelled to Georgia in America as a missionary. This was an unhappy and unsuccessful venture and Wesley sailed home. On this dangerous journey he was deeply impressed by the strong faith, in the face of death, of a group of Moravians.

On 24 May 1738 he attended a Moravian meeting in London's Aldersgate Street, where he felt his 'heart strangely warmed'. This gave him assurance of salvation and a renewed desire to preach. Throughout a long life, he travelled thousands of miles on horseback, preached thousands of sermons (often in the open air) and founded the Methodist Church. His last known letter was to William Wilberforce, encouraging him in the campaign against slavery.

As we have seen, spiritual experiences are not confined to the past. Nor are they confined to Christian believers. The eminent zoologist Sir Alister Hardy set up a research centre to investigate such phenomena. Dr David Hay has built on these foundations. As a result, a remarkable number of people have recounted experiences of this kind.

Such experiences can lead to dramatic changes in life style and attitude. But not always. In his autobiography, the art critic Lord Clark wrote: '*I had a religious experience ... for a few minutes my whole being was irradiated by a kind of heavenly joy.*' This presented him with a dilemma; should he respond to this revelation by repentance and faith? Kenneth Clark could not face such an upheaval. He continues,

> **I was too deeply embedded in the world to change course. But that I had felt the finger of God I am quite sure, and, although the memory of this experience has faded, it still helps me to understand the joys of the saints.** (*The Other Half: A Self Portrait*)

Shortly before he died, Lord Clark was received into the Roman Catholic Church.

Insight

It is quite common for Christians to see 'the hand of God' in the events which make up their lives. One famous example is Nobel Prize winning author Alexander Solzhenitzyn, who believed that God cured his cancer and gave him a long life, for a wider purpose.

Daily life

As already indicated, the experiences outlined above are not confined to a few 'super-saints'. Large numbers of Christians could describe dramatic, 'out of the blue' spiritual experiences which have made a tremendous difference to the quality and direction of their lives. Sometimes they are life-transforming; frequently they leave the person involved with a quiet certainty about the reality and love of God.

But many other believers, probably the majority, do not have experiences of this kind. As a result, some feel 'second-class' in comparison. This is sad, for it is possible to have a strong faith in God without experiencing anything 'dramatic'. For some, the main pointer to the reality of God is a quiet confidence that they are 'accompanied', 'helped' and 'directed' through life by an unseen Presence – and challenged too, to acts of love and service.

In a famous sentence, Jesus promised his disciples that *'where two or three come together in my name, I am there in the midst of them'* (Matthew 18:20). Millions of ordinary believers, who have never had a 'special' encounter with God, testify that these words of Jesus sum up their experience. They affirm that they meet for prayer, worship and fellowship, not to remember a dead hero, but to meet – and to be met by – a living Person. Their testimony is impressive.

The importance of such undramatic experiences of God was captured by Cardinal Basil Hume, Archbishop of Westminster from 1976 to 99:

> **Holiness involves friendship with God. God's love for us and ours for him grows like any relationship with other people. There comes a moment, which we can never quite locate or catch, when an acquaintance becomes a friend. In a sense, the change from one to the other has been taking place over a period of time, but there comes a point when we know we can trust the other, exchange confidences, keep each other's secrets. We are friends.**

There has to be a moment like that in our relationship with God.
He ceases to be just a Sunday acquaintance and becomes a
weekday friend.　　　　　　　　　　　　　　　　　(*To Be a Pilgrim*, SPCK)

Discipleship

As we have seen, powerful life-changing experiences are described
in the Bible. And words of emotion, such as *joy* and *fear*, are often
found there too. In the light of Christian belief in the resurrection
of Jesus and the activity of the Holy Spirit, it is not surprising that
experiences of God (whether gentle or dramatic) continue to be
widespread. But all Christians would agree that the quality of our
discipleship matters more than any particular spiritual experience.

What really counts is the response of the individual believer.
Such experiences are 'given' for practical purposes: to broaden
our understanding, to deepen our faith, to enlarge our compassion
and to secure our obedience.

Insight

'Spiritual experiences' can make a radical difference to the
quality and direction of people's lives. But the majority of
believers do not have dramatic experiences to relate. However,
in prayer, worship and fellowship they do not remember a
dead hero – they affirm that they encounter their risen Lord.

C S Lewis became a leading Christian 'apologist' (defender of the
faith), part of whose story was told in the film *Shadowlands*. He
was Professor of Medieval Literature at Oxford, and he wrote a
series of famous children's books set in Narnia, including *The Lion,
the Witch and the Wardrobe*. He also wrote science fiction, as well
as many books about Christianity. He was converted from atheism
after a long period of intellectual wrestling. C S Lewis described one
striking experience in his autobiography *Surprised by Joy* (Collins):

I was going up Headington Hill on the top of a bus. Without words
and (I think) almost without images, a fact about myself was

somehow presented to me. I became aware that I was holding something at bay, or shutting something out. Or, if you like, that I was wearing some stiff clothing, like corsets, or even a suit of armour, as if I were a lobster. I felt myself being, there and then, given a free choice. I could open the door or keep it shut; I could unbuckle the armour or keep it on. Neither choice was presented as a duty, no threat or promise was attached to either, though I knew that to open the door or to take off the corset meant the incalculable. The choice appeared to be momentous, but it was also strangely unemotional.

C S Lewis wrote a great deal about Christian faith, religious experience and obedience. He believed that God is often most obvious to the emotions and senses at the *beginning* of our Christian pilgrimage, to help get us started on our journey of faith. He argued that Christians sometimes make greater progress during periods when they have no direct sense of the presence of God. Only then are they really living 'by faith, not by sight' (2 Corinthians 5:7) – learning to trust the promises of God in the Bible, 'not in the teeth of reason, but in the teeth of lust, and terror, and jealousy and boredom and indifference'.

For Lewis, the *truth* of Christianity is everything. We are called to follow Jesus Christ whether we experience his presence or not, because he is 'the Way, the Truth and the Life' (John 14:6). He summed up his position like this:

> 'Christianity is a statement which, if false, is of no importance, and if true, of infinite importance. The one thing it cannot be is moderately important.'

The Doctrine of the Trinity

May the grace of the Lord Jesus Christ, and the love of God, and the fellowship of the Holy Spirit be with you all. (2 Corinthians 13:14)

The Christian doctrine that there are 'three Persons in one God' developed over the first few Christian centuries and is found in the Creeds hammered out at Church Councils: Nicaea (325), Constantinople (381) and Chalcedon (451). But the building blocks are found in the New Testament and in the experience of the early disciples. As they reflected on the significance of Jesus they became aware that he was 'the man Christ Jesus' (1 Timothy 2:5) and 'My Lord and my God' (John 20:28). On the day of Pentecost they were filled with the Holy Spirit. They understood these experiences as actions or manifestations of the One True God – Creator and Redeemer of the World (page 16).

This doctrine is linked with the Christian view of *revelation*. God is too good and too great for us to comprehend. But in his mercy he has revealed himself to us – in creation, through prophets and poets, and through Scripture. Supremely he has revealed himself in his Son (Hebrews 1:2) and by his Spirit within us (Galatians 5:22). It would have been impossible for the Jewish disciples of Jesus – with their tenacious belief that 'the Lord is One' – to *invent* this idea of One God as Father, Son and Holy Spirit. They were *forced* to this belief through their experience of Jesus, and the events of Easter and the first Christian Pentecost. This understanding of God as 'Three in One' was not worked out by lonely academics in libraries, but by men and women making sense of their experience in active lives and dangerous times.

The Doctrine of the Trinity makes God accessible. He is not locked away from us in heaven. God has become one of us in Jesus; he continues to live within us, and among us, by his Spirit.

Insight

The Doctrine of the Holy Trinity sums up widespread Christian experience of God. Christians believe that they are strengthened by the risen Christ who 'walks' with them – unseen but real. And they experience God's Spirit within, bringing comfort, inspiration and challenge. God is 'in heaven' – and hence 'transcendent'. But, through his Son and his Spirit, God is near us and within us.

10 THINGS TO REMEMBER

1 *Many people in the Bible narrative had a direct experience of God.*

2 *Two famous Old Testament examples are Abraham and Moses, each of whom received a direct instruction from God.*

3 *A famous New Testament example is the first Christian Pentecost, when God's Holy Spirit came in power on the early disciples.*

4 *Throughout history people have had conversion experiences, leading to a dramatic change in lifestyle and attitude.*

5 *Other people claim to have experienced God's guidance and protection.*

6 *These experiences continue to be widespread in the modern world – including 'near death' experiences, which some view as a foretaste of heaven.*

7 *Christians experience God as Father, Son and Holy Spirit – hence the 'Holy Trinity'.*

8 *Mysticism is a term which describes a direct experience of God.*

9 *Most Christians do not have a dramatic experience of God, but many have a sense of God's presence in their lives.*

10 *Key to all this is the promise of Jesus, 'I will be with you always' (Matthew 28:20).*

7

Prayer and worship

In this chapter you will learn:
- *different styles of prayer*
- *the significance of worship*
- *about the Christian calendar.*

> **Insight**
>
> Christian prayer is usually offered to God the Father through Jesus Christ, the Son of God, under the guidance of God's Spirit in our hearts. But prayer can also be offered directly to Jesus or to the Holy Spirit.

Christian prayer is characteristically offered to God the Father, through Jesus Christ, under the leading of the Holy Spirit. To use a traditional term, it is 'trinitarian' in form. This is no accident of history. It springs from the nature of God's revelation, the supreme moment of which is the life, death and resurrection of Jesus Christ.

Christian prayer is offered on the basis that Jesus cleared away the 'road-blocks' between God and human beings, for on the cross he endured and overcame the alienation caused by our sin. And it is offered in full recognition that what Christ did was the work of God, on behalf of the human race and the whole creation. This work was devised by God and carried through by him out of sheer love and compassion.

Christian prayer also recognizes that the Holy Spirit is the member of the Trinity who enables us to approach God as *Abba*, Father. God's Spirit can be regarded as the bond of love between the Father and the Son. The Spirit guides and intercedes for us because we do not know what to pray for, or how to pray (Romans 8:15, 26). But the trinitarian shape of Christian prayer is also seen in the fact that, because Christianity holds Jesus Christ and the Holy Spirit to be fully divine, prayer is addressed to:

▶ **God the Father**
Most notably in The Lord's Prayer, the prayer which Jesus taught his first disciples, beginning 'Our Father in heaven ...' (page 12). It is God the Father who is most commonly addressed in prayer, through Jesus Christ, in the power of the Holy Spirit.

▶ **Jesus Christ the Son**
A remarkable fact, when we recall that the first disciples were Jews who believed that 'the Lord our God, the Lord is One' (Deuteronomy 6:4; page 22).

> 'Thanks be to thee, my Lord Jesus Christ,
> For all the benefits which thou hast won for me,
> for all the pains and insults which thou hast borne for me.
> O merciful Redeemer, Friend and Brother;
> may I know thee more clearly, love thee more dearly
> and follow thee more nearly, day by day. Amen'
>
> (St Richard of Chichester: 1197–1253)

▶ **The Holy Spirit**
In the form of invocation as in the ancient hymn, 'Come Holy Ghost, our souls inspire' (which has the Latin title *Veni Creator*).

Doing God's will

Insight

Prayer is not magic. We are not trying to change God's mind! Rather, we seek to align our wills with the Divine Will. We 'make space' in our busy lives to think about God, and his loving purposes for our world. And we bring into the presence of God those individuals and events on our minds and in our hearts.

Christianity is deeply concerned with the world as it is. Christians are called to live in the 'here and now'. But they live and pray out of the inspiration gained by *looking back* and *looking forward*. The events of the life, death and resurrection of Jesus Christ are seen as fully relevant at all times. Indeed, he himself is believed in as the ever-living and ever-contemporary Lord. Christians believe that what happened 2000 years ago affects the whole world, since God then set in motion a new order. God will eventually bring this to perfection when he makes 'all things new' (Revelation 21:5).

So there is for Christians a backward look and a forward look, reminding them that all history is in the hands of God. This is why Christian prayer seeks to 'key in' to the will and work of God, who is leading his creation towards a future of restoration, renewal and glory. *Prayer is not a matter of persuading God to do things which he might not want to do. Rather, it is a matter of aligning ourselves with his purpose.* Even when (as is often the case) his will in detail is far from clear, the desire of the praying person is to bring his or her will into conformity with God's will; to want *his* will to be done.

The Khouds of North India have a prayer which reads: '*Lord, we don't know what is good for us. You know what it is. For it we pray. Amen*'. It is a prayer of confidence in God, a prayer which rests in his perfect, loving will. But what if we fear that we do not really want God's will to be done in some particular situation? Writers on prayer tell us that our 'fear' shows that we know we ought to want it. So they encourage us with the thought that God, who knows our hearts, mercifully accepts our *wanting to want it* and gently leads us into a fuller desire for it.

Jesus Christ taught his followers to pray to the Father, '*May your will be done on earth as it is in heaven*' (Matthew 6:10). From this we understand that the very best that could happen 'on earth' at any time, is that God's will should be done. Furthermore, the Holy Spirit is always at work, guiding those who genuinely want the will of God to be done. The confidence that God is active in the world (and will one day make all things new, permeating every part of his new creation with his glory), spurs the believer on to pray and work to make this world a better and a fairer place. This is in anticipation of the future consummation of God's Kingdom. So prayer is best thought of as an active response to the will of the God of history.

In the Bible Abraham and Moses prayed, so did Naomi and Hannah, David and Elijah, Jonah and Daniel, Elizabeth and Mary. Jesus prayed. His disciples asked him to teach them, and he did. He emphasized privacy, trust, honesty, brevity and forgiveness.

Most churches regularly use the Lord's Prayer. If any part is harder than the rest, it must be the words about forgiveness. Jesus developed this great theme in parable and instruction – and by example.

Aspects of prayer

There are various kinds of prayer:

Adoration and praise

The wonder of God's being and character evokes adoration. He is beyond our understanding; but he has revealed himself, supremely in Jesus Christ. God is seen as the One before whom heart and mind must bow, because in him is all perfection and beauty. Prayer may be expressed in words; but sometimes it goes beyond words into an attitude of silent and wordless devotion. A great medieval theologian, Thomas Aquinas, when at prayer in front of a crucifix, heard a voice saying, 'You have written well of me. What reward would you like to have?' He replied, 'No reward, but you yourself, Lord.'

Thanksgiving

This is closely related to adoration. We reflect on everything which enriches our lives, sometimes giving thanks to God for specific blessings. But it does not stop there, for the whole work of God, past and present, occasions, thanksgiving.

Almighty God, Father of all mercies,
we thine unworthy servants do give thee
most humble and hearty thanks
for all thy goodness and loving-kindness
to us and to all men.
We bless thee for our creation, preservation,
and all the blessings of this life;
but above all for thine inestimable love
in the redemption of the world by
our Lord Jesus Christ,
for the means of grace, and for the hope of glory...

From the General Thanksgiving (*Book of Common Prayer*)
by Bishop Edward Reynolds (1599–1676)

Confession

This begins with an awareness that nobody is without sin in
God's sight. In addition to 'sinfulness' (a shared failure to love
God wholeheartedly and our neighbour as ourselves), there are
particular sins of thought, word and deed to be acknowledged
and repented of, if God's forgiveness is to be received and a fresh
start made. While it is undesirable to 'rummage' in our lives to
try to uncover every fault (as if this could be done), confessing
particular known sins is important and can be therapeutic.
However, in the course of Christian worship (i.e. worship in a
Christian congregation) the prayer of confession must necessarily
be general in character. The brief and beautiful 'Jesus Prayer'
from the Eastern Orthodox tradition is used by many
Christians: 'Lord Jesus Christ, Son of God, have mercy on
me, a sinner.'

Many people find it helpful to share with another human being,
in strict confidence, those things which are burdening their
conscience. Some Christian traditions (such as Roman Catholic and
Orthodox) commend the practice of personal confession to God
in the presence of a priest. Some believers find that they come to
an assurance of divine forgiveness more readily when they hear a
declaration of that forgiveness from an authorized representative of
the Church (page 149).

Intercession

This looks out at the world. It is the prayer of concern for individual people, groups of people, causes and events. Since God, in his love, wants the best for his whole creation, the intercessor prays with confidence, asking that God's perfect will may be done. Intercession is based on whatever information is available. The blessing asked for is what seems to the intercessor to be needed, but the prayer is offered essentially as a contribution (itself God-inspired) to the realization of God's will. Just why God should wish to involve us in his purposes through prayer, is a mystery. But, encouraged by Jesus' example and teaching about prayer, Christian believers gladly accept it as a mystery of love – and as a great privilege.

Petition

The Bible encourages us to make specific requests to God. There are three important considerations:

▶ *As the Lord's Prayer shows (page 12) the prayer of asking is meant to bind us ever more closely to God in our daily lives. We come to recognize that we are entirely dependent on him for everything.*
▶ *Jesus taught his disciples to make their requests in his name: that is, to pray as he would pray. This prevents petition from becoming selfish. As always, we pray with the proviso, 'Your will be done.'*
▶ *A loving parent might answer a child's request with 'Yes', 'No' or 'Wait'. In the same way, any one of these three words might be the answer to a particular prayer. St Paul experienced disappointment when he prayed for the removal of a 'thorn in the flesh'. But with the 'No', God reassured Paul with a promise: 'My grace is sufficient for you, for my power is made perfect in weakness' (2 Corinthians 12:7–10).*

Lamentation

The Psalms cover the full range of human emotions, from joy to despair. These poems include deep expressions of sorrow and sharp questions to God about his apparent silence and inactivity (e.g. Psalms 10 and 13). In this way we are encouraged to be totally honest in prayer, telling God 'how it is for us'.

Extemporary prayer

Over the centuries, thousands of written prayers have been composed for all the above modes of prayer. Some are very beautiful; some very famous. But many Christians use *extemporary* (or *extempore*) prayer – praying in their own words rather than from a written text. In some traditions (such as Roman Catholic, Orthodox, Anglican) written prayers are usually preferred in public worship. In others (such as Baptist and Pentecostal) extemporary prayer (sometimes very passionate) is more usual.

PLACE AND POSTURE

Many Christians find it helpful to return to a familiar place which they associate with prayer. This might be a church building; it might be a favourite chair in a particular room. Some people use visual or audio aids – music perhaps, or a cross, a candle, a picture, an icon …

Again, posture can be important. Some choose to kneel; others prefer to sit in a comfortable chair. Many pray in bed. But prayer can be offered anywhere: while walking or driving or ironing… Many Christians offer quick 'arrow prayers' throughout the day, and find prayer a comfort if they cannot sleep at night.

MEDITATION AND CONTEMPLATION

Attention has been given by Christian writers on spirituality to states of mind in prayer and methods of praying. *Meditation* and *contemplation* are defined in various ways and contemplation is often seen as a stage beyond meditation.

In *meditation* we reflect on a text or story or image (often from the Bible or from nature). A famous example comes from the Breton peasant who spent long hours before the crucifix. Asked to describe his experience he replied, 'I look at him; and he looks at me.' Such reflection, in which we try to 'listen' to God, may lead to conclusions which then result in action.

In *contemplation* the reasoning processes are stilled; the person praying gives attention to God through a single act of love and self-offering. This attitude has been described as 'simple attention' and 'one-pointedness'. While some people do move through meditation into contemplation, there are those who experience contemplation at an early stage in their spiritual journey. A parallel may be seen in the wonderment of a child when confronted by something new, lovely and fascinating. The child is completely absorbed, captivated, filled with delight. Since contemplation has something of this character (rooted as it is in adoration), it would be surprising if it were not experienced by some Christians at an early stage, as well as by more mature believers.

Meditation makes use of words and visual images. Contemplation can dispense with both, though it may use a short form of words, or a single word often repeated. Perhaps it is best understood as a 'wordless' approach to God, which has no need of the usual thought processes. Christian mystics down the centuries have done their best to write about it, but have freely admitted that it defies adequate description.

> So if you are to stand and not fall, never give up your firm intention: beat away at this cloud of unknowing between you and God with that sharp dart of longing love.
>
> from *The Cloud of Unknowing*, a fourteenth-century mystical work

Insight

Christians often use written prayers, perhaps within a formal Service. Or we might use our own spontaneous words – sometimes alone, perhaps in the company of other believers. Or we might keep silence and meditate on a passage of Scripture or a Christian symbol, such as a candle or a cross.

Christian worship

Christian worship is from God to God. Worship comes from God in two senses:

▶ *it focuses on who God is and what he has done*
▶ *God himself puts into people's hearts and minds the desire for prayer and praise.*

It is, of course, a human activity; but it is motivated, sustained and inspired by God himself. And so we can say truly that it is 'from God, to God'.

Because worship has this character, it can be seen as a kind of 'conversation' between God and the worshipping community. Through the reading of the Bible, the preaching of a sermon, the singing of psalms, canticles, songs and hymns, and in various other ways, God makes use of human words to speak to his people. He comforts and encourages them, he challenges and inspires them, and he calls them to particular acts of service.

The congregation, hearing God's message in this way, responds in creed, prayers and hymns, and with adoration, confession and thanksgiving. The prayers which are offered for the world, and for particular people and causes, are in themselves a response to God. It is our way of declaring interest in, and loving concern for, the world which God 'loved so much that he gave his only Son' (John 3:16).

It would be mistaken, however, to think that worship is exclusively verbal, though it sometimes seems like that. We need only to think of the *Sacraments* (Chapter 8) to see how wide of the mark this is. The sacraments have at their centre materials and actions, such as water poured, bread and wine consumed. Silence can be an important feature of worship. Some Christians (notably Quakers: pages 150 and 231) make silence central to their Sunday gatherings, as they 'wait upon God'.

Many churches are concerned that the gifts distributed by God's Spirit among the worshippers should be as fully used as possible – gifts of reading and speaking; gifts of music and the visual arts; gifts of leadership and teaching. Word and action belong together.

Insight

Christian worship can be seen as a 'conversation' between God and the worshipping community. We listen to God through Bible readings, sermons and times of silence. We respond with prayer, creed and songs of praise. Worship takes various forms and can be in various moods – from exuberant joy to quiet, even sorrowful, reflection.

All worship is rooted in its culture

Worship among Presbyterians in Scotland will be a more sombre experience than worship in a Pentecostal Church (page 232) in Barbados. Many people (particularly young people but some adults as well) feel the need to express themselves in a style of worship which may differ markedly from that of more traditional believers. 'Alternative worship' is organized in many places; use is made of music groups, synthesizers, videos, dance and drama. In Britain in the third millennium there is no 'typical' church service. Variations within the Church of England alone would have astonished earlier Anglicans. But the same criteria apply: wherever worshippers give thanks and praise to God, confess their sins, and seek to serve and follow Jesus Christ in the world, *there* genuine worship is found.

As with the prayer of the individual Christian, corporate worship is 'trinitarian' in shape. It is offered:

- to God the Father *who makes himself known as the Father of the family of believers*
- through God the Son *on whose life and work the Church depends*
- in the power of God the Holy Spirit, *who inspires the worshippers, and bestows gifts on them 'for the common good' (1 Corinthians 12:7).*

Prayer has blossomed and fruited in every conceivable way – from the silence of Trappist monks or the Society of Friends (Quakers) to the formal intonations of the priest; from the succinctness of the Sunday Collect (to 'collect' our thoughts) to the different freedom of the extempore worship-leader. Methodists are better than most at incorporating hymns into their private devotions. Some Christians pray by the book, as in a 'Daily Office' with its mix of constants and variables; others pray spontaneously.

Worship is not confined to services in church; it involves the entire life of members of the congregation, during the week as well as on Sundays. What happens in a church service is a focus for the worship which believers offer through their everyday activities. *This point is all important.* In the Bible we find a solemn warning: if what happens outside formal worship contradicts what is said within it, then the act of worship is invalidated (Isaiah 1; Amos 5). Worship, properly understood, is the offering of the whole of our lives to God.

Therefore, I urge you, brothers, in view of God's mercy, to offer your bodies as living sacrifices, holy and pleasing to God – this is your spiritual act of worship. Do not conform any longer to the pattern of this world, but be transformed by the renewing of your mind.

(Romans 12:1–2)

Send us now into the world in peace, and grant us strength and courage to love and serve you with gladness and singleness of heart; through Christ our Lord. Amen.

From *The Book of Common Prayer* (USA Episcopal Church)

'One of my most vivid memories of praying came from a visit to Namibia during the war there. I was with Bishop James Kauluma driving from Windhoek to visit the main part of his diocese in the north of the country … It meant driving without lights to avoid getting caught breaking the curfew by the South African army, on tracks through the bush which had been extensively mined. As we went along the two of us not driving said the office of evening prayer so that the driver could hear and take part. The psalm was one of those imploring God to save us from danger. I found myself praying fervently words that I had been used to re-interpreting in my usual condition of comfort and safety.

The experience showed what I have learned elsewhere in Africa, that … what might be called the resources of Christian spirituality were really designed to sustain people facing difficulty and danger. That has actually been most people's lot all through human history.'

(Bishop Humphrey Taylor)

ESCAPISM?

Critics might argue that prayer and worship are an escape from 'the real world'. Christians would reply that it is necessary to withdraw from the world from time to time, in order to serve the world. Of course, not all acts of worship are inspiring and challenging. But some visionary writers have seen prayer and worship as nothing less than *a bridge between heaven and earth*.

Thomas Merton was one of the great spiritual writers of the twentieth century. In 1941 he visited an American monastery called Gethsemani, shortly before joining that community. It was a dark and troubled time in world history, especially in Europe where the Nazis were causing havoc. As he watched the monks at prayer, he came to see that activity as a focus of spiritual power. In his *Secular Journal* he wrote:

This is the center of America. I had wondered what was keeping the country together, what has been keeping the universe from cracking in pieces and falling apart. It's places like this monastery – not only this one; there must be others… This is the

only real city in America – and it is by itself, in the wilderness.
It is an axle around which the whole country blindly turns, and
knows nothing about it. Gethsemani holds the country together:
What right have I to be here?

In Thomas Merton's view it was prayer – that mysterious and powerful means by which human beings are caught up in the plans and purposes of God – which holds the universe together and checks chaos.

Michael Ramsey (100th Archbishop of Canterbury) made the same point. He asserted that *worship brings healing* into a broken world, because it is a channel through which the love of God flows into our lives. He wrote about some of the great problems facing our world and continued with this 'parable':

There was once a man who had three nasty big boils, and he went
to the doctor and asked for each of them to be treated or removed.
And the doctor said 'My dear fellow, I can do nothing permanent with
these boils unless we get rid of the poison in your system which is
causing them.' So, too, the human race, very sick and having at least
three terrible boils in the social and moral order [great poverty,
inequality, injustice ...], wants to be rid of them. But this human
race does not grasp that the trouble is a poison in the system and the
sickness is that of a deep derangement in the relation of mankind
to the Creator. Go to the root. The root is the right relation of man
to Creator: and when Christians are concerned about what they call
worship they are concerned, not with something remote or escapist,
but with the root of the world's predicament.

(*Introducing the Christian Faith*: SCM Press)

High points in the Christian year

Anybody who is found observing, by abstinence from labour,
feasting, or any other way, any such days as Christmas Day, shall
pay for every such offense five shillings.

(Massachusetts 1659, General Court of New England)

As this statement indicates, some Christians have been suspicious of keeping special 'holy' days. For every day is a gift from God. This attitude is held by some Christians even today – in certain Brethren (formerly Plymouth Brethren) churches for example. During the nineteenth century one such Christian was so appalled at being served with Christmas pudding that he threw it into his garden!

However, most churches observe the Christian year, finding its rhythm and changes of mood a helpful aid to devotion, faith and life. Most of these days and seasons relate to events in the life of Jesus Christ. 'Saints' Days' recall notable Christians down the centuries – from the first disciples onwards.

Advent
This is the four-week period before Christmas. The title comes from a Latin word meaning 'Coming'. In Advent, Christians prepare themselves for the celebration of Christ's coming at Christmas – and for his 'Second Coming' at the end of this age, when he will judge the world. This season is longer in the Eastern Orthodox Churches (Chapter 12) than in the West (one example of a number of variations in the Christian calendar between the Eastern and Western Churches).

Christmas
The anniversary of the birth of Christ is celebrated by most Christians on 25 December, though the actual date of Christ's birth in Bethlehem is unknown. Many Eastern Orthodox Christians celebrate Christmas on 7 January (Armenians on 6 January) because of the difference between the Julian and Gregorian calendars. This most popular of all festivals replaced an older, pagan mid-winter festival.

Epiphany
The word is Greek in origin and means 'manifestation'. The date of this festival is 6 January. The Western Church recalls and celebrates the visit of the Magi (the wise men) to the infant Jesus. Matthew's

Gospel (2:1–12) tells us that they presented gifts: gold, frankincense and myrrh. This story is taken to represent the coming *to* Christ of the Gentile (non-Jewish) world, and the coming *of* Christ for all humanity. The Eastern Orthodox Churches focus on the baptism of Jesus at this time, and baptismal water is blessed.

Lent

This is the period of 40 days immediately preceding Easter. The name probably has an Anglo-Saxon origin. It comes from a word meaning 'Spring', which refers to the lengthening days. Christians reflect on the 40 days which Jesus spent in the wilderness after his baptism. Lent is a solemn time, traditionally marked by fasting, when Christians consider the disciplines of their faith. Lent starts on *Ash Wednesday*, the day after *Shrove Tuesday* (from the old English verb 'shrive' – to obtain absolution for sins by confessing and doing penance). The latter is also known as 'Pancake Day', from the old custom of using up all the items of food which were forbidden in Lent.

Holy Week

At the end of Lent, a week is set aside for focusing on the death of Christ and its meaning for the salvation of the world. In this week occurs *Maundy Thursday*, when the institution of Holy Communion is commemorated. 'Maundy' comes from the Latin phrase '*mandatum novum*' (new commandment) and refers to John 13 when Jesus washed his disciples' feet and added, 'A new commandment I give you … As I have loved you, so you must love one another.' *Good Friday* follows *Maundy Thursday*. This is the most solemn day of all, as we reflect on the cost of our redemption. All the prayers and devotions concentrate on the crucifixion of Jesus (Chapter 2).

Easter

This is *the* major festival of the Christian year, when Christians celebrate the resurrection of Jesus Christ from the dead, after his crucifixion and burial. Every Sunday is a festival occasion because it is a 'little Easter' – the weekly celebration of the resurrection of

Jesus Christ 'on the first day of the week'. On Easter Sunday, many churches include a joyful liturgical response:

> *'Alleluia! Christ is risen.*
> *He is risen indeed. Alleluia!'*

Ascension Day

This celebrates the ascension of Jesus into heaven, where he 'sits at the right hand of the Father' and prays for the world. We are reminded that Jesus took his, and our, humanity into heaven. This festival marks the end of Jesus' post-resurrection appearances which lasted for 40 days. For this reason it is celebrated 40 days after Easter Sunday, and falls on a Thursday.

Pentecost

The account of the bestowal of the Holy Spirit on the early Church is given at the beginning of The Acts of the Apostles. Each year at Pentecost, 50 days after Easter, the Church recalls this event. Christians pray that, by his Holy Spirit, God will guide and strengthen the Church for its work and witness in the world. As with some other Christian festivals and dates, Pentecost has its roots in the Jewish tradition. Pentecost is the name given to a Jewish celebration of the first-fruits of the corn harvest, 50 days after the Passover. An alternative name for the Christian festival is *Whitsun*.

Trinity Sunday

The theme of this day (one week after Pentecost) sums up all the observances in the Church's calendar from Advent to Pentecost. On Trinity Sunday, the Church is reminded of God's eternal nature – that he is Father, Son and Holy Spirit; three Persons in One God (pages 18 and 114).

Trinity Sunday to Advent

During this period, sometimes referred to as 'Ordinary Time', many aspects of Christian life and witness are brought to the Church's attention. All these are based, in one way or another, on the life, death and resurrection of Jesus Christ and his continuing presence with us.

'We in England live in the chill religious vapours of Northern Europe, where moribund religious establishments loom over populations that mostly do not enter churches for active worship, even if they entertain inchoate beliefs. Yet these establishments guard and maintain thousands of houses of God, which are markers of space and time. Not only are they markers and anchors, but also the only repositories of all-embracing meanings pointing beyond the immediate to the ultimate. They are the only institutions that deal in tears and concern themselves with the breaking points of human existence… They offer moral codes and exemplars for the creation of communal solidarity and the nourishment of virtue … They welcome schools and regiments and rotary clubs; they celebrate and commemorate … They offer spaces in which solemnly to gather, to sing, to lay flowers, and light candles. They are – in Philip Larkin's phrase – "serious places on serious earth".'

(Professor David Martin)

10 THINGS TO REMEMBER

1 *Christian prayer is usually offered to God the Father.*

2 *Prayer is offered through Jesus Christ, under the leading of the Holy Spirit.*

3 *Prayer can also be offered directly to Jesus and to the Holy Spirit.*

4 *Prayer is not magic; it means seeking to align our wills with God's will.*

5 *Prayer has many aspects – praise and adoration, thanksgiving, confession, petition, lament ...*

6 *In prayer, we can use the carefully crafted words of other people – making them our own as we say them.*

7 *Equally, prayer can be spontaneous and extemporary.*

8 *Worship varies in mood, from deep solemnity to exuberant joy.*

9 *The Christian year expresses this wide spectrum of emotions.*

10 *This spectrum takes in the penitence of Ash Wednesday, the grief of Good Friday and the joy of Easter Sunday.*

8

The Sacraments

In this chapter you will learn:
- **about the New Testament background**
- **the significance of Baptism and Holy Communion**
- **about other sacraments and symbols.**

Insight

Christianity is a sacramental religion. That is to say, physical objects and actions convey spiritual truths. The two central sacraments are Baptism – the rite of Christian initiation – and Holy Communion, by which God nourishes and sustains our spiritual life in fellowship with other believers.

In times of conflict, a nation's flag assumes great significance. Indeed, people are sometimes willing to die rather than deny their national emblem. Viewed in one way, this is absurd. Who in their right mind would exchange life for a little bit of coloured cloth? But to those on the inside of that experience it is completely understandable. They see a 'little bit of coloured cloth', but they also see, represented in their flag, the past history of their nation and all that it stands for at its best. This notion of ordinary objects taking on deep significance is a helpful picture to hold in mind as we consider the sacraments of the Church.

When we call Christianity a 'sacramental religion', we refer to the fact that certain actions (eating, drinking, pouring) and physical objects (wine, bread, water) 'speak' powerfully of spiritual truths. This insight is found throughout the Hebrew Scriptures and in the Gospels. Later, the Church attempted various definitions. One of the most famous can be traced back to Augustine of Hippo: 'a sacrament is an outward and visible sign of an inward and spiritual grace'.

Christianity has two central sacraments: *Baptism* and *Holy Communion*. Both of these are representations of events in the life of Jesus Christ, but with a specific and personal significance for Christian worshippers today.

> In the New Testament, the Greek word '*mysterion*' (mystery) refers to a truth which was hidden but is now revealed in Jesus Christ – and especially through his death. In the ancient Latin Bible (Jerome's Vulgate: fourth century) this term was translated as *sacramentum*; it is from this that we get the English word 'sacrament'.

Baptism

THE BAPTISM OF JESUS

The Gospels tell us that John the Baptist (the cousin of Jesus) 'preached a baptism of repentance for the forgiveness of sins' (Mark 1:4). Crowds went to be baptized in the River Jordan; among them was Jesus. John expressed reluctance to baptize the One who was so much greater than he. But Jesus insisted and John agreed. When Jesus came up out of the water, *'he saw the Spirit of God descending like a dove and lighting on him. And a voice from heaven said, "This is my Son, whom I love; with him I am well pleased"* ' (Matthew 3:16,17).

John's was a baptism of repentance for sin and this raises a question for Christians, for the New Testament teaches the sinlessness of Jesus (1 Peter 2:22). He was the one human being who had no need to repent. But in submitting to baptism, Jesus was not declaring his own sinfulness; he was endorsing John's ministry. He was also identifying himself with the people.

Jesus could have stood with John, calling the people to repentance. Instead, he associated himself with the people; a fitting start to the ministry of the One who would be called 'friend of sinners' and who would die on a cross between two criminals.

BAPTISM IN THE CHURCH

Baptism features strongly in the New Testament, and in subsequent Christian history, as a vital aspect of Christian initiation. *But Christian baptism is a much richer concept than John's baptism. For, as John declared, Jesus would 'baptize with the Holy Spirit'.*

The Acts of the Apostles gives several examples of people being baptized, among them an Ethiopian official (Acts 8:38) and a Philippian jailor, together with his family (Acts 16:31–34). These show that a lengthy period of preparation was not required. Following confession of faith in Christ, baptism was the immediate next step. In the years following the New Testament period, a lengthy preparation and 'apprenticeship' became common, with most baptisms taking place at Easter or Pentecost. Those being prepared for Christian initiation were called *catechumens* or the *catechumenate*, terms still in use today.

WATER

A key passage for understanding Christian baptism is found in St Paul's letter to the church in Rome. He describes baptism as a burial! (Romans 6:4) Baptism links believers with the crucified Saviour – it illustrates the call of Jesus to 'take up your cross'. This call to 'die to self' is a central aspect of Christian discipleship and it is signified in baptism when candidates go under the water. But baptism is also a symbol of resurrection; the candidates come up out of the water, signifying that they have received new life in Christ.

Water has many other rich associations in the Christian tradition. It signifies that a person has been washed clean from sin. And it points to a promise of Jesus – that he will give the 'water of life' (John 7:38). Baptism also reminds those present of God's great saving act in the Old Testament in bringing the people of Israel safely through the divided sea, pursued by their Egyptian captors (the *Exodus*). They remember too, that Jesus referred to his impending death as 'a baptism' (Mark 10:38). The sacrament or ordinance of baptism evokes all these associations.

Insight

Christian baptism is modelled on the baptism of Jesus by his cousin, John the Baptist, in the river Jordan. Water is usually poured onto the candidates. Or the candidate might be immersed in water by the officiating minister. Baptism is administered in the name of the Father, Son and Holy Spirit.

DIFFERENCES

Different customs have grown up around baptism. These differences, the subject of some controversy between the Churches, focus on:

▶ *the candidates for baptism*
▶ *the mode of baptism.*

Who may be baptized?

Nobody is too old for baptism and all churches baptize adults who come to faith in Christ. But most churches baptize babies too, usually on the understanding that they will be given a Christian upbringing. These churches assert that infant baptism speaks clearly of the grace of God – indicating that his love is for all, even those who cannot consciously respond to it.

> *The sheer gratuitousness of the grace of salvation is particularly manifest in infant Baptism. The Church and the parents would deny a child the priceless grace of becoming a child of God were they not to confer Baptism shortly after birth ... For all the baptized, children or adults, faith must grow after Baptism.*

(Catechism of the Catholic Church)*

*Note: This modern Catechism (1994 and 2000) – the first for 400 years – will be quoted frequently in this chapter. These quotations will be in italic and referred to as (CCC).

While it is usual for baptism to be administered by a priest or ordained minister during a church service, Churches encourage lay people to baptize where there is danger of death.

Some Protestant Christians, notably Baptists and Pentecostalists, believe that baptism should be reserved for believers. Parents take newborn babies to church for a special act of thanksgiving and dedication to God. But baptism by water, in the name of the Father, the Son and the Holy Spirit, is delayed until the child grows up and requests it. The Baptism service then becomes a powerful act of personal witness to faith in Jesus Christ.

This approach does have attractions even for some churches which traditionally baptize infants. One problem for many churches is 'nominal' Christianity. Parents who have little contact with the Church and no real intention of raising their children in the Christian faith, nevertheless desire a 'christening' (a popular term for baptism) to celebrate the birth.

Churches are torn between a desire to welcome everyone into the life of the Church, however fleetingly, and a concern to assert that the Christian faith has content and 'bite'. For in choosing the Christian way, we become disciples of Jesus Christ – with a commitment to serve and witness to our world, through his strength and in his name. To use a phrase made famous by Dietrich Bonhoeffer, who was martyred under the Nazis, there is no 'cheap grace'.

The importance of personal choice and radical discipleship as inescapable features of Christianity, are emphasized by those who practise *believers' baptism*. Many Christians who hold that there are good reasons for infant baptism nevertheless welcome the fact that the centrality of personal commitment to Christ is focused so clearly by their Baptist and Pentecostal brothers and sisters. But they point out that those baptized in infancy also have to make a personal choice as they grow up. They should be encouraged to view their baptism as a call to follow Christ.

Different modes of baptism

Many churches baptize by *affusion*. This means that the minister pours water on the head of the candidate (child or adult) and administers baptism 'in the name of the Father, and of the Son and of the Holy Spirit'. Other churches baptize by *immersion*. Immersion is almost always the mode of baptism employed by churches which restrict baptism to believers. Their church buildings often contain a 'baptistery' – a sunken area which contains enough water for candidates to be fully immersed. Some churches offer both modes of baptism. Baptisms are sometimes held in the sea, or in a river or swimming-pool. Eastern Orthodox Churches baptize infants by immersion. The baby is immersed three times (reflecting the Holy Trinity). Not surprisingly, some candidates protest loudly!

To settle these differences, baptismal practice in the New Testament has been closely studied. But it is not spelt out in enough detail to put the issues beyond doubt, and some would argue that this gives validity to a range of practices. The Bible certainly records the baptism of entire households. While it seems likely that such households would have included babies and children, this is not explicitly stated. But there is clear evidence that infant baptism was practised from the second century onwards. As for the *mode* of baptism, some paintings depict Jesus standing in the River Jordan while John the Baptist pours water over his head – a neat way of solving the *either/or* problem!

In practice, there is widespread mutual acceptance among Christians of the baptism administered by other churches. Even when individuals change allegiance and move from one denomination to another, most churches do not insist on 're-baptism'. Indeed, Ephesians makes it clear that there is only 'one baptism', just as there is only 'one Lord' (Ephesians 4:5), so most Christians would argue that 're-baptism' is a theological nonsense.

However, some individuals, on experiencing a profound conversion experience, feel the need to express their new-found faith in baptism, despite having been baptized as infants. Many Baptist and Pentecostal churches encourage this. And as these churches believe that infant baptism is not real baptism, some *insist* on believers' baptism for would-be members, even if they were baptized ('christened') as infants. However, this is not universal. Paul Beasley-Murray (a Baptist) comments: 'Unlike the vast majority of other Baptist groups, most British Baptists have been prepared to make one concession towards other Christians: their practice of "open membership". In many English Baptist churches, it is not necessary to have been baptized as a believer to become a member.' This practice of 'open membership' goes back to the time of John Bunyan (1628–88), the Baptist tinker who wrote *Pilgrim's Progress* while in prison for his non-conformist beliefs.

Holy Communion

> ### Insight
> Holy Communion is modelled on the last supper which Jesus ate with his disciples before his betrayal and crucifixion. Bread is broken and wine is poured by the officiating minister, then shared with the congregation (sometimes just the bread is shared – communion 'under one kind').

Jesus spent the week leading up to his crucifixion in Jerusalem. The Jewish Passover festival fell during that week – when Jews ate (as they still do today) a special family meal to celebrate their escape from Egypt. They view this event as a great saving act of God. The appropriate Scriptures are read (from the book of Exodus) and various dishes are eaten in a specified order.

On the night before his crucifixion Jesus ate this meal with his disciples (pages 15 and 27). When he broke the bread, he also broke with tradition, for he added the mysterious – and shocking – words, *'This is my body.'* He then took wine and added, *'This is my blood.'* As he gave the bread and wine to his disciples, he went on to say, *'Do this in remembrance of me.'* That instruction has been joyfully obeyed throughout the centuries. The Last Supper was to become the first of many, many more.

From the beginning, a fellowship meal in remembrance of Jesus Christ, and especially his death, resurrection and promised return in glory, was a central feature of the Christian Church (Acts 2:42). It soon became less of a meal and more of an act of worship, in which the eating and drinking became nominal and symbolic. Regulations gradually developed as to who might preside at the meal, who might participate in it and in what circumstances. The main celebration was held on Sundays, for the Christian community kept that day special (rather than the Jewish Sabbath or Saturday), to honour the Lord's resurrection.

Descriptions of the Last Supper are found in five places in the New Testament. An account is found in each of the Synoptic Gospels (Matthew 26, Mark 14 and Luke 22), in John 13 and in Paul's first letter to Corinth (1 Corinthians 11:23–32). Paul includes a note of warning. Members of the church were abusing the Lord's Supper. He made it clear that to eat the bread and drink the wine 'in an unworthy manner' was a very serious matter. From then on, Christians were encouraged to prepare themselves by prayer – and sometimes by fasting too.

Paul also links the Lord's Supper with the return of Christ in glory, '*For whenever you eat this bread and drink this cup, you proclaim the Lord's death until he comes*' (1 Corinthians 11:26). This connects with the Gospel accounts, where Jesus tells his disciples that he will not drink wine with them again until '*I drink it anew with you in my Father's kingdom*' (Matthew 26:29). This theme is picked up in some modern liturgies with the affirmation:

Christ has died:
Christ is risen:
Christ will come again.

The fourth Gospel includes the Last Supper (page 15) but does not describe the breaking of bread and sharing of wine. Instead, it describes how Jesus took a towel and washed his disciples' feet as an example of humble service. But John does use sacramental language. Following the miraculous feeding of the 5000, he records a discourse in which Jesus says, '*I am the bread of life … Your ancestors ate the manna in the wilderness, and they died … I am the living bread that came down from heaven. Whoever eats of this bread will live forever …*' (John 6:48–51).

ONE MEAL, MANY NAMES

Jesus' words about remembrance were frequently repeated when believers met to 'break bread' together. Other words, spelling out the significance of Jesus' death, also became part of the liturgy of Holy Communion. Gradually, full liturgical texts were developed for these gatherings around the Lord's Table. Various names for this sacrament or ordinance have come into common usage over the centuries, as follows.

Holy Communion
This title stresses the fellowship aspect of the service or meal. Sharing the bread and wine fosters communion between the worshippers and God, and between those present. Holy Communion is a corporate experience. Believers are encouraged to think not only of 'making my communion' but of sharing one loaf and one cup at the Lord's Table, with their brothers and sisters in Christ.

Eucharist
This comes from the Greek word for 'thanksgiving'. It reminds us that when Jesus took bread at the Last Supper, he 'gave thanks'. It also focuses upon the fact that this is a sacrament of the gospel. Christians who gather at the Lord's Table wish to express their gratitude to God for his saving love. The focus of the service is upon Jesus, the crucified Saviour and risen Lord. But believers are required to express their gratitude, not only with their lips but with their lives. At the end of the Eucharist, worshippers commit themselves afresh to serve God in the world. Worship is only a temporary withdrawal from the pressures of life and the duty (sometimes joyful, sometimes difficult) of loving service.

The Lord's Supper
This title reminds us of the origins of the sacrament; it was a meal shared between Jesus and the original twelve disciples.

The Mass
Holy Communion in Roman Catholic churches is in the language of the people. But this is a recent development: an initiative taken

at the Second Vatican Council (1962–5). Before that this service was in Latin, as it had been for centuries. At the end of the Latin Rite, the priest dismissed the people with the words: *Ite, missa est* ('Go, you are dismissed'). The word 'Mass' – the commonest word for Holy Communion among Roman Catholics and some Anglicans and Lutherans – derives from this phrase. The term contains a challenge. As the Catholic Catechism puts it, '*the liturgy in which the mystery of salvation is accomplished concludes with the sending forth (missio) of the faithful, so that they may fulfil God's will in their daily lives*'.

The Breaking of Bread

This term comes directly from the New Testament and speaks for itself. A famous verse (Acts 2:42) makes clear that breaking bread together was one of the key features of the early Church.

> 'The spirituality of the Catholic and Orthodox Churches is dominated by the Eucharist, though in very different forms. The Orthodox emphasis is much more on the assembled people being brought within sight and sound of the heavenly altar, while in the West sacramental devotion is more personal.'
>
> (Gordon Rupp)

Transubstantiation

Over the centuries, differences in emphasis and in understanding of what happens in Holy Communion emerged – especially as theologians wrestled with the meaning of the phrases 'This is my body' and 'This is my blood'. Strong differences over possible interpretations have been expressed. On the one hand are those who see the breaking of bread and sharing of wine as a powerful means of recalling the focus of our salvation. A highly significant change takes place. It occurs within the hearts and lives of the worshippers, as they consider afresh God's love revealed in the life and death of his Son.

On the other hand are those who believe that something vital happens, not only in the hearts of the worshippers, but to the bread and wine too. This is sometimes referred to as *transubstantiation*. This is the belief that when the priest says the prayer of consecration over the bread and wine, these actually become the body and blood of Christ. In 1551, the Council of Trent put it like this: 'After the consecration of the bread and wine, our Lord Jesus Christ is truly, really and substantially contained in the venerable sacrament of the holy Eucharist under the appearance of those physical things.' This spells out a belief in the *Real Presence* – Jesus present in the elements of the sacrament in a real, not simply symbolic, way.

Insight

Differences in understanding of the sacraments have been sharp and divisive. Most contentious has been the doctrine of 'transubstantiation'. Churches in the modern world have drawn closer in understanding, but full inter-communion with other Churches is still not permitted by the Roman Catholic hierarchy.

The following points should be noted:

▶ Those who take this view do not deny that the communicants eat actual bread and drink real wine. *They employ the Greek philosopher Aristotle's distinction between 'substance' and 'accident'.* Substance *refers to the essential nature of a material;* accident *to its outward appearance (colour, shape, taste). On this view, the accidents of the bread and wine remain – they still look and taste like bread and wine. But the substance changes to that of the body and blood of Jesus Christ.*

▶ The sixteenth-century Reformers (Chapter 17) criticized this view, although they did not agree among themselves on every detail. *Martin Luther held to* Consubstantiation – *the view that the substance of both bread and the body of Christ are present together. When placed in a fire, iron glows because iron and heat are both present. A simple analogy like this helps as we consider the Eucharist, said Luther, who emphasized that the fact of Christ's presence is more important than any explanation or theory. Others pointed to the nature of the language used by Jesus. They argued that he was using the vivid language of metaphor. 'This is my body' means, 'Pay close attention. This bread represents my body which is broken for you.' Bread it remains; but it is set apart for a holy and special purpose.*

▶ This was a very sharp debate. What people believed about the Real Presence in Holy Communion could determine whether they lived or died in sixteenth-century Europe. *Mercifully, much of the heat has now gone out of the argument. Many Catholics and Protestants believe that it does not matter whether all Christians believe in precisely the same way. Some modern Catholic theologians have reworked old ideas and coined new words. Edward Schillebeeckx, for example, speaks of* trans-signification – *the view that the consecration of the bread and the wine is primarily concerned with a change of meaning.*

▶ Church leaders have made efforts to understand each other better and to draw closer together. *The World Council of Churches convened an inter-Church conference in Lima in 1982 to consider* Baptism, Eucharist and Ministry. *ARCIC (Anglican-Roman Catholic International Commission) began in 1970 and ensured that high-level discussions between Roman Catholics and Anglicans continued for some 35 years. It has been succeeded by IARCCUM (International Anglican – Roman Catholic Commission for Unity and Mission).*

But Holy Communion, together with related questions of ministry and priesthood, continues to be one of the main issues dividing the churches. Most denominations welcome members of other churches to the Lord's Table. In contrast, the Roman Catholic Church officially forbids its members to receive holy communion in other churches, and will not offer communion to non-Catholics.

Perhaps Mother Teresa's simple words, with which all Christians can agree, show that the underlying unity is more important than the obvious divisions.

When Jesus came into the world, he loved it so much that he gave his life for it. And what did he do? He made himself the Bread of Life. He became small, fragile, and defenceless for us.

Two or seven?

Almost all churches observe the two great sacraments of Baptism and Holy Communion. These are called *Dominical Sacraments* because they originate directly from commands of Jesus ('Dominical' means 'of the Lord'). All Christians agree that these two are supreme. But the Roman Catholic and Orthodox Churches (and some Anglicans) use the word 'sacrament' to refer to five other ceremonies, in addition to baptism and holy communion. *The Catechism of the Catholic Church* explains these very clearly.

Confirmation

In Western churches this is a service of commissioning and full church membership, involving laying on of hands with prayer, always by a bishop in Anglican churches. This marks a conscious decision by candidates to follow the Christian way. An important feature is prayer for the strength of the Holy Spirit in the candidates' lives.

> *Confirmation brings an increase and deepening of baptismal grace:*
> *– it unites us more firmly to Christ;*
> *– it increases the gifts of the Holy Spirit in us;*
> *– it renders our bond with the Church more perfect;*

> *– it gives us a special strength of the Holy Spirit to spread and
> defend the faith by word and action as true witnesses of Christ,
> to confess the name of Christ boldly, and never to be ashamed of
> the Cross.* (CCC)

Many Anglicans would agree with this exposition. In the Eastern Orthodox Churches, confirmation is usually administered by a priest, not a bishop, immediately after baptism. This means that even infants are confirmed as well as baptized. They are also given their first holy communion on the same occasion. The service which includes these three sacraments is called *Chrismation*.

Marriage

Christians view marriage (or matrimony) as more than a contract or exchange of promises. It is a vocation and calling, requiring God's grace.

> *The consent by which the spouses mutually give and receive
> one another is sealed by God himself ... Authentic married love
> is caught up into divine love. Thus the marriage bond has been
> established by God himself. By its very nature it is ordered to the
> good of the couple, as well as to the generation and education
> of children ... The sacrament of Matrimony signifies the union
> of Christ and the Church. It gives spouses the grace to love each
> other with the love with which Christ has loved his Church.* (CCC)

Ordination

All Christians are called to serve – to exercise 'a ministry'.

> *Christ, high priest and unique mediator, has made of the Church a
> kingdom, priests for his God and Father. The whole community of
> believers is, as such, priestly ...* (CCC)

But many churches 'set aside' some men – and sometimes women too – to exercise leadership, to teach the faith and to administer the sacraments. In Catholic theology, an ordained priesthood has a vital place, especially in relation to the sacraments.

> *Through the ordained ministry, especially that of bishops
> and priests, the presence of Christ as head of the Church is
> made visible in the midst of the community of believers ...
> This priesthood is ministerial. That office ... which the Lord*

> *committed to the pastors of his people, is in the strict sense of*
> *the term a service.* (CCC)

Absolution or reconciliation

Absolution involves receiving assurance that God will forgive all who come to him in prayerful humility, with penitence and faith. No sin is too bad for God's mercy and forgiveness. Reconciliation involves confession, and this sacrament is sometimes called *penance, conversion, confession* or *forgiveness*. Lutherans have a tradition of absolution as a third Dominical Sacrament (based on John 20:23), though this is sometimes seen as an extension of baptism. We may offer the prayer of repentance in solitude, within congregational worship, or in the presence of a priest. It is the last-named that is regarded as sacramental (page 121).

> *The movement of return to God, called conversion and*
> *repentance, entails sorrow for and abhorrence of sins committed*
> *and the firm purpose of sinning no more in the future. Conversion*
> *touches the past and the future, and is nourished by hope in*
> *God's mercy.* (CCC)

Anointing of the sick

Anointing the sick with oil in the context of prayer and thanksgiving, conveys assurance of God's love and ability to heal. This is based on the New Testament letter of James (5:14–15). Over the centuries the practice came to be associated with dying and it is sometimes called *extreme unction* or the *last rites*. But health, wholeness and healing have been emphasized since the Second Vatican Council (page 220).

> *The Anointing of the Sick is not a sacrament for those only*
> *who are at the point of death. Hence, as soon as any one of the*
> *faithful begins to be in danger of death from sickness or old age,*
> *the fitting time for him to receive this sacrament has certainly*
> *already arrived.* (CCC)

....

Insight

Baptism and Holy Communion are called 'Dominical' Sacraments ('of the Lord') because they are based on

(Contd)

commands of Jesus. Some Churches – notably the Roman
Catholic Church – use the word 'sacrament' for five other
ceremonies too.

OTHER TRADITIONS

In contrast to the tendency to multiply sacraments, the Salvation
Army and Quakers (Society of Friends) have no specific sacraments
at all. Rather, Quakers see all life as sacramental.

On this view, *all* good things – the natural world, laughter, food,
love, life itself – speak to us of the love of God. Salvationists
view every meal as a sacrament; an opportunity to remember the
crucified and risen Lord. This is summed up in the challenging
hymn of Albert Orsborn, a member of the Salvation Army:

> **My life must be Christ's broken bread,**
> **My love his outpoured wine,**
> **A cup o'er filled, a table spread**
> **Beneath his name and sign...**

Moved to tears

Examining the nature of the sacraments by reading about them in a
book cannot lead you to the centre of their significance and power.
For the sacraments are essentially a *shared experience*. In an
attempt to convey this, I will end this chapter on a personal note.

BAPTISM

One Saturday evening I was invited by a 20-year-old to a
Pentecostal church where he was to be baptized. There were
17 candidates – mainly teenagers, but also one entire family. The
minister stood up to his thighs in water, in the baptistery at the
front of the simple church building. Before plunging the candidates
under the water, he invited them to say what had led up to that
moment of public witness to faith in Christ.

The church was full. We sang and prayed; many smiled and hugged; a few wept. It was a powerful occasion and I was moved by the deep sincerity and infectious faith of the candidates.

I have attended somewhat similar occasions within the Church of England – student baptisms conducted by the chaplain in a college swimming-pool. But more often I have attended baptisms, of adults and babies, in Anglican and other churches, where water has been poured upon heads. Less dramatic, but equally profound.

HOLY COMMUNION

> 'Twas God the word that spake it,
> He took the Bread and brake it;
> And what the word did make it;
> That I believe, and take it.'
>
> (Queen Elizabeth I on Christ's presence in the sacrament)

I confess that I am not always deeply moved at Holy Communion. Sometimes I struggle to maintain concentration; sometimes I am too aware of a cold building, or aching knees! This does not worry me unduly, for I believe that receiving the elements of bread and wine, out of simple obedience to the Lord's command, has spiritual value. But I have experienced some wonderfully moving services.

▶ I was invited to take part in a Sunday Eucharist in a prison chapel. *It was a high-security prison; many of the prisoners had committed terrible crimes of violence. As I knelt with those prisoners to receive the bread and the wine, I was keenly aware that I, too, came as a penitent sinner, in need of God's grace and forgiveness.*
▶ I recall another occasion, when I stood with a hundred young people *around an altar, with a hundred flickering candles, as we shared deep silence and wonderful singing. And I remember gathering with a group of 40 around a communion table under an oak tree to shade us from the hot sun. During the passing of the peace – an ancient custom, now re-introduced into the Eucharist by many churches – people broke ranks and informally hugged and*

shook hands. I also recall gathering with two others around the bed of a dying woman, and breaking bread and drinking wine in remembrance that Christ had died for each one of us.

▶ I remember attending Mass in a Roman Catholic monastery, *where I was warmly welcomed but not invited to receive the sacrament. I think too, of a Sunday 'Breaking of Bread' service with the Christian Brethren (formerly Plymouth Brethren). About 60 (men, women and children) sat around a central table on which was placed a huge loaf and unfermented grape juice. There was no appointed leader and different members (men only) read a Bible passage, spoke, or chose a hymn, before the bread was broken and shared.*

▶ I think back to a service with a Russian Orthodox congregation in London. *Marvellous singing, no chairs, people coming and going. Some lit a candle, some kissed an icon, others prostrated themselves. Many just stood and watched and listened and prayed. I think back, too, to countless more ordinary services of Holy Communion, where in some indefinable way I have been sustained by receiving bread and wine, by fellowship with other believers, and by the reading and preaching of the Scriptures.*

▶ And I remember too, reading a moving passage about Holy Communion *in the nineteenth century, in which Bishop F J Chavasse recollected the 'Communion Sundays' of his boyhood: 'My father would be extra quiet all day, and shut himself up in his room both before and after the service. I have seen him come down from the rail with tears in his eyes.'*

Tears are an appropriate response to Holy Communion. Tears of *sadness* – as we recall the coolness of our commitment to Christ, to his Church and to his world; tears of gratitude as we reflect upon the cost of our salvation; tears of joy as, in fellowship with other believers, we ponder the wonder of God's great love for us, revealed supremely in the death and resurrection of Jesus Christ.

Note: *The Archbishop's School of the Sacraments* by Simon Stanley is a succinct but helpful survey of this topic. The booklet is published by York Courses (www.yorkcourses.co.uk).

Other signs and symbols

In addition to the sacraments, Christianity is rich in signs and symbols. Each Gospel has its own symbol: Matthew a man with wings; Mark a lion; Luke an ox; John an eagle.

Three common visual symbols are:

▶ Chi-Rho, based on the first two letters of the Greek word for 'Christ' (Christos)

The Chi-Rho

▶ IHS, a monogram for the name Jesus in Greek   The IHS

▶ INRI, taken from the initial letters (in Latin) of 'Jesus of Nazareth, the King of the Jews.' It reminds us that Pontius Pilate ordered this title to be placed on the cross, written in Aramaic, Latin and Greek.

Most famous of all is the ancient fish symbol. As some of the first disciples were fishermen, this is clearly an appropriate sign. But its early, widespread use runs deeper than this. The Greek word for fish is 'Ichthus' and each letter points to a name or title for Jesus.

I	Iesous	Jesus
Ch	Christos	Christ
Th	Theou	Of God
U	(H)uios	Son
S	Soter	Saviour

There are some 50 titles for Jesus in the New Testament and artists have delighted in this rich quarry. Early Christian paintings in the catacombs focus on the Fish and upon Jesus as the Good Shepherd. They were reticent to depict the Cross, which portrayed their Lord and Saviour as a common criminal. Later, of course, the cross became *the* Christian symbol above all others. Nor did the earliest paintings depict Christ in triumph (which later became a popular theme). Rather 'they conceive salvation in the gentle laws of friendship with Christ' (John McManners).

10 THINGS TO REMEMBER

1 *Christianity is a sacramental religion. This means that certain acts and objects bear witness to spiritual truths.*

2 *The two central sacraments are Baptism and Holy Communion. These are called 'Dominical' sacraments – meaning 'of the Lord'.*

3 *Jesus was baptised by his cousin, John the Baptist, in the river Jordan.*

4 *Baptism is the sacrament of Christian initiation.*

5 *Baptism can be administered at any stage of life – from immediately after birth to just before death.*

6 *Holy Communion is based on the last supper which Jesus shared with his disciples.*

7 *This 'Last Supper' has given rise to many famous paintings.*

8 *Holy Communion is also called the* Eucharist *(Greek for 'thanksgiving'), the Lord's Supper, the Breaking of Bread, and Mass.*

9 *Some Churches use the word 'sacrament' for five other ceremonies: confirmation, ordination, marriage, absolution, anointing.*

10 *In addition to the sacraments, Christianity is rich in other signs and symbols e.g. the cross, the* chi-rho *and the fish.*

9

Facing death: the four last things

In this chapter you will learn:
* *about the four last things*
* *about the glory of heaven*
* *about funeral rites and human dignity.*

Every religion is concerned with life; every religion is concerned with death. Each religion makes its own distinctive emphasis as its adherents grapple with deep and profound questions raised by our mortality. Traditional Christian theology speaks of *The Four Last Things: death, judgement, heaven and hell*.

> In December 2007 Pope Benedict XVI issued an Encyclical on eternal life, *Spe Salvi*, in which he addressed questions of judgement, purgatory, hell, faith, hope and heaven. Taking St Paul's letter to the Romans as his starting point, Pope Benedict wrote about the Christian virtue of hope: 'The one who has hope lives differently; the one who hopes has been granted the gift of a new life.'

Death

The Christian faith sets its face against escapism. Even in the joy of a wedding service, the couple are reminded that the promises they make are 'till death us do part'. This note contrasts sharply with Western culture in general, in which many people are shielded from the harsh reality and supreme mystery of death. Mark Twain, the American humorist, caught the Christian emphasis on realism when he said, 'No-one gets out alive'!

Thomas Hobbes (1588–1679) could say that life is 'solitary, poor, nasty, brutish and short'. In his world, most families knew the sorrow of death, including the death of a child. Relatives would observe the dying process, for most people died at home and many, including children, would have seen a dead body. Today, most people are not exposed to such experiences, and some do not attend a funeral until their adult years. Furthermore, our life expectancy is much longer. The biblical 'three score years and ten' (itself rather generous in those days) would seem a meagre ration to today's many octogenarians!

Almost all these changes are for the better. But they do push into the background the necessity to consider our own death. This point has been made by many people, not just Christians. The existentialist philosopher Martin Heidegger insisted that we are not authentically human unless and until we have considered our own mortality. This can be seen as morbid, but it need not be. Indeed, it can be enlightening and liberating.

In the modern world, many people would prefer a quick death, because it is the *process* of dying which is widely feared. Significantly, Dame Cicely Saunders, a Christian doctor with vast experience of care for the dying (Chapter 14), spoke of the value of time and space in which to contemplate eternity, and to take practical steps to 'close the book' on this life. This will include saying 'thank you' and 'sorry' as well as ensuring that a valid and up-to-date will has been made.

Insight

The New Testament is rich in teaching about life beyond the grave. The origin of this teaching is in the four Gospels, which tell us that God raised Jesus from death to new life. The Gospels declare that Jesus' tomb was empty, and that he appeared to his disciples in various places during the forty days following his crucifixion.

JUDGEMENT

In the New Testament we find this terse statement: we are 'destined to die once, and after that to face judgement' (Hebrews 9:27). The fourth-century Apostles' Creed picks up this theme when it says that Jesus Christ 'will come again to judge the living and the dead'. Alongside its joyful stress on resurrection, the Bible teaches that we are accountable to God. One day we shall be called to account for the way we have used our gifts, our opportunities and our energies. Above all, we shall be required to account for the way we have behaved in relation to the poor, the needy and the marginalized (Matthew 25:31–46).

But despite the reminder of Judgement and the call to consider our own mortality, every Christian funeral service includes a strong note of hope – even joy. For the gospel assures us of God's grace and forgiveness. This does not mean that tears and grief are out of place. Far from it; the bereaved are encouraged to mourn. There is a moving example of this in the New Testament. Following the death of Stephen, the first Christian martyr, we read that 'godly men buried Stephen and mourned deeply for him' (Acts 8:2). Their tears were not for Stephen, who died with a radiant faith and who was 'on another shore and in a greater light' (Eric Milner-White). They wept for themselves. Their spokesman and close friend had been taken from them. They would miss him deeply, and so they grieved.

GOD'S GRACE

For Christians, hope and peace in the face of death are not based upon faith in human goodness; they are rooted in the grace of God. The Bible has a rich doctrine of humanity. It gladly acknowledges our great dignity as creatures fashioned in the image of God – evidenced in our ability to reason and reflect, to communicate and create, and above all to love and to cherish. The scriptures also focus on the darker side of human nature: 'all have sinned and fall short of the glory of God' (Romans 3:23). A popular misconception sees God adding up the good deeds in our lives in one column and the bad deeds and omissions in another. He then subtracts one from the other and our eternal salvation depends upon being 'in credit'. This is a crude description of a not uncommon view.

But the Christian God is not a 'score-card' God. According to the Bible, none of us could achieve heaven if this were the basis of our salvation. But it is not. What counts is real faith and true repentance for our sins, and the grace and forgiveness of a loving God. The thief who died on the cross next to Jesus gives encouragement to us all. 'Lord, remember me when you come into your kingdom', was his request. Jesus responded with a gracious promise: 'Today you will be with me in paradise.'

HELL

Insight

There is teaching about judgement – even hell – in the New Testament. Harshest words are reserved for those who are indifferent to the needs of the poor, the marginalized and the young. In this way we are challenged to examine our own lives and motives.

When Jesus taught about hell, he had in mind an actual place – the Valley of Hinnom (Jesus would have used the Aramaic word '*gehinnam*' – Greek *Gehenna*; Hebrew *ge Hinnom*). This valley, south-west of Jerusalem, was where pagan worshippers once sacrificed children to Molech (Leviticus 18:21). This practice was hated by the prophets, and Jeremiah spoke of it as a place of shame and punishment by God. In the first century BC, Jews were using this valley of shame as a metaphor for the place of everlasting punishment for the wicked. By Jesus' day it had become a rubbish dump.

By the Middle Ages, this notion had become very literal, very picturesque, and very frightening! This can be seen by looking at depictions of hell on stained glass, watching the medieval mystery plays or reading Dante's *Divine Comedy*. Dante's classic text (*c.* 1300) portrays hell as nine circles at the centre of the earth. On the gate at the entrance is the inscription, 'Abandon hope, all ye who enter here.'

Teaching about hell continued down the years. On 8 July 1741 Jonathan Edwards preached a sermon entitled *Sinners in the hands of an Angry God*, which contains the following passage:

> **It would be dreadful to suffer the fierceness and wrath of Almighty God for one moment; but you must suffer it for all eternity. There will be no end to this exquisite horrible misery ... You will know that you must wear out long ages, millions of millions of ages, in wrestling and conflicting with this almighty merciless vengeance.**

Jonathan Edwards was not a bloodthirsty monster; he was equally eloquent on the great themes of mercy, forgiveness and divine love. Indeed, his preaching on hell was motivated by love; he had an overwhelming desire to warn those whom he feared would be lost, unless they were given a clear warning. His words were not unusual in the eighteenth century, and there are modern preachers who would say much the same thing in much the same way. In general, however, the twentieth century saw a move away from such harsh ideas, which do not square easily with the notion of the love of God, so clearly and frequently spelt out in the New Testament. Various views have been put forward.

▶ 'Universalists' argue *that the love and grace of God must ultimately conquer every human heart. In the end,* all *will be saved.*

▶ Others disagree. *Yes, it is clear from the Bible that* 'God desires everyone to be saved' *(1 Timothy 2:4). But God's will can be frustrated by human choice. They point out that of the 12 occurrences of the word 'Gehenna' in the New Testament, 11 are on the lips of Jesus. Jesus was particularly harsh on those who led 'little ones' astray (Luke 17:2).*

▶ Today's theologians *wish to dispense with medieval literalism. They remind us that Jesus was using picture language based upon an actual rubbish dump in the Valley of Hinnom. Hell does not literally involve fire and darkness (which are mutually exclusive!). Those who believe that we cannot reject the concept of hell simply because we do not like it, sometimes speak about 'separation from God', freely chosen.*

▶ The above point has been put with dramatic force. *On the Day of Judgement, four words will be spoken:* 'Your will be done.' *Addressed by us to God, they assure us of heaven. Spoken by God to us, they have an awful finality. If we insist on enthroning ourselves at the centre of our personal universe, God will allow this to happen. To change the image: the prison door is open but we must decide to walk out if we are to be free.*

▶ Some theologians *speak of 'conditional immortality'. In their view, hell does not involve eternal punishment; it means ceasing to exist.*

▶ Some stress the outrage *that we feel in the face of naked evil. Hitler, Stalin, Saddam Hussein and Osama bin Laden have caused untold suffering; should they 'get away with it'? And what about less well-known people who spread misery throughout their lives? At the very least, would not extinction be a just outcome – if not actual punishment? Others ask why these people behaved as they did. Cruel or indifferent adults may have lacked love in childhood; many child abusers have themselves been abused. Perhaps 'to know all is to forgive all'?*

▶ On the other hand *we might ask, 'Would Hitler be happy in heaven?' Without a massive change of heart, would he not find it intolerable to spend eternity worshipping Jesus the Jew? And might not bitter, self-centred people dislike and despise the love and openness which characterize life in heaven? A change of heart is precisely what the gospel requires. Christians call this* repentance. *In giving human beings a measure of real choice, God knowingly places limits on his own power. To over-rule our fundamental freedom of choice is something which God will not do.*

▶ There is no evidence *that Hitler repented before he died. Might it be possible for him to repent after his death? The notion of a further opportunity to respond to God's love after death was developed by some Protestant theologians in the nineteenth century – but resisted by others.*

> 'All sin tends to be addictive, and the terminal point of addiction is damnation. Since God has given us the freedom either to accept his love and obey the laws of our created nature, or to reject it and defy them, he cannot prevent us from going to hell and staying there if that is what we insist upon.'
> (W H Auden)

JESUS' DESCENT INTO HELL

In the Apostles' Creed we find the mysterious phrase 'he (Jesus) descended into hell'. The twentieth-century Swiss Roman Catholic theologian Hans Urs von Balthasar took this as a major theme. He raised the question: what happened between the death of Jesus on Good Friday and his resurrection on Easter Sunday? His answer? 'The outreach of God [through Jesus] to the furthest possible limits of human lostness' (1 Peter 3:18–22; Ephesians 4:9–10).

Commenting on this, Archbishop Rowan Williams says:

> *So wherever you are, however lost you are, however much darkness there is around you, you have not got beyond the reach of God because if God is Father and Son then the embrace of God can go right round and bring you back...*
>
> *I was visiting Uganda when I was invited to preach in the condemned section of Lisiro Jail in Kampala, to about 300 people under sentence of death. Well, there are congregations and congregations – and this wasn't one of the easier ones. And all I could think of to say was – there is nowhere where Jesus is not. And if there's nowhere where Jesus is not, there's nowhere where God's transforming openness is not...*

He goes on to quote von Balthasar:

> *The Trinity is revealed in the giving of God's Son to divine abandonment and hell, which is the greatest possible conception of God. He is so full of life that he can afford to be dead. No religion or worldview has dared to think and proclaim something of this kind about God, human beings and the world. Therefore, Christianity remains without analogy and it rests not on an idea, but on a fact – Jesus Christ – which in the unity of claim, cross and resurrection, remains an unsplittable atom.*

PURGATORY?

Purgatory is seen as a 'staging post' between this world and heaven, providing further opportunity for sanctification. The idea is found early in the history of the Church. The stress on torment in Purgatory was developed in the Middle Ages. With this came the notion of multiple 'Masses for the dead' and 'indulgences', from which concepts many were glad to be released at the Reformation (Chapter 17).

Most Protestants believe that we shall be changed 'in a flash, in the twinkling of an eye' (1 Corinthians 15:52). At death we pass from time to eternity, where everything is *now*. The life of heaven lies just beyond death. Catholics continue to believe in a period of preparation and purification before we enter heaven; but purgatory '*is entirely different from the punishment of the damned*' (CCC). In traditional Catholic theology, purgatory does not afford a 'second chance' for initial repentance.

In general, Catholics believe in purgatory and Protestants do not. But the lines are not distinct. The Anglican apologist, C S Lewis, wrote an imaginative defence of purgatory in *The Great Divorce*. In this book, Lewis argued that the possibility of hell (seen as separation from God) does not fly in the face of the love of God. Indeed, he argued that our freedom to choose whether to respond to, or reject, God's love, is in itself an indication of that love. The grey world which Lewis represented as hell relates to the thinking of the Belgian Roman Catholic scholar Edward Schillebeeckx. He rejects the notion that heaven and hell can in some sense be 'balanced'. Heaven has glorious substance; hell is the terrible absence of all that gives zest to life. Heaven is radiant with glory; hell is dismal and joyless.

In *The Weight of Glory*, C S Lewis reminds us that a consideration of heaven and hell can be an extremely practical matter:

'It may be possible for each to think too much of his own potential glory hereafter; it is hardly possible for him to think too often or too deeply about that of his neighbour. The load, or weight, or burden of my neighbour's glory should be laid daily on my back, a load so heavy that only humility can carry it, and the backs of the proud will be broken. It is a serious thing to live in a society of possible gods and goddesses, to remember that the dullest and most uninteresting person you can talk to may one day be a creature which, if you saw it now, you would be strongly tempted to worship, or else a horror and a corruption such as you now meet, if at all, only in a nightmare. All day long we are, in some degree, helping each other to one or other of these destinations. It is in the light of these overwhelming possibilities ... that we should conduct all our dealings with one another, all friendships, all loves, all play, all politics. There are no ordinary people.'

(From *Screwtape Proposes a Toast* (Collins))

HEAVEN

The distinctive feature of Christian thought as it faces the brevity of life and the reality and meaning of death, is *resurrection*. Because of his firm belief in this, St Paul claimed to look forward to the world to come, asserting that to die is 'to be with Christ, which is better by far' (Philippians 1:23). In his *Journal*, Pope John XXIII wrote that his bags were packed and he was ready to go. The twentieth-century journalist, Malcolm Muggeridge, picked up this theme. He suggested that dying is rather like checking out of a seedy boarding house and being welcomed into a glorious palace, with all expenses paid!

Christians deny that this is wishful thinking, for the Christian hope is grounded in the love and forgiveness of God, and it is based upon the resurrection of Jesus Christ. Easter celebrates the wonderful fact that Jesus was too good and too great to be held by death. God raised him from the grave.

Some ancient 'nature religions' focused upon belief in a dying and rising god, for example Osiris (Egypt) and Baal (Canaan). By enacting and reciting their great myths, they sought to ensure that a season of barrenness would once again give way to harvest and fertility. But there is a striking contrast between those religions and the Christian faith. In fertility religions, resurrection operated at a *mythological* level: it was *story* not history. Christians believe that in Jesus Christ, the 'myth became fact'. What 'happened' annually in those nature religions, *actually happened* once for all in Jesus Christ, according to the Bible. The idea became an event – erupting into history and transforming the future. This is the Christian claim and it is for this reason that Easter is the supreme Christian festival.

Insight

New Testament teaching about eternal life is not mere speculation. It is rooted in history and evidence (Chapter 3). The Bible claims that when God raised Jesus from the grave he defeated death for us all. He is the 'first fruits' of a great harvest. We are that harvest.

If true (Chapter 3), the resurrection of Jesus Christ is clearly a *wonderful* event. From a Christian viewpoint it is also a highly *significant* event. For it was not a question of one man overcoming death for himself. Rather, by raising Jesus from the dead, God defeated death itself. Things would never be the same again. *It was a decisive moment for the whole human race.*

In the New Testament, Jesus' resurrection is described as the 'first fruits' of a great harvest. We are that harvest. To change the image: Jesus threw wide open the gates of glory. John Donne (1572–1631), Dean of St Paul's, caught this in his sonnet 'Death be not proud':

> *Death be not proud, though some have called thee*
> *Mighty and dreadful, for, thou art not so...*
> *One short sleep past, we wake eternally,*
> *And death shall be no more. Death, thou shalt die.*

This does not mean that facing death is necessarily easy for Christians. Derek Worlock, Roman Catholic Archbishop of Liverpool, died of lung cancer in 1996. He wrote honestly and movingly about his pain and his faith.

> *I remained cold as a stone spiritually and desperately troubled by nightmares ... Our own sufferings and difficulties can seem cruel and pointless unless they are related to the work of salvation. In our hearts we know that properly directed, they can be a way in which we are drawn into the life and purpose of our Saviour. That is never easy for us but it is part of our faith.*

(With *Hope in Our Hearts*: Hodder & Stoughton)

When Cardinal Basil Hume, a former Abbot of Ampleforth, rang to tell Abbot Timothy Wright that he was dying of cancer, the abbot said: 'Congratulations! That's brilliant news. I wish I was coming with you.' The Cardinal was relieved by his brother monk's response: 'Thank you, Timothy. Every one else has burst into tears.'

REDEMPTION

What a wretched man I am! Who will rescue me from this body of death? Thanks be to God – through Jesus Christ our Lord!

(St Paul: Romans 7:24–25)

For the first time I examined myself with a seriously practical purpose. And there I found what appalled me; a zoo of lusts, a bedlam of ambitions, a nursery of fears, a harem of fondled hatreds. My name was legion. (C S Lewis: *Surprised by Joy*, Collins)

When the 'book of life' is opened, we may expect to find all those nasty, spiteful and selfish things that we did, said and thought, recorded there in black and white. Even worse perhaps, we might expect to find there all the good things that we failed to do, through indifference or pride or hostility.

To our amazement and joy, the book will contain page after page of blank, white paper. Not because we did nothing wrong, but because our sins have been forgiven. God really does 'forgive and forget'. Because of his love for us, and all that Jesus did for us, our sins will be blotted out.

This great truth can be illustrated by a homely story. A man lost his temper. 'Please forgive me, Lord', he prayed. The following day he lost his temper again. 'Oh Lord, I've done it again', he wailed in anguish when he cooled down. At that point a voice from heaven asked, 'Done what again?'

Though your sins are like scarlet, they shall be as white as snow; though they are red as crimson, they shall be like wool.

(Isaiah 1:18 – see also 1 John 1:8–9)

The life of the world to come

> **Insight**
>
> We are not given details of the glories of heaven and eternal life. But by vivid picture language we are told that it is a 'place' of rich fellowship, love, truth, laughter and praise.

What is heaven like? The Bible speaks of this ultimate mystery in hints, pictures and parables. It *is* a mystery. Paul reminds us that in this life 'we see but a poor reflection' (1 Corinthians 13:12) and John admits that 'what we will be has not yet been made known' (1 John 3:2). But from time to time the Bible pulls back the curtain and we glimpse the glory of heaven.

Heaven will be a place of light, beauty and joy. 'There will be no more death or mourning or crying or pain, for the old order of things has passed away' (Revelation 21:4). Jesus spoke about a great banquet. Heaven will be a place of friendship and conviviality, where Jesus will drink wine with his disciples – his promise given at the Last Supper. All present will be bathed in the light of the presence of God and glorious music will be sung in worship of 'the Lamb upon the throne'. Professor Alister McGrath points out that 'the New Testament parables of heaven are strongly communal in nature; for example, heaven is portrayed as a banquet, as a wedding feast, or as a city – the new Jerusalem'.

In heaven we shall know as we are known, perfectly ourselves and perfectly related one to another. It is because heaven is such a participation in the communion of God's love that it is right to believe that we shall see and know those whom we have loved, but we shall see and know them in God ... Human destiny in heaven will not be attainment of an eternal and static perfection, but rather an everlasting participation in the exploration of the inexhaustible riches of the divine nature. From *The Mystery of Salvation* (Church of England report)

> Christian belief in eternal life and heaven depends upon the
> grace and mercy of the God who forgives us. Christians place
> their trust, not in their own 'goodness', but in the love and
> forgiveness of God.

The notion of 'reincarnation' is not taught in the Bible. This is the
Hindu and Buddhist belief that, after death, some aspect of the self
or soul can be reborn in a new body (human or animal). Nor is the
popular notion of heaven as a place of 'disembodied spirits' to be
found in the New Testament. The Bible is much more *earthy*.

The Old Testament does talk of the human spirit surviving death,
but when it does so it usually speaks with dismay. 'Sheol', the
shadowy place of departed spirits sometimes referred to in the
Psalms, was to be feared, for it was viewed as a twilight world
without zest or vitality.

> *The New Testament paints a much richer picture of life beyond
> death, with its stress on resurrection and glory.*

The Christian faith strongly discourages mourners from attempting
to 'get in touch' with deceased loved ones. It is understandable that
we should wish to attempt to do so, but Christians believe that the
Spiritualist route of mediums and seances is a road to heartache.
There are strong condemnations of such practices in the Bible
(Leviticus 19:31; Deuteronomy 18:10–13). Christianity encourages
us to commit our loved ones to God and to trust in his faithfulness
and enduring love.

The scientist Arthur Peacocke reflected on the puzzle of how we might be
resurrected, and drew an analogy from computers. He suggested that 'the
pattern in our brains which constitutes the essential you and me' is rather
like software. 'We know that software programs can be embodied in
many different kinds of hardware – and yet the software is real enough.'

The historian Gillian Evans considers the modern concern that heaven
will be 'beautiful but dull'. She affirms that 'we should be envisaging
a freedom from the confinement of time and space which will make

(Contd)

it possible for us to be with all our friends at once and individually, to be enjoying an infinite variety of things as we choose, without delay or hurry, crowding or isolation. It is something new, a new quality of life.'

RESURRECTION OF THE BODY

When it talks of the glories of heaven, the Bible does so in terms of *bodily resurrection*, rather than spiritual survival or the 'immortality of the soul'. The Apostles' Creed emphasizes this: '*I believe in the resurrection of the body and the life everlasting.*' By 'resurrection', the New Testament writers do not mean mere 'resuscitation'. What is raised will be far more glorious than what is sown – just as the butterfly is much freer and more interesting than the chrysalis, and the daffodil more beautiful than the bulb. Personal resurrection is set within the context of cosmic renewal. 'Behold I make all things new.' There will be 'a new heaven and a new earth' (Revelation 21:1).

Modern minds addressing this difficult, but fascinating and important, subject often find it helpful to focus on the word 'personality'. The teaching of the Bible is that we shall retain our personalities – refined and purified – for all eternity. You will still be recognizably you. We shall be much more interesting and glorious than we are now, but there will be a definite link between you-as-you-are-now and you-as-you-will-be-then.

Every aspect of life and personality which we offered to God during our earthly lives, will be gloriously raised – and handed back to us. Life in the glory of heaven will be full of substance, colour and zest. We shall not lose our identities in an ocean of consciousness. Indeed, it is only then that we shall really find and possess our true selves. For the gifts which make us what we are, are on loan now. They will be given to us then and they will be ours forever – to be shared in the rich fellowship of heaven.

'I implore you, good Jesus, that as in your mercy you have given me to drink in with delight the words of your knowledge, so of your loving kindness you will also grant me one day to come to you, the fountain of all wisdom, and to stand forever before your face. Amen.' (A prayer of the Venerable Bede)

Funeral rites

Because the Christian faith has taken root in so many cultures, each with its own rich traditions, funeral services vary in outward detail, as do weddings and baptisms. In some countries, the coffin is left open until the time for burial and the bereaved are encouraged to view the body. In other cultures the body is not seen except sometimes by the close family. In some places the coffin remains in the home until burial; in others it is taken to a church or chapel between death and the funeral service.

For centuries, burial (usually in the ground; sometimes at sea) was the Christian custom, unless there were exceptional circumstances such as the plague – and even then burial was often practised. But the industrial revolution gave rise to large towns and cities, with pressure on space. So the practice of cremation began around 1875 – amid suspicion and criticism. Indeed it was condemned by the Roman Catholic Church until 1963. In its early days, 'free-thinkers' promoted cremation in the hope that the practice would destroy belief in the resurrection of the body. '*It appeared to have no such consequence. In some cases reverence for the human body was more evident in burning than in burial*' (Owen Chadwick).

Burial and cremation are equally appropriate ways of marking the end of a person's life as the solemn words are pronounced: '*earth to earth, ashes to ashes, dust to dust, in sure and certain hope of the resurrection to eternal life through our Lord Jesus Christ'.*

Some funeral services are very simple; others are lengthy and may be set within a Requiem Mass. Every funeral reminds us of our own mortality – and of the wisdom of fashioning our lives in the light of this awesome fact. Despite differences, the really essential features are common to all Christian funerals: the dignity which is afforded to the body; the atmosphere of mourning and loss; the sense of Easter joy bursting through; the note of confidence in the love of God and the fact of eternal life.

J G Ballard's autobiographical novel *Empire of the Sun* (Gollancz) was made into an award-winning film. It tells the story of Jim – a boy who survived life in a Japanese prison camp. At one point, he describes how he and two Christian missionaries were burying a dead companion.

> *The women pulled Mr Radik from the cart. Although wearied by the effort, they handled him with the same care they had shown when he was alive. Was he still alive for these two Christian widows? Jim had always been impressed by strong religious beliefs. His mother and father were agnostics, and he respected devout Christians in the same way that he respected people who were members of the Graf Zeppelin Club or shopped at the Chinese department stores, for their mastery of an exotic foreign ritual. Besides, those who worked hardest for others, like Mrs Philips and Mrs Gilmour and Dr Ransome, often held beliefs that turned out to be correct.*

Insight

A note on 'near death experiences': In recent years great interest has been shown in 'near death experiences'. Some people who have nearly died claim to have felt warmth, light and a deep sense of peace. The cause and significance of such experiences is debated, but many are convinced that they have enjoyed a foretaste of heaven and, because of their near-death experience, they have no fear of death.

10 THINGS TO REMEMBER

1 Like all religions, Christianity is concerned with the 'big questions' of life – including the fact of death.

2 Every Christian funeral service includes a strong note of hope – even joy – amidst the sorrow.

3 This joy arises from the Christian belief in heaven and eternal life.

4 The Christian gospel – the 'good news' – assures us of God's grace, love and forgiveness.

5 Jesus taught about heaven and hell.

6 When Jesus taught about hell he had in mind an actual place – a rubbish dump outside Jerusalem.

7 Christian belief in heaven is based on Jesus' resurrection.

8 The Bible teaches that through his resurrection, Jesus defeated death and flung wide open the gates of heaven.

9 The New Testament talks of the glories of heaven in terms of bodily resurrection, not spiritual survival.

10 Many people claim that, because of a 'near death' experience of light and warmth, they have no fear of death.

10

Christian faith in a scientific age

In this chapter you will learn:
- *about the Christian origins of science*
- *about the 'conflict' between Christianity and science*
- *about Christianity, science and ethical dilemmas.*

> 'In the beginning God created the heavens and the earth...' (Genesis 1:1). These opening words from the Bible were read to the world by the crew of Apollo 8 on Christmas Eve, 1968, as their spacecraft circled the moon – the first human beings to do so.

The Vatican has its own observatory (*Specola Vaticana*) – one of the oldest astronomical institutes in the world. Several religious orders have contributed personnel to the observatory and the nineteenth-century Jesuit, Father Angelo Secchi, was the first to classify stars according to their spectra.

Nevertheless, as science has grown in stature, so religion in Europe (the cradle of modern science) has become less central to many people's lives. There is a likely connection between these two facts.

The explanation for the existence of the world given in the Bible focuses on *purpose*. It affirms that the universe was created and is sustained by the will of a loving God. Science also gives an explanation: a different kind of explanation which excludes purpose, and focuses on *cause and effect*. It is sometimes assumed that these *why* and *how* explanations are mutually exclusive.

If so – if they really are in competition – there is no real contest. It is game, set and match to science.

A recent survey taken among British teenagers revealed that a large number believe that science has disproved religion. Clearly, if they are right, then Christian believers have no credibility in the modern world. A book entitled *Teach Yourself Christianity* will be read only by those interested in lost causes! Before conceding this, however, we need to examine some significant facts.

Science is a self-limiting activity – as single-minded about what it *excludes*, as what it *includes*. Science raises many fascinating issues but, by definition, it does not address some of the most important questions we face as human beings – about love, duty, honour and meaning, for example. Off duty, scientists are as concerned with these non-scientific questions as anyone else. Questions such as:

▶ Does my life have any ultimate meaning and purpose?
▶ Was I dumped here by chance, or loved into existence?
▶ Where does my sense of duty – and of beauty – come from?

It is because Christianity addresses these in a 'real' way, without offering easy answers, that it convinces many – though certainly not all – scientists.

The origins of modern science

In a remarkable statement, the philosopher John Macmurray asserted that 'science is the legitimate child of a great religious movement, and its genealogy goes back to Jesus'. This is not to deny other important influences: Greek, Chinese, Egyptian, Arabian mathematics, the Old Testament (with its Wisdom literature and Creation narratives) … But it is to affirm the importance for the rise of science of a widespread and particular way of looking at the universe, which Christianity gave to the Western world. Others have made the same point. For example, the philosopher A N Whitehead and the historian Herbert Butterfield both affirmed that science is a child of Christian thought.

As already indicated, some ancient civilizations were deeply interested in mathematical and scientific questions. There were important advances. But in the event it was Christian civilization which, following the Renaissance in Europe (Chapters 17 and 18), brought scientific thought to birth. Dr Peter Hodgson, Lecturer in Nuclear Physics at Oxford, put it this way: *'Christianity provided just those beliefs that are essential for science, and the whole moral climate that encourages its growth.'*

On this view, modern science could only 'take off' when certain factors were present. An eagerness to ask questions and a willingness to doubt received wisdom, were crucial. So was a wide range of accepted beliefs about the nature of the universe. Central among these were the belief that:

- *the material world is good, because it is created by God*
- *the same physical laws apply throughout the universe*
- *time moves forward rather than round in circles (Einstein gave us the concept of the curvature of space-time, but this does not undermine the biblical view that history is shot through with purpose)*
- *there is order in the universe because God is One and God is rational and loving.*

These views are expounded in the Bible. In contrast, some religions teach that matter is evil; or that we should be detached from the world; or that different gods rule different aspects of life; or that time goes round in endless cycles; or (in ancient Greek thought) that there is a given pattern to which the 'demi-urge' creator had to conform.

So it comes as no surprise to learn that the prestigious Royal Society (founded by a gathering of leading British scientists in the seventeenth century) is dedicated 'to the Glory of God the Creator, and the benefit of the human race'. Two centuries later the British Association for the Advancement of Science held its first meeting in York. Those who gathered at that meeting in 1831 paid tribute to the Church, 'without whose aid the Association would never have been founded'. They went on to declare that 'true religion and true science ever lead to the same great end'. The Association's first two presidents were clergymen.

Several famous early scientists were devout Christians, some of whom wrote theological books as well as scientific works. Among many others we note: Isaac Newton (1642–1727), thought by many to be the greatest scientist of all time; Robert Boyle (1627–91), famous for Boyle's Law; Michael Faraday (1791–1867) who harnessed electro-magnetism; and Gregor Mendel (1822–84) who laid the groundwork for modern genetics while Abbot of a monastery. James Young Simpson (1811–70) was the first surgeon to employ the anaesthetic properties of chloroform. When asked to name his greatest discovery, his reported reply was, 'It is not chloroform. My greatest discovery has been to know that I am a sinner and that I could be saved by the grace of God.'

Insight

The widespread view that Christianity and Science are opposed is false. Many of the founders of modern science were Christian believers – as are a significant number of modern scientists.

THE PRESENT DAY

Professor Arnold Wolfendale, when appointed Astronomer Royal in 1991, declared, 'I think the hand of God can be seen everywhere'. This is not an isolated viewpoint, for many professional scientists believe in God and a number are convinced Christians. *Christians in Science* (formerly *The Research Scientists' Christian Fellowship*) has some 700 members in Britain; its American counterpart has about 2,000.

In Britain there is a flourishing Society for Ordained Scientists. Both Oxford and Cambridge universities have recently established centres to explore the interface between science and religion. Somewhat similar initiatives have been taken in the USA – at

Berkeley, California and in Chicago, for example. Many believing scientists, including Professors Ian Barbour, John Lennox, Arthur Peacocke, John Polkinghorne and Russell Stannard, have written about the relationship between Christianity and science. (Paul Davies writes from a less orthodox standpoint.) From a very long list, we might also mention geneticists Professor 'Sam' Berry and Dr Francis Collins, the American who led the Human Genome Project for many years.

Professor Sir John Houghton is another eminent scientist who is a convinced Christian. A former Professor of Atmospheric Physics at Oxford University, he is an international figure in the vital field of climate change. On 7 December 2007 he was a member of the UN delegation which, alongside Al Gore, received the Nobel Peace Prize for outstanding work on global warming.

Of course, none of the above *proves* that Christianity is true. What it *does* show is that Christianity and science are not opposed. They are certainly not mutually exclusive.

If two teams really are in competition, no key player can be on both sides at the same time. And because scientists are intelligent people, the significant number of scientifically literate Christians also suggests that Christianity is not just a fairy story, suitable only for those who are unable to think for themselves.

The seeds of conflict

In view of all this, why has the notion that science has disproved religion become so widespread? We shall consider six reasons.

First, the notion of *purpose* lies outside scientific endeavour, by definition and choice, i.e. science is a deliberately 'self-limiting' activity. So science as an enterprise excludes the concept of God. Early on, the notion that the intervention of God was necessary to explain the gaps in scientific knowledge ('God of the Gaps') was rightly seen to be false. In principle (much harder in practice) it was claimed that *everything* could be explained in terms of cause and effect. From there it was a short (but inaccurate) step to the conclusion that, because concepts like 'God' and 'purpose' are outside the scope of science, they are unimportant or non-existent or even anti-science. While many of the founders of modern science were convinced believers, some of the later popularizers of science were militant atheists or agnostics. They spread their views with missionary zeal.

A second factor was the Galileo debate. **Galileo Galilei** (1564–1642) remained a Catholic throughout his life, but his harsh treatment at the hands of church officials is well known. Galileo built on the work of Copernicus (who was a canon in the church) in suggesting that the earth is not at the centre of the universe – an idea which was resisted by the church leadership of his day.

Insight

The Catholic Church's dispute with Galileo (who was a member of that Church) is a blot on the Church's reputation. The Vatican now supports scientific research and has its own world-famous observatory.

At stake was scientific method itself. Observation, followed by hypothesis and experimentation, could not be contained within limits already laid down by religious authority. Although it is over 300 years old, memories of the Galileo dispute live on because it is such a dramatic story (Bertolt Brecht, among others, wrote a play based upon it). This reinforces the popular view that religion is anti-science and that science is a threat to religion.

A third factor was the controversy over **Charles Darwin**'s research. *His Origin of Species by Means of Natural Selection* (1859) gave a very different account of the origins of life from that given in the Bible. At a famous debate in 1861 (not with Darwin himself but with T H Huxley), the Bishop of Oxford suggested that it was 'either-or' (*either* Darwin was right *or* the Genesis account of Creation in the Bible was right). Battle lines were drawn up.

Two centuries after Galileo, Charles Darwin's views rocked Victorian society. Several leading Christians supported Charles Darwin – and some leading scientists argued against him. To describe the dispute as 'science versus religion' is wrong.

Some Christians were unhappy with the Bishop of Oxford's debating stance (although it should be noted that careful research has shown that the Bishop was, and still is, inaccurately reported; he was more subtle than is commonly supposed). They looked again at the Bible and came to the conclusion that the beautiful poetic language of Genesis is just that: *beautiful poetic language, written in a pre-scientific age*. This does not mean that it is unimportant; it does mean that it is not a scientific treatise.

Genesis describes and explains the human situation in a most profound way. The glory and the tragedy are both there. It raises deep questions about our relationship with God, with Nature, and with one another. The rest of the Bible shows the solution to these vital questions being worked out in the lives of individuals and nations. Such literature is quite different from a scientific treatise on the origins of the universe – but no less important.

Charles Darwin himself was not an opponent of Christianity. It is true that he gradually lost his faith (partly through the death of his young daughter, Annie). But in 1872 (13 years after the *Origin of Species*) he gladly accepted honorary membership of the Anglican South American Missionary Society, because he was so impressed with their work. In reply to their invitation, he wrote, 'I shall feel proud if your committee think fit to elect me an honorary member of your society.' 'SAMS' continues to do excellent work today.

A fourth factor relates to the above. Some modern fundamentalist Christians are keen to keep the Darwinian controversy alive. They assert that evolution is a discredited theory and that the chapters on Creation in Genesis should be read literally (page 244).

A fifth factor arises from the work of **Sigmund Freud** (1856–1939), who made an immense impact upon the way we view the world.

Freud has given us a new vocabulary (unconscious, ego, id, superego, Oedipus complex, Freudian slip) and a new understanding of ourselves. Freud maintained that he was making a *scientific* analysis of human behaviour – a view contested by many, including non-Christians.

He wrote about religion and asserted that a key Christian insight should be inverted. God has not made us in his image; rather, we have made God in our image – according to our deepest needs (see *wish-fulfilment* in Glossary).

Carl Gustav Jung, another of the founders of modern psychology, was much more sympathetic to religion. He made the following remarkable statement:

> *During the past 30 years people from all the civilized countries of the earth have consulted me ... Among my patients in the second half of life – that is to say over 35 – there has not been one whose problem in the last resort was not that of finding a religious outlook on life.*

But Freud's views are firmly established in popular thought. His insights have been modified and criticized by psychologists and philosophers, but he raises significant challenges for religious believers. Together with Darwin and Marx (in their very different ways), he gave considerable impetus to a secular way of viewing the world, in which religion is marginalized or excluded.

Finally we note the hostility or indifference towards religion of some articulate present-day exponents of science. As we have seen, many scientists are practising Christians. But some non-Christian scientists have captured the popular imagination. Richard Dawkins with *The Selfish Gene* and his bestseller *The God Delusion* is the best known. Such aggressively atheistic scientists may appear to be speaking 'on behalf of science'; in fact, they are private individuals, whose views on religion are opposed by many of their fellow scientists. Significantly, despite its huge popularity, *The God Delusion* received some bad reviews from both atheists and scientists for its belligerent 'atheistic fundamentalism'.

Perhaps the most famous of all modern scientists is the cosmologist Stephen Hawking, whose *A Brief History of Time* leaves the door firmly open to the possibility of God, in a teasing conclusion.

Insight

'Creationists' are those Christians who believe that the accounts of creation in Genesis should be taken literally. In contrast, many modern Christians believe in God as Creator and Sustainer of the universe, and *also* in evolution. They believe that the accounts of creation in the Bible are not scientific records, but are stories carrying deep insights into 'the human condition', our relationships with one another, with Nature – and with God.

RESOLVING THE TENSION: 'COMPLEMENTARITY'

'Reductionism' refers to the process of 'reducing' complex areas of life to a simple one-level explanation. Notable among such explanations is Professor C E M Joad's description of human beings.

'Man is nothing but:

- ▸ *FAT enough for seven bars of soap*
- ▸ *LIME enough to whitewash one chicken coop*
- ▸ *PHOSPHORUS enough to tip 2200 matches*
- ▸ *IRON enough for one medium-sized nail*
- ▸ *MAGNESIUM enough for one dose of salts*
- ▸ *POTASH enough to explode one toy crane*
- ▸ *SUGAR enough for seven cups of tea*
- ▸ *SULPHUR enough to rid one dog of fleas.'*

In this tongue-in-cheek description, Professor Joad (who came to embrace the Christian faith in later life), provides a classic example of *reductionism*. The flaw is in the phrase 'nothing but'. His description gives a perfectly legitimate description of a human being. But it is not complete; other kinds and levels of description are required.

We need to add *psychological* categories, for human beings have emotions and ideas. We will wish to add *sociological* categories, for human beings function in communities. And these descriptions do not rule out the possibility of *spiritual* categories, for human beings experience love and have an instinct for worship. These various levels of description and explanation are 'complementary': each adds to the others and together they give a fuller and more accurate account.

This approach applies to everything. Music is vibrations in the air and ink dots on paper (even cat-gut or steel on horse hair, if we are listening to a cello). But it is not *just* these things. Ask the audience. And we are bound to ask how it is that music and art have the power to inspire and disturb us. The same approach is true when we consider the universe itself. We might describe it in terms of its origins in 'the big bang' some 14,000 million years ago. But this explanation, which uses the categories of modern physics, does not rule out the possibility of explaining the universe as the creation of a God of love.

Why does the earth support life? An answer in *scientific* terms will discuss factors like the importance of carbon, the immensity of space, the size of the earth (just right to support an atmosphere) and the theory of evolution. But it is equally possible to give an explanation in *theological* terms – by maintaining that God designed the earth so that these factors apply. If this is the case, then scientists are discovering the way in which God has designed the world – 'thinking God's thoughts after him' as the early astronomer Johannes Kepler put it. Science itself can help us to see the grandeur of God.

Of course, this theological explanation may be untrue. But not *because* of the fact that Nature can be explained in scientific terms.

'It is the contention of the Christian that, in order to do full justice to the totality of his experience, he finds it necessary to see and interpret the overall pattern of his experience not only in biochemical, physiological or psychological terms, but also in religious terms.'

(Malcolm Jeeves, former Professor of Psychology at St Andrews and Adelaide Universities)

In a recent radio discussion, a member of the panel asserted that science is about facts, and religion is about faith. Now of course all religions involve faith. But they include facts too. This is certainly true of Christianity which, like science, is based on *interpreted facts*. One fact is the Bible's account of Jesus of Nazareth which, as C S Lewis put it, is very difficult to explain in other than Christian terms. Another fact is the rise of the Christian movement in apparently impossible circumstances (with a shrinking number of demoralized disciples and an executed leader: see Chapter 3). And so we could go on. There are plenty of facts; and faith builds on these.

Conversely, there is plenty of *faith* in science. Scientific method can be described as observation, hypothesis and experimentation, leading to inference and theory. But it can equally well be described in terms of hunch, intuition, gamble, accident, teamwork, flashes of insight, patient slog, with plenty of faith mixed in; and numerous conversations over coffee and beer! Both sets of factors are present all the time. The great Albert Einstein asserted that '*God does not play dice*.' And his statement of faith, that there is a constancy and reality about nature, is fundamental to the scientific enterprise.

> 'Science and religion both seek to understand ourselves and our place in the cosmos, albeit by rather different means. I suspect that very frequently the apparent differences between science and religious faith are of scale, rather than of kind. So, for example, although it is sometimes said that religion is a matter of faith, whilst science deals with facts, I would urge that there is generally some experience, some matter of fact, that undergirds religious faith and that some element of belief must underlie scientific statements too.' (Dr Michael Fuller)

Humility

Strictly speaking, there is no such thing as Science. Rather, there are lots of human beings tackling a whole series of interesting puzzles and important questions. Despite their hugely impressive achievements, most modern scientists have a greater humility than many of their predecessors. They do not believe that nature is a book simply waiting to be read. They acknowledge mystery and contemplate with awe the inexhaustible riches within nature which they have only begun to glimpse. The awe-inspiring universe in which we live is both beautiful and terrifying – and full of surprises.

Despite astonishing progress, modern scientists realize their own practical limitations. 'Chaos theory' (an intriguing but misleading name for a vital insight) suggests that science will never be able to deliver an accurate long-term weather forecast!

Humility is linked with *wonder*. Science is a deliberately self-limiting enterprise. It excludes consideration of widespread human experiences of goodness, beauty and obligation. 'But the experience of wonder at the structure of the world is an authentic part of the scientist's experience, quite as important and fundamental as anything that can be measured in a laboratory or seen through a telescope' (Professor John Polkinghorne). The distinguished theoretical physicist Vicky Weisskopf wrote a book on this great theme, entitled *Knowledge and Wonder*.

Christians were forced to take their own journey into humility long ago. The days when theology was 'Queen of the Sciences', and every facet of life came within an overarching system of Christian belief and explanation, have long gone. But Christians do claim to have some insights into the nature and ways of God – whom they believe to be both Creator and Redeemer – not because they are clever but because God is gracious. He has revealed himself in Nature and in Scripture – and supremely in Jesus Christ. And so we glimpse his glory and recognize that he is 'full of grace and truth' (John 1:14). But many questions remain for 'now we see but a poor reflection' as St Paul puts it (1 Corinthians 13:12).

Meanwhile, new ideas surface and buzz. The suggestion of a 'multiverse' (containing parallel universes) is fascinating; the possibility of detecting intelligent life on other planets is exciting. Christianity is open to truth from every quarter and welcomes speculation and research into these, and other, intriguing possibilities.

Faith involves living with questions which we cannot answer. But this is not 'blind faith'. We live with these questions in the light of the great answers which we *do* possess. To the questions 'Does life have meaning?' and 'Is it all heading somewhere?' Jesus Christ is God's resounding 'Yes!'.

Design?

Many people are impressed by the beauty and order in our universe, observing that many factors are 'just right' to sustain life on earth. Some of these are built into the fabric of the universe; others are 'local happy accidents'.

- ▶ *Our sun has been burning steadily for billions of years, thus providing energy for the evolution of the earth.*
- ▶ *The unique properties of water as it nears its freezing point – it expands as it cools – means that lakes freeze top down, not bottom up. This is vital for aquatic life, but bad for lead water pipes on freezing nights!*
- ▶ *If our moon were bigger, we would suffer huge tidal waves caused by its gravitational pull.*
- ▶ *Without the massive planet Jupiter in our solar system, we might well be bombarded by large meteors. (Jupiter's gravitational pull acts as a kind of life-saving 'magnet'.)*

Factors like these, together with the beauty and rich variety in our world, convince many people that our universe has a Designer. Also significant is the fact that mathematics 'matches' reality. Equations on paper (human constructs) enable us to produce sophisticated technology in the 'real world'.

One enduring test of a scientific theory has proved to be whether it is 'elegant' or 'beautiful'. To some scientists all this is highly significant. A rational world suggests a rational God. A world with beautiful mathematics suggests a caring God. Others are less sure. They point to the chaos and destruction which also mark our universe.

Vigorous debate continues. Recent discussion has focused on the *anthropic principle*. This comes from the Greek word *anthropos* (meaning human being) and draws attention to the fact that our world is a good 'home' for life in general and especially for the human race. The odds against this are very high. Three writers spell this out for us:

> *The anthropic principle ... is a massive piece of circumstantial evidence pointing to meaning and purpose in the universe... The precise values of the speed of light, Planck's Constant, the mass of protons compared with neutrons, the total quantity of hydrogen and helium – all apparently unconnected conditions which have controlled every detail of the universe's development – seem to have been exactly programmed at or just after the first moment of time, and all to one end: humanity. Any deviation (and the odds on such deviations were tremendous) would have made the development of the universe as you know it, life included, impossible ... If in the course of an experiment a scientist produced a result against odds this large, he certainly would not dismiss it as an accident. He would look for a cause.* (Clifford Longley in *The Times*)

> *Scientists have discovered that the laws of nature have to be 'finely-tuned' to allow the possibility for life to develop. If the power of gravity, or the charge on the electron, or the nature of nuclear forces, were even a little different from what they actually are, no life could have come into being ... Life is not possible in 'any old world'; it requires a universe in a trillion.*
> (Professor John Polkinghorne, mathematical physicist)

> *The more I examine the universe and the details of its architecture, the more evidence I find that the universe in some sense must have known we were coming.* (Freeman Dyson, theoretical physicist)

'Intelligent Design'?

Christianity is based on Jesus Christ, not on the so-called 'argument from design'. Evidence for design in the universe is significant, but not decisive, for believers in God. They are not

(Contd)

surprised that scientists use words like 'beautiful' and 'elegant' to describe equations and explanations, for they believe that the universe is created and sustained by a rational and loving God. But most scientifically literate Christians do not subscribe to the recent theory called 'Intelligent Design', which started life in America. Its critics argue that it is one more version of the discredited 'God of the Gaps' approach. God as Creator stands behind the whole of Creation, not just those bits of 'the puzzle' which we do not, as yet, understand. Professor Sir John Houghton touches on this in *Climate Change & Christian Faith* (a CD conversation with the author of this book – available at www.yorkcourses.co.uk).

Ethical dilemmas

Science has given the world many blessings. Most of us would not wish to live in a world without anaesthetics, without television and without toothpaste. But science has presented us with enormous problems too. The possible destruction of our planet, whether by nuclear explosion or global warming, is not just the stuff of science fiction. Some commentators are very pessimistic. David Bosch wrote:

> *It is becoming increasingly evident that the modern gods of the West – science, technology and industrialization – have lost their magic. Events of world history have shaken Western civilization to the core... we are heading for an ecological disaster on a cosmic scale... progress was, in effect, a false god.*

Medical science, too, presents us with great problems as well as numerous blessings. To take just one example: we now have the ability to discern early in pregnancy whether a baby is likely to have certain grave health problems and whether it will be male or female. This means that we also have the ability to decide which babies will actually be born. With such knowledge comes a threat to the gender balance – already a practical concern in some societies today.

Numerous new ethical and practical decisions press in upon us in the early decades of the twenty-first century. Scientists themselves do not wish to carry the burden of decision-making on their own. This is a task for all of us. It is a task which Christians, together with many others, take very seriously (Chapter 14). We believe that prayer and a study of the wisdom to be found in previous generations – especially in the ancient Scriptures – have a practical part to play in seeking to ensure that science enriches, and does not destroy, life on planet Earth. In particular, the biblical teaching that God has given us stewardship of our world, is a vital insight. Nature is not a treasure-trove to be ransacked; it is a delicate network to be respected, cherished and left in good order for future generations.

> *Science ... does not deal in certainties. The best it can do is convince us, on the basis of strong probabilities – and that depends on trust.* (Professor Lisa Jardine, BBC R4, 5 February 2010)

> 'It is indeed a sobering thought that the early writings of the Jewish people (i.e. our Old Testament) encompass all the basic recommendations of world conservation strategy.'
> (Professor David Bellamy)

NATURAL ALLIES?

The above quotation from botanist David Bellamy indicates that some scientists view religious faith and scientific endeavour as natural – perhaps essential – allies. The following statements show that this belief is not uncommon.

> *Religion without science is blind. Science without religion is lame.*
> (Albert Einstein, who revolutionized modern physics with his Theory of Relativity)

> *Religion and natural science are fighting a joint battle in an incessant never relaxing crusade against scepticism and against dogmatism, against disbelief and against superstition, and the rallying cry in this crusade has always been, and always will be: 'On to God'.* (Max Planck, awarded the Nobel Prize for his work on Quantum Theory)

Science brings man nearer to God.

(Louis Pasteur, who revolutionized microbiology and gave his name to pasteurized milk)

... In the self-organization of molecules leading to life, there seems to have been considerable built-in design.

(Professor Ian Barbour, scientist–theologian)

Historically, religion came first and science grew out of religion. Science has never superseded religion, and it is my expectation that it never will supersede it. (Arnold Toynbee, historian)

There is evolution, and indeterminacy, and generosity, and chance. There is risk and beauty and joy. Gambling on the God who has so gambled on us does not seem so risky in the end.

(Sara Maitland, novelist)

I'm not an atheist. We are in the position of a little child entering a huge library filled with books in many different languages. The child knows someone must have written those books. It does not know how. The child dimly suspects a mysterious order in the arrangement of the books but doesn't know what it is. That, it seems to me, is the attitude of even the most intelligent human being toward God. (Albert Einstein)

The eternal mystery of the world is its comprehensibility ... The fact that it is comprehensible is a miracle. (Albert Einstein)

10 THINGS TO REMEMBER

1   *In today's world, many people believe there is a conflict between science and Christian faith.*

2   *This view is fuelled by famous historical debates, especially those featuring Galileo and Charles Darwin.*

3   *However, science has Christian origins and many founders of modern science were Christians.*

4   *A significant number of today's professional scientists are also Christian believers.*

5   *These scientists argue that science and religion, properly understood, are not in conflict.*

6   *Albert Einstein said: 'Religion without science is blind. Science without religion is lame.'*

7   *Charles Darwin became an honorary member of a missionary society some thirteen years after publishing* On the Origin of Species.

8   *Science is a 'self-limiting' activity, which deliberately excludes deep questions about God and whether life has meaning.*

9   *Modern scientific advances raise immense ethical dilemmas about life and death issues.*

10 *Some Christians are 'creationists'. But many are not, because they believe in God and in evolution.*

Part three

The Christian Church

11

Saints, martyrs, sins and virtues

In this chapter you will learn:
- *about martyrs – ancient and modern*
- *the significance of Mary and other saints*
- *about deadly sins and glorious virtues*.

Before his terrible death by crucifixion, Jesus warned his followers that some of them would die in his service. His grim prophecy has been grimly fulfilled. Throughout the centuries millions of men, women and children have given their lives because of their allegiance to Jesus Christ. This is not confined to the past (see box below). And, of course, adherents of other faiths have shared in this carnage, and suffered for their beliefs too.

70 million martyrs

Dr David Barrett has undertaken detailed research into the extent of martyrdom in Christian history up to the present day. He calculates that 70 million Christians have been killed for their faith in 220 countries across 20 centuries. He added, 'the effect of Christian martyrdom on evangelization over the centuries has been profound'. The nineteenth and twentieth centuries saw more mass martyrdoms of 100,000 or more than all previous centuries put together. 'Martyrs are not just a handful of special saints and heroes, they are 500 ordinary Christians being murdered every day for their witness.'

The first Christian martyr

The Greek word for 'martyr' simply means 'witness'; it soon came
to be associated with 'witness unto death'. The first Christian
martyr was Stephen, a deacon of the church in Jerusalem. A Jew
who was well versed in the Scriptures, Stephen reflected on the
significance of Jesus. He came to realize that by fulfilling the old
prophecies, Jesus had made redundant some of the key institutions
of the Jewish nation. Stephen's outspoken views were seen as an
attack upon *the law* and *the temple* and he was stoned to death.

As Stephen died he saw Jesus, 'the Son of Man', standing to receive
him into heaven (Acts 7:56). Like his Master, Stephen prayed that
God would forgive his executioners. Shortly after this, James,
the brother of the apostle John and an important leader in the
Jerusalem church, was beheaded by King Herod. The blood had
started to flow. It was that blood which became, as Tertullian
(*c*. 160–220) put it, 'the seed of the Church'.

Insight

The Greek word for *martyr* means 'witness'. From the time of
Stephen (the first Christian martyr) this became understood
as 'witness unto death'. Stephen was soon followed by others,
including St Peter and St Paul, who died under the Emperor
Nero.

ENTER NERO

The Roman Emperor Nero (AD 37–68) accused Christians of
putting Rome to the torch in AD 64. Many wild rumours circulated
about this new sect. For example, the Christians were accused
of cannibalism, because they ate the body of Christ! They were
sometimes called atheists, because they did not believe in the
Roman gods (page 260). And while they honoured the Emperor
(Romans 13), Jesus – not the Emperor – was their Lord. All this
was very convenient for a leader looking for a scapegoat. Paul and
Peter were almost certainly martyred under Nero. Many other
believers died too, some as human torches.

After that, many Roman Emperors persecuted Christians, who – with captives, slaves and other despised minorities – provided sport for the masses in arenas in various cities throughout the Roman empire. There are several passages in the New Testament which illustrate how the early church leaders encouraged Christians to cope with persecution. They were exhorted to live humble, simple lives – for love and integrity were their only weapons. In the long term such weapons proved to be extremely powerful and a growing number came to embrace Christianity, including the Roman Emperor Constantine (d. 337).

A problem arose concerning the desire for martyrdom. Some members of the Church coveted 'the martyr's crown' and felt that an early death was a small price to pay. This attitude was always opposed by the Church at large. Martyrdom might be 'given'; it was not to be sought.

> *Dear friends, do not be surprised at the painful trial you are suffering, as though something strange were happening to you. But rejoice that you participate in the sufferings of Christ, so that you may be overjoyed when his glory is revealed.* (1 Peter 4:12, 13)

In AD 156 (possibly 155), old Bishop Polycarp of Smyrna was placed in a Roman arena. He was challenged to deny Jesus Christ and embrace the pagan gods. He declared, 'For 86 years I have been his servant and he has never done me any wrong. How then can I blaspheme my King who saved me?' He was burnt to death.

Relics and shrines

The public veneration of Christian martyrs has been practised since the second century; Bishop Polycarp is the first clear example of such veneration. The practice developed in local communities, usually around the martyr's tomb. It was based on:

▶ *the long-standing Jewish practice of venerating the memory of patriarchs, prophets and martyrs by building monuments over the places where their bones lay*
▶ *the belief that Christian martyrs were in heaven, and therefore able to pray for those who invoked their help.*

The veneration of saints soon involved 'holy relics'. Tombs contained bones; and bones were visible – and portable. The bones of Polycarp were considered 'more precious than jewels of great price'. The cult of any individual saint could be moved from one place to another. This 'opened European routes to sacred travel, sacred commerce, and eventually, sacred theft' (Robert Markus). And, we might add, sacred fraud.

The relics of a saint were regarded as a source of healing and an agent which gave protection to the church which possessed them. Bones, commerce, superstition and local prestige made a powerful, and sometimes corrupting, combination. Reverence for saints and martyrs was often positive. No doubt many believers were encouraged in their discipleship of Christ, by pondering the deeds of those who had gone before. But concern about malpractice emerged early on. In the fourth century, Augustine of Hippo stressed the immense difference between devotion directed to martyrs and worship offered to God. He wrote, 'We build temples to our martyrs, not like temples for the gods, but as tombs of mortal men, whose spirits live with God.'

Items other than bones were – and are – venerated. Perhaps the most famous (certainly the most intriguing) in today's world, is the Turin Shroud. Shrines continue to attract thousands e.g. Walsingham – even millions, e.g. Lourdes and the Padre Pio Pilgrimage Church (see page 356).

The early saints

It was natural that stories of heroic deeds, courageous deaths and godly lives should be treasured and passed on. Indeed, this process had already begun in the New Testament (Hebrews 11, 12). From this grew a desire to honour such men and women with official recognition – rather as we award medals today. In this wish we find the seeds of *canonization*, by which certain individuals are honoured with the official title 'Saint'.

The choice of that particular word was confusing, for it already had a different, though related, meaning. Several of the New Testament letters are addressed to 'the saints', a term which means 'dedicated to God for holy living'. It is a common New Testament term for *all* believers, much as we use the word 'Christian' today. To pick out a few particularly distinguished believers as 'saints' led to ambiguity.

The popular gospel song, 'O when the saints go marching in', gives the word its biblical meaning. 'I wanna be in that number' runs the lyric. This is not a desire to be a special 'super Christian'; rather it expresses a devout wish to be included in the festival of heaven with *all* of God's people. As one writer put it: 'the Church canonizes a few believers; the Bible canonizes all.'

The New Testament understanding is caught in the Christian festival entitled *All Saints' Day* (1 November). In the modern Church this is often taken as a celebration of all Christian lives – well-known and unknown, ancient and modern. This great festival enshrines another important emphasis – the *Communion of Saints*. This belief unites *all* believers – past, present and future – in the family of God.

Insight

The word 'saints' is commonly used in the New Testament to describe ordinary church members, all of whom are called to holiness of life. Over time, the word 'saint' was attached to outstandingly heroic or holy followers of Jesus Christ.

PRAYING THROUGH THE SAINTS

The Christian centuries have seen many faithful lives and heroic deaths; it is challenging and inspiring for modern Christians to reflect upon these. For this reason, the Christian calendar commemorates individual saints on particular days. The first disciples of Jesus are given special honour, but many others are included too.

Some ancient saints have a dubious background. St Olave was not a godly woman but a fierce Norse king! St George, patron saint of England (also of Istanbul and the Italian cavalry!), fares slightly better. George, probably a soldier, certainly died as a martyr around 303. But little else is known of him and the story of the dragon is a late arrival on the scene. Alas, St Valentine's route to fame is also shrouded in uncertainty.

One controversial question is whether Christians should pray through – and even *to* – the saints. Some Christians do, feeling their near presence.

They point out that it is natural to ask living Christians to pray for us; so why not ask saints of old, who lived holy lives, who died in the faith of Christ, and who are in heaven? Others believe that there is a danger in praying through, or to, the saints, who were sinners like us. In their view this obscures the uniqueness of Jesus, who prays for us (Romans 8:34; Hebrews 7:25) and through whom – and to whom – we pray.

Thomas Becket, Archbishop of Canterbury from 1162–1170, opposed King Henry II. He was exiled to France but returned to Canterbury in 1170. Thomas was murdered in Canterbury Cathedral by knights from the Royal Court, although the King protested his innocence. The episode caused a sensation throughout Europe. Churches from Iceland to Sicily were dedicated to *Saint Thomas*. (He was canonized in 1173.) Within ten years, 703 miracles had been reported at his tomb.

Mary, the Mother of Jesus

A special place is accorded to Mary, the Mother of Jesus, by all Christians but especially by Roman Catholics. Great devotion has been offered to her, countless statues made in her honour and thousands of paintings perpetuate her memory. The *Annunciation*, the occasion when the angel Gabriel announced to Mary that she would bear a son (Luke 1:26–38), is a scene depicted on countless canvases, some of them very famous.

At some periods in history (and in some places today) her prayers have been thought to be so effective that she has been called the 'lawyer of sinners'. Other titles given to Mary over the centuries are Mother of God ('Theotokos'), Queen of Heaven, Mother of Humanity, Mother of Angels, even Co-redeemer with Christ. It should be added that popular titles and devotion sometimes go further than official teaching, requiring this correction: *'This very special devotion (to Mary) ... differs essentially from the adoration which is given to the incarnate Word and equally to the Father and the Holy Spirit"* (Catechism of the Catholic Church).

Other beliefs that have developed over the centuries are the Immaculate Conception of Mary (not to be confused with the virginal conception of Jesus – more commonly known as the Virgin Birth), her perpetual virginity and her Assumption (body and soul) into Heaven. The last named was not officially promulgated until 1950, by Pope Pius XII. A Bull (official statement) from the Vatican in 1854 defined 'Immaculate Conception' as the belief that 'From the first moment of her conception the Blessed Virgin Mary was... kept free from all stain of original sin'.

These are official doctrines within the Roman Catholic Church, but many Protestants object on three grounds. First, they argue that there is no historical evidence for these views. Second, they contend that these beliefs do a disservice to Mary, who is special enough without these false elaborations (as they regard them). Third, Protestants are concerned that these doctrines draw attention away from Jesus who is the only and unique Saviour. All Christians agree that what is truly inspiring about Mary is:

▶ *her humility and reticence to believe that she could be honoured by the visit of an angel and the birth of such a special child*
▶ *her obedience and willingness to serve God (Luke 1:38)*
▶ *her grasp of God's priorities – his 'bias to the poor'. In the Magnificat (Luke 1:46) Mary declares, '... he has scattered those who are proud ... but has lifted up the humble'*
▶ *her loyalty to Jesus, seen not only at the wedding in Cana (John 2:5) but by her presence at his death. We learn that to be chosen by God carries sorrow and pain, as well as joy and privilege.*

The *Oxford Dictionary of Saints* gives a balanced assessment:

> *In both East and West Mary is accounted pre-eminent among all the saints. The unique privilege of being the mother of one who was, according to Christian belief, both God and Man is at the heart of the special honour paid to Mary, described by Aquinas as 'hyperdulia', i.e. a veneration which exceeds that paid to other saints, but is at the same time infinitely below the adoration (latria) due to God alone, which it would be blasphemous to attribute to any creature.*

Reformation martyrs

The sixteenth century saw an enormous upheaval in Europe (Chapter 17). Medieval unity, already cracking, was split apart and the Church was divided. Controversy was often bitter and it produced martyrs on both sides. Among Protestants who died were Thomas Cranmer and William Tyndale, both of whom helped to shape the English language.

Thomas Cranmer (1489–1556) was a quiet, scholarly man and a liturgical genius who wrote The Book of Common Prayer (slightly amended in its final version in 1662). He was elevated to Archbishop by Henry VIII and lived during three turbulent reigns. He piloted the Reformation throughout the reign of the young Edward VI but was denounced as a heretic under the Catholic Queen Mary. Cranmer hesitated but eventually signed a recantation – an action which did not save him. As he was burning at the stake, he thrust the hand that had signed the recantation into the flames.

William Tyndale (1494–1536) was appalled at the ignorance of many clergy and set himself the task of making the Bible available to ordinary people. The English Bible had been banned since 1408 but Tyndale translated Hebrew (Old Testament) and Greek (New Testament) texts into English. Though banned, his translation had enormous influence upon the King James or 'Authorized' Version

(1611), which became *the* standard English Bible for more than 300 years (page 97).

He completed the New Testament and substantial sections of the Old Testament before he was betrayed and arrested near Brussels in 1535. English Church leaders feared his Protestant ideas and a year later he was strangled and burnt at the stake. Tyndale died with a prayer on his lips: 'Lord, open the King of England's eyes.' His prayer was answered. In 1538, Henry VIII – for reasons rather different from Tyndale's – ordered that an English Bible should be placed in every parish church.

Many devout Catholics were equally courageous during those turbulent years. These included Edmund Campion and Margaret Clitherow.

Edmund Campion (1540–81) was a Catholic priest (a Jesuit: Chapter 17) who worked hard in Protestant Britain to sustain the faith of his fellow Catholics. He was betrayed, tortured and condemned to death. When sentence was declared he sang the *Te Deum* ('We praise thee, O God …'). Edmund was visited in his cell by the man who betrayed him. His own life was in danger and he needed Father Edmund's help. Campion wrote a letter of introduction to a nobleman in Germany. His betrayer escaped; Edmund Campion was dragged through the streets to Tyburn where he was hanged and quartered.

Margaret Clitherow (1556–86), a butcher's wife, was described by her contemporaries as good-looking, witty, merry and caring. She was a devout Catholic who lived in the ancient city of York. Accused of harbouring priests, she was brought to trial. Margaret refused to defend herself in court because in this way she could save her children from being forced to testify against her. She was crushed to death under immense weights. Her hand – a holy relic – is held in the Bar Convent just outside the city walls of York. Edmund Campion and Margaret Clitherow were canonized by the Roman Catholic Church in 1960.

Modern saints

The practice of *canonization* – the declaration by the Pope that the Church shall recognize an individual as an official saint – continues within the Roman Catholic Church. A rather less formal procedure for declaring 'saints' operates within the Eastern Orthodox Churches. In modern times strict criteria are applied by the Vatican – no Norse warrior-king need apply!

One of the most recent saints to be canonized was the Polish Roman Catholic Franciscan priest, Maximilian Kolbe. Maximilian was arrested by the Nazis during the Second World War. In the infamous concentration camp of Auschwitz, his dignity and faith sustained many of his fellow sufferers. After an attempted escape, several prisoners were condemned to death by starvation. One victim, a sergeant called Francis Gajowniczek, was very distressed. He had a wife and children, so Maximilian volunteered to change places.

The guards agreed to this grisly act of barter. The married man was spared; the rest were locked away in Cell 18 without food. Two weeks later all were dead except four men. Only Maximilian was fully conscious, and on 14 August 1941 he was given phenol poison. He was 47. On 14 August 1982 Maximilian was declared an official saint by the Polish Pope John Paul II. This was a moving occasion attended by Francis Gajowniczek, the man whom Father Kolbe had saved.

Canonization is preceded by *Beatification,* the means by which a person receives the title 'Blessed'. The Pope permits the person to be venerated, though not all who are honoured in this way go on to be canonized. **Mother Teresa of Calcutta** and **Pope Paul II** have both been beatified (in 2003 and 2005 respectively) in response to public acclaim. Letters in which she expressed her doubts, published in 2007, raised questions about the suitability of Mother Teresa. To her defenders these letters prove the genuineness of her faith, which was tested so rigorously. They argue that she continued to follow Christ in a way which inspired millions, despite being plunged into 'the dark night of the soul' – experienced by many true saints throughout the centuries.

HEROES BUT NOT ALWAYS 'SAINTS'

Maximilian Kolbe's story reminds us of the tens of thousands of men and women who, in the twentieth and twenty-first centuries, have given – and are giving – their lives for their faith. Comment has been made elsewhere on the Church in the USSR, in Nazi Germany (page 26) and in China (pages 218–9). Relatively few of the martyrs under those regimes, or the rest of the 70 million (page 193), have been formally canonized.

One notable death from another continent was that of the Roman Catholic Archbishop Oscar Romero of El Salvador. He sided with the poor and denounced the abuses of a state which was locked in a struggle against Marxist guerrillas. As he celebrated Mass in March 1980, he was shot through the heart. A few years before this, in Uganda, the Anglican Archbishop Janani Luwum had been assassinated for speaking out against the atrocities perpetrated by Idi Amin in the 1960s. The west front of Westminster Abbey carries a memorial, in stone carvings, to 40 modern martyrs.

Uganda has a distinguished place in the history of martyrdom. In 1885 a tribal leader named Mwanga waged war against Christianity. One day, 19 men (all under 25 years old) were asked if they wished to remain Christians. Following their reply, 'Until death', they were wrapped in reed mats and burnt alive. Their courage and remarkable serenity remind us of many early martyrs, including Stephen. More Ugandan deaths were to follow – both Roman Catholic and Protestant. In the twentieth century, Stephen Neill, a well-travelled Anglican scholar-bishop, found their memorial site outside Kampala to be the most moving place on earth. The bishop of the diocese of Uganda commented to him, 'I think the Baganda [the local people] would be ready to die for Christ today; it is living for him that they find difficult'. The Ugandan martyrs were formally canonized in 1964.

Whatever their views on the formal canonization of saints, in all churches the memory of martyrs and other distinguished believers is kept alive, as a challenge and inspiration. Indeed, some Christians are 'canonized' unofficially by the world at large; for example Dr Martin Luther King (a Baptist pastor) and Mother Teresa (an Albanian nun who was beatified in 2003 – page 202). Some churches occasionally authorize new liturgical calendars, with additional names to be remembered on particular days.

The writer of the New Testament letter to the Hebrews gives a long list of heroes of the faith (Hebrews 11). He has a particular purpose in mind. '*Since we are surrounded by such a great cloud of witnesses*', he writes, '*... let us run with perseverance the race marked out for us. Let us fix our eyes on Jesus, the author and perfecter of our faith*' (Hebrews 12:1–2). Look at them, he says, then look at Jesus. Draw inspiration from their example, and keep on keeping on in your discipleship.

Insight

The practice of 'canonization' continues within the Roman Catholic Church. After research into the prospective saint's life and a period of 'beatification', the Pope declares that the individual shall be recognized as an official Saint. The twentieth-century Pope John Paul II created more Saints than any other Pope in history.

Sins and virtues

'Holiness' is what makes a saint. So when we use the word 'saint' in its biblical sense we see that holiness should characterize *every* Christian. Holiness means 'set apart for God'. It involves avoidance of sin, victory over temptation and the cultivation of Christian virtues.

SEVEN DEADLY SINS?

The centuries have seen the development of the popular notion of *seven deadly sins*: pride, covetousness, lust, envy, gluttony, anger and sloth. The Bible does not limit the number of sins to seven, but it certainly speaks of sin's 'deadliness'. '*For the wages of sin is death, but the gift of God is eternal life*' (Romans 6:23). Sin is serious. At root it is hostility or indifference towards God, his truth and his standards, which results in alienation. It is so serious that, according to Jesus, we can be enslaved by sin: locked into it and unable to break free from it (John 8:34). But by the death of Christ we may be forgiven and set free. And by the Spirit of Christ we may be sanctified – given strength to struggle and overcome.

The Cathedral of Notre Dame in Paris displayed the following pithy sentence: '*Sin is a refusal to grow bigger.*' This captures another important truth. We sin when we lower our horizons and our moral and spiritual ambitions. We sin when we ration our love and act out of self-interest. We sin when we settle for second best and become small-minded. From such an approach to life come those many manifestations of sin – irritability, greed, laziness, selfishness – which damage our relationship with those with whom we live and work. Ultimately, these things seriously diminish us as human beings.

Salvation involves being set free to be fully human. Jesus Christ bids us take the risk of following him. He points us to a world in need; and he calls us to love and serve it in his name and with his strength. '*The glory of God is a human being fully alive*' (Irenaeus: *c.* 130–200).

Sin and guilt

The New Testament call to repentance is linked to a sense of guilt – and feeling guilty is often thought to be unhealthy. On the other hand, the modern concept of restorative justice is built on the notion that acknowledging guilt is the first step to rebuilding good relationships and a new life. Vague, unfocused feelings of guilt are indeed unhealthy and unhelpful, but guilt is an important emotion with a practical purpose. People who live entirely without it are called 'psychopaths'.

(Contd)

Christianity is not really interested in sin; it is far more interested in salvation and liberation. This is expressed cogently by Dr Giles Fraser: 'St Paul runs sin and death together. We are saved from sin/death, because sin is a form of death. Real sin – rather than the watered-down, overly-sexualized version we too often employ as a substitute – is cold, and hollow, and meaningless. Hence it is death. Furthermore, real sin is not a terribly religious thing. One does not have to be a believer to feel threatened by the deathly chill of human self-absorption.'

THREE GLORIOUS VIRTUES

All this can be put positively. Christian discipleship involves opening ourselves to God's Spirit, that we might grow in *faith*, *hope* and *love*. These virtues, above all, are the marks of holiness – of sanctity or 'sainthood'.

Faith

In one sense, faith is universal because all human beings base their lives on assumptions which cannot be proved with mathematical certainty. *Every* human being lives by probability, so no one can opt out of believing. This applies to the 'big' questions: questions about God and whether life has purpose and ultimate meaning. Christians *believe* that God exists. Atheists *believe* that God does not exist. Agnostics *believe* that we do not have enough evidence to decide either way. The indifferent person *believes* that it does not matter anyway ('Theism and atheism are equally leaps of faith' – Professor Jonathan Clark). Total certainty – mathematical proof – is out of the question, though most people can give some reasons for their beliefs.

Faith is important in other areas of life too. It applies to our convictions and commitments, e.g. 'I believe in abortion on demand' or 'I believe the rights of the unborn child are supreme'. And it applies to our relationships: 'I trust him' is the highest form of praise.

Christians are called 'believers', not because they alone live by faith, but because they live by *faith in Jesus Christ*. Faith is not a substitute for reason but it can be firmly based on reason.

Christians argue that they have good reasons for believing in Jesus (Chapters 1 and 3). Arising from those reasons and that belief come active faith, commitment and obedient action.

Of course, some Christians have doubts. Many would argue that these can have a positive outcome: Dr George Carey (Archbishop of Canterbury 1991–2002) testified that 'doubt has stirred me to deeper faith'. A helpful parallel can be drawn from personal relationships. If we doubt a friend's loyalty, we put our reasons for doubting our friend alongside our experience of his or her faithfulness. Christians do the same in their relationship with God. They consider afresh God's love and faithfulness; they reflect again upon the significance of Jesus. Then they put their doubts within this framework.

> Relating the story of his conversion, US President Barack Obama said: 'The questions I had didn't magically disappear. The sceptical bent of my mind didn't suddenly vanish. But kneeling beneath that cross on the South Side [of Chicago], I felt I heard God's Spirit beckoning me.'

Faith has a passive element: 'Let go and let God.' This is caught in a famous prayer of Reinhold Niebuhr: '*God grant me the serenity to accept the things I cannot change, the courage to change the things that I can, and the wisdom to know the difference.*' But as that prayer shows, faith has an active side too: it involves obedient action. Dr John Vincent captures this: '*Our word "believe" does not get the force of the Greek word. It really means give yourself over to, risk your life on.*'

Hope

Christian hope is captured by Mother Julian's great affirmation, '… all shall be well and all shall be well and all manner of thing shall be well'. We shall not consider this at length here, for 'the hope of heaven' is spelt out in Chapter 9. At this point we simply note two points:

- ▶ Christian hope means facing the future with confidence. *In ordinary speech, the word 'hope' can be a weak concept. 'I hope I will win a fortune on the national lottery' is a sentence running through many minds, although they are* fairly sure that they will not. *Christian hope has a much more confident quality. It enables believers to face the unknown future in quiet confidence that 'all things work together for good for those who love God' (Romans 8:28). The Christian hope of life in heaven is rooted in history, and focused on Jesus Christ. It is as strong as the evidence for Jesus and his resurrection: readers must evaluate this for themselves (Chapters 1 and 3).*

▶ Christian hope is joyful. *Christians are not often optimistic about this world, where realism sometimes makes us feel gloomy and sad – even desperate. There are good reasons for tears (James 4:9) as we ponder the state of our world, the spiritual poverty of our lives, and the cost of our redemption. But, overall, the New Testament is a joyful book. Saints are often thought of as other-worldly, solemn figures, associated with pain and death. But people who live close to God are often joyful and serene, with wide concerns. God's saints can be good fun. (Note: In his research, the social psychologist Michael Argyle found that church-goers tend to be more than usually happy. Medical researchers in South Carolina found that going to church appears to be good for the health of our hearts. Not the best of reasons for attending perhaps, but interesting none the less!)*

Love

Ancient Greek had several different words which we translate by 'love': *philia* (deep friendship), *storge* (family affection), *eros* (erotic love – celebrated in the *Song of Songs*: page 66). But the most frequent word for love in the Greek New Testament is *agape*. This refers to self-giving, sacrificial, practical love. Jesus himself showed deep compassion to those in need and especially to people who experienced rejection. He demonstrated that love must sometimes be heroic: he died on the cross. He showed that love must often be small-scale and domestic: he washed the disciples' feet. The New Testament insists that love is practical and creative, and that it includes forgiveness.

> **Love is patient, love is kind. It does not envy, it does not boast, it is not proud. It is not rude, it is not self-seeking, it is not easily angered, it keeps no record of wrongs. Love does not delight in evil but rejoices with the truth. It always protects, always trusts, always hopes, always perseveres.** (1 Corinthians 13:4–7)

> *Therefore, as God's chosen people, holy and dearly loved, clothe yourselves with compassion, kindness, humility, gentleness and patience. Bear with each other and forgive whatever grievances you may have against one another. Forgive as the Lord forgave you. And over all these virtues put on love, which binds them all together in perfect unity.*
> (Colossians 3:12–14)

Christian love (*agape*) is Christianity's greatest gift to the world. Tony Bridge, when Dean of Guildford Cathedral, posed the question, 'Why value love at all?' He went on to say that after 2000 years of Christianity, this question sounds idiotic. It is taken for granted that love is a wonderful quality, even if we do not often live up to its high demands. But he then made an important contrast. '*Other civilizations have assumed no such thing. Courage, stoic endurance, the search for wisdom, intellectual integrity, strength, detachment – these are the virtues normally worshipped by mankind and preached by his many religions. And love is a contradiction of many of them.*'

Ultimately, and rightly, outsiders judge Christianity by its fruit. Does it 'deliver the goods'? How many bitter people have been softened by its influence? How many nervous people have been given courage? How many selfish people have been so touched by the love of Christ, that they too have been inspired to loving service? How evident in the life of Christian believers are 'the fruit of the Spirit – love, joy, peace, patience, kindness, goodness, faithfulness, gentleness and self-control' (Galatians 5:22). This is the key test which faces Christians in every generation.

Insight

The three greatest Christian virtues are celebrated in a famous passage by St Paul (1 Corinthians 13). They are faith, hope and love. Following Jesus' teaching, the apostle insists that 'the greatest of these is love'.

There have been many failures in the Church. But the chapters in this book on history and society reveal some triumphs too. Thousands of unloved children have been rescued from death by exposure, tens of thousands of desperate people have been given a listening ear, millions have been helped to die with peace and hope.

Perhaps the clearest testimony comes from those who do not belong to the Church. In Chapter 14 we shall consider the witness of the Roman Emperor Julian. He complained that his attempts to reintroduce pagan gods failed because of the love of the Christians who 'care not only for their own poor but for ours as well' (page 260).

A somewhat similar testimony comes from modern Russia. Staff from a hospital were invited to a service of worship in a Baptist church. The chief physician, Valentin Kozyrev, an atheist, was invited to speak. He said that the formula for curing sick people is 'chemistry with love'. He went on, 'We can provide the first part, but are incapable of fulfilling the second. Only you can provide that and we have very much appreciated your contribution' (from *Gorbachev, Glasnost and the Gospel* by Michael Bourdeaux).

Ruben Gallego bears witness to this same truth. Born without the use of hands and feet, he spent years in a state orphanage in Russia. The quality of care was poor but there were exceptions, as he recalls in his award-winning memoir *White on Black*: 'The good ones [the carers] believed in God – all of them.'

Love is the supreme test and the supreme mark of the saint, whether formally canonized or living in obscurity in your street. It is the most important quality of all. The apostle Paul ends his great hymn about love with this summary: '*And now these three remain: faith, hope and love. But the greatest of these is love*' (1 Corinthians 13:13).

'If the world is to be saved, it will be saved by the spirit. Politicians, or bankers, or soldiers, or businessmen, or even authors and artists are not the essential people. We need saints. The most relevant figures are not those who understand the world but those who can bring to the world something from outside itself, who can act as the transmitters of grace... God does not force humanity to survive, but at least we are sent enough saints in each generation to show us the possibility. A world guided by saints and the spirit would not only be a better world but also far, far safer into a much longer future.' (Lord Rees-Mogg, in *The Independent*)

10 THINGS TO REMEMBER

1   *The word* martyr *comes from the Greek word meaning 'witness'.*

2   *This shows that openly following Jesus Christ can be dangerous.*

3   *The first Christian martyr was Stephen; Peter and Paul also died for their faith in Christ.*

4   *In the New Testament, the word 'saints' refers to all believers – as in the song,* O when the Saints go marching in …

5   *Over time the word 'saint' took on a narrower meaning; it was applied to Christians who lived especially heroic or holy lives.*

6   *'Canonization' is the process by which the Catholic Church declares someone to be an official Saint.*

7   *This practice continues today in the Roman Catholic and Orthodox Churches.*

8   *Mary, the Mother of Jesus, has a special place of honour in the Church.*

9   *Christianity is not really interested in sin. It is much more interested in liberation from sin's power and effects.*

10 *The three greatest Christian virtues are faith, hope and love (1 Corinthians 13).*

12

One Church, many churches

In this chapter you will learn:
- **statistics for the largest movement in history**
- **about the world's many Churches**
- **about a shifting centre of gravity.**

> ### Insight
> The Church of Jesus Christ is the largest movement in all
> history. Modern-day disciples of Jesus are to be found
> on every continent, and about one third of the world's
> population would call themselves Christian.

The Christian Church is like a great mountain. If we stand looking at
it, and even if we are on it, we cannot see all sides at the same time.
The view from another vantage point may be very different from
ours. The aim of this chapter is to walk round and up the mountain
to gain a fuller impression of the whole; an institution, a community
of peoples and a vital factor in any view of world history.

If it is One Church, one mountain, why are there so many
different churches? All Christians, whatever their race or status,
are united 'in Christ' – in his love, grace and forgiveness. So there
can only be One Church, one body of Christians, spread through
all generations and throughout the world (for which the Greek
word is 'Katholikos'). Hence the phrase in the Nicene Creed – an
important ancient summary of belief – 'We believe in one holy,
catholic and apostolic Church.'

But this Church consists, and always has consisted, of people with different histories and cultures, living in different places. When local believers gather together they are the church there; not the same body as a group meeting in another place halfway across the world. So the language about 'One Church but many churches' makes sense. It already occurs in the New Testament – for example, the churches of Asia, the churches of Galatia, the churches of the Gentiles.

The differences are not only of place. Differences in modes of worship, beliefs and ethical requirements are found between different denominations. Such differences were apparent even in the first few decades covered by the New Testament writings: differences between the Jewish Christians and Gentile Christians (Acts 6:1) and between the apostles Peter and Paul (Galatians 2:11).

As the centuries wore on, Christianity spread through all the nations of the known world and its detailed beliefs and practices were hammered out. Different opinions and claims about authenticity and authority caused some groups of Christians to separate from others. At times they even fought and persecuted each other. One encouraging feature of the twentieth century was that Christians with a different history and tradition recognized each other again. They came together in discussion, in mutual agreement and, in some cases, in visible reunion (Chapter 13).

But great Christian 'blocs' remain and in this chapter we shall outline the main distinctive features of:

▶ *the Roman Catholic Church with 1,143 million members (including some 6 million Catholic Christians who do not owe allegiance to Rome)*
▶ *Protestant Churches with 277 million members*
▶ *the various Orthodox Churches with 220 million members*
▶ *Independent Churches with 438 million members*
▶ *Anglican Churches with 83 million members*

Across these various denominational groups are spread the many Christians who belong to different Pentecostal or Charismatic churches or groups. In addition there are about 35 million members of groups that claim to be Christian but which are outside mainstream Christianity (such as Jehovah's Witnesses, Mormons, Christian Scientists, Unitarians, Spiritualists and British Israelites), called 'Marginals' on the pie chart (see below).

All the above together make up some 2,200 million church members, or 33 per cent of the world's total population. Muslims make up about 21 per cent, Hindus 13 per cent, Buddhists 6 per cent and Jews 0.2 per cent.

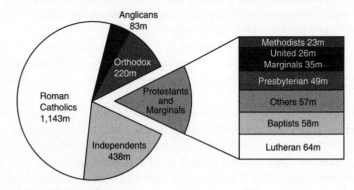

Figure 12.1 Churches of the world 2007.

Church statistics

More statistical accounting of a precise nature takes place each year among the Christian world of denominations and agencies than for any other global movement. However, it is important to note the exact definitions of all categories thus enumerated. Almost every church has more members than regular worshippers and a few have more attenders than members!

▶ Many *who do not* formally *belong profess publicly to believe in Jesus Christ, and many of these regard themselves as 'belonging' to the Church in a loose sense. Britain illustrates this. Regular church attendance (about 7 per cent) is lower than in many other countries, but the 2001 Population Census showed that 72 per cent said they were Christian. Sample* surveys reveal that about 60 per cent claim to believe in God and some 40 per cent say that they pray regularly. Many of these people regard themselves as 'belonging' to a church or denomination, even though they seldom attend.

▶ Statisticians *attempt to distinguish 'cultural Christians' from 'committed Christians'. The former are defined in the preceding paragraph; the latter are defined by varying degrees of attendance, profession of faith, giving of money and so on. The scene is by no means static. As the world population increases rapidly, so does the number of church members.*

▶ The Church worldwide *is currently growing by some 70,000 members every day, calculated as follows: 133,000 new Christians added daily (74,000 births into Christian families plus 59,000 converts from other religions or 'irreligion'). At the same time, each day 44,000 Christians die and 19,000 (mostly in the West) defect to other religions or 'irreligion'.*

▶ The number of churches *is increasing all the time. Recent research has revealed more than 275 different denominations in Britain; there are far more than this in the USA (some 5100). Out of the world total of around 39,000 distinct denominations (many of them relatively small), the World Council of Churches (WCC) now has 347 member denominations from 110 countries. This figure of 347 includes most mainline 'historic' Churches (but not Roman Catholic –* page 219)*, so the WCC does ensure that a sizeable proportion of the world's churches keep in touch.*

Most statistical information in this chapter was provided by Dr David Barrett and Dr Peter Brierley, leading Church statisticians, and relates to 2007. I am extremely grateful for all their help. A second edition of Dr Barrett's monumental *World Christian Encyclopaedia* was published in 2001 (OUP). I also strongly recommend the latest edition of *Religious Trends*, edited by Dr Peter Brierley (Christian Research: 2007). Dr Brierley kindly supplied the pie chart on page 214.

Author's note: *The following material attempts to give a 'feel' of the distinctive features of the various Churches around the world. But it is important to note the diversity that is also to be found within all these great traditions. For further information* *see* The Christian Church, *ed. Paul Avis (SPCK) and Diarmaid MacCulloch's magisterial* A History of Christianity *(Allen Lane).*

The Orthodox Churches

We start with those Churches which have preserved ancient structures and forms most tenaciously throughout the centuries. These are the Churches of Eastern Europe: the Greek, Balkan and Russian 'Orthodox Churches'. 'Orthodox' means right teaching. These Churches maintain they have kept the apostolic faith most faithfully, while alleging that Catholics and Protestants have diverged from it – by adding what is new or non-genuine, or subtracting what is original and authentic.

To go into an Eastern Orthodox church is like stepping back a thousand years or more; neither the furnishings nor the ritual seem to have changed at all. Often the building itself is centuries old and crumbling, with clouds of incense surrounding the worshippers. Religious paintings (icons) are placed around the church. They are surrounded by candles, with people bowing in reverence in front of them and kissing them. Behind an elaborate screen (the *iconostasis*) priests and deacons move about in glorious vestments, engaged in ancient ceremony.

And a small choir, often at the western end, raises you to heaven with the rise and fall of persistent chanting, in Greek or Old Church Slavonic, with the deepest of bass voices you have ever heard coming through to shiver your timbers in ecstasy. Often there are no pews; just seats around the edge for the infirm (as in medieval churches; hence the phrase 'the weakest to the wall').

Insight

The Orthodox Churches form a large body within the worldwide Church. Their main sphere of influence is found East of Rome e.g. the Russian Orthodox and Greek Orthodox Churches. Orthodox worship is traditional and colourful with incense, choral singing and icons.

To be a faithful Orthodox Christian you should attend the liturgy, pray to God, Jesus, Mary and the saints, and heed your parish priest. The parish priest is usually a married man of local origin. He is likely to remain in his village all his life; in this too he is much like his flock. In general, learning belongs not to the parish clergy but to the monasteries, where celibacy, poverty and total obedience to superiors are required. All bishops come from the monasteries, although there is a long tradition of lay theologians – highly educated lay people who are teachers and writers. A number of Orthodox congregations – often small, but usually growing – have established themselves in Britain and the USA.

Similar to the above churches are the ancient groups of Christians known as Oriental Orthodox, found in Egypt, Ethiopia, Syria, Iraq, Iran, South India and Armenia. These Churches felt obliged to leave the mainstream in the fourth and fifth centuries. They did so because they could not agree with various definitions of the faith hammered out by the majority at great Councils of the Church, such as Nicaea (325), Constantinople (381) and Chalcedon (451). The Eastern and Western Churches alike tended to regard these other groups as 'heretical', and for this reason they have lived in isolation from other Christians. The term 'heretical' originally meant separate, different, cut-off, but came to mean 'having wrong beliefs'. To be an Oriental Orthodox Christian is to be like the Eastern Orthodox in many ways, but to be even more tenacious in holding to inherited traditions. This tenacity comes from the fact that they feel challenged by other Christians, or by Muslims who form the majority in most of these countries.

The Russian Orthodox Church

It experienced great hostility with the Revolution in 1917 and 70 years of Communist (officially atheistic) rule – as did most churches throughout Eastern Europe. Religion was strictly controlled. Many active believers were persecuted and imprisoned; large numbers were martyred (David Barrett calculates a staggering 16 million).

(Contd)

The Orthodox churches survived by making an uneasy truce with the ruling powers. If they were willing to keep out of politics, to concentrate on the devotional life and curtail evangelism, they were allowed to function. Of course, this policy was controversial and some members (such as Alexander Solzhenitsyn, the Nobel Prize winning author: page 108) encouraged the church leadership to be more courageous.

With the demise of the totalitarian state, doors are now open to travellers, and the Orthodox Church faces what it sees as a new threat – missionaries from some Protestant and Pentecostal churches, as well as from some Western sects and cults, are gaining a following, especially among younger people.

FURTHER EAST

The churches of India, China and Japan tend not to be Orthodox but more closely aligned with the Western churches. India and Japan have minority churches (about 7 per cent of the population in India; 4 per cent in Japan, of whom the majority are Catholics in communion with Rome).

These churches reflect the divisions of Western Christendom, since they were founded largely through missions from the West during the last few centuries. The Philippines (page 231) is the only Asian country which is predominantly Christian (Roman Catholic), though the situation throughout Asia is fluid and many churches are growing. South Korea has the largest single church in the world: the Yoido Full Gospel Church in Seoul with a membership of some 900,000.

China has a striking story to tell.

China, Korea and India

We are getting used to a stream of amazing statistics from China. But none is more striking than a report that 10,000 Chinese become Christians every day. In August 2007 a US magazine, the *National Catholic Reporter*, estimated that by 2150 the number of Christians in China will have doubled to 200 million – the largest concentration of Christians in any one country. This is largely the result of 'fearless grass roots evangelists'.

We have already noted impressive Bible publishing figures in China (page 95) but all is not sweetness and light. Pastor Zhang Minguxan, president of the Chinese House Church Alliance, was asked to close down his church, school and orphanage. In 2007 he wrote an open letter to President Hu Jintao, complaining about corrupt officials and the persecution of unregistered Christians.

While South Korea boasts the largest congregation in the world, reports from North Korea speak of tens of thousands of Christian believers enduring torture and starvation in labour camps.

India is the world's largest democracy. Mainly Hindu, it has a sizeable Muslim minority and is home to many other faiths. Christians make up about 7 per cent of the population. A national day of prayer for persecuted Christians in India was held in November 2007. The All India Catholic Union (AICU) published figures reporting an increase in attacks – some 190 in 2007. Dr John Dayal, president of the AICU, said that, in general, secular people are tolerant of Christians in India, but some political parties are not.

The Roman Catholic Church

When Christianity started, the known world was under the control of the Roman Empire. The two greatest Christian leaders, Peter and Paul, were executed in Rome under the Emperor Nero, probably in AD 64 and 65. There is a strong tradition that Peter asked to be crucified upside down, because he felt unworthy to die exactly like his Lord. A Church (believers, not a building) was founded early in Rome, through evangelism by 'ordinary' believers whose names are not recorded. Before long the bishop of Rome was asserting his position as supreme leader in the whole Church. Other patriarchs, such as those of the great Christian centres of Jerusalem, Alexandria, Antioch and Constantinople, disagreed. They could not accept that the teachings and practices of Rome should be definitive for the whole of Christendom, nor that Rome had authority over them.

This was one of the main causes of the Great Schism of 1054, when the Eastern and Western Churches finally divided, each declaring the other not to be the one true catholic and apostolic Church. As we have just seen, we call the Eastern Church 'Orthodox'. The Western Church took to itself the name 'Catholic' and remained broadly unified for five more centuries. But the Western Church was not always united even before the Reformation (Chapter 17), because there were substantial groups which remained separate from Rome. These included the early Celtic churches (responsible for evangelizing Ireland, Scotland, Wales and much of northern and south-west England, together with Flanders and north Germany). These churches remained distinct until the seventh century when they were absorbed by the greater power of Rome (Chapter 16).

The Bishop of Rome came to be called *Pope* (from Latin *Papa* or *Father*). The Church which remained faithful to his supremacy through all the changes of the Reformation period, is now known as the Roman Catholic Church. It has spread from Europe to most parts of the globe and is the largest of the Christian Churches. If the main characteristic of the Eastern Churches is *conservatism*, that of the Roman Catholic Church is *central authority*. The papal system keeps a strong hand over new ideas and threatened changes, but when it approves of them, it imposes them vigorously and quickly. Some modern Catholics, especially those in the USA and Europe, are prepared to question papal authority and even to ignore it (for example, in matters of contraception: Chapter 14).

Roman Catholics today live with the heritage of the **Second Vatican Council** (1962–5), which instituted considerable changes in the hitherto rigid structures and practices of that Church. Most obvious was the shift from Latin to national languages for the Mass. At the same time, Catholics were given strong encouragement to read the Scriptures.

This influential Council led to a greater openness within the Catholic Church. As a result, in 1968 the Pope and the Orthodox Patriarch of Constantinople mutually lifted the dual excommunications which had divided the Eastern Orthodox and Catholic Churches since 1054.

To be a Roman Catholic is to be conscious of belonging to a Church of immense size and global spread, which claims to be the nearest to the sort of Church that Christ wants. It is also to be part of a long tradition of colourful worship and deep spirituality. Worship styles vary despite the rigid outward structures.

The Roman Catholic Church has often been able to tolerate and live with local customs, religions and beliefs to such a degree that some other Christians accuse it of compromise – even of encouraging pagan practice and superstition. But Pope John Paul II spoke out against astrology and horoscopes as being incompatible with Christian faith. Even so, they remain popular throughout the Western world, including Italy.

The *monastic movement* has always played a significant role in Roman Catholicism. At their best, monasteries have been powerhouses of prayer, worship and evangelization, and centres for experimental change. Because the vast majority of parish priests are required to be celibate, the distinction between monks and parish priests is not so obvious as in the Eastern Churches.

Whether clergy should be celibate is keenly debated within the Roman Catholic Church. Some of its members believe that papal insistence on this is one cause of an alarming fall in vocations to the priesthood. At the same time many priests are not allowed to exercise their priesthood, because they have married after ordination. One estimate puts this figure as high as one-fifth of the total number of priests worldwide. (*Note: There are some married Roman Catholic priests but they are the exception e.g. some married Anglican priests, who left the Church of England because of the ordination of women priests, were later ordained as priests in the Roman Catholic Church.)*

The teaching of the Roman Catholic Church since the Reformation has been largely focused in three Councils: Trent (1545–63), the First Vatican Council (1869–70) and the Second Vatican Council (1962–5).

From time to time decrees ('Bulls' or 'Encyclicals') are issued by the Pope on specific matters – most famously in recent years on sexual morality. Decrees of the First Vatican Council were the cause of a breakaway church by those Roman Catholics who could not accept what they saw as the novelty of *papal infallibility*. Today they constitute small groups known as 'Old Catholics'. They are found mainly in Holland, Germany and Austria, and are in communion with Anglican churches.

Three recent Popes

When **Pope John XXIII** (1958–63) was elected by the College of Cardinals it was assumed that, at 76, he would be a 'caretaker Pope'. From an Italian peasant family, he was a warm and popular figure. Pope John XXIII convened the Second Vatican Council, which ran from 1962–5 and 'opened the windows' to allow the Holy Spirit to blow through the Church. Among the results were the replacement of the Latin Mass with vernacular services, warmer relationships with other Churches and strong encouragement to read the Scriptures.

Pope John Paul II (1978–2005) was the first non-Italian Pope for over 400 years. The first-ever Polish Pope, he had personal experience of the suffering Church, having lived under Nazi and Marxist regimes. A fine linguist and poet, Pope John Paul II was popular and charismatic. He travelled much more widely than his predecessors – kissing the soil when he landed in a new country. He encouraged good inter-faith relationships but was very conservative and would not yield on contraception, nor on celibacy for priests. Some Christians from other Churches believe this stance on contraception to be profoundly wrong and, in a world decimated by AIDS, extremely damaging (page 273). He was shot and seriously injured in 1981 but recovered from this assassination attempt. As a result of popular acclaim at his funeral in 2005, his papal successor agreed to 'fast-track' John Paul II towards beatification.

Pope Benedict XVI (Pope from 19 April 2005) is an academic theologian, who has called on the nations of Europe to turn back from secularization to Christian values. Less charismatic than his predecessor, he appears to be gentle and calm. In his preaching he emphasizes 'Friendship with Jesus Christ'. Like Pope John Paul II, he is conservative in outlook and theology. Critics claim that the cause of good inter-church relationships was damaged when, in June 2007, the Vatican referred to the Roman Catholic Church as the one true Church of Christ – while acknowledging that salvation can be found within other Churches. In April 2008 he was warmly received during an official visit to the USA where he apologised for child abuse by priests. In a church procession on Christmas Eve 2009 Pope Benedict was attacked and pulled to the ground, but not seriously injured. In 2010, in Malta, the Pope was deeply moved when he met seven men who had been sexually abused by priests while growing up in an orphanage. He expressed his shame and sorrow over their suffering.

Protestant Churches

In the sixteenth century there was turmoil in Europe. The Reformation – a movement for reform within the Medieval

Church – was the inspiration and ultimate cause of most Churches other than Orthodox or Catholic. The Reformation resulted partly from the rediscovery of the ancient languages of Hebrew and Greek, which meant that the Scriptures could be read in the original. For the previous 12 centuries, the Latin tradition had totally dominated the West. A second cause of the Reformation was the growing nationalism in various European countries; this led to a desire for freedom from the influence and power of Rome. A further cause was reaction to the abuses which developed in the Catholic Church, during the latter decades of the Middle Ages (Chapter 17).

The Reformation could have resulted in reforms in teaching and practice *within* the Catholic Church, had it not met total resistance from the central authority in Rome. All attempts at reconciliation failed and new church groupings emerged. Each of these protested at the claims and power of Rome, hence 'Protestant' Churches. (The term was first used at the Diet of Speyer in 1529.) These Churches emphasized different elements in the practices and beliefs of the Church before it was corrupted (as they saw it) by Rome. Because of this, and since they emerged in different countries at a time when nationalism was so strong, they fell into four main groups:

- *Lutheran*
- *Reformed (or Presbyterian)*
- *Baptist*
- *Anglican.*

In later centuries they were joined by two other 'breakaway' Churches: Methodist (eighteenth century) and Pentecostal (twentieth century). All these churches placed great emphasis on the Bible as the controlling authority for belief and practice. They wished to make the Scriptures readily available and easy to read. And they wanted to simplify worship, so that important elements would stand out and not be overwhelmed by trivial or misleading ceremonies, or by ornate music. They emphasized the importance of preaching alongside, or above, the administration of the sacraments. Many churches in the sixteenth century (including the Church of England) substituted the authority of the local monarch for that of the Pope in Rome.

Lutheran Churches

The Lutheran churches (now estimated at about 64 million members) were at first dominant in northern Germany and Scandinavia. They are now also found in Africa, America, Asia and many countries in Europe. Martin Luther (1483–1546) in northern Germany was the principal protagonist of the Reformation. Many of the features listed in the previous paragraph owe their force to his preaching and writing. The Lutheran tradition allows old customs to stay, as long as they are not deemed to be contrary to New Testament teaching. So, in many Lutheran churches, customs, vestments and furnishings are still maintained – as well as an episcopal ministry (bishops) – from the old days of the united Western Catholic Church.

The teachings of the Lutheran churches are historically summed up in the *Augsburg Confession* (1530). This is a moderate statement of the universal Christian faith with an emphasis on the grace of God, which is to be responded to by faith. It is *faith* which is seen as the 'justifying' or saving factor, not good works: these must follow as a thanksgiving for God's grace. Lutherans practise a faith which has strong roots in the home, with family prayers.

In church, Lutherans worship with quiet dignity: hymns, Bible reading, preaching and the sacraments are the most important elements. The clergy are well trained in theology and there is a comprehensiveness which allows quite varied practices to exist. In the twentieth century, monasticism was revived within the Lutheran Church, but the numbers remain small. Lutherans have made a distinguished contribution to the Ecumenical Movement, i.e. the moving together of Churches to talk, to cooperate, and even to unite (Chapter 13).

Presbyterian Churches

As Lutheran churches were banding together against Rome, John Calvin (1509–64) was teaching similar doctrines in Geneva.

But he was more radical in breaking with past customs in organization and liturgy. With great rigour, he regarded the Bible as the sole authority in all matters of faith and practice. This led him to reject the ministry of bishops and all forms of decoration in the churches, as well as most music and ceremony.

These Churches, founded by John Calvin and his followers (called Calvinist, Reformed or Presbyterian), have a membership of some 49 million and are the dominant form of Christianity in Scotland, Holland and Switzerland. They are well represented in most countries in Europe, America and Africa. Calvinism is usually an austere form of Christianity with dignified, simple worship and deep spirituality. Its members have made a strong contribution to Christian missions worldwide and to honesty, fairness and hard work in public life.

The ecumenical movement of recent decades has led to some churches in the above two major Protestant traditions coming together locally. This has resulted in United Lutheran and Reformed Churches in many parts of the world. So, to the 64 million Lutherans and the 49 million Reformed Christians, we must add about 26 million in these united Churches.

Baptist Churches

The above two Church groupings were not the only ones to emerge from the Reformation. Some felt that true Christian discipleship had been largely displaced by nominal Christianity. Virtually everyone was baptized in infancy and these new churches rebelled against this (Chapter 8). They came to be called Baptists because they insisted on the practice of plunging believers under the water (total immersion) not just pouring water over the forehead of infants. Baptists now number around 58 million and are particularly strong in the southern states of the USA.

William Carey is often credited with starting the modern Protestant missionary movement when he sailed from England to India in 1793.

He was a Baptist cobbler with little formal education. Carey had a brilliant mind and during his lifetime he translated the Bible (whole or part) into 25 languages and dialects. These emphases – love for the Bible and enthusiasm for evangelism – characterize modern Baptists. So does William Carey's challenging motto: '*Expect great things from God; attempt great things for God.*'

Anglicanism

In England, the Reformation took a different path from the rest of Europe. The English Church was greatly influenced by both Luther and Calvin but did not join either of those two Church groupings. So the Church of England maintained a position which was Luther-like in its conservative attitude to tradition and Calvin-like in its doctrine. Some Anglicans dislike being called Protestant, arguing that they are both Catholic and Reformed. Its basis was defined in the Thirty Nine Articles (1563 Latin; 1571 English) and the English Book of Common Prayer (finalized in 1662 but based on the work of Archbishop Thomas Cranmer a century earlier).

The British (and other European) churches expanded widely to other parts of the globe during the seventeenth, eighteenth and nineteenth centuries. This expansion arose from:

▶ *the colonizing process which resulted in the British Empire (although some missionaries found it necessary to oppose some policies of the colonizers)*
▶ *missionary zeal which wanted to take the gospel to new areas.*

One result is a great worldwide network of churches called the Anglican Communion, which numbers some 83 million members. Most of today's Anglicans live in Africa. Anglican churches are sometimes called Episcopal or Episcopalian (from the Greek word *episkopos* meaning 'bishop' or 'overseer'). Anglicans are distinguished by having created a fellowship which allows for considerable doctrinal and liturgical differences, within a recognizable organizational unity. Anglican provinces are autonomous, but still look to the Church of

England as the founding Church and to the Archbishop of Canterbury as 'first bishop among equals'. Every ten years, Anglican bishops from around the globe gather for the Lambeth Conference, hosted by the Archbishop of Canterbury. The first Conference was held in 1867.

> 'A bishop from Tanzania was telling me that he stops for lunch in the middle of a confirmation, so as to do 1,000 candidates in the morning and then another 1,000 in the afternoon.'
>
> (Bishop Michael Doe)

The ordination of women to the priesthood was debated and accepted in many Anglican churches in the final decades of the twentieth century (for example, the Church of England ordained its first women priests in 1994). This initiative, welcomed by the majority, nevertheless caused controversy and division, which persists into the twenty-first century as the question of female bishops is debated.

CATHOLIC, LIBERAL AND EVANGELICAL

There are three broad, sometimes overlapping, streams within Anglicanism: Catholic, Liberal and Evangelical.

▶ *Anglo-Catholics (or 'Catholic Anglicans') are 'high church' in worship. They stress the mystery and awesomeness of God, using colourful vestments and incense (hence the affectionate nickname 'smells and bells' for high church worship).*

▶ *Liberal theology lays stress upon questioning the tradition and requiring the Faith to respond (sometimes radically; hence 'radical theology') to changes in culture and outlook in the world outside the Church.*

▶ *Evangelicals (not to be confused with fundamentalists – Chapter 13) stress the importance of the Bible and the need for conversion and commitment. In recent years, evangelicals have become strong within the Church of England. Their worship tends to be 'low church' in style with minimal ceremony, in an attempt to make Church services accessible to outsiders. In recent years evangelicals have been relatively effective in attracting young people, a task with which most European churches struggle.*

It is important to stress that the boundaries between these three approaches are not rigid. The Charismatic Renewal Movement (Chapter 13) has influenced all three streams, especially the evangelical. As a result, the 'feel' of Anglican worship today is much more relaxed than hitherto, with bands and music groups featuring alongside pipe organs and choirs.

The Oxford Movement (Chapter 18) resulted in the foundation of Anglican monasteries and convents. Some continue to flourish and do distinguished pioneering work (e.g. Helen House, the first Children's Hospice, was founded by Sister Frances Dominica). However, many of these religious communities struggle to survive, with few younger members joining.

Other types of Christian community have been established (such as Lee Abbey in Devon; Scargill House in Yorkshire). Taizé (France) and Iona (Scotland) are flourishing communities which attract many Anglicans – though these communities are essentially ecumenical. They involve many lay people (often young) who commit themselves to communal life for a year or so; few stay in these communities for life.

Britain today

Research shows that about 7 per cent of the population attend church on Sundays. Of these:

- ▶ about 1.7 per cent attend a Church of England service
- ▶ about 1.9 per cent attend a Roman Catholic church
- ▶ most of the remaining 3.0 per cent attend a range of Protestant churches: Baptist, Methodist, Presbyterian or United Reformed, Pentecostal, Salvation Army, Quaker, Independent or 'New Church'.

There are strong regional variations in church attendance: less than 1 per cent in some parts of some cities; about 10 per cent in Scotland and perhaps 25 per cent in Northern Ireland.

(Contd)

In 2005 there were 48,328 churches in the UK, of which 37,846 were in England.

Four or five new congregations are founded in Britain each week because 'church planting' is a policy adopted by most mainstream and independent churches. These new congregations often meet in schools and community halls, even pubs. However, about six churches close each week.

On 23 December 2007 the media announced (based on information from *Christian Research*) that for the first time in 500 years there are more Roman Catholic than Anglican worshippers – partly as a result of Polish immigrants. The Church of England's Statistical Department pointed out that these figures relate to Sunday worship only – a large number of services and activities are also held on weekdays.

Britain has not become a nation of atheists. In the 2001 Census, 72 per cent claimed Christian allegiance. A *Tearfund* survey in 2007 showed that 42 per cent pray and one-third of the population believes that God watches over them. And a 2007 MORI poll showed that 63 per cent of women and 49 per cent of men believe in God. In addition, Dr David Hay's research reveals that a growing number of British people claim to have had a spiritual experience.

Other world faiths are found in Britain, mainly as a result of immigration in the 1950s and subsequently, especially since the mid-1990s. Numbers are not huge but are increasing: adherents of all other faiths taken together amount to about 8 per cent of the British population.

Methodist Churches

The Church of England was not always comprehensive and open. When a reform movement began in the eighteenth century, led by two Anglican priests, the established Church resisted it. John and Charles Wesley and their followers were nicknamed 'Methodists' because of their orderly (methodical) approach to life and faith. So a new church grouping was created which took that name with pride.

Today there are Methodist churches around the world with 23 million members. Methodists have developed strong lay leadership and a travelling ministry. They are distinguished by the prominent place given in worship to hymn singing. Many of the fine hymns written by Charles Wesley are sung wherever English is used in worship, regardless of denomination (Chapter 20).

Around the world

- In the USA 'about 22 per cent of Americans attend religious services in any given week, in contrast to the 40 per cent commonly found from opinion polls'. (Professor David Voas in *Religious Trends* published by Christian Research in 2008)
- In Italy 41 per cent attend church every week. (Professor Grace Davie, 2002)
- In the Republic of Ireland the figure is 57 per cent. (Professor Grace Davie, 2002)
- In the Philippines there are nearly 2 million baptisms a year. (Kenneth Hylson-Smith, 2007)
- Assuming current trends continue, by 2050 the world will have 3 billion Christians, and only 20 per cent of them will be non-Hispanic whites. (Kenneth Hylson-Smith, 2007)

Salvation Army and Quakers

Some smaller groups have made an impact beyond their size. For example, the Salvation Army, with 2.4 million members, is renowned for a combination of outdoor evangelism, brass bands and social action among the homeless and others in desperate need. It has a highly effective (and confidential) ministry in tracing missing persons and offering the possibility of reunion with their families.

'The Army' was started by William Booth, a Methodist living in Victorian London, in an attempt to bring the gospel to the thousands living in poverty, following the Industrial Revolution. The Salvation Army, with its musical, practical and evangelistic concerns, has spread to other countries and is especially strong in the USA. Salvationists (together with some other Christians) have taken a clear stand against what they perceive as the damaging effects of alcohol.

The Quakers (more correctly, the Religious Society of Friends), founded by George Fox (1624–91) have no ordained ministers. Silence is central to their tradition, as they 'wait upon God' in their Sunday meetings. Anyone may speak, under the prompting of the Spirit. Quakers have a distinguished record of pacifism and heroic war service in non-combatant roles – usually para-medical. In this they are like the Christian Brethren (formerly 'Plymouth Brethren'), a group of autonomous churches with no ordained ministers. Quakers number 400,000 (16,000 in Britain) and the Brethren 3.4 million (71,000 in Britain).

Pentecostal Churches

Pentecostalists take their name from Acts 2, where God's Spirit came in power on Peter and the other disciples ('the Feast of Pentecost': page 284). God's Spirit enabled the disciples to go out with zeal to spread the gospel, and gave them miraculous powers to speak in 'other tongues' and to heal the sick (Chapter 15). Pentecostal Christians believe that such powers are still available today, through the Holy Spirit. Pentecostal churches were established early in the twentieth century and are growing fast throughout the world. Their worship is informal, exuberant and partly unplanned, because of their belief in the immediacy of the gifts of the Spirit. The word 'charismatic' is often used for this expression of Christianity, but charismatic worship of an exuberant kind is often found in the older 'mainstream' churches too (Chapter 13).

Independent Churches

Independent Churches (indigenous or locally founded churches) are springing up around the world. Some African and Asian churches have arisen partly in adverse reaction to the Western elements which inevitably became associated with the missionary work of previous centuries. They are strong numerically but diverse in character. Often they are Pentecostal in emphasis but some stress the practices (and sometimes also the teachings and culture) of their countries before the missionaries arrived. Throughout the world, Independent, Pentecostal and Charismatic churches are growing faster than any other tradition. Taken together, they number about 438 million, although their independent character makes them difficult to enumerate.

Older independent churches, for example, Seventh Day Adventists, Moravians, Mennonites and Nazerenes, have long been an important part of the Christian landscape.

A shifting centre of gravity

Insight

Sociologists speak about the 'European exception'. As church-going in Europe declines, there is fast expansion elsewhere, especially in Africa, Latin America and above all – and perhaps surprisingly – in China.

Christianity started in the Middle East and was found very early in North Africa (see Acts 8:27). But throughout most of its history Europe has taken the lead, dominating both its thinking and its expansion – although the USA took over this leadership role during the twentieth century.

The eighteenth, nineteenth and early twentieth centuries saw a remarkable burst of missionary zeal. Britain, the USA and other countries sent missionaries to the four corners of the earth. As a result, the Christian Church has been planted in every continent and in almost every country. Christianity has shown itself capable of adapting to all cultures. In every society there are customs which need to be challenged in the name of Christ. But in every place, aspects of local custom and culture are found to be effective vehicles for Christian teaching and worship. Today, it is the relatively young churches which are flourishing. So the Christian Church worldwide is growing and the Christian faith continues to spread (page 215). Meanwhile, the Church's centre of gravity has shifted:

- from *Europe and (to a lesser extent) the USA*
- to *Africa, Asia, and Latin America.*

> Population trends in these continents mean that the Church in the twenty-first century is increasingly young, energetic, non-white, and Pentecostal/Charismatic. The sociologist David Martin speaks of the 'massive shift to Pentecostalism and the global South'. In the coming decades this is likely to be hugely significant, not only for the World Church, but for the world in general. This century is likely to see a culture shift, as the younger churches in the developing world become more influential, shape the future and send missionaries and mission-partners to other continents, including Europe.

Disharmony

The mainstream historic churches moved closer together throughout the twentieth century. But some of the newer churches are aggressive in their evangelism and ready to 'proselytize' – to win converts from other churches. We have noted the problems caused

by this policy for the Russian Orthodox Church (page 218).
A similar problem – the rapid spread of Pentecostal churches –
faces the Roman Catholic Church in Latin America.

Many Independent Churches, in whichever country they are found,
are not interested in working with other Christians. So, while
there is a strong movement towards unity within many 'historic'
churches, there is also a counter-movement towards independence
and fragmentation among the newer churches.

Insight

In Britain over the past few decades, relationships between
the different denominations have grown warm. Local
churches co-operate on a number of ventures, from centres
for homeless people to united services and shared church
buildings. But full unity still seems a distant goal.

Conclusion

At the beginning of this chapter, the image of a mountain was used
to illustrate the one Church in its different aspects. Another image
is the river which flows from one single spring. The spring is Jesus
Christ himself, who gives 'living water' (John 4:10). At first it was
concentrated into a small area but gradually it spread out over a
wider bed. Some streams are deep and narrow, others shallow and
wide, eventually dividing into separate streams which themselves
divide again later. All the water flows from the same source, but it
forms many streams. Separate as we are, we acknowledge that the
water matters more than any particular river.

10 THINGS TO REMEMBER

1 The worldwide Church is made up of a network of local churches, which belong to different 'denominations'.

2 The largest Church is the Roman Catholic Church, with over a billion members.

3 People who would describe themselves as Christian make up some 33 per cent of the world's total population.

4 Other large worldwide faith communities are Muslim (21 per cent) and Hindu (13 per cent).

5 In Eastern Europe the Orthodox Church is numerically strong, totalling some 220 million.

6 During the sixteenth-century Reformation in Europe, the unity of the mediaeval Catholic Church was broken.

7 As a result of the Reformation, several Protestant (from 'protest') Churches were formed.

8 In Britain about 7 per cent of the population attends a Christian church each week – more than attend football matches.

9 The centre of gravity for Christians is shifting from Europe to Africa, the Americas and Asia (especially China).

10 In today's world a typical Christian is not elderly, prosperous and white – but young, non-white, poor, energetic and Pentecostal.

13

Modern movements

In this chapter you will learn:
- *about influential modern movements*
- *about the rise of fundamentalism*
- *about the Church and sexuality.*

As we have just seen, individual Christians belong to a particular
local church, and (very often) through that to a 'denomination' or
worldwide Communion of churches (Roman Catholic, Anglican,
Lutheran and so on). But it would be a mistake to think that
these bodies are self-contained, or sealed off from one another.
Some are, but there is a great deal of communication between the
various Churches. So, in addition to belonging to a local church
and a denomination, many Christians are influenced by widespread
movements which cross denominational boundaries. In this chapter
we shall consider some of the movements which are influential in
church life today.

The ecumenical movement

Unity among the disciples of Jesus is a key theme in the New
Testament. Jesus prayed for his followers *'that all of them may be
one, Father, just as you are in me and I am in you'* (John 17:21). The
apostle Paul urged the Christians in Ephesus to *'Make every effort to
keep the unity of the Spirit through the bond of peace'* (Ephesians 4:3).

However, as the centuries passed and the Christian movement grew, serious divisions occurred (Chapter 12). Throughout the twentieth century, a new spirit of togetherness developed. This was anticipated by the formation of the Evangelical Alliance. In 1846, individuals from more than 50 American and British Protestant denominations agreed to pursue religious liberty and to cooperate in various evangelistic and educational endeavours. But the intended unity was selective: one aim was to unite Protestants in resistance to Catholicism.

The Evangelical Alliance (EA) continues to flourish. In Britain the EA has pioneered Spring Harvest, which mixes holiday activities with worship services and seminars on different aspects of Christian faith. These annual gatherings, based in holiday camps, are attended by tens of thousands from a wide range of churches, mainly Protestant and Anglican.

The twentieth-century ecumenical movement attempted to bring together churches with widely differing approaches to the Christian faith. In 1910, at an international missionary conference in Edinburgh led by the American Methodist John R Mott, 1000 delegates shared his desire for Christian unity. Structures were established in an attempt to give shape and substance to their vision. Eventually this initiative gave rise to the formation of the *World Council of Churches* (WCC). 351 delegates from 147 denominations and 44 countries gathered for the first General Assembly in Amsterdam in 1948. The movement was earning the right to call itself 'ecumenical' – from the Greek word *oikoumene*, meaning 'the whole inhabited earth'.

Further General Assemblies were organized every six years or so. At New Delhi in 1961 there were two important developments: the Russian Orthodox Church joined the Council and a formal *Confessional Basis* was adopted. This stated that:

> **The World Council of Churches is a fellowship of Churches which confess the Lord Jesus Christ as God and Saviour according to the Scriptures and therefore seek to fulfil together their common calling to the glory of one God, Father, Son, and Holy Spirit.**

In the 1960s, the WCC caused controversy by its involvement in political issues. The Council made grants to 'freedom fighters' in national struggles, arguing that they were oppressed minorities in a 'just war'. Some member churches expressed strong disagreement with the leadership of the WCC on this matter. Critics pointed out that the WCC leadership was selective in the causes it championed – appearing to be less critical of Marxist and Maoist regimes. They also argued that the WCC is not a 'super Church' but should be a servant of all the churches; it has no mandate to take sides in this way.

> Conspicuous by its absence from these ecumenical endeavours has been the Roman Catholic Church. Issues such as the primacy of the Pope, the nature of the priesthood and the meaning and practice of the Eucharist have made it difficult for that Church to participate fully. However, from 1961 senior Roman Catholics have attended WCC Assemblies as official observers. Under the leadership of the reforming Pope John XXIII, the Second Vatican Council (1962–5) opened the door to closer ecumenical activity. For the first time a Roman Catholic Council acknowledged that there are authentic Christians ('separated brethren') outside the Roman fold. Reflecting this new spirit, in December 1968 the Patriarch of Constantinople and the Pope mutually lifted the excommunications which had divided the Catholic and Eastern Orthodox Churches since 1054.

Several churches have entered into bi-lateral or multi-lateral talks – sometimes on specific issues (e.g. Baptism, Eucharist and Ministry), sometimes about the possibility of uniting. Organic unity has been achieved in some cases: for example in 1947 several churches united to form the Church of South India (CSI). Not all attempts at formal unity between churches have succeeded. Critics of such schemes argue that variety in worship and church order is a good thing (matching different histories, theologies and personalities), provided there is an underlying unity of spirit and purpose.

In Britain and some other countries, relationships between members of different churches at a local level is often warm, and united endeavours in outreach and social action are common (but see page 234). Some commentators believe that this is where the future lies: cooperation at a local level rather than grand schemes for reunion.

Liberation theology

Liberation theology emerged in Latin America in the 1960s. In 1968, at a conference of Roman Catholic Bishops from Latin America held in Colombia, some members insisted that the starting point for theological reflection must be the situation of the poor. Liberation theology was born. At the forefront of this movement is the belief that the God of the Bible is on the side of the downtrodden and marginalized. Liberation theologians remind us that:

- ▶ *God heard the cry of the children of Israel when they were enslaved in Egypt.*
- ▶ *The Old Testament prophets were passionate in demanding social justice.*
- ▶ *Mary's song ('the Magnificat') based on Hannah's Song (1 Samuel 2:1–10), is revolutionary: God 'has filled the hungry with good things but has sent the rich away empty' (Luke 1:53).*
- ▶ *Jesus showed particular concern for the poor and those on the edge of society.*
- ▶ *Christianity is a 'this-worldly' religion, concerned with the welfare of mind and body, as well as redemption of the soul.*

The Bible is seen as a very practical book, concerned with freedom from physical oppression and freedom for the human spirit. Liberation theology is concerned with reflection, action ('praxis') and raising the awareness of poor people concerning issues of justice. Something of its mood is caught in these statements:

- ▶ *As a sign of the liberation of humankind and history, the Church itself in its concrete existence ought to be a place of liberation … The point is not to survive, but to serve. The rest will be given (Gustavo Gutiérrez).*
- ▶ *The poor man, the other, reveals the totally Other to us (Gutiérrez).*
- ▶ *Theology has to stop explaining the world and start reforming it (J Miguez-Bonino).*
- ▶ *The Church in liberation theology is rooted in a faith in God and an option for the poor (Marilyn J Legge).*

> *The God of the future is the crucified God who submerges himself in a world of misery. God is found on the crosses of the oppressed rather than in beauty, power or wisdom (D D Webster).*

Alongside the rise of liberation theology came the formation of Christian **Base Communities**, a separate but related phenomenon. This movement arose in part as a way of coping with a chronic shortage of Catholic priests in Latin America. It is essentially a lay movement flourishing among largely uneducated Christians, often in shanty towns. Small groups (usually around 10 or 20 strong) gather weekly for worship services, Bible study, discussion, pastoral care and social awareness. In Brazil in 1985 there were over 100,000 base communities. Similar communities have developed within Protestant churches. Within these groups, liberation theologians have attempted to raise awareness of the power of ordinary people working together for change ('conscientization').

The Vatican has often expressed unease at what it sees as the Marxist overtones of liberation theology. In December 2009 Pope Benedict called liberation theology 'deceitful and Marxist' and told Brazilian bishops to steer clear of it. This declaration was regarded with dismay by campaigners for reform in the Roman Catholic Church. Anglican Bishop Michael Doe commented, 'I was myself in Brasilia two or three years ago in one of the shanty towns … The Anglican priest there celebrates the eucharist, leads the campaigns for water and electricity, and helps people to seek change by hearing what the Bible says about God, who wants to free his people.'

In the 1970s and 1980s many priests in repressive Latin American states opposed those regimes. Several paid with their lives. We have already noted the high profile assassination of Archbishop Oscar Romero (page 203). He was one among many. While Rome did not like 'politicized' priests, it disliked the persecution of priests even more. Modern Popes do not encourage priests to get involved in direct political action, but they frequently emphasize human rights and often speak out against war (e.g. the war against Iraq in 2003).

Liberation theology has spread around the world and in some places (such as South Africa) it has become a powerful force.

Always there are those who argue that Christianity should confine itself to matters of the spirit. In reply, Archbishop Desmond Tutu spoke for many when he said: '*I am puzzled about which Bible people are reading when they suggest that religion and politics don't mix.*' This approach has spilled over into the life of more affluent churches too – for example in feminist theology, which views women as an oppressed majority within the Church (page 253).

Needless to say, liberation theology has its critics inside and outside the Church. It has been viewed by some conservative Christians as a Marxist political movement rather than a spiritual movement. Archbishop Helder Camara answered his critics by saying, '*When I give food to the poor they call me a Saint. When I ask why they are poor, they call me a Communist.*' Liberation theologians argue that to rest content with the status quo in unjust societies is to side with the oppressors against the oppressed.

'Structural sin' (i.e. unjust systems and structures in society) rather than personal sin is emphasized. Critics argue that liberation theology reduces salvation to political liberation and neglects the transcendent and eternal dimensions of Christianity. Others (such as Professor David Martin) argue that intellectual liberation theologians do not serve the real needs of poor local communities. The feminist theologian Professor Rosemary Radford Ruether, while being sympathetic to the movement, asserts (controversially) that early liberation theologians omitted 'women, nature and indigenous peoples' from their concerns. But the influence of liberation theology remains strong and many Christians endorse its challenge to the view that the Church should concentrate only on 'spiritual matters'. They argue that Christian faith, and hence the Church, must be concerned with the *whole* of life, because the God of the Bible is concerned with the whole of life.

Insight

The modern worldwide Church is marked by a wide range of movements and emphases. One of these is liberation theology, which began in Latin America in the 1960s. It stresses that the God of the Bible has a special concern for the poor and marginalized.

Fundamentalism

Fundamentalism is often in the news and fundamentalists usually get a bad press, because they are perceived as dangerous. Sadly, this suspicion is sometimes well placed.

Doctors who practise abortion have been attacked by Christian fundamentalists. Mosques have been destroyed by Hindu fundamentalists. The peace process in Israel has been obstructed by Jewish fundamentalists who insist that land must not be traded for peace. The world was shaken when, in 1995, the Israeli Prime Minister Yitzhak Rabin was shot by a Jewish fundamentalist. The assassin Yigal Amir claimed that he was acting on orders from God, and in the best interests of Israel.

Islamic fundamentalists ('Islamists') have become notorious since 9/11 (2001) and 7/7 (2005); both are dates which evoke images of carnage. 12/27 (2007) has joined this tragic shortlist – the day on which Benazir Bhutto was murdered in Pakistan. Al Qaeda and Osama bin Laden are feared around the world – and admired by a growing number of radicalized young Muslims who despise the West. Some commentators argue that 'the War on Terror' has resulted in yet more suicide bombers willing to embrace 'martyrdom'.

Thus fundamentalism has become synonymous with bigotry, with unshakeable certainty and with a passionate, and often violent, commitment to a range of dubious causes. Some commentators see fundamentalism within the world's various religions as a major challenge to international peace and stability. But is this fair?

Insight

Fundamentalism is often in the news. The word has Christian origins and describes those in every world religion and ideology who stress certainty, and have little empathy with other views.

The term 'fundamentalism' originated in a series of tracts written in America between 1909 and 1915. These pamphlets were called *The Fundamentals*. They were written by scholarly conservative Protestant Christians who wished to re-state 'the fundamentals' of the Christian faith. The authors would be amazed at the journey taken by their title.

Christian fundamentalists claim to follow the Bible in all matters of life and belief. Sometimes they oppose modern science, asserting that evolution is a discredited theory and attempting to replace it with a 'young earth' view, known as Creationism. (Similarly, many Muslims do not believe in evolution.) Many Christian fundamentalists claim to have, from the Bible, a clear outline of the events leading to the end of the world, and the return of Jesus Christ in glorious majesty. Some would argue that this has exerted an influence on US policy in the Middle East – especially on its strong support for the State of Israel.

Interestingly, the term 'atheistic fundamentalism' has been applied to the stance of some enthusiastic atheists – a term which they resist.

As noted above, deep suspicion of some fundamentalists is well placed. *But relatively few modern Christian fundamentalists espouse violence and many are loyal church members and good citizens.* Following the lead of their influential leaders, many fundamentalists have espoused a political agenda, especially in the USA. On some issues, such as abortion, assisted suicide and stem-cell research, they have made common cause with Roman Catholics, even though their understanding of 'church' is very different in many ways. (However, they do share an emphasis on the authority of church leaders.)

Evangelicals and fundamentalists

Due to its bad press, the word 'fundamentalist' has become a term of abuse. Labelling someone 'a fundamentalist' is sometimes used as a substitute for sound argument, to dismiss opponents out of hand. The word is often applied to Christians who hold a 'high' view of the Bible as the Word of God, but do not share the negative characteristics described above. Such Christians protest, and prefer the term 'evangelical' (or, in some cases, 'conservative evangelical') although the terms are increasingly used interchangeably by secular journalists.

Evangelicals, unlike fundamentalists, accept biblical criticism (see Chapter 5), while insisting that it be applied responsibly. Most evangelicals accept evolution and they recognize that not all biblical passages should be read literally. Evangelicals are not usually committed to a detailed timetable concerning the return of Christ in glory and the end of the world. And while they are realistic about human nature and sin, evangelicals do not dismiss modern culture as being in the grip of the devil, as many fundamentalists do.

A number of distinguished scholars, bishops and other leaders within the historic churches are happy to embrace the term 'evangelical', but they object to being called fundamentalist. Notable among them is the Anglican Dr John Stott, Rector Emeritus of All Souls' Church in London's Langham Place. Through writing, preaching, travelling and organizing, he exercised a remarkable worldwide ministry during the second half of the twentieth century. Other widely respected evangelicals include climatologist Professor Sir John Houghton (page 176) and Jim Wallis. An American church leader with a passion for social justice, Jim Wallis' counsel and vision have been sought in the White House.

Insight

Despite their vilification, most Christian fundamentalists are not violent. On the contrary, most seek to be good citizens and helpful neighbours, because that is what the Bible teaches.

Evangelization

Go and make disciples of all nations. (Matthew 28:19)

Always be ready to give a reason for the hope that you have.

(1 Peter 3:15)

Christianity, like Buddhism and Islam, is a missionary religion. In this it is unlike Judaism, from which it sprang. To be a Jew is essentially a matter of birth (the mother's line is vital in this regard). Jews have little interest in persuading others to join their ranks. In contrast, Christians are committed to sharing the good news ('the gospel') of God's saving love revealed in Jesus Christ.

In the 1980s, church leaders began to consider appropriate ways of marking the new Millennium, with its 2000 years of Christian history. Pope John Paul II suggested that the 1990s should be a Decade of Evangelization. And the 1988 Lambeth Conference of Anglican Bishops worldwide declared a Decade of Evangelism. Most mainstream churches supported these initiatives, with their vision of 'a renewed and united effort to make Christ known to the peoples of the world'.

For many people, evangelism is closely associated with the famous evangelist Dr Billy Graham (b. 1918) – a widely respected American preacher who concluded his huge meetings with an invitation to 'get up out of your seat'. In this way 'enquirers' were invited to come forward to receive Jesus Christ as Saviour and Lord. The word 'evangelism' also evokes images of American-style 'televangelists', some of whom have an affluent lifestyle and questionable methods and morals.

Neither of these models was uppermost in the minds of most Christian leaders when they called for a Decade of Evangelism. They were more concerned to make outreach with the gospel a natural feature of local church life. Their concern was to help ordinary Christians to know their faith more deeply, hold it more securely and share it more confidently. The Catholic Catechism (1994) states: 'Lay people also fulfil their prophetic mission by evangelization, that is, the proclamation of Christ by word and the testimony of life.'

The Anglican Bishops made a similar point at the 1988 Lambeth Conference: 'Every Christian as an agent of mission.' They did not wish to make individual Christians 'pushy' and aggressive.

They were concerned that churches should be warm in their welcome, with adventurous and attractive programmes, accessible and inspiring worship, and blurred boundaries, to ensure that enquirers and visitors feel included.

In the twenty-first century *all* churches are in a missionary situation, including (perhaps *especially*) churches in so-called 'Christian countries' in Europe. It is acknowledged, too, that in the modern world there are many voices seeking to gain people's allegiance. Some of these are benign; others are pernicious, damaging and exploitative. The call to evangelize is an attempt by Christian leaders to say to all the churches: 'alongside these other voices, let the Christian voice be heard'.

Most churches in multicultural situations are sensitive to adherents of other faiths (in Britain about 8 per cent of the population). It is recognized that the gospel is for all, but dialogue is preferable to preaching in such circumstances. Jesus was 'full of grace and truth'. So evangelism must be marked by courtesy, humility and attentive listening.

Many churches are keenly aware of the importance of hospitality and a warm (but not suffocating) welcome. 'Fresh Expressions' is one key example of this. In *Rowan Revealed*, a York Courses' CD conversation with the author in 2009, the Archbishop of Canterbury said, 'There's one thing I'd like to be remembered for in the Church of England – it's putting my shoulder behind 'Fresh Expressions'. That's the thing that's most cheered me and encouraged me, in recent years.' 'Fresh Expressions' encourages churches to offer services and events which local people find attractive and appropriate. 'Back to church Sunday' is another example of Christian hospitality – as is the encouragement to Christians to meet people away from the 'safety' of church premises.

Why evangelize?
Enlarging the Church – or, in the West, stemming the decline – is only one reason for evangelism. The main concern is truly to be the 'Servant Church'. Christians believe that they have good news

to share: good news that can bring hope, confidence and courage to people who often 'live lives of quiet desperation'. At times of distress and reflection many people ask deep questions:

- *Is the universe friendly? Can we really find God, meaning, truth and love at the centre of our universe?*
- *Or do we live in a cold, uncaring world which grinds relentlessly on, reducing us all to rubble and dust in the end? Worse still, do we live in a 'cosmic madhouse'?*
- *'Is that all there is?' runs the lyric of Neil Simon's wistful song. This all-important question was answered by John Donne some 400 years earlier (page 164). If he is right, the triumphant final words of his sonnet 'Death be not proud' are the most significant two lines in all English literature.*
- *Like everyone else, Christians have to grapple with many questions that do not have easy answers. C S Lewis once observed that Christianity is not a 'filleted religion'. It is coherent but it comes to us with loose ends and 'bones'. Like life itself, it is not 'tidy'.*

> But Christianity does claim to shed light on life's deepest mysteries. Because Jesus has defeated death (Chapter 3), we can be assured of eternal life. Because of God's revelation of himself in Jesus Christ, we can find meaning, truth and love at the centre of our world. Even more important, we can find these great qualities at the heart and centre of our individual, personal lives.
>
> These vital insights are to be shared with humility, boldness, love, sensitivity and friendship. D T Niles, an Asian Christian, gave this pithy definition: 'Evangelism is one beggar showing another beggar where he found bread.' Mother Teresa is credited with an equally beautiful affirmation: 'Evangelism means to carry Jesus in your heart, and to give the presence of Jesus to someone else.'

One bracing feature of evangelization in the West today is that the gloves are off. The majority continues to believe in God, but at the same time militant atheism is widespread. Deference has departed and Christianity no longer has a privileged place in society. Indeed, even some atheists protest that things have gone too far when Christmas is termed 'Winterval' and schools are nervous about staging nativity plays. All this – and the fear of militant 'Islamism' (not to be confused with mainstream Islam) – makes religion a widespread topic for conversation, and for the Letters pages of newspapers.

The Sea of Faith – and Alpha

In the last decades of the twentieth century a small but articulate group of intellectuals formed the *Sea of Faith* movement. Most members of this movement take a very radical approach to Christian theology. There is no 'party line' and members are free to believe, practise and write as they wish. Don Cupitt, former Dean of Emmanuel College, Cambridge, was a founder member. He believes that God and heaven have no reality outside human language and imagination. These concepts, and the Bible stories which carry them, are useful (and for some, perhaps, essential) symbols and myths enabling us to construct and lead purposeful and moral lives.

Don Cupitt is happy to use traditional Christian terminology like 'Christ is Lord of my life.' But he means something very different from more orthodox believers; he means 'a commitment to values, that's all'. And when he talks about resurrection, he does not mean that God raised Jesus from the dead but, 'I choose to live the risen life.' By the 'risen life' he means 'solar living'. Like the sun we burn for a while, spreading light and heat. Then we burn out – forever.

An articulate 'Vicar who doesn't believe in God' has news value and his views have been given considerable space in the media. Supporters of this approach to Christianity argue that it is bracing: facing bleak reality without offering escapism. There is no God 'out there'; life after death is an illusion. We must face squarely the glory and the tragedy of being a human being.

Critics raise the obvious point that Christian faith without a real God and with no hope of heaven, is very anaemic indeed. Some question whether it can properly be called Christianity. They also argue that for all its bleakness and boldness, this theology lacks a true sense of the depth of human tragedy and helplessness. It 'works' for people who – through upbringing and temperament – are upright, moral and interested in religious ideas. But the gospel is for everyone. Malcolm Worsley (page 103) would argue that he could not 'choose to live the risen life'. Without a real God, who offers real strength, grace and forgiveness, he would still be in the gutter.

Insight

One of today's best-known methods of Christian outreach is *Alpha*. This is very different from the 'large meeting' approach used by Billy Graham and other evangelists. *Alpha* gathers a dozen or so people in a home or hall for a shared meal, friendship and discussion.

Alpha is based at Holy Trinity Church, Brompton ('HTB') – an Anglican church in London, evangelical and charismatic in emphasis. Their simple formula is to invite people for a good meal, and a presentation of one aspect of the Christian faith, followed by open discussion. Some critics assert that *Alpha* over-simplifies; others say that it is too cerebral! This approach is now used in many countries and Nicky Gumbel, the leader of Alpha, is warmly welcomed by many senior Roman Catholic leaders, including Cardinals.

Alpha is now established in many prisons, as Michael Emmett's story illustrates: 'It's odd going to prison with your dad. I'm a loud-mouthed Cockney with scars on my face. There were 11 of us [who responded to Alpha] and we were known as the God Squad.' Michael stopped taking drugs overnight ('It's amazing what you can get in prison') and on release he sorted out his complicated family life and ran a flower business. 'If I could give a word of encouragement to anyone who feels they are failing, it would be: "Don't worry how far you fall: you can always get up again." Sometimes we can be in danger of raising the bar too high as Christians. None of us is perfect.'

The charismatic movement

In 1960 Dennis Bennett, an Episcopal (Anglican) rector in California, became national news. Things were happening in his church which were usually associated with Pentecostal churches founded some 40 years earlier. Church members claimed to be 'baptized in the Spirit' and to 'speak in tongues'. Similar phenomena took place elsewhere, and the movement spread around the world with remarkable speed.

At first this movement influenced Anglican and Protestant Churches; but by the late 1960s it had made an impact upon the Roman Catholic Church too. In the early 1970s its influence was also felt within the Greek Orthodox Church. This is remarkable, given the stress on tradition and the inbuilt resistance to change and innovation which mark the Eastern Orthodox Churches (Chapter 12).

Within the 'charismatic movement' (sometimes called the *renewal movement*), emphasis is placed upon openness to the influence of the Holy Spirit. Charismatic worship is usually informal, with prayer, singing and 'ministry' – one or two people (often lay people) praying for individuals within the congregation. Speaking or singing in tongues ('glossolalia') is common: words are uttered, not in a language usually spoken by the person involved, but in a language of transcendent prayer and praise. Worship is often exuberant but fine singing and silence are significant features in some churches.

The importance of a direct experience of God's Holy Spirit is stressed and charismatic worship generates a sense of warm fellowship. All members of the congregation are invited to participate; even to take a lead. They might feel moved by the Spirit to offer prophecy, 'a word of knowledge' or to lead the congregation in prayer, perhaps using 'a tongue'. Or they might offer an interpretation of someone else's prayer in tongues. The gifts of the Spirit (1 Corinthians 12–14) are encouraged, including the gift of healing through prayer – and 'power evangelism' through 'signs and wonders' (especially healing).

The large number of charismatic Christians in every denomination has forced the mainstream 'historic' churches to take the charismatic renewal movement seriously. Since 1960, well over 100 official denominational documents on the movement have been produced. Assessments have become increasingly positive and it has been espoused by some leading figures, such as the late Roman Catholic Cardinal Suenens from Belgium.

In Britain, one result of the charismatic movement has been the formation of House Churches (sometimes called New Churches). Frustrated by what they perceived as the straitjacket of traditional Christianity, but not attracted to the classical Pentecostal churches, in the 1960s and 1970s some Christians began to meet in homes, schools, community centres or pubs. Some of these have grown into well-organized networks of churches, such as the Ichthus Fellowship in London. The charismatic Vineyard Fellowship from California spread to other countries under the leadership of John Wimber.

The impact of charismatic renewal on the mainstream Churches has been considerable. In some places it has been divisive and some church members are suspicious of what they perceive to be an excess of emotion and enthusiasm. However, many Christians and churches are less formal and more open to spontaneity than hitherto – even if they do not see themselves as 'belonging' to the charismatic movement.

The laity

Most of the above movements are, in one way or another, a move away from a priest- or minister-centred Church, to a more biblical notion of the Church as 'the body of Christ'.

'Laity' derives from a Greek word (laos) meaning 'people'. In most churches today, the unity of all Christian believers – clergy and laity together – as 'the people of God' is stressed, along with the doctrine of 'the priesthood of all believers' (page 148). The key Bible passage on the Church as 'the body of Christ' is

1 Corinthians 12: 12–30. This stresses the fact that all members have gifts to be exercised 'for the common good'. Bishop John Robinson put it like this: *'The laity are not the helpers of the clergy, so that they can do their job. The clergy are the helpers of the laity so that they can be the Church in the world.'*

One remarkable lay-led initiative is to be found within universities. Several student-led religious societies are in evidence and an evangelical Christian Union is the largest single student society in some British universities.

Insight

Two features of the modern world Church are the importance placed upon the laity ('every member ministry') and vigorous debate about sexuality and gender e.g. 'inclusive' language in worship and Scripture, homosexuality, women priests and bishops ...

Issues of gender and sexuality

Issues of gender and sexuality are currently being widely discussed in many churches, particularly in the West. Although not focused within a single movement, it will be convenient to consider some of these important matters at this point. (See also page 228.)

GENDER AND LANGUAGE

God as Mother?

Throughout this book we have encountered traditional language for God; God is thought of as Father and referred to as 'he' (or, in older usage 'He'). Some Christians believe that this is too narrow. They do not deny that this usage is to be found in the Bible – including the teaching of Jesus, where it is central – and throughout most subsequent Christian history. But they argue that such language is culturally determined. In their view, it does not arise from essential theological considerations.

Strictly speaking, God is not a 'Person'. 'He' is supra-personal (not sub-personal). But, because personal categories are the highest we can imagine, we rightly use these. For centuries, following the teaching of Jesus, Christians have referred to God as 'Father'. But, runs the argument, it is equally valid to refer to God as 'Mother' or 'She'. Indeed, they point out that the Bible illustrates God's love by using pictures from motherhood: '*As a mother comforts her child, so will I comfort you*' (Isaiah 66:13; see also 49:15).

We cannot avoid using images and metaphors when describing God. Motherhood suggests compassion, faithfulness and sacrifice – all highly appropriate to the God revealed in the Scriptures. Some advocates of this view also remind us that the word for Spirit in Hebrew (ruach) is feminine and in Greek (pneuma) it is neuter. Neither word is masculine. None of this is new. Anselm, Archbishop of Canterbury from 1093–1109, wrote, '*Jesus … you are gentle with us as a mother with her children.*' In the fourteenth century Mother Julian of Norwich spoke of 'Mother Jesus' and wrote, '*As truly as God is our Father, as truly God is our Mother.*'

In response, opponents of change argue that the concept of the Fatherhood of God is persistent and central in the New Testament and throughout Christian history, and that we are not at liberty to create a new and fashionable 'tradition'. They are concerned, too, that the notion of God as Mother has overtones of paganism and New Age thinking. Some are uncertain and hesitant about these issues. (I recall a conversation with a well-known and controversial bishop who frequently followed the word 'God' with the qualifying phrase, 'He, She or It'!)

The debate is not a 'battle of the sexes'. Men and women are to be found on both sides of the debate (Or, more accurately, all sides of the debate. As with most issues in this section, there are more than two viewpoints.)

Sons or daughters of God?
Some Christians object to 'inclusive' language. For centuries, the word 'men' has been a commonplace for 'all human beings'. This will not do, say the objectors: men are men and women are

women. Some recent versions of the Bible translate 'brothers' as 'brothers and sisters'. Modern liturgical texts are taking these concerns into account by reworking such phrases as 'for us men and our salvation' (in the Nicene Creed) and 'against our fellow men' (in the Confession).

Some also find difficulty with the biblical term 'Sons of God' when referred to women as well as men. They prefer 'children of God', which is also found in the New Testament. Some feminist writers feel the force of all this very keenly. Dorothy McMahon expressed their viewpoint with great clarity:

> *There is no doubt in my mind that women sit in the pews of the churches year after year and fail to hear the gospel. They listen to the Word like observers – they appreciate it, but they never claim it as their own. I believe that sexist language, that which excludes women and offers them only a male image of God, is a salvation issue. To ignore it is to be careless and half-hearted about the communication of the gospel.*

While many men within the Church endorse this viewpoint, some women strongly disagree, arguing vigorously for the retention of traditional language. Once again, advocates and opponents are not divided according to gender.

It remains true that more women than men attend church in the West (in contrast to Islam, where Friday prayers draws large numbers of men). Within the Anglican Church, an increasing number of women are hearing – and heeding – God's call into the ordained ministry.

SEXUALITY

Jesus and women
Contrary to the norms of his society, Jesus appears to have been unmarried. This is an inference from silence; the Bible says nothing definite either way. It is clear that he enjoyed the company of women and that he was at ease with them. As Hans Küng points out, Jesus' attitude to women was in striking contrast to the prevailing attitudes of his day.

Jewish men were advised to talk very little with women, including their own wives. Women were to be withdrawn from public view as far as possible and were required to avoid men's company in public. In the Temple they had access only to the women's forecourt. They were regarded (by Josephus, for example: page 23) as inferior in every respect. Jesus confronted these attitudes. His behaviour on some occasions was regarded as scandalous by many of his contemporaries – for example, when he allowed a prostitute to wash his feet with her tears and wipe them with her hair (Luke 7:36–50).

> 'If you read the Bible through women's eyes you find out that women are really quite prominent. Jesus' attitude to women was quite revolutionary. He treated them entirely on an equal level … I think Paul has been maligned really: I don't think he was as anti-women as he is made out to be.'
> (Dr Pauline Webb)

Christian history

History shows that the Church has often fallen short of Jesus' example. Women came to be regarded as a source of temptation; much was made of Eve's part in Adam's downfall. Sexual intimacy became suspect; virginity and celibacy were exalted. There was a proper reaction against these attitudes in the twentieth century. Sexual intimacy within marriage is now welcomed as a gift from God. The Song of Solomon, a celebration of erotic love in the Old Testament, has come into its own again.

Some argue that the pendulum has swung too far. They assert that traditional Christian values and practices are under attack – from the secular world in which the Church is set *and* from some within the Church itself. One thing is clear: issues of gender and sexuality are high on the agenda. The Anglican bishops debated polygamy at the 1988 Lambeth Conference because this is a live issue in parts of Africa. Marriage, cohabitation and divorce are under debate in the Western churches.

The notion of a celibate priesthood is often criticized from within the Roman Catholic Church. But the Vatican shows no signs of yielding to this pressure, even though one estimate suggests that around 20 per cent of priests marry and therefore cannot function as priests, and many would-be priests choose work where celibacy is not a requirement.

Homosexuality

This is another matter which challenges many churches. Some Christians argue that a homosexual orientation is 'given' by nature and, therefore, by God. All agree that promiscuity is wrong (whether heterosexual or homosexual). But in their view, faithful, loving relationships are blessed by God, whatever the gender of the parties. Others strongly disagree. From certain Bible passages (few, they would concede, but in their view decisive) they argue that same-sex genital acts are sinful. Those with a homosexual orientation are welcome within the Church, but their calling is to sexual abstinence.

Both viewpoints were expressed (strongly) during the 1998 Lambeth Conference of Anglican Bishops. In general, bishops from the developing countries tended to be against homosexual practice; many Western bishops took a more liberal stance. The resolution was worded in cautious terms, and drafted along traditional lines. The media continued to focus on this issue during the 2008 Lambeth Conference, despite a very wide Conference agenda.

Not all Churches and faith communities are riven by open debate. Homosexuality is a crime in many Islamic countries – carrying the death penalty in some. The firm official line taken by the Roman Catholic Church rules out the debate raging openly within the Anglican Communion. But this does not mean there are no gay Muslims or Catholics, and some are brave enough to express dissenting views.

It is clear that this issue could tear the Anglican Communion in two, despite the heroic efforts of Rowan Williams, the 104th Archbishop of Canterbury. But perhaps it is not homosexuality *per se* which is dividing the Communion. Rather it is the underlying question of the way in which the Bible should be interpreted and applied in the twentieth-first century. **Note:** *Rowan Williams speaks about this in a wide-ranging conversation on the CD* 'Rowan Revealed' (www.yorkcourses.co.uk).

10 THINGS TO REMEMBER

1 Today's Church is marked by many 'movements', each with a distinctive emphasis.

2 The ecumenical movement attempts to increase understanding and fellowship between churches with differing histories and approaches to the Christian faith.

3 In Britain, relations between local churches of different denominations are often warm and marked by strong co-operation.

4 Liberation theology emerged in Latin America in the 1960s. It stresses that the God of the Bible sides with the downtrodden and marginalized.

5 'Fundamentalism' is found in all religions – and even within atheism. It is marked by dogmatism and a refusal to work closely with those of a different mindset.

6 While some fundamentalists are dangerous extremists, most are good, law-abiding citizens.

7 There is widespread 'Pentecostal' influence within many modern churches and denominations – sometimes called the 'charismatic movement'.

8 Recent decades have seen a sharp emphasis on lay ministry. Christian leadership is not just for the clergy.

9 Increasingly, Christians are keen to ensure that language (including language used in worship) is 'inclusive'.

10 Attitudes to homosexuality continue to be divisive within the worldwide Church.

14

Church and society

In this chapter you will learn:
- *about the Church under persecution*
- *about modern Christian initiatives*
- *about Christianity and other faiths.*

In modern Britain

David (19): 'The first person I saw commit a murder was my dad. I was seven. In all, I've seen around 15 people murdered. A boy I was friends with borrowed a CD and one of my shirts and didn't bother to give me them back. So I broke into his house and stabbed him while he was asleep ... I got out of it because I was given a chance. I was raised all my life to think I was worthless. But then, when I was living in a shared house, there was another family from Mauritius. They knew I wasn't really all right. They took me to church and that's how I learned a lot more about morals and remorse. The pastors helped me a lot. A lot of middle-class people think that youths are unreachable, but that's not the case – these 13- and 14-year-old boys are scared, they are looking for guidance and they're going to anyone who can provide it, whether that's a 30-year-old gang leader or a 20-year-old church member. That's why I love the family. They couldn't even speak English, but they still managed to help me. They took a chance and said, "I'm not going to judge you."'

From the earliest days the Church has needed to work out its position in relation to society. At first it was a minority group, often persecuted. The small but growing band of disciples developed a distinctive lifestyle based on love for God and neighbour, and witness to their risen Lord, within a suspicious and hostile society. They recalled the vivid images used by Jesus; they were to be 'salt', 'light' and 'peacemakers' within their communities.

A radical change took place when the Emperor Constantine embraced the Christian faith in AD 312 (Chapter 15). No longer outlawed or marginalized, Christians had to learn how to wield secular power. There were attempts to turn back the clock. The pagan Emperor Julian ('the Apostate', c. 331–363) wished his subjects to honour his gods and worked hard to bring this about. He failed, and in a moving testimony he paid tribute to the power of Christian love. It is a clear example of the Christian faith at its best, making an impact on society. Julian referred to Christian believers as 'atheists' and 'godless Galileans', for they worshipped one invisible God and denied his gods.

> *Atheism [i.e. Christian faith] has been specially advanced through the loving service rendered to strangers, and through their care for the burial of the dead. It is a scandal that there is not a single Jew who is a beggar, and that the godless Galileans care not only for their own poor but for ours as well; while those who belong to us look in vain for the help that we should render them.*

Power and persecution

Jesus came 'not to be served but to serve'. At the Last Supper he washed his disciples' feet as an example of humble service (John 13:15). But the Church has not always stayed close to its Founder's intentions. In its strength the Church has often betrayed its Lord. This is partly due to the fact that Christians share the prejudices and many of the assumptions to be found in every culture and period of history. It has also resulted from corruption within the Church. Men far from the Spirit of Christ, and with little regard for the teaching of Christ, nevertheless found positions of power within the Church of Christ. As a result, the impact of the Church on Society has sometimes been harmful.

But the Church itself has been subject to tyranny. Over the centuries Christians have had to work out how to live under a range of repressive regimes. Should they seek to co-exist or to resist? In the twentieth century, the Church in Europe found itself in the shadow of two especially hostile ideologies.

Nazism

Like many politicians and ordinary citizens, Church leaders found it difficult to see the shape of things to come, when Hitler took power. Within the Roman Catholic Church, leadership was sometimes weak and uncertain. But some bishops and priests stood firm and several were martyred. The Catholic dean of the cathedral at Berlin, Lichtenberg, protested from his pulpit against the persecution of Jews; he died on the way to a concentration camp. Opposition by Church leaders caused Hitler to drop his 'euthanasia for incurables' plan. And 'Pope Pius XII secretly allowed himself to be used as a channel of communication between the German conspirators against Hitler and the British government' (Professor Owen Chadwick).

Among German Protestants, the Confessing Church opposed the Nazi regime. The Lutheran pastor Martin Niemöller (page 61) was a leading member who was imprisoned in a concentration camp by Hitler in 1937. He refused offers of conditional release and stayed there until 1945. Dietrich Bonhoeffer was another important figure (page 21). Tragically, he was executed by the Nazis just before the end of the Second World War.

> **The resistance of the Confessing Church to the policies of Hitler continued into and through the war years. It also survived the bitter attack on all opposition and non-conformity, and raised its voice constantly in 2,000 pulpits and in every possible way.**
>
> (E H Robertson)

Marxism

Karl Marx (1813–83) declared religion to be 'the opium of the people' because it could be used by the wealthy to exploit the poor, by promising better things in the world to come. Following the Russian Revolution of 1917 the Church entered turbulent waters as it came under an atheist dictatorship. Some 8000 priests and nuns were assassinated during Lenin's lifetime. Under Stalin (1879–1953) it was difficult for Christians in the USSR even to meet for worship.

Subsequent leaders proved little better – especially those with a KGB (secret police) background. There was tension in Communist lands between those Christians who felt that they should oppose an atheistic regime, and those who believed that it was possible to make an uneasy alliance with the State (pages 217–8).

Christians in China and especially North Korea continue to face the problems arising from following Christ in an officially atheistic state. Despite this, as we have seen (page 218), there is clear evidence that the Church in China is growing rapidly.

Insight

The relationship between the Church and the society in which it is set has swung like a pendulum. In some situations (e.g. sixteenth-century Europe) the Church exercised immense power. In other situations it has been fiercely persecuted, for example by Hitler, in the USSR and in North Korea today.

Christian initiatives

Today in the West, the Church wields influence rather than power. Individual believers have to take a stance with reference to 'the world'. Some see the secular world as essentially evil; in their view the Church is called to be an active counter-culture. Most believers have a more favourable attitude towards secular power, seeking to work for the Kingdom of God in the midst of the kingdoms of this world. They are willing to consider individual issues on their merits and wish to work with all people of good will, regardless of creed.

Sadly, the churches have often lacked urgency and vision. But in nineteenth-century England individual Christians were at the forefront of those who opposed the slave trade (William Wilberforce) and regulated working hours for children (Lord Shaftesbury). A wide range of other issues exercised Christian consciences: the treatment of mental illness (also Lord Shaftesbury); chimney boys and effective drains (Charles Kingsley); nursing methods (Florence Nightingale); prison reform (Elizabeth Fry); social conditions in the fast growing towns and cities (William Booth).

Individual Christians were deeply involved in the care of children, many of whom were homeless in Victorian England. Most successful was 'Dr' Barnardo, in whose name homes for children have been established around the world. Other distinguished organizations which were started then and continue to serve children now, are the Children's Society (Anglican), the National Children's Homes (Methodist), Spurgeon's Homes (Baptist) and Müller Homes (Christian Brethren).

Modern critics of Victorian values can be harsh, and those early reformers are certainly not above criticism. It is also true that many other Christians lacked their vision and that some non-Christians made a vital contribution to a range of reforms: Christians do not claim a monopoly on compassion and justice. But many of the initiatives outlined above were visionary and desperately needed. Lord Clark (not himself a Christian at that time) in *Civilization* described Wilberforce and Shaftesbury as two of the greatest names in the history of humanitarianism. Of Elizabeth Fry, he wrote that her *'spiritual influence on the prisoners at Newgate was really a miracle'*.

Insight

The impact of the Church on society has been enormous. The Church founded universities and hospitals in mediaeval Europe and pioneered schools in Victorian Britain. Throughout Europe, Protestant Christianity gave rise to the liberal democratic state.

The impact upon society of Christian individuals and groups continued into the twentieth century. Christian Socialists like Archbishop William Temple helped prepare for Britain's Welfare State (page 340) and many modern caring agencies have Christian origins, as follows.

Samaritans began as a result of the concern of an Anglican rector in London. Chad Varah became aware that a large number of people were in despair and suicidal. He invited them to ring Mansion House 9000. Within 20 years this telephone ministry of listening and befriending had grown into an international movement.

Shelter is an influential pressure group for good housing in Britain. It began on 1 December 1966 as the result of the united concern of five housing organizations, three of which contained the word Catholic, Christian or Church. Christian leaders were key figures in those early days and Shelter's first chairman, Bruce Kenrick, was a Christian minister.

Habitat for Humanity is an American initiative which builds subsidized homes for needy families in the USA. It has also pioneered 'appropriate technology' homes in other continents and countries (Tanzania, for example).

Several Christian organizations work among refugees and in areas struck by famine, drought and endemic poverty. In addition to bringing emergency aid, many of these organizations seek to influence long-term policy. Christian missionaries have a record of distinction in the fields of education (as witnessed by Nelson Mandela: page 268) and medicine, especially in the fight against leprosy (Matthew 10:8).

The Hospice Movement was started in Britain under the inspiration of Dame Cicely Saunders. She pioneered pain control and saw the need for small, intimate units, where terminally ill patients could be cared for and families and friends welcomed. Dame Cicely gladly acknowledged that without the inspiration and power of Jesus Christ, she would have lacked the strength needed to establish the movement. Her vision and practical ideas caught on and hospices are now found around the world.

Insight

Christians have founded many well-known modern caring organizations. These include Shelter, Samaritans, Save the Children, Amnesty International and the Hospice movement. These are not 'Christian organizations' but welcome people of all faiths and none, as volunteers and as clients.

Amnesty International was founded by Peter Benenson, a Christian lawyer. Concerned at the plight of prisoners of conscience, he prayed in the crypt of St Martin-in-the-Fields in London's Trafalgar Square. He developed the idea of a network of people who would write to, and about, prisoners of conscience, and speak on their behalf. At a practical level, the existing network of churches was important. Peter Benenson launched the movement on Trinity Sunday 1961 to emphasize 'that the power of the Holy Spirit works to bring together people of diverse origins by influencing their common conscience'.

> *When the first 200 letters came, the guards gave me back my clothes. When the next 200 letters came, the prison Director came to see me. When the next pile of letters arrived, the Director got in touch with his superior. The letters kept arriving, and the President was informed. The letters still kept arriving, and the President called the prison and told them to let me go.*
>
> (From a letter by a former prisoner of conscience)

The above movements are not limited to Christian believers. In most cases a wide range of views and beliefs are to be found among their activists. But it remains true that these organizations were built on Christian foundations, with Christian vision and energy.

Church and Society today

Many Christians are regularly involved in voluntary community service outside the Church. In 2006 their contribution was calculated as amounting to some 23.2 million hours of community service. 'Churches and other faith-based organizations represent a formidable proportion of the voluntary sector in Britain.'

(Professor Elaine Graham)

Church schools account for one-quarter of all primary schools in England. Of the 100 top scoring English schools in 2007, 40 were C of E and 20 were RC foundations. Speaking in November 2007, Lord Adonis, the Schools Minister, said, 'Strong evidence from OFSTED (Office for Standards in Education) pointed to the contribution of C of E schools in disadvantaged communities.'

Secondary schools with a religious foundation contribute more to community cohesion than other schools, according to an independent study of OFSTED inspection data published in November 2009. They outperform even 'community schools' in this respect, and also in tackling inequality and discrimination.

The media in modern Britain often depict the Church as a rather sad, dying cause. While it's true that numbers of church-attenders declined during the twentieth-century, many Christians do not recognize the picture that is often painted. Many churches are growing and new congregations are regularly planted. There is plenty of energy for new initiatives such as Nightstop UK (page 344) and Street Pastors (see below).

In 2007, 2.7 million people in Britain attended a Church of England Christmas service, compared with about 1.2 million in a typical week. Over 4.4 million Britons went shopping online on Christmas Day.

Street pastors: This initiative was pioneered in London in 2003 by the black Pentecostal pastor Les Isaac. Representatives from churches go into city centres across Britain at 'binge drinking' time, armed with compassion – and flip-flops! They offer practical care to distressed young people. Police and local councils have been warm in their praise for such initiatives, which make city centres safer at night. Street Pastors have received numerous civic awards (www.streetpastors.co.uk).

A focus for dissent

The Christian Church has often been a natural focus for dissent against established authority. In the twentieth century this was extremely important in many places and for many issues.

Martin Luther King (1929–68)

Few individuals are honoured shortly after death by the creation of an annual public holiday in their name. This honour marked the achievements of Martin Luther King – Pastor of Ebenezer Baptist Church in Atlanta. By personal charisma, courage, brilliant organization and moving rhetoric, he led a massive non-violent movement in an attempt to establish equality for black citizens in the USA. The achievements of the civil rights movement were considerable, and related issues (such as positive discrimination) are still on the political agenda in the USA. Like Gandhi, upon whom he based his campaign of non-violent resistance, Dr King was assassinated.

The Berlin Wall

As Marxism came to a swift end throughout Europe in the late 1980s, the Christian churches were a natural rallying point for dissent from the old order. Large prayer vigils were held, with flickering candles, communal singing and inspiring addresses. The churches in Eastern Europe are finding life in the new order easier (in that they are no longer persecuted) but more complex.

Materialism, commercialism and hedonism may yet prove more corrosive than Marxism. Some Eastern Europeans look back to the old order with nostalgia.

Insight

One example of the Church's impact on Society was the fall of the Berlin Wall in 1989, when prayer meetings and vigils became rallying points for dissent. Other celebrated examples were resistance to apartheid by Archbishop Desmond Tutu and other Christians, and the Civil Rights movement in the USA, led by the Baptist Pastor, Martin Luther King.

South Africa

The old white-dominated order in South Africa claimed to be Christian, and the ruling white party was closely linked with the Dutch Reformed Church. But dissent often found expression in the Christian churches. Best known among black Christian leaders is Archbishop Desmond Tutu (a Nobel Peace Prize winner), but there are many others.

The new democratic South Africa is, thus far, a 'success' story, but there is a long road to travel and levels of violence – a legacy from the days of apartheid – are still extremely high. In his autobiography (*Long Walk to Freedom*) Nelson Mandela is not uncritical of the churches, especially the Dutch Reformed Church. But he speaks affectionately of the church of his childhood: '... *the Church was as concerned with this world as the next: I saw that virtually all of the achievements of Africans seemed to have come about through the missionary work of the Church*'. He pays special tribute to his black Methodist housemaster (the Revd S S Mokitimi) and to Archbishops Trevor Huddleston and Desmond Tutu.

Failure

As with all human endeavours, we find the bad alongside the good. To take just one recent example, no Christian can feel anything but shame when contemplating 'the troubles' in Northern Ireland. This was not essentially a religious conflict; it was about power, tribalism, independence and nationalism. The causes were complex and embedded in history, but the divisions were strongly related to religious allegiance.

Some Christians (e.g. Gordon Wilson) made a distinguished contribution to the peace and prosperity now flourishing in the island of Ireland. But others failed to live up to their high calling to be 'salt' and 'light' in society. Many failed to be peacemakers; some engaged in violence. Of course, not all 'cultural Christians' are active disciples of Jesus Christ. In some situations, terms such as 'Christian militia' are used to distinguish soldiers, terrorists or freedom fighters from those of a different cultural background. The need for careful consideration of 'faith labels' is illustrated by the young man from Ireland who was asked about his religion. 'I'm an agnostic', he replied, 'but I'm a Protestant agnostic'!

A quite different area of failure and disgrace is that of child abuse. A number of priests have been accused of this and some have been found guilty. Church leaders have been accused of a 'cover-up'. This appalling scandal continues to rock the worldwide Catholic Church (see page 223).

In December 2002 Cardinal Bernard Law was forced to resign as Archbishop of Boston (USA) as a result of losing the confidence of the Catholic laity and priests. He was accused of protecting priests known to have abused children. In February 2010 Pope Benedict XVI convened a two-day summit with 24 Irish bishops at the Vatican, following two damning reports published in 2009 (the Murphy and Ryan Reports), and the subsequent resignation of Irish bishops involved in a long-term 'cover-up'. The Pope called this sexual abuse 'a heinous crime' and 'a grave sin which offends God and wounds the dignity of the human person'. Almost every Church now has a policy of openness, with child protection measures in place. (For a happier scenario from childhood, featuring Sir Alec Guinness, see page 104.)

Current issues

Insight

In modern Britain, state and Church are sometimes in conflict over key ethical matters. But Christians do not speak with one voice. The Roman Catholic stance on contraception and (to a lesser extent) abortion is rejected by many other Christians.

The pace of change continues to accelerate and new ethical questions are surfacing all the time. In this section we shall touch upon a few of the most pressing issues facing society and consider the Christian response – or in most cases, the Christian responses. As we shall see, with the possible exception of the Roman Catholic Church, there is a solid Christian 'party line' on very few issues. In the Western churches in particular, lively debate is often regarded as a healthy sign. Christians are encouraged to work things out for themselves on the basis of:

▶ *principles drawn from the Bible and Christian tradition – giving special attention to compassion and justice*
▶ *prayerful dependence upon the Holy Spirit*
▶ *consultation and discussion based on up-to-date information*
▶ *pragmatic implications.*

The Churches have been energetic in thinking and acting on a wide range of issues. At international and national levels the Churches have eminent Christian specialists, with a wide range of expertise, upon whom they can call. But concern is also shown at the local level. For example, several Roman Catholic churches have a 'justice and peace' group. And in many British cities and towns Christians have practical schemes to help homeless people (e.g. Nightstop UK for vulnerable young people).

Detailed consideration of these issues would require at least a book, if not a series! Here we can do no more than note some of them and briefly consider a few – to give some idea of the way in which Christians approach these questions. Over the past few decades, the Churches have been involved in debate about the following:

- *can there be a 'just war' in a nuclear age?*
- *terrorism: is a freedom fighter a criminal or a soldier?*
- *the expanding world population: food, water and other resources, world trade and third world debt*
- *ecology, climate change and the integrity of creation*
- *the welfare of children; women's rights; female circumcision*
- *gambling; the use and abuse of alcohol/drugs; animal rights*
- *human sexuality, including homosexuality*
- *human fertility: the status and protection of the human embryo; abortion; stem-cell research*
- *bio-ethics: DNA, cloning, 'designer babies'; organ donation*
- *marriage, cohabitation, polygamy, divorce and the family*
- *HIV/AIDS; assisted suicide/euthanasia*
- *life in a multicultural and multifaith society.*

This list could be extended. We will briefly consider four issues: abortion, contraception, euthanasia and Christian attitudes to other faiths.

An issue often in the news – and sometimes in the law courts – is whether the Christian faith any longer has a public role, or whether it should be confined to the sphere of private preference. Advocates for public influence point out that European law and custom is based on Judeo-Christian ethics, including the Ten Commandments. Opponents urge that this is no longer relevant in what they see as a secular society. Writing in 2010 John Atherton summed up like this: 'We are now living in an emerging post-secular world. It is a world in which two contrasting views jostle for power: on the one hand, the secularization position held by many in government, media and universities, that religion, especially Christianity, is dying, and should be relegated to the private world of individuals and churches; and, on the other hand, the growing significance of religion globally and in the UK, and its claim to take a full part in public as well as private life.'

As the world at large debates this issue, so do the Churches. Some Christians are 'pro-choice'. They see abortion as a question of women's rights. They argue that the main focus must be upon the woman rather than upon the embryo, which they see as no more than a potential human being. But many Christians strongly disagree; they are pro-life rather than pro-choice. The Roman Catholic Church and the 'Christian Right' (i.e. conservative Christians, especially in the USA) in particular, have taken a strong stance. They argue that life is God-given and that a human being is brought into existence at conception, not at birth.

To this issue they apply the Bible's emphasis on care for the vulnerable. In the Old Testament, protection for powerless people (widows, orphans and strangers) is emphasized. Nothing is more vulnerable and less able to defend itself than a fetus. So the Church must fight on behalf of the unborn child. Those who perform abortions are called 'baby-murderers'. The notion that a woman has the right to choose what she does with her own body (the pro-choice stance) is dismissed on the grounds that the fetus is an independent life, not simply a disposable organ of the mother. With medical advances the question of the viability of the fetus becomes more important – and with it the stage in the pregnancy at which an abortion might be legally (if not morally) acceptable.

For some, the rights of the fetus are absolute. Others would make exceptions for exceptional cases, such as pregnancies resulting from rape or incest, and those which threaten the mother's life.

For many other Christians, pragmatic considerations are decisive. To make abortion illegal would not stop abortions; it would drive the practice onto the backstreets. Illegal operations would endanger desperate, vulnerable women – especially teenagers. Christians who take this stance argue that abortion should remain legal – but kept under careful review. This is the view of Lord (David) Steel. He was the Christian MP who, in 1967, introduced the Private Member's Bill which legalized abortion in Britain.

- *In Britain there were some 600 legal abortions carried out each day in 2007.*
- *Worldwide, according to a 2007 report in* The Lancet, *there are some 20 million unsafe abortions carried out each year.*

CONTRACEPTION

This sharply divides the Churches. The official teaching of the Roman Catholic Church is that all contraception is wrong, apart from abstinence and the use of the 'rhythm method' (tuning into a woman's monthly cycle). Leaders of the Roman Catholic Church argue that it is sinful for mere mortals to interfere with God's sovereign will by preventing conception in any other way. Sexual intercourse should always carry with it the possibility of procreation. '… each and every marriage act must remain open to the transmission of life' (CCC: 1994). Most other Churches strongly disagree on four grounds:

1 *Population explosion is a major issue. It is irresponsible to encourage large families – especially in the 'developing world' (a term often used for the world's poorest countries, which masks the fact that some nations are growing poorer).*
2 *Responsible stewardship requires adults to plan their families according to their means, their preferences and their health.*
3 *Sexual intimacy within marriage is good in itself; the fact that it need no longer be linked with the possibility of conception is to be welcomed with thanksgiving.*
4 *HIV/AIDS is an immense problem. Its spread is more likely to be stemmed by widespread use of condoms than by unrealistic calls for sexual abstinence.*

It is evident that even within the Roman Catholic Church, private judgement on this matter is widespread. In Italy, some 80 per cent of the population claims to be Roman Catholic. But Italy has a very low birth rate. This illustrates the fact that one strand of Christian ethics acknowledges the supremacy of the individual Christian's conscience – even over official Church teaching.

While these two issues are clearly related, it is the call for legalized assisted suicide ('aid in dying') that grows ever stronger in Britain. Some celebrities have added their voice to this – Sir Terry Pratchett, in his 2010 BBC Richard Dimbley Lecture, is one example.

Advances in medical science have made it possible to prolong the lives of very sick people. Some individuals live on in a coma ('persistent vegetative state' or PVS) for years. Should such people be kept alive artificially for long periods, or is this a case for 'mercy killing' (euthanasia)? Many people are clear that the answer is 'Yes'. Others point out that some individuals thought to be beyond recovery have resumed an active life. In February 2010, research using MRI scanning showed that some people apparently in a prolonged coma can, in fact, play 'mental tennis'. It seems that they are in a 'locked-in state' – mentally aware but unable to communicate.

Christians urge that a human being remains a human being – even in a PVS. And every human being has a right to food, drink and air. Many believe that to withhold nutrition is wrong, while acknowledging the extreme difficulty of making wise and compassionate judgements in such circumstances. Such debates are new. Until late in the twentieth century this was not an issue. Victims would have died because of inadequate knowledge and technology – a clear illustration of the way in which advances in medical science raise new ethical issues. Few people believe that very sick people should be kept alive by all possible means. But improvements in medical care mean that, in the developed world, most people live much longer than hitherto. Clearly this is good news, but not for everyone; it does mean that some people live for long periods in severe ill health, pain and distress. From this springs the desire to legalize assisted suicide – to make possible an 'easy death' for those who request this. The Netherlands, Belgium and Switzerland have already passed such legislation (which includes strict controls).

Christians have sympathy with this viewpoint and some have felt the force of it within their own families. But while some Christians support the growing call to legalize assisted suicide in Britain, many are against this. Rather more would be against legalizing euthanasia. The differing views within the Church echo divisions within the nation as a whole. The Christian response is based on theological principles and practical considerations.

- ▶ The sanctity of life: *which is a gift from God.*
- ▶ Concern: *that human beings should not 'play God' in matters of life and death.*
- ▶ Compassion: *on a practical level, the hospice movement (pioneered by the lay Christian Cicely Saunders) has made enormous advances in pain control. And it has helped countless patients, and their families, to face death.*
- ▶ Care for the vulnerable: *the unintended outcome of such legislation might be counterproductive, causing widespread distress for sick and elderly people. It is a short step from legalizing assisted suicide to causing elderly people to wonder if they have a duty to die, in case they are (perhaps unwittingly) a burden on their families.*
- ▶ Human sinfulness: *although most advocates of euthanasia have good motives, society is not to be trusted with such a fundamental change in the law. Those who argue against euthanasia on these grounds (as did Dame Cicely Saunders), sometimes point to abortion. What began as carefully worded legislation for hard cases has virtually become 'abortion on demand' in some societies. Slopes can be slippery and steep.*

'Euthanasia is not something for which I can make a case; in a way I wish it were otherwise… Once the law has changed on this there's bound to be pressure – social and economic pressure – on people who are being told that their existence is now superfluous… Some of the pressure about euthanasia comes not so much from a question of pain as from a sense of uselessness. That's where Christianity has something to say. As long as you are an object of love – to God and others – then you can't simply be written off as superfluous to requirements.'

(Archbishop Rowan Williams in *New World, Old Faith*, www.yorkcourses.co.uk)

One world, many faiths

It is impossible to consider the Church in society without giving thought to the various Christian responses to other faiths. We are accustomed to the notion of a 'global village'. Through travel and television, we have insights into other nations and cultures which were impossible before the middle of the twentieth century. As a result, many people have some acquaintance with a few of the world's various religions.

For the most part these are situated in clearly identifiable cultural blocs. Burma is predominantly Buddhist; Saudi Arabia and Pakistan are strongly Muslim; India is predominantly Hindu, with some Buddhists, Muslims, Christians and others; Europe has its roots in Christianity. Some Western nations experienced a great cultural mix during the twentieth century. Many immigrants came to Britain in the 1950s, 1960s and 1970s – and they naturally wished to keep their own culture and religion. Christians from the West Indies often found traditional British Christianity rather reserved, so they formed Black Churches. Muslims and other faith or ethnic groups established communities in certain urban areas, such as Bradford, Birmingham, Leicester and Southall.

> Today Britain is home to many faiths, but I hope it doesn't lose its own – the Christian faith that inspired its greatest poetry, its finest architecture, and its bravest battles in defence of freedom.
>
> (Chief Rabbi, Sir Jonathan Sacks)

In relation to Britain's population (60 million and rising – and ageing), the number of adherents of non-Christian faiths is relatively small. Some towns and cities have many temples, gurdwaras, synagogues and mosques to cater for Hindus, Sikhs, Jews, Muslims and others. The total number following faiths other than Christianity in Britain is about 8 per cent – a figure that is growing. Some Christians are keenly aware of the need to understand other faiths and to communicate across cultural and religious boundaries. Indeed, many commentators see constructive interfaith dialogue and environmental issues as two of the most pressing issues facing modern civilization. The need for dialogue between the great faiths is seen as even more pressing in the light of the events of 11 September 2001 and 7 July 2005 (see page 243).

Multicultural discussion is often focused on social concerns – on issues such as racism, policing and education. But sooner or later members of different faith groups must tackle questions of ultimate truth. How much do the different religions have in common? Indeed, are all religions really saying the same thing? If not, can they all be true? As Christians have grappled with the relationship of Christianity to other faiths, three broad responses have emerged.

An exclusive approach

'*God has revealed the Way and the Truth and the Life in Jesus Christ and wills this to be known throughout the world*' (Hendrik Kraemer 1885–1965). Jesus Christ is not merely a teacher or a prophet. He is the Son of God, Lord of Lords and the Word made flesh. He is also *the* Saviour of the world, not one saviour among many.

Some who take this view believe that those who do not turn to Christ will not find salvation – whether or not they have heard the gospel of redemption. From this belief they have found great energy for evangelism and missionary endeavour. 'To save the lost' was a driving force for many Christians during the missionary expansion of the nineteenth century. In the 1830s the Church Missionary Society advertised in London for missionaries for West Africa, warning that life expectancy in the 'white man's grave' was not more than six months. Scores volunteered to go.

Others who hold an exclusive position about Jesus Christ nevertheless take a different view on salvation: the great Swiss theologian Karl Barth (1886–1968) for example. He declared that salvation is only possible through Christ. Christian faith is God's revelation; all other religions are human constructs. However, 'at the end of history… God's grace will triumph completely, and all will come to faith in Christ' (Alister McGrath's summary of Barth's view).

An inclusive approach

The Roman Catholic scholar Karl Rahner argued that Christianity is unique and absolute, for Jesus Christ is the self-revelation of God. But God's will is that all should be saved (1 Timothy 2:4). So Rahner maintained that despite their shortcomings, non-Christian religions are capable of mediating the saving grace of God to their members. Faithful followers of other faiths are to be regarded as 'anonymous Christians' – they are saved because they are inspired by Christ, without realizing it. 'More know him (Jesus) than know him by name', as one summary puts it.

Critics of Rahner's view argue that it is 'triumphalistic' – a Christian takeover bid. Others argue that it is the only approach which does justice both to the authentic experience of God to be found in other religions *and* to the Christian conviction that in Jesus, God is revealed in a unique way.

A pluralist approach

John Hick argued for the need to move away from a Christ-centred approach to a God-centred approach. On this view, all religions lead to the same God. Christians have no 'special access': God is universally available through all religions. John Hick's critics argue that his desertion of Christ as a reference point means that he has abandoned any claim to speak from a *Christian* perspective.

As Christians ponder these important questions, the following practical steps are open to us.

> ▶ It is important that in dialogue, the various faiths should be true to themselves. 'Fudging' issues is not helpful. Of course the great world religions have features and teaching in common, especially the three great monotheistic ('Abrahamic') faiths – Judaism, Christianity and Islam. Muslims, for example, honour Jesus as a prophet. But there are fundamental differences too. It is for this reason that some adherents of the various faiths, including Christians, are unenthusiastic about multifaith worship. It leaves too many questions hanging in the air, and too many traditional forms of prayer must be excluded in order to prevent

giving offence. Of course, this does not mean that members of different faiths should not gather together to mark great occasions or terrible tragedies. At such times, shared silence can be very powerful.

▶ No one pretends that dialogue is easy. How can a Muslim progress in conversation with a Christian, when the Muslim believes that Jesus did not die on the Cross, and that the doctrine of the Trinity verges on blasphemy? But conversation is vital, especially as in some parts of the world relations between different faith communities are bound up with land, property, prestige and political power: an explosive mixture. In some countries, with the rise of fundamentalism, relations between Muslims, Hindus and Christians have deteriorated seriously in recent years: a cause for concern and prayer.

▶ It is important, too, that followers of the world's various faiths should accept the best possible representation of religions other than their own. It is too easy to take aberrations as the norm and to allow caricatures of other faiths to form the popular view. Many Muslims are not fundamentalist; not every Hindu is happy with all aspects of the caste system; few Christians endorse the Crusades or the Spanish Inquisition.

Perhaps, in the end, only one thing is more important for the future of our world than interfaith dialogue. And that is inter-faith friendship.

Archbishop Rowan Williams sets before us a Christian approach that marries confidence in the gospel with humility towards those who hold a different viewpoint, or believe a different creed:

'There is a confidence that arises from being utterly convinced that the Christian creed and the Christian vision have in them a life and a richness that can embrace and transfigure all the complexities of human life. This confidence can rightly sit alongside a patient willingness to learn from others in the ordinary encounters of life together in our varied society.'

10 THINGS TO REMEMBER

1 *From the beginning the Church has had an impact on society – and society has had an impact on the Church.*

2 *Over the centuries, Christians have learned to live under repressive regimes, from Roman emperors to Nazi and Communist dictatorships.*

3 *The Church was instrumental in founding the first schools, universities and hospitals.*

4 *When the Church was very powerful, its impact on society was sometimes harmful, e.g. the Crusades and Inquisition.*

5 *According to Professor Basil Mitchell, the liberal democratic state 'owes its existence very largely to Christianity in its Protestant forms'.*

6 *Christians have been instrumental in founding several great caring movements – Samaritans, Shelter, the Hospice movement, Amnesty International, Save the Children ...*

7 *In Britain today, Church schools account for about one quarter of all primary schools.*

8 *Prayer meetings were a crucial focus for dissent from Communism in Eastern Europe, and the destruction of the Berlin Wall in 1989.*

9 *Christians are involved in all the major moral issues of our time, sometimes opposing governments.*

10 *The churches are in dialogue with all the other main world faith communities – at both local and national level.*

Part four
Key events in Church history

15

The first five centuries

In this chapter you will learn:
- **about the birth of the Church**
- **about life in Roman days**
- **about the Church and the Roman Empire.**

Author's note: *Some readers will welcome an outline of the history of the Church. It will, of course, be very sketchy and it will involve some repetition of material contained in previous chapters. But setting ideas and developments within a historical framework will, I hope, be helpful.*

Insight

Within 500 years of Jesus' life the Church had spread and grown. The small group of original disciples, initially demoralized by the death of Jesus, had swelled into a widespread, buoyant, well-organized movement.

The Church is born

The Jewish religion at the time of Jesus was made up of many groups. They disagreed sharply on some issues but all groups owed allegiance to the One God and to the sacred institutions of Law and Sabbath (and most of them to the Temple, too). In those early days following his death and resurrection, all the disciples of Jesus were Jews; they observed the ways of Judaism and often met in the precincts of the Temple in Jerusalem. Their one distinguishing feature was allegiance to Jesus. The opening of The Acts of the Apostles in the New Testament shows a group of about 120, waiting in Jerusalem. They did this in response to an instruction of the risen Christ, just before his ascension into heaven (Luke 24:49).

PENTECOST

The Feast of Pentecost was an important Jewish Festival which brought many visitors – Jews from various countries (the 'Diaspora') – to Jerusalem. The disciples of Jesus were 'all together in one place' when God's Holy Spirit came upon them. The result was a noisy and undignified exhibition. There were 'tongues of fire', a strong wind, and an ability to speak 'in other tongues as the Spirit enabled them' (Acts 2:4).

A crowd gathered. The confusion was so great that some cynics accused them of being drunk. Peter took the opportunity to preach. He drew on the Jewish Scriptures, explaining that the words of the prophet Joel had just been fulfilled: '*In the last days, God says, I will pour out my Spirit…*' (Acts 2:17; Joel 2:28). He went on to assert that:

- *Jesus, a descendant of King David, had been raised from the dead by God*
- *God had made him 'both Lord and Christ' (Messiah)*
- *He is now seated at God's right hand*
- *Their own nation had crucified this Jesus*
- *They could be forgiven through repentance and baptism.*

About 3000 responded.

A famous New Testament passage (Acts 2:42–7) describes the lifestyle of those early followers of Jesus.

The main features were:
- the Apostles' teaching
- supportive fellowship
- breaking bread together
- prayer
- sharing possessions
- joyfulness.

PERSECUTION

Throughout this period there were many outstanding leaders such as John the apostle, James the Lord's brother, Barnabas the missionary, Philip the deacon and Stephen the first martyr. But Peter was the main teacher and leader. This comes as no surprise, because Jesus himself had told Peter that he would be the rock on which Jesus would build his Church (Matthew 16:18).

Future generations of Christians were to draw strength from the fact that Peter was used by God in this way. For according to the Gospel accounts Peter often failed: in particular, he denied Jesus just before the crucifixion (Mark 14:66–72). In describing Peter's failings with such honesty, the Bible assures us that God has a place for the weak as well as the strong; for the coward as well as the hero.

The rapid growth of this new group caused unrest among the Jewish leaders. They thought they had stopped a dangerous movement by crucifying Jesus, but now it seemed stronger than ever. They issued threats; they imprisoned Peter; they stoned Stephen; James, the brother of John, was beheaded by King Herod. But the courage and confidence of these leaders only encouraged others. *Persecution resulted in dispersal. And dispersal meant that the gospel spread far and wide* (Acts 8:4). It spread, not only through the energy and commitment of named leaders, but through the enthusiasm, integrity and love of 'ordinary' believers. For example, the Christians who founded the Church in Rome itself at an early date are unknown to us.

One man, a Roman citizen from Tarsus in Cilicia, took a strong lead in attempting to stop the spread of this new movement. Saul was a Jew of 'the dispersion' – the name given to the many Jews who lived outside Israel. He turned his enormous energy and single-minded determination against the followers of 'the Way', until his famous conversion to Jesus Christ while travelling to Damascus (Acts 9:3–6). The seeds of his conversion may have been sown at the stoning of Stephen, the first Christian martyr.

Saul hated all that Stephen stood for, but it is likely that Stephen's courage and faith made a deep impression upon him.

Following his conversion, Saul of Tarsus became Paul the apostle to the Gentiles. His decision to take the gospel to the Gentiles – to all people regardless of race or rank – was of the utmost importance. Indeed, Paul would not have called it a 'decision'. It was, he claimed, a task given to him by God. Paul's dynamic energy, his single-minded vision, his brilliance as a debater, his persistence as a pastor and letter writer, and his courage as a traveller, ensured that the gospel was preached in many countries around the Mediterranean before he died (probably executed in Rome under the Emperor Nero in AD 65).

Insight

The growth of the Church was based on the attractive lifestyle of the early Christian believers. They became a strong 'counter-cultural' movement – practising love and forgiveness in a world marked by harsh repression and revenge.

CROSSING BOUNDARIES

At first it was Jews who joined this new movement. But soon Gentiles (a term for all non-Jews) were converted to Christ, in Antioch in Syria where believers were first called 'Christians'. Gentiles presented the young Church with major problems. Should it be preaching to non-Jews at all? In a remarkable vision, God made it abundantly clear to Peter that Gentiles should be incorporated into the Church (Acts 10; page 102). But then came another issue. Was it necessary to become a Jew before following the Jewish Messiah? Should Gentiles who wanted to join the Church be required to convert to Judaism first – by embracing the Jewish Law, including dietary rules and the practice of circumcision?

The answer of Paul, the great missionary strategist and theologian, was 'No'. This was highly contentious for many Jewish Christians. They had simply never imagined that it might be possible to follow the one true God, except by being a devout Jew. The key contention of Paul was that salvation was a release from 'law'. Being a Christian was a matter of being 'saved', or put right with God, through faith in Jesus Christ and what he has done. God's grace was central. This being so, nothing else could contribute to salvation. So it seemed both unnecessary and misleading to expect Gentiles to be circumcized. A great controversy ensued. This led to the Council of Jerusalem in about AD 49, at which the views of Peter, Paul and Barnabas (endorsed by James), triumphed (Acts 15).

These very early events in the life of the Church were momentous in ensuring that Christianity crossed national, cultural and social boundaries. A different decision would have meant that the 'Jesus movement' remained as one strand within Judaism, with little potential for growth.

This kind of problem was to recur frequently: the need for the Church to distinguish between the core tradition and matters of cultural or religious addition. The latter may be good in themselves but are not essential to the gospel. They can become subtly dangerous, standing in place of the message of salvation through Christ. And they can be used by one group in the Church to impose its authority over another.

REMEMBERING THE STORY

It thus became a matter of the utmost importance to have a record of the life and teaching of Jesus, as a touchstone in debate. The four Gospels were completed in the last 40 years of the first century (some scholars would date them rather earlier). The Evangelists – Matthew, Mark, Luke and John – were interpreters, or 'portrait painters', who wanted the authentic voice of Jesus to be heard.

As the apostles and their successors died, and as the challenge of heretics became more acute, it was necessary to define what was to count as authoritative Scripture. Which books focusing on Jesus should be regarded as Holy Scripture ('New Testament'), alongside the Jewish Scriptures ('Old Testament')? The broad outlines of an answer to this pressing question were quickly established (Chapters 4 and 5).

Confronting heresy and division

Meanwhile, as the first century wore on, the Church continued to expand rapidly because of:

- ▸ *the significance of the gospel of God's love shown in Jesus Christ*
- ▸ *the power of the Holy Spirit*
- ▸ *the attractive lifestyle of ordinary Christians*
- ▸ *the vision and energy of Christian leaders.*

Growth sometimes took place in the teeth of fierce persecution. This was sporadic and local; there was no official Imperial policy because the early Christian movement was insignificant to those who governed the Roman Empire. So the Church had a vital breathing space in which to develop policies and structures to deal with its own internal problems – particularly heresy and schism.

Heresy

This is already detectable in the New Testament period. It was evident in the Church in Corinth, where knowledge and spiritual gifts were thought to be more important than love; and in Colossae, where angels were worshipped. These are two of the cluster of Greek ideas which characterize Gnosticism – a term which comes from the Greek word for knowledge (*Gnosis*). Gnostics believed that there was an esoteric, secret knowledge available to some, which would enable them to pass beyond the present evil world and achieve salvation. 'Christian' Gnostics saw Jesus as the redeemer but argued that he could not possibly have taken our material, human flesh, which they considered to be evil. Gnosticism is a word which covers a wide range of ideas, many of which presented a considerable threat to genuine Christianity. The Church's defence against heresy was threefold:

- ▸ *heretics were disciplined and sometimes excommunicated*
- ▸ *the spiritual riches of the Christian faith were explored more deeply*
- ▸ *a renewed emphasis was placed on sound, effective teaching.*

Church leaders insisted that the gospel was not a secret way available only to some, as the Gnostics believed. It was open to all. Hence the importance of:

▶ *a grasp of the basics (creeds)*
▶ *authoritative sources (New Testament Scriptures)*
▶ *sound teaching (a recognized ministry).*

In the New Testament there is no prescribed structure for ministry in the Church. But during the second century a pattern of authorized ministry developed, which came to be widely accepted. This had a threefold order: deacon, priest (or presbyter) and bishop.

Schism

Breaking away from other Christians usually resulted from dissatisfaction with the spirituality, order or discipline within the Church. As the Church became more structured, there was a loss of fervour and distinctiveness. As it was 'institutionalized' it became more concerned with consolidation than with advance; more concerned with the definition of office than with the spontaneity of shared gifts. Some Christians resisted this.

In the second half of the second century Montanus began to prophesy, speaking in 'tongues' in Phrygia. His followers included two women, Prisca and Maximilla. Montanists reacted against the perceived intellectualism, formalism, compromise and authority of the official Church. They included at least one outstanding theologian, namely Tertullian (*c.* 160–*c.* 220). This movement raised an important question: how far does authority lie with those who hold office within the Church? And how far does it lie with prophets who claim a direct 'word' from the Holy Spirit – a word which sometimes goes beyond anything which the tradition allows?

Insight

Anonymous Christians, as well as Church leaders, were confronted by many difficult problems. These included harsh persecution from without, and coping with heresy and division within the Church.

Christianity and culture

Other controversies arose. There were those who regarded the State as the abode of Satan. They saw martyrdom as the highest honour – a means of immediate fellowship with Christ in heaven. But others looked forward to a time when the dominant culture would understand and accept Christ. The former were world-renouncing; the latter world-affirming. The latter presented the Christian message in a way which was sympathetic to the dominant Greek culture. Their most important representative was Justin Martyr (*c.*100–*c.*165).

The growing impact of Christianity is evident from the fact that a leading pagan intellectual called Celsus published a sharp attack upon it (*c.* 178). This, in turn, was countered by a great Christian theologian, Origen (*c.*185–*c.*254). He was the outstanding representative of '*a new tradition, that of the sophisticated Christian scholar who could match any pagan philosopher*' (David Bosch).

ORDINARY LIFE

Then, as now, the real test of Christianity is to be found in ordinary homes, towns and local churches. What was it like to be a Christian in those early days?

There were many distinguishing features. While pagan men slept with their slave girls as of right, Christian husbands were expected to be faithful to their wives. Attitudes to children were markedly different too: Christians opposed the killing of unwanted babies by exposure, actively rescuing foundlings. They deplored abortion, putting it on a level with infanticide.

Sex appears to have caused unease within the Church, as it did in later centuries. The Bible celebrates erotic love in The Song of Solomon. But by the mid-second century, the apocryphal Acts of John felt it necessary to present St John as a life-long virgin. Around AD 400, 'Jerome was confident that even married apostles lived in mutual continence, after the example of their unmarried Lord and his ever virgin mother' (Henry Chadwick).

From early days, Christians were reticent to become soldiers. The vivid military imagery in the New Testament is about spiritual warfare. One aspect of this battle was against poverty. The Church sought to protect widows and orphans, and provide hospices for the sick. By AD 250 the Roman Church was feeding 1,500 distressed persons; late in the fourth century the Church in Syrian Antioch had feeding programmes for 3,000, complete with a register of names (page 297).

Perhaps the most remarkable feature of Church life was the way in which, at its best, it overcame barriers of race, class and gender. *'There is neither Jew nor Greek, slave nor free, male nor female, for you are all one in Christ Jesus'*, wrote St Paul (Galatians 3:28). Slaves sang hymns with slave owners. Some women, such as Lydia and Priscilla (Acts 16 & 18), played a leading role in church life.

Coming to terms with the Roman Empire

Insight

In AD 306, the young Constantine was declared Emperor by his troops in York. Two pivotal moments occurred when he embraced the Christian faith, and then declared religious toleration in the Edict of Milan (313). Very soon the Church was no longer a persecuted minority, but a powerful force within the Roman Empire.

As the Church grew, persecutions were more sustained. Those in the third and early fourth centuries were particularly severe, culminating in the Great Persecution under the Emperor Diocletian in 303–312. This was really a vain attempt to roll back Christianity which was becoming ever stronger. In 312 Constantine became sole Emperor, having declared his allegiance to Christ before a decisive battle with his main rival. In 313 he issued his famous *Edict of Milan* giving religious toleration.

Very soon the Church was given special privileges. Many of the most accomplished leaders and thinkers were Christians and, though sporadic opposition continued, the Church's position was very strong. It now had to cope with being popular – a friend of the State rather than a foe. Secular and political considerations entered into Christianity in a new way. Problems in the Church were no longer a matter of indifference to the State. Decisions of the Church in matters of discipline or doctrine might have an enormous impact on the unity of the Empire.

One major issue of discipline was how to treat those Christians who had denied their faith under persecution ('apostasy'). This was no academic debate. In North Africa, Caecilian was made Bishop of Carthage in 311 and one of the consecrating bishops present was a 'traditor' (i.e. he had surrendered the Scriptures under threat). Caecilian was tainted by association and unacceptable to many. So they elected Donatus as bishop. There was a deep schism fuelled by local dislike of the Roman (pro-Caecilian) colonists and by economic unrest.

The question for the State was how to put down a rebellion inflamed by Christian convictions. The question for the Church was ultimately one of authority. When the Church was divided, was its true voice the local congregation or the wider majority? This issue rumbled on for hundreds of years. Distinctions between Church and State became blurred. Constantine made a judgement against the Donatists and tried (unsuccessfully) to enforce it by arms. Christian leaders such as St Augustine of Hippo (354–430) urged that the judgement of the whole Church had authority over any particular part: if necessary, schismatics should be suppressed by force. All this greatly weakened the North African Church, which was virtually wiped out by the advances of Islam in the seventh and eighth centuries.

Church, State and doctrine

Two major theological questions came to divide Christians:

- ▶ *the doctrine of the Trinity (pages 18 and 114)*
- ▶ *the relationship of the human and divine natures within Christ.*

Arius (*c.* 250–336) was an Alexandrian priest who taught that Christ was inferior to the Father. His views split the Eastern Church and again the State became involved. The Emperor Constantine called the Council of Nicaea (325), the first really international, or 'ecumenical', Council of the Church. It affirmed that Christ was 'of one substance with the Father'. The Council left ambiguities and the conflict continued. The doughty guardian of orthodoxy throughout this debate was St Athanasius (*c.* 296–373), Bishop of Alexandria.

He suffered for his stand, being exiled from his See (official 'seat') five times. Again, the State, in the shape of Constantine's successors, played a key role, often against orthodoxy. Eventually the Emperor Theodosius convened the Council of Constantinople (381). This Council, in the process of giving us the Nicene Creed, strongly asserted that both the Son and the Holy Spirit were of 'one essence' with God the Father. These Christological controversies (questions about Jesus Christ) centred around two great cities:

- ▶ **Alexandria** *emphasized the divinity of Christ: sometimes, as with Apollinarius (c. 310–390), in a way which denied that Christ was fully human.*
- ▶ **Antioch** *emphasized Christ's humanity, but in a way which sometimes suggested that Christ had a 'split personality': one human nature, one divine nature, always kept distinct. The matter was further complicated because it became part of a bitter conflict for supremacy between the Sees of Constantinople and Alexandria.*

A decision was reached at the Council of Chalcedon (451). The Council declared that Christ was '*acknowledged in two natures, without confusion, without change, without division, without separation*'. But he was acknowledged as one Person, not '*parted or divided into two persons*'. Though a definition was worked out which still remains the touchstone of orthodoxy, it was far from satisfactory to a significant group called *Monophysites*. They maintained that Christ had only one nature, which was divine. Despite many efforts, they could not be reconciled. They eventually emerged as the Syrian, Coptic and Abyssinian Churches (Chapter 12).

However necessary, the definitions of Nicaea, Constantinople and Chalcedon were purchased at a high price. Philosophical abstractions could too easily obscure the sense of a personal relationship with God through Jesus Christ. Politics, whether in the (sometimes unseemly) rivalries of theologians, bishops and great ecclesiastical centres, or in the different agendas of emperors, could too easily become dominant. The Church was discovering that it is perhaps more difficult to be true to its Lord when it is large and influential, than when it is ignored or persecuted – a lesson which was to be repeated down the centuries.

Ministry, Eucharist and authority

The threefold structure of ministry – bishops, priests and deacons – emerged in the second century. (It was noted by Ignatius of Antioch as early as AD 106.) Two further ideas began to dominate:

▶ *the importance of bishops being in line of apostolic succession from the first apostles*
▶ *the use of priestly language in relation to the administration of Holy Communion (Chapter 8).*

The idea of apostolic succession was first applied to all leaders and teachers, for they taught the apostles' doctrine. But by the time of Cyprian (Bishop of Carthage d. 258), it focused on the claim of a bishop to be standing in a direct line of succession, through the laying on of hands, reaching back to the apostles. This became important in disputes with those who questioned a bishop's authority.

The early Church did not define ordained ministry in relation to the sacraments. Gradually the term 'priest' began to be applied to presbyters (*presbyter* is derived from the Greek New Testament term for minister). With this shift came the notion that the minister's central role was in relation to the Eucharist. Bishop Cyprian saw the priest as a *'cultic official, offering sacrifice ... the sacrifice of Christ himself in the consecrated elements'* (A T Hanson). This was a far cry from the idea of the whole people of God offering a sacrifice of praise and a life of service. It gave justification to the emergence of a priestly 'caste'.

Rome naturally had a certain supremacy, because of its central place within the Empire. But in the middle of the third century, Bishop Cyprian of Carthage argued vigorously with the Bishop of Rome about the equality of all bishops. The conversion of the Emperor Constantine (AD 312) inevitably made Rome even more important. Paradoxically, this increased in the fifth century, as the Empire went into marked decline and fall.

In 410 Rome was sacked by Alaric the Visigoth and the Roman Empire began to crumble. In contrast, the Bishop of Rome represented permanency and authority in the midst of collapse. Leo I (Pope from 440–61) was very powerful. He advanced papal claims considerably by his assertion that the apostle Peter spoke through him. His claims were, in turn, backed by the Empire, which saw him as a bulwark against the advance of the barbarians. But the Eastern Church did not accept his claims and the seeds of future conflict were sown.

The birth of monasticism

The idea of renouncing everything for Christ ('asceticism') runs deep in the New Testament. By the second century it began to be linked to virginity. Here were the beginnings of monasticism, a movement advanced by the conversion of Constantine and the consequent ending, or so it seemed, of the self-sacrifice of martyrdom (but see page 193). The very popularity of Christianity was a problem for some. They wished to escape from church politics; to find a place for prayer and discipline. Growing numbers had a thirst for God and a determination to do battle with the forces of evil, away from the temptations of everyday life.

Around 285, Antony of Egypt (*c.* 250–355) went into the desert as a hermit. He became a well-known role model whose story was recorded by Athanasius. The next development was from *hermit life to community life*. This came through another Egyptian, Pachomius (*c.* 290–346), who laid down rules for communal monasteries. The movement spread rapidly. Through Basil of Caesarea (*c.* 330–79) these communities developed a concern for the poor and deprived, as well as for the development of the interior spiritual life. Evagrius (346–99) added a more contemplative, mystical and intellectual strand.

The movement which started in the East was encouraged in the West by John Cassian (*c.* 360–435). Monasticism was later given its classic definition by St Benedict (*c.* 480–550), who laid down the Benedictine rule. This struck a sensible balance between work and prayer and became definitive for Western monasticism. By the fifth century, the foundations of monasticism had been laid, with all its strengths (self-sacrificial service to the Lord and to the needy) and with its weaknesses, namely a tendency:

▶ *to regard its expression of Christianity as superior*
▶ *to put a greater emphasis on human 'works' than on divine grace.*

A great challenge

By the fifth century, Christianity was *the* credible spiritual and intellectual force in an Empire which was crumbling fast in the West. It was St Augustine of Hippo who, in his influential book *City of God*, was able to give a coherent explanation of what was happening. Yes, the barbarians might be about to come through the gates; but the Kingdom of God was not bound to the Roman Empire. Indeed, it lay beyond time. This knowledge would prevent

Christians from falling into undue pessimism, in the face of the collapse of existing institutions.

In any event, the barbarians were not the end of everything that was important. Rather, they were a challenge to the Church. Could it find ways of converting them? It had the organization and motivation to undertake this task. As the Empire collapsed, the Church was the only credible institution remotely able to take its place. This was a tribute to the achievements of the previous 500 years. It was also a heady and dangerous power. The next chapter reveals how imperfectly and patchily it responded to these challenges.

The Christians sought to protect the destitute, or those who had fallen in status and resources, like widows and orphans. They provided hospices for the sick or for raising the innumerable foundlings. In the mid-third century the Roman church was feeding 155 church officials of various grades, and more than 1,500 widows and distressed persons. At Antioch in Syria late in the fourth century, the number of destitute persons beings fed by the church had reached 3,000. It became common for a register or *matricula* of names to be kept.

Christians were strongly opposed to child exposure, actively rescuing foundlings, and deplored abortions which they did not think defensible except with arguments that equally justified infanticide.

(Professor Owen Chadwick in *The Oxford Illustrated History of Christianity*, OUP)

10 THINGS TO REMEMBER

1 *Jesus and his disciples were Jews – the Christian Church began as a small group within Judaism.*

2 *The Jewish Scriptures (the 'Old Testament') have been key texts for Christians from the time of Jesus onwards.*

3 *On the first Christian Pentecost in Jerusalem, the Holy Spirit came down in power on the early followers of Jesus.*

4 *These first followers of Jesus – a rapidly growing band – were known for joyful sharing of possessions and supportive fellowship.*

5 *They 'broke bread' and prayed together, and attended to the apostles' teaching.*

6 *A decisive – and difficult – decision was taken shortly after the death of Jesus, when Gentiles (non-Jews) were welcomed into the Church.*

7 *As a result of persecution the early Christians scattered, spreading the gospel as they travelled and settled.*

8 *In the early days after his death and resurrection, Jesus was remembered through conversations, shared memories and preaching.*

9 *Before all the companions of Jesus died, a written record of the oral accounts of his life, ministry and resurrection became essential – hence the four Gospels.*

10 *Each new generation of believers has wrestled with different questions – theological, pastoral and practical.*

16

One thousand turbulent years:
AD 500–1500

In this chapter you will learn:
- *about Celtic missionaries in Britain*
- *about the rise of the papacy*
- *about monks and friars.*

The turbulent centuries between 500 and 1500 can be seen as the Church's most glorious era. It dominated Europe and witnessed the building of breathtaking cathedrals, the production of superb works of art and much fine music (Chapters 19 and 20). But the same period also brought shame on the Church – with the Crusades, the Inquisition, anti-Semitism, the degradation of women, and the spiritual poverty of many of its leaders.

The 'Middle Ages' brought immense pressures and temptations to the Church. It was the one remaining institution in a society facing endless waves of invaders (Vikings, Arabs, Moguls). The challenge came first from the barbarians who rolled back the Roman Empire, at any rate in the West. But, in time, the Church was able to convert the barbarians.

A much more serious and long-lasting threat came from the forces of Islam. Muhammad (570–632) established the Muslim community which, together with economic factors, led to conquests of huge Christian areas (Persia, Syria, Egypt, North Africa, Spain and Palestine – including Jerusalem itself in 638). Muslim forces threatened the whole of Europe. Only the victory of Charles Martel at Tours in 732 turned them back.

The plundering raids of the Vikings were a further problem. The result of all this was that the West was inferior both to the Christian East ('Byzantium') and to Islamic nations, in organization and culture. Hence, from a Western perspective, this period is sometimes called the 'dark ages'.

Evangelization of and from England

The Christian faith came to Britain shortly after the death of Jesus, as soldiers, traders and other travellers in the Roman Empire lived and shared the gospel. The *Edict of Milan* (AD 313: page 291) had encouraged an embryo organization. Indeed, three British bishops travelled to the Council of Arles in southern France (Gaul) in 314. Invading Saxons drove the Christian Britons west into Cornwall, Wales and Strathclyde. It is the descendants of these invaders who were evangelized by Augustine and the Celtic missionaries. *Note: St Augustine, first Archbishop of Canterbury (d. 604 or 605), should not be confused with the great theologian, St Augustine of Hippo in North Africa (354–430: pages 103 and 296.)*

Pope Gregory I (*c.* 540–604) had, as a youngster, seen Rome sacked several times. A man of great ability, born to nobility and wealth, he was an urban prefect at the age of 30. He gave this up to become a monk and he became Pope in 590. He used the vast powers of the papacy (the greatest landowner in Italy) to good effect. He reformed the Church, made peace with those who threatened Rome, engaged in acts of charity and wrote books of pastoral guidance.

Gregory encouraged missionary work, and sent a reluctant Augustine to England. After a false start, Augustine arrived in Kent in 597. He and his 40 monks came into Canterbury carrying a cross and singing an antiphon for God's mercy; they would have preferred to be in Rome! But they were well received. Augustine found a Christian Queen (Bertha from Gaul) and a cautious King (Ethelbert) who was soon converted. Kings were influential and, according to a letter written by Gregory, within a year of Augustine's arrival, 10,000 Saxons had been baptized.

Gregory's commission to Augustine represents a change from the very confrontational approach towards paganism of earlier missionaries. Martin of Tours (d. 397), for example, insisted on a complete break with the pagan past. In contrast, Gregory urged that temples and other holy places should not be destroyed but rather *'converted from the worship of devils to the service of the true God'*. The Venerable Bede (*c.* 673–735) records that the first Canterbury Cathedral was a one-time Roman basilica (Chapter 19).

Insight

The great Pope Gregory I (*c.* 540–604) sent Augustine to evangelize England in 597. He found a cautious but welcoming king – and a Christian queen, for Christianity had already reached Britain via Christian traders and soldiers, soon after the resurrection of Jesus.

Celtic missionaries

St Patrick

It was, however, *Celtic* missionaries who achieved most in the conversion of Britain. This began with Patrick who was born, probably in Scotland, around 390. He had a tough apprenticeship as a slave for six years. Then, after studying in France, he was made a bishop, and he travelled to Ireland to spearhead its conversion. A century later, it was Ireland which was sending missionaries to mainland Britain.

St Columba

Columba (*c.* 521–97) sailed to Iona in the Hebrides where he established a monastery. From this centre, missionary monks sallied forth to convert most of Scotland and northern England. Of particular importance was the way in which they adapted their methods to the social and cultural customs of the tribal societies which they encountered. Scholars today point to this as a good example of the process of 'inculturation' – presenting the gospel in ways appropriate to the culture of the people being evangelized and not importing 'cultural baggage'.

St Aidan

One of the most celebrated of the Iona missionaries was Aidan (c. 600–651) who established his base at Lindisfarne. This monastery on the Northumbrian coast became the centre of Celtic Christianity in the north. From there, missionary monks evangelized the area. Lindisfarne is famous for the beautifully scripted and illustrated *Lindisfarne Gospels*.

Thus England was evangelized: on the one hand, Celtic missionaries from Ireland and Scotland; on the other, missionaries from Rome based in Canterbury.

But the Celtic and Roman understandings of the way in which the Church should be organized were significantly different. The Celts emphasized a loose structure of monastic communities, with a high degree of freedom and mobility. The Romans preferred a more highly organized, settled and hierarchical Church structure.

There were other differences: about the dating of Easter, the organization of monasteries and the shape of the tonsure (a monk's haircut). These matters were debated at the **Synod of Whitby** in 664. At Whitby the Roman views gained the ascendancy, though the Celtic understanding continued to be influential. This important Synod was hosted by **St Hilda,** the founding Abbess of Whitby – a woman of great influence, praised by the Venerable Bede as a skilled administrator and teacher.

Insight

Celtic missionaries were largely responsible for the conversion of Britain. Key figures were Patrick, Columba, and Aidan. Boniface from Devon took the good news to Germany, where he was martyred.

St Boniface

Those who had been converted to Christ wanted to take the gospel message to others. So missionaries soon began travelling *from* England. Here the outstanding figure is St Boniface (680–754) who evangelized Germany. Born in Devon, he was trained under the influence of Canterbury and went to Germany as the representative of the papacy. He was highly successful. Indeed, the new overarching political institutions which began to emerge under the Emperor Charlemagne (*c.* 742–814) were, in some measure, built on Boniface's achievements. In 754 he joined 'the noble army of martyrs', protecting himself from his attackers with nothing more than his Gospel book.

> *When Boniface wrote to other bishops, he had a way of invariably reminding them that Christian authority meant service. The service of the pastor was exemplified in Christ's washing of his disciples' feet, and so, whatever little present he might have received from another bishop, back went a towel from a seemingly inexhaustible linen cupboard.* (Professor Henry Mayr-Harting)

Expansion

The coronation of Charlemagne as Holy Roman Emperor by Pope Leo III in 800 represented something of a triumph for the Church – and particularly for the papacy. But it brought problems. For many centuries, the question of the relationship between Emperor and Pope was to be a matter of contention. Further, Charlemagne was a soldier who was willing to use forceful methods to expand the Church. This policy was openly criticized by the scholarly Alcuin of York (*c.* 735–804), an advisor to Charlemagne. Charlemagne regarded himself as another King David, and his military methods help to explain why the expansion of this period was often superficial.

This was made worse by the fact that Church leaders were not concerned to translate the Bible or the liturgy into local languages. For example, none of Augustine's party spoke English; nor did they think it important to learn it - or to produce an Anglo-Saxon Bible or Service Book. This Roman mind-set is evident in the unbending commitment to the Latin liturgy on the part of the Western Church (which continued until the Second Vatican Council: 1962–5).

Missionary expansion in the East took a different character. On the one hand, it was even more an arm of the government. On the other hand, those missionaries were concerned to understand the language and culture of the people. The two great evangelists to the Slavs, the brothers St Cyril (826–69) and St Methodius (c. 815–85), translated the Bible and the liturgy into the vernacular. Because of this, they became key figures in the development of Slav culture.

The papacy

By AD 800, the Church had immense and dangerous powers. Within the boundaries of the Holy Roman Empire, it reigned supreme. Great figures in the Church were often great figures of State too. They grew increasingly remote from their own clergy and people. This corrupting effect can be seen most clearly in the papacy itself.

In the ninth century, a forged document called *The Donation of Constantine* began to circulate. It claimed that Constantine (the first Christian Emperor) had granted to the Pope not only power over all the churches but imperial power in Rome, Italy and all the provinces of the West. In effect, this 'historical' document made the Pope a powerful temporal, as well as spiritual, lord. Nobody realized that it was a forgery and it was used to bolster papal authority, until its falsity was demonstrated in the fifteenth century.

The late ninth century through to the mid-eleventh century was a low period for Western Christendom. It was a time of general breakdown within political institutions, particularly in the face of threats from the expansionist Vikings. Famine was an additional problem. As the year 1000 approached, some people expected the end of the world. Popes were often just one more warring force, sometimes noted for their lack of moral scruple. What was true of popes was also true of archbishops and bishops. Inevitably, their poor example had an adverse effect on ordinary clergy. In addition, many monasteries had become lax. The Church was in desperate need of reform.

Insight

By AD 800, the Church had great power. Church leaders often held high positions in the State. Great power corrupted – though reform came from a new Benedictine monastery at Cluny in France under Hildebrand (later to become Pope Gregory VII).

Reform

The first sign of reform was the founding of a new monastery in the Benedictine tradition at Cluny in France in 910. It freed itself from lay control and returned to the old ideals. Cluny had a succession of outstanding and influential abbots. Its ideals spread to other houses. Most importantly, it influenced the papacy. The key figure in this regard was a monk called Hildebrand (c. 1020–85) who became Pope Gregory VII in 1073. He set reform in motion and was against both 'kings who oppose divine justice and bishops who set a bad example'. In the pursuit of the first aim he became involved in a violent dispute over whether the Emperor, Henry IV, had the right to appoint bishops – a practice called lay investiture.

There were moments of high drama, with the Emperor pleading for absolution, standing barefoot for three days in the January snow at Canossa in 1077. It remains a matter of debate whether Pope Gregory gained anything lasting from this conflict. But he certainly bolstered papal claims to domination over the State and he pressed forward with his reform of the Church. Gregory opposed simony (the purchase of benefices) and clerical deviations from celibacy.

Mutual excommunication

Tensions between Greek-speaking Christians (East) and Latin-speaking Christians (West) had always been present. In the early Middle Ages these strains were considerably reduced, as old Rome and new 'Rome' (Constantinople) found common cause against the new threat from Islam. Between 654 and 752, most popes came from the East or from areas with Greek influence such as Sicily. But the accord was fragile.

In 668, St Theodore (602–90), a Greek-speaking monk from Tarsus, was sent to be Archbishop of Canterbury – this showed that a measure of harmony had been achieved. But Theodore was accompanied by Hadrian (d. 709) from Africa, to ensure that Theodore would introduce '*no Greek customs contrary to the true Faith*'. The old suspicions and rivalries were still alive.

These grew, particularly as the axis of the Western Church began to move northwards when France, Germany and England became influential. The coronation by Pope Leo III (AD 800) of Charlemagne as the first Emperor of the 'Holy Roman Empire' constituted a challenge to the Eastern Empire. His coronation was a symbol that the political unity of the old Empire was finally broken. It was only a matter of time before this would be expressed institutionally.

Insight
A key – and tragic – event took place in 1054 when the Eastern (Orthodox) and Western (Catholic) Churches each excommunicated the other. This 'Great Schism' had been brewing for centuries and took centuries to mend.

When the separation of East and West eventually took place, almost nobody noticed. The trigger was the Western Church's addition of the '*filioque* clause' to the Nicene Creed – a clause which states that the Holy Spirit proceeds from the Father '*and the Son*'. This became a major difference between the Eastern and Western Churches. It reached a climax in 1054 when each side excommunicated the other (the 'Great Schism'). Ironically, disunity came at a time when reviving trade in the Mediterranean was bringing East and West back into contact. But contact did not bring understanding and the pressure from the West was for total uniformity (on its terms!). Any such notion was unacceptable to the urbane, sophisticated, Greek-speaking Christians.

Everyday Christian life

Writing under this heading in *Christianity* (SCM Press), Hans Küng points out that the Middle Ages were complex (*'they were by no means a unitary Christian culture!'*). But life for all was dominated by the Church. Church bells tolled the time and marked festivals. Church buildings were highly visible. Sundays and feast days broke the routine of hard work. The people were united in collective joy and collective anxiety.

Life was hard and life-expectancy short, especially when pestilence or famine struck. But the Church was there. *'It did not let people die alone; they died in the midst of the community, surrounded by members of their family and strengthened by prayer and the church's rites for the dying'* (Hans Küng). Perhaps surprisingly in such a tough world, atheism and suicide were extremely rare.

Care for the sick and the poor was organized, and a leading role in this was played by women. Education, political influence and leadership in the Church were closed to most women. However, noble women would exercise power and were sometimes more educated than their husbands, who were often illiterate. Nunneries were numerous (and in the early Middle Ages, virtually closed to all but the aristocracy). There were several female mystics: the Cistercian convent of Helfta in Germany became an important centre for mysticism – and there were others. Sexual intimacy was discouraged even within marriage, apart from the purpose of procreation.

Contraception was regarded as sinful, on a level with abortion and the abandonment of unwanted children.

While acknowledging the distortions of New Testament faith which developed, such as the flagellant movement, Hans Küng strikes a positive note: '*And yet there were countless medieval people who wanted to live out an* authentic discipleship of Jesus *unpretentiously in everyday life.*'

Crusades and corruption

Insight

The Crusades marked a very dark period in Church history. Encouraged by popes, Christian soldiers tried to capture and rule the Holy Land. On a positive note, however, St Francis and his friars lit a torch for simple faith and practical love.

The Turks were pressing in the East. Pope Gregory VII had contemplated a *Crusade* and the idea was taken up by his disciple and successor, Pope Urban II (*c.* 1042–99). The first Crusade set out in 1096, aiming at the conquest of Jerusalem. In 1099 it succeeded '*and by 1153 the whole Syrian coastline from Ascalon to Antioch was in Latin hands*' (Colin Morris). This first Crusade roused fanatical enthusiasm, fed by Urban's declaration that Crusaders who died in a state of repentance and confession would gain immediate entry to heaven. But Islam was united under Nureddin and his successor, Saladin, and Muslims ruled Jerusalem again in 1187. The idea that the Church could conquer by the sword was bound to corrupt; thus began another slide downwards. This Crusade and its successors (they continued until the fifteenth century) brought little glory and much shame on the Church.

A whole succession of popes made claims to vast power. They had no desire to be 'the servant of the servants of God'. By the middle

of the twelfth century it was common for popes to take the title
'Vicar of Christ' rather than 'Vicar of St Peter'. But the higher the
claim, the more it required political methods to promote it. By
the thirteenth century the political ambitions of the papacy were
undisguised. The need to raise money was consequently acute and
its commitment to reform was slight.

In 1296, Boniface VIII (Pope: 1294–1303) issued a 'bull' declaring
that secular powers could not impose taxation without the
permission of the papacy. Such claims debased the power of the
papacy and triggered strong opposition by powerful rulers. The
so-called 'Babylonian Captivity' of the papacy (1309–77), when it
was 'imprisoned' in Avignon, is a good example of this. During this
period, successive popes lived in France rather than Rome. When
the papacy moved back to Rome, a rival claimed to be the one true
Pope – hence another 'great schism' (page 306). At one point there
were three rival claimants.

There were attempts within the Church to curtail the power
of the papacy. *The Conciliar Movement* of the late fourteenth
and early fifteenth centuries tried unsuccessfully to assert the
authority of Councils over the Pope. The papacy won, but
the damage to the spiritual integrity of the Church was
considerable.

The Renaissance prince-popes left a glorious artistic legacy. Sixtus
IV (1414–84) built the Sistine chapel and supported charities. The
warrior Pope Julius II (1443–1513) engaged Raphael to decorate
the Vatican and Michelangelo as architect for the rebuilding of
St Peter's. But their lifestyle was notorious. 'The most notorious
of these Renaissance prince-popes was the Spaniard Roderigo
Borgia, who as Alexander VI presided at his daughter's wedding and
flaunted a young mistress within the Vatican itself. His son, Cesare,
the model for Machiavelli's Prince, gave a party in the Vatican in
1502 at which 50 prostitutes danced naked, picked chestnuts off the
floor with their teeth and were competed for by the men present'
(Professor Eamon Duffy).

Monasticism

As we have seen, the driving force for reform in the tenth century came from monasticism. This was true for much of this period. In 1098, a group went to a most inaccessible place (Citeaux), where they determined to follow the Benedictine rule as literally as possible.

The Cistercians (as these monks are called) had some outstanding early members. Stephen Harding (*c.* 1060–1134), one of the earliest abbots, expressed their ideals in enduring form in the *Carta Caritatis* (the Charter of Charity). He even found ways of bringing the laity (albeit in an inferior role) back into monasticism. Bernard of Clairvaux (1090–1153) was another leader of immense and magnetic spiritual influence. By 1300 there were 694 Cistercian abbeys.

Monasticism was a truly pan-European movement. Before the dissolution of the monasteries under Henry VIII (from 1536) there were more than 500 abbeys and priories in England. Only one order could be described as 'purely English' (i.e. founded by an Englishman). The Gilbertines were founded by Gilbert of Sempringham (1083–1189) but even he borrowed ideas from the Cistercians.

In 1131, Bernard of Clairvaux sent monks to found the Cistercian Rievaulx Abbey in Yorkshire. In its heyday, Rievaulx had 140 monks and more than 500 lay brothers. At its dissolution by Henry VIII in 1538 it had only 22 monks.

The Carthusians were founded in 1084; they placed great emphasis on silence. In general they avoided the decline which the Cistercians and most other monastic orders experienced in the late Middle Ages. (*Note:* The 'Reformed Cistercians' (1664) became known as 'Trappists'.)

It is difficult to exaggerate the importance of monasticism. Monasteries were 'the symbol of stability and immutability in a world of flux' (R W Southern). They provided the inspiration for reform as well as intellectual and spiritual leadership. They cared for the deprived and marginalized. They included craftsmen and architects of distinction.

A visit to the great Cistercian Abbeys in Yorkshire (Byland, Fountains, Jervaulx, Rievaulx ...) reveals the remarkable commitment, energy and organization of these communities, which were dissolved by Henry VIII (1491–1547).

However, from the twelfth century monasticism was in decline. Perhaps some monasteries were victims of their own success. They had civilized some of the wildest areas of Europe and good management brought great wealth. At the same time, other institutions such as schools and universities were developing. In these, *the friars* played a crucial role.

Two monks tell their story

Everything here and in my nature are opposed to each other. I cannot endure the daily tasks. The sight of it all revolts me. I am tormented and crushed down by the length of the vigils, I often succumb to the manual labour. The food cleaves to my mouth, more bitter than wormwood. The rough clothing cuts through my skin and flesh down to my very bones. More than this, my will is always hankering after other things; it longs for the delights of the world and sighs unceasingly for its loves and affections and pleasures.

Our food is scanty, our garments rough, our drink is from the stream and our sleep often upon our book. Under our tired limbs there is but a hard mat; when sleep is sweetest we must rise at a bell's bidding. Such unity and concord is there among the brethren, that each thing seems to belong to all, and all to each ... To put all in brief, no perfection ... is lacking to our order and our way of life.

(From Walter Daniel's *Life of Aelred*)

St Francis and the friars

From the eleventh century onwards, there was an economic recovery. With this went the growth of towns and the emergence of universities. The institutional Church was ill-equipped to deal with the challenges of a new, freer, less respectful, more uncertain society. Francis of Assisi (1181/2–1226) embraced poverty and renounced everything else, including learning. He was fresh and spontaneous and gathered a group of 'friars' around him. Unlike monks, friars were not tied to one monastery by a vow of 'stability'; they were able to move more freely.

In *'showing how the destitution of the towns could be accepted with joy and made serviceable for salvation, he touched some deep emotional springs in an urban society'* (R W Southern). Francis believed in the importance of preaching and in engagement with the world rather than retreat from it. He was not a good organizer and after his death the Franciscans soon lost their simple lifestyle. They became clericalized and as much involved in the university world as were the Dominicans.

St Dominic (1170–1221) was a less charismatic figure than Francis. Like Francis, he stressed the importance of preaching and involvement with the world. In contrast, however, he was also convinced of the place of learning. His followers soon included some of the foremost theologians in Europe. They were particularly influential in the new university centres of the West, which provided a major catalyst for the study of theology. Many of the great names in medieval theology until the mid-fourteenth century were friars. By the fourteenth century, both movements had declined from their early ideals – but they had been important new instruments for ministry, and had made a powerful impact on the Church and the world at large.

Intellectual developments

The eleventh century saw the beginnings of a revival in theology, which was to continue for centuries. The Italian,

Anselm (*c.* 1033–1109), 36th Archbishop of Canterbury, pointed the way to a new confidence in reason, based on faith. His phrase '*fides quaerens intellectum*' (faith seeking understanding) is a good guide to what he sought to do.

The Frenchman **Peter Abelard** (1079–1142) was a brilliant scholar. He was confident enough to use his intellectual skills to question received ideas on key concepts such as the Atonement and the Trinity. His fundamental principle – '*by doubting we come to enquiry, by enquiring we perceive the truth*' – indicates the distance that had been travelled from the simple, received theology of the earlier period. He is also remembered for a famous and tragic love affair with Heloise, who later became a nun. Abelard lectured to large audiences in Paris, playing an important role in the emergence and growth of universities in twelfth-century France, Italy and England.

Ancient Greek ideas, particularly those of the pre-Christian philosopher Aristotle (384–322 BC), became very influential. To some, Aristotle represented such a threat to orthodox belief that they burned copies of his works. To others, he was an intellectual challenge. Was it possible to reconcile reason and faith? **St Thomas Aquinas** (*c.* 1225–74), a Dominican theologian, brilliantly achieved this synthesis. He wrote extensively ('Thomism') and set out a series of 'proofs' for the existence of God.

Throughout this period, mystics were influential. They were less concerned to analyse theological ideas than to describe religious experiences. One famous example from England is **Mother Julian of Norwich** who, in 1373, had a series of 'revelations' or 'shewings' (Chapter 6).

Inspired by a rediscovery of Graeco-Roman art and literature, intellectual interest turned to artistic, literary and historical questions. The Renaissance (a 'Rebirth' of classical culture and learning) started in Italy and spread northwards. There was a flowering of artistic creativity. Scholars returned to the Hebrew and Greek texts of the Scriptures. They began to see the Bible in its historical context, rather than as a collection of proof texts for particular doctrines. Thus they were able to compare their own world with previous historical periods: the age of the apostles, for example. Their own times did not emerge with credit. Perhaps the greatest scholar in this respect was the Christian 'humanist' Desiderius Erasmus (pages 322 and 373). Himself a priest, he was also a powerful satirist. In his writings the corrupt, self-seeking and clericalized Church emerged in a sorry and often ridiculous light.

Movements for change

As we have seen, the medieval Church had many low points, often followed by movements for reform. Sometimes such movements were on the edge of, or were forced out from, the mainstream Church. Some were remarkably similar to the Reformation of the sixteenth century – looking to Scripture rather than tradition for their authority.

In southern France, the Waldensians (followers of Peter Waldo – d. *c.* 1210) wanted reform. They emphasized poverty, rejected the doctrine of purgatory, engaged in lay preaching and survived to be incorporated into Zwinglianism (Chapter 17). In Bohemia, **John Hus** (*c.* 1369–1415) was put to death (despite being promised safe conduct) for challenging the Church. His followers survived to be linked with the Lutherans (Chapters 12 and 17). In England, the followers of **John Wycliffe** (1329–84) became known as Lollards. They:

- ▶ *stressed the place of preaching*
- ▶ *attacked corruption in the Church*
- ▶ *rejected papal claims to authority over secular rulers*
- ▶ *encouraged Bible reading in English.*

'A deep, unquiet spirit'

Throughout this period the Church acquired vast power, far exceeding its previous, or subsequent, influence. Nobody doubts that this corrupted the Church; but how extensive was this corruption? Vigorous debate persists about the spirituality of the late medieval Church.

Certainly there was immense vision and energy, as the beautiful, large and rich churches built during this time testify (Chapter 19). Certainly too, there was deep spirituality, particularly among those who sought to develop an inner personal spiritual life. But many of the laity were restive – increasingly disinclined to accept the power and privilege of some clergy; increasingly hungry for a richer spiritual diet. Their 'deep, unquiet spirit' (A G Dickens) was to bring a momentous transformation.

10 THINGS TO REMEMBER

1 *During the Middle Ages the Church grew very strong. It had to learn to live with power rather than persecution.*

2 *For much of this time, Christian civilization was under attack – from barbarians, Muslims and Vikings.*

3 *Christianity reached Britain shortly after Jesus' death, through traders and Roman soldiers.*

4 *In 597 Pope Gregory sent Augustine to Britain, where he became the first Archbishop of Canterbury.*

5 *From then on, the influence of Roman Christianity would rival – and eventually dominate – Celtic Christianity.*

6 *Celtic missionaries like Patrick and (later) Columba and Aidan were highly effective missionaries.*

7 *Tension between the Eastern and Western Churches resulted in a split in 1054 – hence Catholicism (West) and the Orthodox Churches (East).*

8 *Sponsored by popes, the Crusades were a shameful (and unsuccessful) attempt to establish Christian domination in Jerusalem and the Middle East.*

9 *Through discipline and hard work, monasteries tamed wild countryside throughout Europe, becoming wealthy and powerful.*

10 *A new movement of wandering friars emerged around 1200. Pledged to poverty, they were led by Francis of Assisi (Franciscans) and Dominic (Dominicans).*

17

....

The Reformation

In this chapter you will learn:

- **about the medieval Church**
- **about Martin Luther's rebellion**
- **about the English Reformation.**

> *The religion of the late Middle Ages was a rich and complex thing.*
> *Decline is evident in many of its institutions, but more striking are*
> *its vitality and diversity.* (Professor Eamon Duffy)

In the Atlas of the Christian Church (Equinox), Eamon Duffy lists
some of the corruptions:

1 An inefficient Church riddled with inequalities

Of 670 European bishoprics, 300 were in Italy; Germany and
central Europe had only 90. The Bishop of Winchester received
1200 florins; the Bishop of Ross in Ireland received 33 florins.

2 Uneducated parish clergy

Many priests were unofficially 'married' and poor.

> *'Concubinage was widespread: impecunious clergy with a*
> *household of children, presiding over a half-coherent liturgy on*
> *Sundays… as they worked their farmland for the rest of the week,*
> *were common all over Europe.'*

3 Monastic decline

'In England comfortable mediocrity prevailed. Elsewhere, as in Italy and part of France, there were many openly scandalous houses. There was everywhere a decline in numbers, and handfuls of monks lived in luxury on incomes intended to maintain hundreds. Sexual laxity was not uncommon.'

But there were good things too:

1 Reform groups

These existed within all religious orders and there were some saintly bishops. Some individuals practised a meditative piety based largely on the Gospels. This movement (the *Devotio Moderna*: 'Modern Devotion') found classical expression in *The Imitation of Christ* by Thomas à Kempis (1380–1471).

2 Preaching

Preaching was popular and sermons by Franciscan and Dominican friars drew large numbers.

3 A strong communal element among the laity

Every parish had a least one 'confraternity' – a religious brotherhood of lay people. In Italy in particular, the brotherhoods were concerned with works of mercy: help for the dying, the poor and prisoners. They provided orphanages, hospitals and almshouses. Above all – driven by a belief in purgatory (Chapter 9) – they organized and funded masses and prayers for the dead.

Insight

The Middle Ages were marked by corruption and laxity within the Church, but alongside this ran deep devotion and sincere discipleship, as illustrated by Thomas à Kempis in his book *The Imitation of Christ* (c. 1418).

It is against this background that we must understand the struggles of a young German monk which found an echo in the deep feelings of thousands throughout Europe.

Martin Luther (1483–1546)

Martin Luther's dominating concern was to find peace with God. To this end he became a monk. Luther did penance, sought indulgences, read the mystics and theologians of the Church. A wise Vicar-General directed him to the Bible. The Bible was '*the most studied book of the Middle Ages*' (Beryl Smalley). But it was often regarded as a source book to support doctrine, rather than a resource book for living. Martin studied it with an intense, thirsty immediacy as he prepared to lecture at Wittenberg University. He came to see that he did not have to make himself righteous in order to find peace with God.

The all-important breakthrough came as he read St Paul's words, '*the just (or righteous) shall live by faith*' (Romans 1:17). It was, Luther came to understand, through faith in Christ and what Christ had done for him that he could know that his sins were forgiven. *Salvation was a matter of divine grace and not of his own good works*. It was a free gift, resulting from the love, life, death and resurrection of Jesus. 'Justification' was by faith alone.

Luther had no desire to break with the Catholic Church. He did have a desire to preach, teach and apply his fresh understanding of the gospel. So he attacked the whole elaborate system of 'indulgences'. Originally seen as tangible rewards for signs of penance, these had become a commercial racket – pardons for sin were sold, with proceeds going to the material welfare of the Church.

Such an approach obscured the richness of the Christian understanding of forgiveness through Christ, so clear in the Bible. All this drove Martin Luther, in 1517, to publish his famous *Ninety-Five Theses* on the doors of Wittenberg Cathedral. In a quite unexpected and extraordinary way, this document lit a great fire.

Insight

As a devout and brilliant German monk called Martin Luther wrestled with his conscience – and with his God – he

(Contd)

studied St Paul's letter to the Romans. Luther rediscovered 'justification by faith'; he came to realize that salvation is a free gift from God, not a prize to be granted through indulgences.

There was a remarkable response from many ordinary people to this obscure monk. Luther had expressed *their* feelings. There were several reasons for this groundswell:

- *many people were better educated than hitherto*
- *they had new economic, social, national and political aspirations*
- *they increasingly resented interference from Rome*
- *they were disillusioned with the Church hierarchy*
- *the road to salvation seemed to be complex, expensive, arduous and Church-centred*
- *most important of all, many were spiritually hungry.*

The Church was taken aback. It sought to debate. It tried to suppress. It miscalculated at every stage. By the time it made up its mind to oppose Luther, he was in effect protected by his popularity in Germany. At the Diet (Council) of Worms in 1521, he refused to recant unless his position could be disproved from Scripture. He was excommunicated but the movement grew very quickly. This was partly because the Emperor, Charles V, had his mind on the threat to Europe from the Turks. In 1453 they had taken Constantinople; in 1529 they were at the gates of Vienna.

Martin Luther had an unusual brilliance with words. The evidence for this can be seen in:

- *his great translation of the Bible into German (1522–34)*
- *his liturgy (1526) and catechism (1529)*
- *his prolific theological output*
- *his hymn writing.*

Luther wanted to reform the Church from *within*. He remained convinced that his teaching was true to the Bible; and indeed to the

Creeds and the Fathers (the early teachers) of the Church. He was protesting only against later additions and corruption. But once the break came, he had to face the question of how to restructure the breakaway Church. For this, he enlisted the secular rulers.

In the reforms, much was swept away (the Latin Mass, monasteries, all but three sacraments and in some places, bishops). But Luther was instinctively conservative, so much remained. He continued to hold a high doctrine of Christ's presence in Holy Communion (Chapter 8). Consequently, elaborate ritual and vestments often remain in Lutheran churches today.

The Lutheran Reformation spread rapidly, particularly in the north of Germany and Scandinavia. *In this way the Church in the West was divided*. This resulted, very largely, from the failure of the medieval Church to reform itself. Nor did it come to terms with the emerging new world of cities, commerce and better educated, independent citizens. It was in this context that the next stage of the Reformation unfolded.

Insight

Martin Luther was expelled from the Catholic Church and established a new Church, which is named after him. His ideas spread throughout Europe. Because this was a protest movement within the Church, the Reformation Churches became known as 'Protestant'.

Other Reformation leaders

Ulrich Zwingli (1484–1531), reacting to the same spiritual crisis as Luther, reached very similar conclusions. He worked them through in a very different setting: the city state of Zurich. Zwingli was more strongly influenced by 'humanist' forces than Luther. *Humanism* in the sixteenth century was a Christian movement, made up of those who were concerned with the literary and historical heritage opened up by the Renaissance.

The outstanding humanist figure was the Dutchman **Desiderius Erasmus** (1466–1536). He wanted to uncover the heritage of the past and allow it to criticize the present. Erasmus improved understanding of the Bible by producing a Greek version of the New Testament in 1516. For centuries, the New Testament had been known only through the Latin edition – the *Vulgate*. As people came to the text through the original Greek, their eyes were opened to all sorts of nuances which the Vulgate had obscured. For example, they realized that it was not correct to translate Matthew 4:17 as 'do penance', but rather 'be penitent' or 'repent'. Erasmus (a priest) never left the Catholic Church. But in many ways, his critique of its practices (as opposed to its theology) was even more radical and devastating than that of Luther. And there were others who thought as he did.

Zwingli admired Erasmus greatly. The reformation he led in Zurich in the early 1520s was more radical and rationalist than that of Luther. Zwingli rejected any idea of Christ's physical presence (the 'Real Presence') in the elements of the Eucharist (Chapter 8). Reflecting this, Zwinglian churches were as simple as possible: ideally with plain, whitewashed walls. Many of his followers were newly wealthy merchants and artisans. They were attracted not only by the theology but also by the opportunity of challenging the status quo. Zwingli became embroiled in Swiss city-state politics, and died in a battle between Catholic and Protestant cantons.

Like Zwingli, the Frenchman **John Calvin** (1509–64) was heavily influenced by humanism and was converted to a Protestant understanding of God's grace. He was called to help in the Reformation at Geneva and, amid much opposition, he created a Church with clear and definite structures and a sharp separation from the State. He was a systematic theologian of great lucidity and profundity. His writings (*The Institutes* and Bible commentaries) are lengthy but remarkably readable. Calvin established an Academy which sent out many leaders to other parts of Europe. He provided a church structure which was readily exportable and which was able to survive (as Lutheranism was not) within hostile states. Calvinism was often narrower and less tolerant than John Calvin himself. It spread to France, the Netherlands, Scotland, parts of Germany, Poland, Hungary and, in some measure, to England.

The radical Reformation

All these leaders of the Reformation took the Bible as their prime authority. They established churches which were very different from the medieval Catholic Church. They stressed the importance of an educated ministry and, as far as possible, worked closely with the State. In contrast, the more extreme 'radical reformation' claimed to depend on the Holy Spirit and on God's capacity to speak directly to ordinary, uneducated believers. Its leaders tended to be anti-intellectual, to be suspicious of secular government and to be 'restitutional'. This means that they wanted a complete, literal restitution of New Testament Christianity as they understood it:

- ▶ *all things to be shared*
- ▶ *an itinerant ministry*
- ▶ *the baptism of adult believers.*

Some even preached from the rooftops (Matthew 10:27) and tried to develop a precise replication of the New Testament structure of ministry. In contrast, the mainstream reformers were concerned with *reformation* – the reform of the Church according to principles which were grounded in the New Testament and worked out in the history of the Church. They tolerated a range of practices, for they saw that the all-important principles might be applied in different ways, depending on the historical, cultural and social setting.

Under the umbrella of 'radical' there was, in fact, a cluster of movements. These ranged from those which were comparatively orthodox (the *Anabaptists*) to those which were decidedly unorthodox (the *Rationalists*). The latter abandoned central Christian doctrines such as the Trinity. These groups were never numerically strong but they were feared as dangerous by both Catholics and Protestants, and many paid with their lives.

They were seen as a threat to the State, to civic order and to good government. Some were, as can be seen by the involvement of radicals such as Thomas Münzer (*c.* 1490–1525) in the Peasants' Revolt (1525) in Germany, and by the take-over of the German town of Munster in 1534 by radical extremists. They declared that it would become 'New Jerusalem' with Christ's imminent return in glory. They ruled the city in a highly authoritarian, fanatical style, introducing communism and polygamy.

The Reformation in England

Insight

In England these new ideas were caught up in politics – and in the love life of a tyrant king. Although Henry VIII remained Catholic in theology, he defied the Pope and established the Church of England. The First Act of Supremacy, passed in 1534, declared Henry VIII to be 'the only supreme head on earth of the Church in England'.

The Reformation everywhere was a mixture of spiritual rediscovery, political and national self-interest, economic factors and social forces. But in England it took a unique path, nurtured by the presence of:

▶ *the Lollard tradition (going back to John Wycliffe: d. 1384)*
▶ *Christian humanism as exemplified by Erasmus*
▶ *the influence of Luther's ideas in the universities*
▶ *anticlericalism – dislike of an often unspiritual clergy*
▶ *the growth of 'Erastian' convictions (the belief that the State should have greater control over the Church).*

In 1521 Henry VIII wrote against Luther, and the Pope entitled him 'Defender of the Faith' (a title still held by British monarchs). Henry's enthusiasm for the papal office was such that Thomas More warned Henry to remember that popes were not only spiritual leaders, but also Italian princes. (Ironically, and tragically, St Thomas – as he later became – was executed by the King in 1535 for his loyalty to the Catholic Church's opposition to Henry's divorce.) When the Pope refused to dissolve his marriage to Catherine of Aragon, Henry proclaimed himself Head of the Church of England (in 1534) and was excommunicated by Rome. Henry then set about dissolving the monasteries to raise funds and to establish his supremacy in ecclesiastical affairs.

His Act of State plunged England into bloody turmoil (see pages 200–1). His heir (the young Edward VI) was Protestant, but he was soon succeeded by his half-sister, the strongly Catholic Queen Mary. Her successor, Elizabeth I, had no wish to 'make windows into men's souls' and the Church of England eventually emerged as both Catholic *and* Reformed. The Elizabethan Settlement of 1559 found its greatest advocate in the Anglican divine, Richard Hooker (*c.* 1554–1600), a master of English prose.

Henry VIII remained Catholic in theology but he had around him some key people who were driven by strong Protestant convictions. Among these were Archbishop Thomas Cranmer (1489–1556) and the statesman Thomas Cromwell (1485–1540).

The end result of all this turmoil within the Anglican Church was a unique mixture. It had:

- *some members with a strongly Protestant theology*
- *some who emphasized Patristic theology (the early Church Fathers) and tradition*
- *a liturgy and church structure (bishops, vestments and church government) which retained many links with the past.*

The stronger Protestants (often called Puritans) resented this 'compromise' and some eventually departed for America. The Pilgrim Fathers sailed from Plymouth in 1620 in the *Mayflower* (see page 341). Others became 'dissenters' or Nonconformists within England.

The Catholic response

Meanwhile, Catholicism began to reform itself in a Counter-Reformation. In part this was prompted by the emergence of

Protestantism. In part it was the continuation of a process of reform and renewal which had often been evident before. A commission was set up to advise on reform and it produced the *Consilium de Emenda Ecclesia* (Advice on the Reform of the Church) in 1537. It was devastatingly critical of abuses in the Church and its recommendations led to significant reforms.

Earlier, **Ignatius Loyola** (1491–1556) found his own solution to spiritual crisis by way of devotion to Christ and the Church. He published his *Spiritual Exercises* in 1541. These provided a guide to spiritual discipline and became the basis of the Order he founded in 1534: the *Society of Jesus* – 'Jesuits'. (Ignatian Spirituality is still widely practised today.) The Jesuits were modern, practical and world-centred; they were concerned to live in the world, not to escape from it. They were prepared to be involved in politics and intrigue. The Order came to be a most effective instrument for countering Protestant advances – helping to win back Poland for Catholicism for example.

There were still some hopes of a reconciliation with the Protestants. Some Catholic theologians such as Cardinal Contarini (1483–1542) and some Protestant theologians such as the Lutheran Philipp Melanchthon (1497–1560), were able to agree on justification by faith. Sadly, they were unable to carry their constituencies with them. The *Council of Trent* (1545–63) marked a distinct hardening of Catholic attitudes. Its declarations were anti-Protestant:

▶ *justification was not by faith alone*
▶ *tradition was given equal place alongside the Bible*
▶ *the Vulgate (the Latin version of the Bible) was declared to be* the *canonical text*
▶ *the Mass was to continue in Latin.*

The Council of Trent made the Church narrower than it had been before. It marked '*the end of the old, universal comprehensive Latin Church and the emergence of modern Roman Catholicism as one Christian denomination among several*' (G R Elton). One example of the new narrowness, rigour and intolerance was

Pope Paul IV (Pope: 1555–1559). He was as far removed from the Renaissance humanism of popes earlier in the century, as he was from Protestantism. He drove his views forward, using the full force of the Inquisition to destroy opposition. This was ruthless but it created a Catholicism which could survive. Indeed, it was able (sometimes despite leaders like Paul IV) once again to inspire loyalty, passion and devotion, and to produce:

▶ *saints such as St Philip Neri (1515–95)*
▶ *great mystics such as St John of the Cross (1542–91) and St Teresa of Avila (1515–82)*
▶ *people with a passionate concern for the needy such as St Vincent de Paul (1580–1660)*
▶ *martyrs like Margaret Clitherow and Edmund Campion (Chapter 11).*

But, by the path it had chosen, it had ceased to be the Church of more than one section of Western Europe.

Insight

The sixteenth century ended with a number of Churches, as Western Christendom was irreversibly fragmented. But under the direction of the Council of Trent (1545–63), the Catholic Church set in hand far-reaching reforms in the 'Counter-Reformation'.

The wars of religion

Wars of religion raged throughout Europe from the mid-sixteenth to the mid-seventeenth centuries: in France (1562–98), in Germany (1618–48), in England (1642–62). Religious difference was only one factor among many, but it did sharpen divisions. Eventually, the Peace of Westphalia (1648) recognized Protestantism in Germany. In France, the Edict of Nantes (1598) had already declared tolerance for Protestants. But this was revoked by Louis XIV in 1685 and hundreds of thousands of French Protestants (*Huguenots*) were forced to flee.

In 1662, the Act of Uniformity reasserted Anglicanism as the established religion in England. The Church of England took severe action against Roman Catholics and nonconformists such as John Bunyan (1628–88). This Baptist tinker from Bedford wrote *Pilgrim's Progress* and the hymn 'Who would true valour see' in his prison cell (Chapter 20). The 'Glorious Revolution' of 1688 brought William and Mary to power in England and gave Protestant dissenters, but not Catholics, a measure of religious toleration.

Conclusion

Reforms within the Church were inevitably mixed up with social forces, politics and a growing sense of nationalism. All this produced conflict, sometimes prolonged and savage. It is not surprising that people grew weary and frustrated. Some moved their allegiance in other directions.

Sometimes they embraced a rationalism which marginalized or excluded religion. Pietists emphasized an experience of a relationship with Christ, which largely disregarded or dismissed the perceived formalism of the established churches (page 332). Others embraced a 'broad church' inclusiveness which seemed in danger of incorporating so much that it said nothing that was distinctive.

But the young Luther had represented many in his despair at a Church which seemed to block the way to a joyful, liberating faith in the living God. The need to rediscover the gospel message of the New Testament had been urgent. The Reformation led to a divided Europe; but many regarded this as a price worth paying.

10 THINGS TO REMEMBER

1 *The Church of the Middle Ages was marked by corruption and by deep devotion to Jesus.*

2 *Martin Luther, a German Augustinian monk, rediscovered St Paul's emphasis on the grace of God – and called for widespread reforms within the Church.*

3 *Despite excommunication he stood his ground and the Reformation took hold.*

4 *In 1500 there was a single medieval Catholic Church in Europe.*

5 *By 1600 there were many Churches, including Lutheran, Calvinist (Presbyterian), Church of England and Roman Catholic.*

6 *Some enthusiasts with zany ideas pushed the boundaries of reform to breaking point. They sometimes paid with their lives.*

7 *The Reformation in England took a unique path. In addition to ideas from Luther and Calvin, King Henry VIII's divorce shaped events.*

8 *A key doctrine of the Reformation was 'justification by faith' with its strong stress on God's grace, as taught by Paul in his letter to the Romans – and by Jesus (Luke 18:14).*

9 *The Catholic Church responded with a Counter-Reformation, which did not yield to Reformation ideas.*

10 *Four centuries later, the Second Vatican Council accepted many Reformation ideas, e.g. the importance of reading Scripture and worship in the vernacular.*

18

To the present day

In this chapter you will learn:
* *about the Enlightenment and the Church*
* *about challenges to Christianity*
* *about post-modernism and consider the future of the Church.*

The age of reason

Insight

The Enlightenment, with its stress on scepticism and reason, buffeted the Church. In response, some within the Church wanted to strip the Christian faith of miracle and mystery. 'Deism' became influential.

The spirit of 'the Enlightenment' can be summed up in the famous words of the French philosopher **René Descartes** (1596–1650): '*Cogito, ergo sum*' (I think, therefore I am).

Reason was the starting point. All problems could be solved by its application. In particular, there was a growing confidence in scientific objectivity – the capacity to isolate any part of our world, to discover the principles on which it works, and to harness these to our advantage. Earlier scientific study had been driven by a concern to reveal more fully the glory of the Creator, and to glimpse his purposes through Creation (Chapter 10). In contrast, in the world of the Enlightenment, *man* was the measure and centre of all, and the notion of purpose was marginalized.

There was great confidence in progress and the mastery of the world that this would bring. All things were possible. Knowledge, as the English philosopher **John Locke** (1632–1704) maintained, is derived from the five senses – that is, from our experience. Furthermore, humanity (which was capable of knowing all) was, or should be, autonomous and free. Freedom of the individual was, in sharp contrast to any previous age, more important than communal solidarity. Thus *Voltaire* (1694–1778), the brilliant French writer, constantly sided with freedom of thought against any 'orthodoxy', particularly that of the Church.

This new way of viewing the world gradually emerged in the second half of the seventeenth century and throughout the eighteenth. It had no necessary place for a Christian God who had taken human flesh and who remained in a close, intimate relationship with his people through the Holy Spirit. God could easily be excluded altogether. Or he could be regarded as a remote 'watchmaker', who had set Creation in motion and then removed himself from any active involvement – an absentee Deity.

David Hume (1711–76), the Scottish philosopher, argued that if nature is uniform, and if human reason is able to provide all the answers, there is no place for miracles. This presented a great challenge to the Christian faith which is based on belief in the Incarnation and Resurrection of Jesus (Chapters 1 and 3).

The Enlightenment and the Church

Enlightenment ideas made a great impact and the Church was forced to rise to this strong intellectual challenge. In 1736 **Bishop Joseph Butler** (1692–1752) in his influential *Analogy of Religion* complained with irony that Christianity *'is now at length discovered to be fictitious'*. Some within the Church came to terms with Enlightenment thinking by more or less removing the supernatural. *Deism* (the belief that God is a remote Supreme Being rather than 'Our Heavenly Father') became very popular.

Uncertainty entered the hearts of the denominations. Many English Presbyterians became Unitarians (that is, they rejected the doctrine of the Trinity). Within Anglicanism it became possible to hold high office and lean heavily towards Unitarianism, as did **Richard Watson** (1737–1816), Regius Professor of Divinity at Cambridge and later Bishop of Llandaff. The mainland European Protestant churches became defensive and strongly rationalist. As a result they lost the power to arouse emotion, to convert and change people. They retained their Anglican, Lutheran and Reformed identities, but their links with the State became a rather formal reminder of an earlier spiritual and political reality.

REVIVAL!

Insight

Some Christians countered the Enlightenment stress on scepticism with an emphasis on conversion and the transforming power of the Holy Spirit. Central to this revival were the Wesley brothers. Methodism was born through powerful preaching, good organization – and song!

As so often happens in the history of the Church, the Holy Spirit breathed life back into a body which desperately needed reviving, fulfilling once again Ezekiel's prophecy about bones and breath (Ezekiel 37). One of the first signs of this was the Pietistic movement in Germany in the second half of the seventeenth century. The Pietists returned to basic beliefs: a sense of sin, the work of Christ in winning salvation on the Cross, and the importance of faith and forgiveness. While orthodoxy had become cold, cerebral and lifeless, Pietists were warm, immediate and intensely devoted to the crucified Christ. They had little time for the institutional Church.

Their most famous representative was **Count Zinzendorf** (1700–60), a leader of the Moravian Brethren who traced their origins back to **John Hus** (1369–1415). The Moravians in turn influenced **John Wesley** (1703–91) whose heart, he recalled, was 'strangely warmed' when he attended one of their meetings in

London's Aldersgate Street on 24 May 1738. This happened as Wesley listened to a reading from the preface to Martin Luther's commentary on Romans. In that moment he came to a fresh understanding of what Christ had done for him.

Although he had a fine intellect and wide interests, Wesley's faith was essentially a religion of the heart. As he and other evangelicals – such as the great orator **George Whitefield** (1714–70) and, in America, the theologian **Jonathan Edwards** (1703–58) – preached, there was an immense response. Often this came from ordinary working people, more or less outside the established Church. Many of these early Methodists learnt to speak publicly and to organize effectively – a key factor in the formation of Trade Unions and, eventually, of the Labour Party.

Sadly, the Anglican Church was not sufficiently imaginative to find ways of keeping Methodists (as the followers of Wesley came to be called) within the Church. Gradually, they formed another denomination (pages 230 and 371).

This revival came about as a reaction against certain consequences of the Enlightenment. At the same time it was an expression of the Enlightenment, in that it depended heavily on 'evidences' which were grounded in experience – especially transformed lives. It was the Church's response to the challenge of a new culture; or, as those involved would have claimed, it was *God's* response.

Some Christians came under these influences, yet remained in their own churches. One famous example of this is the 'Clapham Sect', a group of distinguished politicians, business and professional people. They were evangelical Christians within the Church of England, and they remained there. They sought to win the middle and upper classes for Christ and to attack social abuses. The MP William Wilberforce (1759–1833), the Cambridge clergyman Charles Simeon (1759–1836) and Lord Shaftesbury (1801–85) were outstanding leaders of a movement which:

▶ helped to bring the slave trade to an end
▶ did much to improve working conditions in factory, field and mine

(Contd)

- ▶ pressed the need to regulate working hours for children
- ▶ together with Methodism, helped transform Britain from the lax moral and religious conditions of the late eighteenth century.

In this way they laid the foundations for the higher moral and religious tone of the Victorian era (1836–1901); an era often (with some justification) accused of hypocrisy, but which also saw many major reforms. Some historians argue that the evangelical revival was a major factor in explaining why Britain did not have an upheaval similar to the French Revolution (1789–95).

The story is told about David Hume, the great sceptical Scottish philosopher, who was hurrying to hear George Whitfield preach in the open air. On telling his friend that he was going to hear Whitfield, Hume's friend responded in surprise, 'But you don't believe what he says'. 'No,' replied the philosopher, 'but Whitfield does'. Clearly, great preaching was the best show in town!

Romanticism

Jean-Jacques Rousseau (1712–78), the French philosopher, was an early Romantic, as was **William Wordsworth** the English poet (1770–1850). The Romantics celebrated the heart as well as the head. The Romantic Movement became a force in the early nineteenth century. It emphasized emotion, intuition, nature and history. As far as religion was concerned, it gave '*a new appreciation of the dramatic, the extraordinary and the otherworldly*' (D W Bebbington).

This was a factor in reviving Catholicism in Europe, after the setback of the mid-century revolutions. In 1846, 38 out of 59 Spanish dioceses had no bishop. Two years later Pope Pius IX fled from Rome in disguise when a mob fired on his palace, killing a priest. Romanticism provided a rationale for returning to the authority of the papacy, which had been derided in the high days of the Enlightenment. It was now seen increasingly as part of the Church's defence against the onslaught of revolutionary rationalism and atheism.

Looking back

The medieval Church no longer appeared to be a disaster to
be avoided. Rather it was seen as a model to be followed. The
immense popularity of all things *Gothic* (such as medieval buildings)
is one example of this. Another is the movement known as
Ultramontanism (literally 'across the mountains') which pressed for
a strong papal role. The most important exponent of these views was
Pius IX (Pope 1846–1878). He denounced nearly all modern or non-
Catholic ideas in the fiercely conservative *Syllabus of Errors* (1864).
He also convened the first Vatican Council (1869–70) which defined
papal infallibility for the first time. In contrast to the evangelicals,
who met their challenges by returning to the Bible and the experience
of the Holy Spirit in daily life, Catholicism sought to return to a very
high view of the Church and the authority of its representatives.

There was a similar revival of interest in authority within Anglicanism.
The parlous state of the Church at this time can be gathered from
Matthew Arnold's comment in 1832 that 'The Church of England
as it now stands, no human power can save.' Some leaders felt the
need to learn from the courage and clarity of the early, and even the
medieval, Church. *The Oxford Movement* which was led by **John
Keble** (1792–1866), **E B Pusey** (1800–82) and **John Henry Newman**
(1801–90), returned constantly to these themes. It is also called the
Tractarian Movement because its leaders issued a series of influential
tracts, in which they vigorously set out their views. This was
essentially a return to a more Catholic emphasis, with a high view of
the Lord's presence in the Eucharist and the central role of the priest.

These emphases were disliked and combated by some other
Anglicans. Controversy was robust and sometimes ended in the
courts. But liturgy and theology within Anglicanism were gradually
transformed. The Tractarians looked back to the medieval Church
and introduced many features which are recognizable today, such
as robed choirs, coloured vestments, ornaments and candles. Some
Anglicans converted to Roman Catholicism – notably Newman and
Henry Edward Manning (1808–92), both of whom became cardinals.

In the same century, famous preachers filled some of the large churches which were built then – sometimes in a spirit of competition – by the various denominations. Most famous was the Baptist, **C H Spurgeon** (1834–92). Called 'the prince of preachers', he filled London's Metropolitan Tabernacle, established children's homes and a theological college. This varied ministry still flourishes today.

Historical and scientific challenges

The challenge of the Enlightenment was sharpened by the application of the tools of historical and critical scholarship to the Bible. Many scholars treated the Bible as if it were simply a human composition like any other book. They appeared to challenge not only questions of authorship, but the whole supernatural undergirding of the Bible. If the Scriptures told of miraculous events which were not part of the experience of modern people, then there must be some other explanation for those events.

So ran the argument. It was taken further by the apparent challenge of science. In particular, the theory of evolution put forward by **Charles Darwin** (1809–82) gave a very different account of creation from that in Genesis (page 177). *Doubt* became a problem for many thoughtful Victorians, for whom religion was a vitally important matter. '*The ship of faith rocked gently at its moorings*' (Owen Chadwick).

The response of many liberal Christians was similar to that in the early eighteenth century. They jettisoned large tracts of traditional belief (miracles, much of the Old Testament and any belief in hell). They saw Jesus primarily as a supreme human teacher and example – and revealer of God in word and deed. Sin tended to be seen as error rather than evil, and salvation as sacrificial living.

Particularly after the First World War, scholars such as **Karl Barth** came to see that it was unhistorical, unscientific and philosophically naïve to reject all possibility of the supernatural. Certainly the evidence has to be weighed, but there should be no assumption that such things are impossible. Furthermore, the sheer power of the Bible to transform those who heeded its message was once again realized. All this became urgent as people faced:

▶ *the challenges of war*
▶ *godless totalitarianism in Nazi Germany (Chapter 14)*
▶ *atheistic Marxism in the Communist states of Eastern Europe.*

Notions of unstoppable progress and human goodness were destroyed by the Great War (1914–18). Biblical doctrines of sin and salvation were seen to be relevant – though the immense suffering of the War severely challenged Christian faith. The scientific challenge was in one sense more easily dealt with, as theologians came to see that much of the Bible was not addressing *how* questions but *why* questions (Chapter 10).

In the twentieth century Nature came to be seen, not as a machine, but as a delicately balanced organism of which we are part. In the twenty-first century, climate change has become a major issue on the international stage, arguably even more important than combating terrorism. Some would argue that Nature is in danger of being destroyed, precisely because religious questions of purpose (the 'why' questions) have been marginalized.

Expansion

Insight

From its earliest days, the Church has been outward-looking. The energetic modern Missionary Movement began in the late eighteenth century. The effects of this continue today in the lively and expanding churches of Africa, Asia and Latin America.

The Church in the West declined before the forces of the Enlightenment. But there was fresh energy for Protestant missionary expansion from the late eighteenth century, with the advent of a new agency: the voluntary missionary society (many of which still flourish in today's very different climate). The motivation for this missionary work was complex, but leading factors were:

▶ *the increasing colonial expansion of Protestant countries – especially Britain and Holland (although some missionaries spoke against the policies and practices of colonial powers)*
▶ *a burning evangelical desire to spread the gospel.*

Catholic overseas missionary work, which had been substantial – particularly in the Americas – declined in the eighteenth century. In the early nineteenth century, Roman Catholic commitment to missionary endeavour began to return.

The cumulative results in Africa, Asia and South America were immense. Although the Church has declined numerically in the West, at the beginning of the twenty-first century Christians represent about one-third of the world's population because of this growth. The Church worldwide continues to be the largest movement in all history (Chapter 12).

> The period since 1830 has been one of the three great ages of Christian evangelization since the first century, so that countries that had hardly heard of Christ in 1800 have flourishing Churches that venerate their own saints and martyrs – Korea, Japan, Australia, Nigeria and Uganda, among others. (A O J Cockshut)

The *ecumenical movement* (the coming together of churches) arose partly out of the missionary movement. Some leaders in the 'sending' churches came to believe that it was foolish and wrong that young churches should reflect church controversies and divisions from another continent. Other factors which gave rise to ecumenism were a deeply-felt biblical vision for unity (based on Jesus' prayer in John 17) and the weakness of the churches in some parts of the world. These churches felt the need to stand together (page 237).

The Church in society

Insight

Evangelicals like William Wilberforce and the 'Clapham Sect' continued to stress the Scriptures. They believed in miracles – and were themselves responsible for a 'miracle' when (after a very long struggle) slavery was outlawed in the early nineteenth century.

The Industrial Revolution brought prosperity to some; it brought poverty, suffering, dislocation and rootlessness to many others. Thousands moved from the country into the new, monochrome, hastily built industrial towns and cities. The response of the churches was patchy; indifference was mixed with committed concern. The latter gave rise to massive church building programmes and engagement with social, moral and educational issues. Christians became involved in a host of ways as they sought to alleviate some of the problems. Founded by **William Booth** (1829–1912), the Salvation Army has become famous for its practical, and musical, Christianity (page 231). Others began to challenge the economic theories which gave rise to so much suffering.

F D Maurice (1805–72), an English Anglican, was particularly influential in questioning:

▶ the cult of individualism
▶ the glorification of competition as an unavoidable law of economics
▶ the uncritical acceptance of the notion of laissez-faire economics (non-interference by governments in the workings of the market) which favoured the rich.

Christianity, Maurice argued, is about cooperation. It has a duty to attempt to persuade people of the relevance of its view of what it means to be a human being, living in community. To this end, in 1848 he founded a movement called *Christian Socialism*. His ideas live on and have influenced many, including some leading modern politicians. Maurice started a tradition of questioning capitalism and some of its practices. Among those who took the same path was **Charles Kingsley**, advocate of 'muscular Christianity' and author of *The Water Babies*. This novel highlighted the terrible plight of chimney boys and the evils of child labour in general.

Leo XIII (Pope 1878–1903) issued an encyclical (*Rerum Novarum*) in 1891. This was a landmark. While it attacked Socialism, it also maintained that employees have rights and employers have obligations, including a fair wage.

Throughout the twentieth century there was pressure from some for capitalism to be replaced or radically modified. One landmark was the Conference on Politics, Economics and Citizenship (COPEC), held in Birmingham in 1924. COPEC challenged economic individualism. **William Temple**, Archbishop of Canterbury from 1942 to 1944, was a leading participant. He laid down important principles of equality and emphasized the need to subordinate the 'profit motive' to the 'service motive'. All this was important for the emergence of the Welfare State in Britain in 1948.

The gospel of personal redemption and the call to social action are both clear in the Bible. Concentration on the former can lead to indifference to poor social conditions. Equally, there is a danger that the so-called 'social gospel', with its concern for questions of political and economic structure, might replace the spiritual challenge of Christ to the individual. This undoubtedly happened at times. At a World Council of Churches conference in Bangkok in 1972, salvation was debated as if it were a concept wholly related to the structural sins of societies, rather than the personal sins of individuals.

But there is widespread agreement that the churches must seek to apply the principles of the gospel to the *whole* of life in society. One example of this was the Church of England report entitled *Faith in the City* (1985), which challenged politicians – and the Church itself – to combat urban deprivation. The report was strongly criticized by some Conservative politicians but it gave rise to the Church Urban Fund which continues to sponsor a wide range of projects. A sequel entitled *Staying in the City* was published in 1995; *Faithful Cities* was produced by the Commission on Urban Life and Faith in 2006. The Church also continues to have a visible and active presence in rural Britain.

Religion in the USA

One striking feature of the USA today is that it is a very religious culture. Many different faiths can be found: from the new ideas which bubble from California, to the large Jewish community in New York. However Christianity – in its wide diversity – is the religion embraced by most Americans. Some 40 per cent claim to attend church regularly, while headcounts indicate about 22 per cent! There is, however, no 'State religion'; the writ of private enterprise runs here too.

The story of American Christianity is too complex to chart here. (Readable accounts can be found in the *Atlas of the Christian Church* (Equinox) and *A History of Christianity* by Diarmaid MacCulloch). Colonizers sought to establish the Church of England in North America as early as 1619 (in Jamestown, Virginia). Most famous of the early English settlers are the 149 who set out from Plymouth on the *Mayflower* in 1620 to escape the straitjacket of the English Church.

Over the years, a wide range of churches has found a place in American society. For example, there are some 60 million Roman Catholics and a large number of Independent, Fundamentalist and Pentecostal Churches. Churches from the USA continue to exert worldwide influence, through a large number of overseas missionaries.

The number of Roman Catholics in the USA (currently around 1 in 5 of the population) is rising with the increasing number of Hispanic citizens. There are some 6 million Jews in the USA, and 4 million Muslims.

Post-modernism

Both the Enlightenment and the Romantic Movement had confidence in our capacity to discover Truth. Modernism and especially post-modernism (the cultural movement of the late twentieth century) rejected such confidence. Some doubt that there is any objective reality which can be known. On this view, all that is left as important is to express one's experiences and inner feelings and to relate to others. Significantly, in this climate a spiritual approach to life enjoyed something of a resurgence in the late twentieth century. This remains strong among many who are outside, or uneasily on the edges of, the traditional churches. It tends to be private rather than corporate and easily degenerates into superstition and bizarre practice, under the umbrella of 'New Age'. Several Christian writers and researchers have explored this important topic, including Grace Davie, John Drane and David Hay (pages 111 and 347).

Articulate atheists use the media to propagate their views. But society has not become atheistic and rationalistic. In most Western countries many people believe in God, angels and prayer (page 230). Many people claim church membership, even though they do not attend regularly. Modern Western society is sometimes described as secular, because throughout the twentieth century organized religion declined and faith in God is seldom a factor in decision-making – in contrast to Islamic nations. But Western society could equally well be described as superstitious. In Europe and in the USA, horoscopes have never been more popular. This presents the Church with a challenge – and with an opportunity to show that reasoned faith in the Living God is a far better way of dealing with an unknown future.

Into the twenty-first century

Writing a few decades ago the Trappist monk Thomas Merton could say: '*We are living in the greatest revolution in history, a huge, spontaneous upheaval of the entire human race... This is not something we have chosen or are free to avoid.'*

In the twenty-first century our world is both exciting and daunting. Many in the West enjoy greater affluence and longer life than their forebears – but a considerable number of families continue to live in poverty. The rate of change is extremely rapid. Terrorism and global warming have moved to the top of the political agenda. It is predicted that the direst effects of the latter will be felt in the developing world, with resulting mass migration, disruption and conflict. In our 'global village', communication and trade are trans-national. While new and exciting developments mean wealth and opportunity for many, life remains very hard for many more.

Of the world's 1.3 billion children:

▶ over 500,000 children have no toilet facilities
▶ almost 500,000 children lack access to published information
▶ over one-third of children live in dwellings with more than five people per room
▶ 376 million children have more than a 15-minute walk to water and/or are using unsafe water resources
▶ 246 million children work, with 171 million engaged in the worst forms of child labour
▶ 134 million children have no access to any school
▶ more than 91 million children under five years of age are growing up with debilitating hunger
▶ 15 million are orphans as a result of AIDS
▶ an estimated 1 million children enter the commercial sex trade every year (and last in it for about ten years).

(Source: Lausanne Forum, 2004)

People continue to die in their millions from tuberculosis and malaria; leprosy disables millions more. Huge numbers still live in abject poverty. In the West the 'fuel crisis' refers to oil; for many in the developing world it means lack of wood for cooking. Clean water is an urgent requirement that would transform millions of lives. 'Water wars' are forecast by some commentators; indeed, tension between India and Pakistan over water supplies was reported in 2010. Enlightened self-interest, as well as compassion and justice, should prompt the wealthy nations to address these pressing issues.

> The Millennium Development Goals will not be met unless poor people have adequate sanitation, the UN Secretary General, Ban Ki-moon, warned in November 2007. Every year the lack of it contributes to the deaths of 1.5 million children.

Given such enormous problems, the call of Jesus Christ to love our neighbour as ourselves has never been more urgent. Such love needs to be worked out in many political arenas of tough debate and informed decision-making, as well as in simple good neighbourliness. Social justice is agape love painted on a large canvas. Non-governmental organizations, some of them Christian (such as CAFOD, Christian Aid, Tearfund, World Vision) play an important part in the alleviation of suffering, and in long-term strategic thinking. At the end of the twentieth century, many churches and Christian charities responded to the need for medical supplies in Eastern Europe, especially Romania.

Nearer to home, soup-runs and shelter for hungry and homeless people in British towns and cities are organized by churches working together ecumenically. 'Nightstop', a church-inspired organization providing short-term accommodation for homeless young people, in ordinary homes, is found in many towns and cities. Street Pastors (sometimes called 'Street Angels') are playing an important role in many town centres (page 267).

A future for the gospel?

Within the churches there has been a movement away from a hierarchical, priest or minister-dominated concept of the Church, to an understanding of the Church as the whole people of God.

This was given impetus by the enormously influential Second Vatican Council (1962–5) convened by Pope John XXIII (page 220). Other significant emphases were discussed in Chapter 13, including the charismatic movement with its stress upon renewal by the Holy Spirit, and liberation theology with its insistence on God's bias towards the poor. In a world of rapid change, the churches continue to adapt and to communicate the gospel. They also contribute vigorously to current debate and action on social and ethical issues.

As the world population explodes so does the size of the Christian Church, which grows by some 70,000 new members every day (page 215). While the Church struggles to hold its own in Europe, there is rapid growth in Africa, Asia and the Americas. The world Church of the twenty-first century will be increasingly young, energetic, poor, non-white and Pentecostal. In some places it will be made welcome, in others it will be persecuted. Sadly, Christian martyrs do not belong only to the past (page 193).

The certainties of the past, particularly those of the Enlightenment, no longer hold sway. Uncertainty brings danger and opportunity. Post-modernism, with its stress on personal choice and experience rather than on objective truth, may mean that the Christian viewpoint will be increasingly disregarded in the West. Bishop Lesslie Newbigin's experience of 'cold contempt for the gospel' may become more common. Much in post-modernism is contrary to Christianity and there is a danger that sections of the Church will simply try to ignore the problems posed by this new way of viewing life and truth. But post-modernism and its legacy cannot be ignored – for ideas are in the air we breathe, the newspapers we read, the television programmes we watch, the social networking sites we visit, and the assumptions we share.

In a million different situations, the challenge to modern disciples of Jesus Christ remains constant. Their calling is to demonstrate afresh that the gospel is a wonderful resource for living, and that faith, hope and love are priceless gifts from God.

A community of hope

Throughout its history, the Church has shown great energy in
crossing boundaries of culture and class. And it has engaged
with many ideas, some of which have been hostile to a Christian
understanding of life. At such times, the Christian calling is difficult
and exciting. Reflection on the past can give us courage to face the
future.

There is much that is ambiguous in the history of the Church,
which is a patchwork of shame and glory. The Church has been
corrupt, compromised and weak, standing in need of God's
forgiveness and strength. It has also ministered to the needs of
the deprived, inspired hope and positive action, spoken for the
voiceless and stood by the powerless. It has preached the good
news of Jesus Christ and made disciples of all nations. It has
survived fierce persecution, often emerging stronger, as in modern
China.

Perhaps the word 'Church' is too general, for the Christian faith
is lived and shared in tens of thousands of local congregations
and by millions of individual Christians. Popes, patriarchs,
archbishops, moderators, councils and synods exercise great
influence and eventually wend their way into the history books.
But the effectiveness of the Church stands or falls with the
quality of fellowship and outreach to be found in churches
on a thousand street corners and in ten thousand fields and
forests.

'*The church is a community of hope, which looks with humble
confidence to the future*' (John Stott). Through glory and shame,
the eye of faith can discern that 'our God reigns'. Time and
again he has breathed life into what appear to be spiritually dead
or dying lives and communities (Ezekiel 37). Sometimes God works
in hidden and obscure ways, but Christians believe that he never
lets go and always beckons us on to his future. Throughout the
third millennium, Christians can continue to have confidence

in that same God, as they reflect upon the promise of Jesus concerning his Church: 'the gates of hell will not overcome it' (Matthew 16:18).

'The secularization thesis assumes that… as the world modernizes, it will necessarily secularize: the two are assumed to be linked, theoretically speaking.

The data, however, are beginning to indicate otherwise. The modern (or modernizing) world has not secularized in the way that had been anticipated. And the material emerging from all corners of the globe suggests that it will not, in the foreseeable future … so it is hardly possible to argue that religion, and specifically Christianity, is incompatible with modernity. The patterns of religion that have emerged in Europe look increasingly like an exception, rather than a global prototype.'   (Grace Davie of Exeter University)

10 THINGS TO REMEMBER

1 *The Enlightenment, with its stress on reason rather than revelation, challenged the Church.*

2 *A revival in the Church's fortunes was kick-started by the Wesley brothers and the rise of Methodism.*

3 *This 'evangelical revival' had strong moral and political emphases, with effective advocacy for better working conditions and the abolition of slavery.*

4 *The nineteenth-century Oxford Movement brought considerable change to the Church of England with vestments, robed choirs, organs replacing gallery bands, and a more Catholic theology.*

5 *The publication in 1859 of Charles Darwin's* Origin of Species *caused vigorous debate about the Bible and Creation.*

6 *At the same time, Biblical scholarship caused many scholars to view the Bible differently.*

7 *During the eighteenth and nineteenth centuries huge energy was poured into missionary work, resulting in a truly worldwide Church.*

8 *While the Church worldwide grows in the twenty-first century, Christianity in Europe struggles. Sociologists refer to 'the European exception'.*

9 *The speed of growth of Christianity in modern China is remarkable.*

10 *As it is confronted by new challenges and a fast-changing world, the worldwide Church continues to possess both energy and adaptability.*

Part five

A great inheritance

19

Holy places, art and architecture

In this chapter you will learn:
- *about buildings – ancient and modern*
- *about art in Western history*
- *about Christian sites and holy places.*

The earliest days

Jesus' ministry took place mainly in the open air. Neither his little group of followers, nor the crowds who flocked to hear him, required a building or needed any visual magnificence. From time to time this has also been true for later Christians, and a meeting for worship in the open air – perhaps beside a lake – is often a treasured memory. But this does not mean that Jesus rejected all holy places and buildings, or their splendid decoration. Indeed, after his resurrection his first disciples met daily in the Temple precincts.

Jesus' ministry rested on the Jewish religion. He and his first followers had been brought up in this, and they remained practising members. The Gospels underline the importance of the synagogue for Jesus and his contemporaries. Judaism was, and is, intensely corporate. Private or group devotions were viewed against the background of the worship and obedience offered by all Jewish people. In Jesus' day that included the sacrifices offered daily according to the law of Moses in the Temple at Jerusalem. This had been newly restored and lavishly decorated by Herod 'the Great' (a brilliant tyrant whose building feats, sometimes in the desert, were breathtaking).

Some Jewish sects were strongly opposed to the Temple and its priesthood. That was not because of the building or its liturgy as such, but because Jerusalem had become tainted in their eyes by too much cooperation with the Roman occupying forces. This represented, for these groups, compromise with pagans who worshipped many gods.

But Christianity quickly separated from its Jewish roots. The early believers soon realized that Jesus' life, death and resurrection had made both Temple and animal sacrifices redundant. The early Christians came to see that on the cross, Jesus had become our Great High Priest, who had offered the one perfect sacrifice for sin: his own life.

At first, Christian worship took place in people's homes or in the open air. That did not last long. Any movement which passes into a second and third generation tends to become an institution. This happened to the Church. As it increased in numbers and spread through different countries and cultures, it developed an organization with identifiable 'places'.

The best known early places are the *catacombs* (burial chambers), where people could meet underground for worship and to commemorate their dead. This invisible meeting place was ideal, for the Church was intermittently persecuted for the first 300 years. As soon as specific places became identified with Christianity, art was employed to beautify and to instruct. The catacomb paintings are the earliest known form of Christian art. They often show Jesus as:

▶ *the Good Shepherd*
▶ *the King who promises salvation*
▶ *the giver of the Communion meal.*

Some of the more wealthy Christians were buried after the Roman manner in ornately carved stone coffins. These carvings show Jesus and his disciples with Christian symbols instead of the gods of Greek and Roman mythologies.

Not all Christian worship had to be secretive, even during the first 300 years. The earliest known Christian church is a house adapted soon after AD 200, in Dura Europos in Syria. Two rooms were turned into a baptistery and decorated with wall paintings. A similar house church, from two centuries later, has been found in Britain at Lullingstone in Kent.

Christians begin to build

Insight

When the Emperor Constantine converted to Christianity early in the fourth century, Christians began to build in earnest. Some fourth-, fifth- and sixth-century buildings still exist, including the Church of the Holy Sepulchre (Jerusalem), the Church of the Nativity (Bethlehem) and the Church of the Holy Wisdom (Istanbul).

Christianity was eventually 'permitted', and then almost immediately adopted as the official religion of the Roman Empire under the Emperor Constantine, early in the fourth century (page 260). So church buildings were not only allowed; they were required. But because there had been no specific form of church building before, the first churches were copied from two different types of building already popular in the Roman Empire. These were:

▶ *the mausoleum*
▶ *the meeting hall or basilica.*

THE HOLIEST AND THE GRANDEST

As soon as the public building of churches was possible, a longing to locate the sites of central events in Jesus' ministry made itself felt. The most holy place in all Christendom is the Church of the Holy Sepulchre in Jerusalem. This vast building stands over the place where Jesus was crucified – and where his tomb was located, according to fourth-century Christians (a claim which has been supported by recent archaeology). Around the remains of the rock tomb of Jesus, there still stands a huge octagonal shape built by Constantine the Great in the fourth century. He also built a basilica over the site of the Nativity in Bethlehem. The great church now standing there, over the cave celebrated as Jesus' birthplace, dates from the next century. (Caves were, and are, used as stables.)

Mausoleums were round or octagonal in shape. This enabled people to gather round a tomb for commemorations and worship (an obvious 'coming out into the open' of the catacomb tradition).

The basilica was a rectangular pillared hall where hundreds, or even thousands, could gather to listen to speeches or witness ceremonies.

Both shapes could be either large or small and both have been used ever since by Christians the world over. The round shape became more common in the Eastern Empire, and this is the form commonly associated with the Eastern Orthodox churches of Greece, Russia and those of the Middle East generally. The rectangular shape, with nave and aisles, became more general in the West – so much so that many Western people today think of it as *the* shape for a church.

The grandest early church still standing is the Church of the Holy Wisdom (*Hagia Sophia*) in Constantinople (Istanbul). Built in the fifth century it is decorated all over with mosaics in gold and other colours. It is huge enough to hold thousands at a time, magnificent even today after centuries as a mosque and now just as a museum. The mosaics show bishops and saints, and emperors and their courts, as God's servants clad in priestly garments. The Eastern Emperors were the 'popes' of Church and State. They were contemptuous of the claims of the bishop of Rome to this position.

The round, or centrally orientated, church was not totally confined to the East. Those which survive in Britain were built by the Order of Knights Templar as copies of the Holy Sepulchre in Jerusalem. Examples can be found in London (the Temple Church), in Northampton, Cambridge, and Little Maplestead in Essex. This influence is seen in modern churches where a central tower dominates.

The most memorable churches are grand buildings in cities and towns, built under the patronage of a king, bishop or other wealthy person. But, of course, most churches were humble buildings in villages. The vast majority of these were of timber, built in the same way as huts and barns. Few have survived from earlier than the thirteenth century. The earliest in Europe is in Greensted, Essex, dating from the eleventh century. There are twenty or so stave (timber) churches in Norway which survive from the twelfth century onwards.

In the early days, stone churches were rare and reserved for wealthy patrons (royal, episcopal, cathedral, civic or monastic). A large stone church was sometimes called 'the white church' (hence Whitkirk or Whitchurch), because it stood out from all other buildings. Some English villages have cathedral-like churches, built out of economic success e.g. Lavenham in Sussex, where the wool trade flourished.

OPEN-AIR SITES

Although the Church of the Holy Sepulchre is nearby, Christians still gather for worship in their thousands in the 'garden tomb' in Jerusalem. This is not the actual site of Jesus' burial but it is a *garden* (not a huge building!) and helps modern pilgrims to visualize – and 'feel' – the events of the first Easter morning.

The desire to visit open-air holy sites as well as buildings grew during the twentieth century, partly as a result of renewed interest in Celtic Christianity. Lindisfarne, Iona, Glendalough and St David's welcome an increasing number of pilgrims, many attracted by the stories of Columba, Cuthbert, Aidan, Dewi, Kevin, Patrick and Brigid. Stone crosses from the days of the Celtic Mission (Chapter 16) may be found in many places in Britain. They served as a gathering place and the characteristic Celtic decoration on the circular cross is often still visible. Some holy places have no strong associations with the past. Since the 1960s, Taizé in the Burgundy region of France has become a place of ecumenical pilgrimage for thousands of (mainly young) people from all over the world and from every Christian tradition – and none.

The most famous holy place in France is the town of Lourdes. Its fame is based on the belief that the Virgin Mary appeared to St Bernadette in 1858 and that it is a place of healing. For over 100 years pilgrims have visited the town – some 5 million each year in the twenty-first century. Many seek healing, but the Roman Catholic Church authorities employ strict criteria before accepting a healing as a gift or sign from God. Some modern sceptics come away impressed by the joy and hope they witness. Research points to a widespread and long-term decrease in anxiety and depression following a pilgrimage.

In southern Italy in 2003, a huge church was dedicated to Padre Pio who died in 1968 and was canonized in 2002. Miracles were attributed to him, he bore the stigmata (wounds like Christ's) on his hands, and some 7 million pilgrims converge on this site each year.

Focal points

Church buildings were influenced by the Christian ceremonies that took place inside them and for which they were built. The basilica, or the great octagon or circle, held the people, but the focal points for worship were:

- *the altar or table for Holy Communion*
- *the lectern or desk – from which the Scriptures were read and sermons preached*
- *the throne (the 'cathedra') for the bishop.*

These were placed together so that the people faced them. The fourth essential focal point was the font for baptisms. Originally a great basin of water, this was sometimes placed in a separate building nearby. In later church buildings it is usually found at the back, near the entrance – to symbolize that it is through baptism that we come into membership of the Church.

The mosaics which covered most of these early churches usually had a gleaming gold background and depicted prophets, saints, bishops and

Christian emperors. Presiding in the centre were Mary holding the infant Jesus, or Jesus reigning in majesty. In the early period, Christ was not depicted as suffering on the cross. Instead, the emphasis was on his humble friendship, or his power and glory as resurrected Lord.

Decoration

> **Insight**
>
> Art of various kinds has adorned church buildings for centuries, notably stained glass and wall paintings. The latter are very vulnerable to the forces of nature, and to the enthusiastic paintbrush of the undiscerning! Such art was designed to beautify – and to instruct.

A wide range of visual arts was employed. Carvings in stone became a feature of Christian decoration from the beginning. These often depicted scenes from the Bible and the lives of saints. Carvings in wood were also made but fewer have survived, since wood is more vulnerable than stone. Work in textiles (including embroidery), gold, silver and jewellery was also commissioned by the Christian Church. The clothes worn by the ministers – and the carpets, draperies and other furnishings – should be, it was felt, the finest possible. Altar frontals, episcopal and priestly vestments, and the vessels for use in the celebration of the Eucharist became very fine – at least the equal of any to be seen in the palaces of kings and emperors.

Monasteries became centres for the production of books – many of them beautifully scripted and illustrated. In Chapter 16 we noted the *Lindisfarne Gospels*. These were made on Holy Island (Lindisfarne) in Northumbria around 700, 'in honour of St Cuthbert'. In 950, a priest called Aldred wrote an Anglo-Saxon translation between the lines of the Latin text.

From the early days in the catacombs, Christians expressed their faith through paintings. In the East this took a unique form – the icon – which has recently become known, admired and copied in the West and worldwide. An icon is a stylized painting on wood of a Christian subject, usually Christ or a saint. Icons are painted according to strict rules which are devotional as well as artistic. The resulting icon (which means 'image') is regarded not just as a picture to inform the mind or excite the emotions: in some ways it is seen as an embodiment of what it depicts. So it can be revered and gazed upon in prayer, for it was created in prayer. There is no more powerful assertion of the place of art in Christian worship than the tradition of making and using icons (but see page 361).

The Cross

In medieval Europe the Church was, at first, the only patron of the arts. So all the early examples of painting, carving and work in stained and painted glass are of Christian subjects. And many great paintings from medieval and Renaissance times are of biblical or church events or people.

In the late Middle Ages, the earlier dislike of portraying Christ's crucifixion in agony had vanished. Instead, there was a concentration on the human suffering that he, as God's Son, underwent to bring salvation to the world. There were frequent representations of episodes from Christ's final days: the whipping, the crowning with a wreath of thorns, and the jeering crowds. The nailed body on the cross was no longer robed in majesty but almost naked, in pain, with wounds and blood in evidence. In this tradition there is a strong appeal to the emotions. Perhaps the most famous early example is *The Crucifixion* by Grünewald, painted in 1515–16. In the twentieth century, Salvador Dali's painting of Christ of St John of the Cross became equally famous.

Insight
The earliest Christian art did not focus on the cross of Christ. Favourite themes were Jesus as the Good Shepherd, the King who promises salvation and the provider of the Lord's Supper. The cross as a subject for art emerged strongly in the late Middle Ages.

COLOUR AND HEIGHT

Art performed another important function; it helped to teach an illiterate population the basic elements of the Christian faith. This is why scenes of Christ's birth, life, suffering and resurrection were so frequent – together with Old Testament figures, saints and bishops. The finest display of original stained glass in situ is probably in Chartres Cathedral in France. In Britain, York Minster has more than a third of the nation's surviving medieval glass. Wall paintings are much more vulnerable and few remain, although Pickering in Yorkshire and Chaldon in Surrey retain impressive examples.

The medieval age produced the most splendid churches in the *Romanesque* (round arch) and *Gothic* (pointed arch) styles. It produced and furnished them in such numbers that in many parts of Europe the local church is more likely to be medieval than of any other period. Some buildings are huge. The cathedrals in Seville, Milan and York are the largest – in that order. Some are very large (most cathedral, collegiate and abbey churches). Even the smaller ones are often the largest building in the town. And there are little country churches by the thousand all over Europe.

The Gothic style aimed at height. Most British builders went for width as well as height. But all Gothic churches aimed to dominate the town with tall towers and spires, pointing to heaven. This was an inescapable sign of the ultimate Power to whom all must give account. The cathedral in Ulm in Germany has the highest medieval spire at 161 metres. Britain's tallest spire is that of Salisbury Cathedral, at 123 metres. Many who have never visited Salisbury are nevertheless familiar with the cathedral through the painting by John Constable (1776–1837).

These great buildings were much more beautiful and magnificent than any other human construction seen by medieval people. The first glimpse would cause them, as it does us, to gasp in wonder and to feel both lowliness and exaltation. In the twenty-first century we marvel at the superb medieval craftsmen and their amazing ability to shift huge blocks of stone. We wonder too at their willingness to work for years on a building which they would not see completed in their lifetime. Some medieval cathedrals, York Minster for example, took more than 200 years to complete.

Insight

Immense cathedrals were built over the centuries – an amazing and costly feat in the days before modern engineering. Reaching to the heavens, they declared – and declare – 'Glory to God in the Highest!'

ART

Art and architecture have been first cousins from the earliest days. Christian churches have been adorned by artists and craftsmen in every possible way. And a great deal of art, also sponsored by the Church, flourished outside these buildings.

A walk around any of the great European art galleries reveals the importance of the Bible as a source of inspiration for painters and sculptors. Supreme among subjects are the annunciation to Mary by the angel Gabriel foretelling the birth of her son, the shepherds and wise men visiting the infant Christ, the Last Supper, the crucifixion and the resurrection. But we instantly think also of numerous great works of art on other biblical themes: Michelangelo's *David*; Masaccio's *The Expulsion of Adam and Eve*; Rembrandt's *Jacob Wrestling with the Angel* ... The list is endless.

In every generation there has been an attempt to make Jesus Christ contemporary. Styles of clothing, buildings and landscape often refer to the time of the artist rather than to the time of Christ. This is an attempt to say that, in a profound sense, those ancient events are 'happening' here and now.

For example, in a seventeenth-century painting in Peru's Cuzco Cathedral, Jesus and his disciples eat guinea-pig (an Andean Indian delicacy) at the Last Supper.

This sense of enduring significance was captured powerfully by Stanley Spencer who, in 1920, painted Christ as carrying his cross through the English village of Cookham.

Simplicity and destruction

From time to time in the 2000-year history of Christianity, there has been a reaction against prevailing artistic trends. Sometimes an attempt has been made to create Christian art and architecture which reflect the humility of Jesus Christ, rather than his glory. Occasionally, Christians have tried to do without holy places or, more often, to do without elaborate art or architecture (or music: Chapter 20).

In the eighth and ninth centuries, in the East, there was a movement against icons. Many were smashed or defaced. The protesters became known as *iconoclasts* or image-breakers. They argued that icons of Christ showed only his humanity. And they feared that people were tempted to worship the icons rather than God himself.

In the twelfth century, a movement for greater austerity in the monastic life spread through the Benedictine houses, and the Cistercian movement began. As well as protesting against laxity in lifestyle, Cistercians also argued for greater simplicity in the art and architecture of abbeys. Their leader, St Bernard of Clairvaux, wrote:

> *Tell me then poor monks, what is gold doing in the holy place? For the sight of these sumptuous and amazing vanities encourages man to give rather than to pray... the poor are allowed to groan in hunger and the money they need is spent in useless luxury.*

Such accusations have often been levelled against elaborate buildings and extravagant acts. We are reminded of Mary's extravagance in pouring expensive perfume on Jesus' feet. Judas rebuked her but Jesus defended her action (John 12:1–8).

In the Reformation of the sixteenth century, some believers, particularly those of the Calvinist persuasion, were so antagonized by pictures and statues that they destroyed or beheaded them. But these destructive phases were intermittent and represent the extremism which occasionally strikes many religious and political traditions. This Protestant influence sometimes improved the medieval buildings. By removing a clutter of statues and altars, they allowed the simple dignity of the architecture to stand out.

The new churches built by these Reformation groups often introduced another form of church architecture. The main focus was on the *pulpit* rather than the *altar*. The seating was arranged so that as many as possible could see the preacher; galleries were often built at first-floor level. This did not mark a complete change, for the other focal points of Christian worship – the communion table, the font, and the seats for the president and his assistants – were retained.

Many of these churches are very beautiful in their simplicity. Examples abound of churches erected during the seventeenth and eighteenth centuries for the Protestant denominations, with somewhat more emphasis being given to the Holy Table within Anglican buildings, such as the Wren churches built in London after the Great Fire of 1666. (Christopher Wren designed 53 churches, including St Paul's Cathedral.) In these buildings, art is still in evidence, if not in statues and vestments, then in monuments and painted patterns around biblical texts and other inscriptions.

Insight

Some Christians reacted against art and ornamentation, believing these obscured and detracted from the spoken word and the essential simplicity of the gospel. *Iconoclasts* sometimes destroyed art and artefacts.

CONTRASTS

During the Middle Ages, the Church was the dominant patron of art and architecture. Gradually, during the sixteenth and seventeenth centuries, power and wealth moved to the royal houses and the aristocracy. The kind of art and architecture favoured in their palaces and public buildings was copied also in the churches.

In southern Europe, a highly elaborate style known as *Baroque* produced some fantastic churches similar to theatres or opera houses. Huge canopies with angels and rays of the sun towered over the altars. Pulpits were as high as 7 metres, with so many curtains and saints and trumpet-blowing angels that the preacher could hardly be seen! The best examples of this exuberant style of decoration are to be found in Austria and southern Germany, although most countries in Europe were touched by this fashion.

There was also at that time an almost opposite enthusiasm for everything in the classical style of ancient Greece and Rome (producing the word 'Gothic' as a term of contempt for the 'barbaric' styles of the Middle Ages). So churches, as well as great houses and public buildings, were built like ancient temples: rectangular, with graceful lines and Doric, Ionic and Corinthian columns. This was the style exported by empire-builders and missionaries to the New World. So most of the older buildings in Canada and the USA are in this 'colonial' neo-classical style.

Back to the future

In the nineteenth century, there was a reaction against simplicity and Gothic once again became popular. Not only churches, but other public buildings – and even houses – started to sprout pinnacles, traceried windows, stained glass and other features of medieval art and architecture.

The great increase in Europe's population at that time led to thousands of new churches being built. Most of them are in this medieval style, although nineteenth-century skills in mass manufacture were fully employed and not much was handmade. Because of the survival of so many medieval churches in Europe, and the large number of nineteenth-century churches built in that style, many people still think that the only 'proper' church building is 'Gothic' (i.e. one that looks 'medieval').

In the twentieth century there were many changes in fashion, in building and in decoration. Modern technology ensured that new materials became readily available, such as fibreglass, concrete (in fact, invented first by the Romans), plastic, aluminium. It was a century which felt free from dominance by the past. There was much greater diversity in buildings, as people experimented with different styles and tried out new combinations.

In recent times, there has been a greater emphasis on abstract art and symbolism. This can be seen most clearly in contemporary stained glass, in textiles for church use and in paintings (and to a lesser extent in sculpture). There has also been a conscious attempt to adjust church architecture afresh to modern patterns of worship. There were disadvantages to the nineteenth-century enthusiasm for the building styles of the Middle Ages. In particular, church buildings were not always suitable for the styles of worship then evolving. They exercised a retrograde influence, for worship had to adjust to the building, rather than the other way round. Large old buildings present real – and expensive – problems for many modern congregations.

Several contemporary churches have abandoned the basilica pattern with its eastward-facing focus, so dominant in the West for 17 centuries. Architects have experimented with the centralized plan of the Eastern tradition, with the focus nearer the centre and the congregation ranged around. One famous example is the Roman Catholic Cathedral in Liverpool. Built in the 1960s, this is affectionately known as 'the Mersey funnel'.

This freedom from tradition has been expressed in some very unusual churches, of which Gaudi's *La Sagrada Familia* (Holy Family) Church in Barcelona is probably the best known. Started in 1882 it is scheduled for completion in 2026. Gaudi worked on the project for over 40 years and is said to have commented, 'my client is not in a hurry'. The first cathedral to be consecrated in the twenty-first century (2 September 2002) was Our Lady of the Angels in Los Angeles, which harnesses solar power.

Glory to God in the highest

In one sense Christianity has no holy places. Unlike a Muslim or a Hindu, a Christian is under no obligation to make a pilgrimage.

God can be experienced with equal power and worshipped with equal validity in every place.

But it is a universal human need, which Christianity in no way denies, that people need a place, usually a building, which is set apart (which is what the word 'holy' means) for the worship of the Creator and Sustainer of the universe. These places remind us of the claims upon us of that which is greater than ourselves. In building and decorating such places, we offer our skills, our labour and our most precious gifts as tokens of our worship. For, as the Bible makes abundantly clear, true worship involves nothing less than the offering of our lives to be 'a living sacrifice' (Romans 12:1–2).

In recent years, interest in church buildings has grown. Many – especially cathedrals – have become extremely popular with tourists. For example, St Paul's Cathedral welcomed 1.82 million visitors and worshippers in 2009, while York Minster welcomed over 700,000. Attendance figures at cathedrals rose by 37 per cent between 2000 and 2007.

The church buildings of these many centuries, with their architecture and artistic contents, witness to the immense contribution that Christianity has made to the universal human need for sacred places. They also bear witness to the billions of hours that have been devoted over the centuries, by thousands of unknown people – in planning, building, carving, painting, weaving... The exercise of these skills has produced some of the most beautiful and magnificent works of human achievement.

Why such massive endeavour? Partly because of the God-given creative drive within human beings. Partly, no doubt, to bring glory to the town or city, the clergy, and the architect. But there is another motive too – a desire to glorify Almighty God, and to raise human hearts in worship, adoration and thanksgiving.

10 THINGS TO REMEMBER

1 *The first Christians met for worship in homes and (in Rome) in the catacombs.*

2 *The earliest known Christian building was a house adapted for the purpose soon after 200 AD.*

3 *A similar house-church in Britain is dated around 400 AD.*

4 *Impressive church buildings were established as early as the fourth, fifth and sixth centuries.*

5 *Fine churches and cathedrals continue to be built in the twenty-first century.*

6 *Open-air 'holy sites' are very popular with modern pilgrims.*

7 *From early days, believers decorated their buildings 'to the glory of God' – with mosaics, carvings, paintings ...*

8 *Icons – stylized paintings on wood of Jesus or the Saints – were developed in Eastern Orthodox churches.*

9 *Eventually the Church became the patron of the arts, although the counter-urge for simple, plain church buildings also persisted.*

10 *Early paintings of Jesus avoided his crucifixion, but from the late Middle Ages this became a common subject.*

20

Music and literature

In this chapter you will learn:

- *about hymns – ancient and modern*
- *about the tension between words and music*
- *about books – ancient and modern.*

Continuity

Jesus came, he said, not to destroy the Hebrew Scriptures ('The Law and the Prophets') but to fulfil them; to bring out their full meaning. The Old Testament Law (or Torah) is itself rich in poetry, from the spectacular rhythms of its opening drama – the Creation story – to the song of Moses in Exodus. Among the volumes of later history, Chronicles goes into enthusiastic detail about the specialized music of the Temple. Elsewhere the prophets, impatient as they are with empty rituals and meaningless songs, themselves soar to heights of lyrical writing as they deliver the Word of God for good or ill.

The highest peaks of Israel's praises are found between the Law and the Prophets, in 'The Writings'. Job, the Song of Songs and Ecclesiastes are outstanding literary works. But the best-known, and best-loved, of all Bible poetry is the collection of Psalms. These 150 Hebrew songs in many moods were sung in the temple and synagogue; they were adopted by Christians from the earliest days of the New Testament Church.

Those who travelled with Jesus for his three public years repeatedly heard him use these already ancient verses as inspired pointers to himself. The singing of a Psalm concluded the last meal before his death; at least two others were on his lips as he hung dying on the cross. After the resurrection they were part of his final teaching, and after Pentecost the widening circle of his followers took up the song. With few exceptions, their successors have kept such music echoing around the globe.

Slip into Evensong in an Anglican cathedral and you will hear the appointed Psalm(s) for that day. Touch down in the Western Isles of Scotland and, in tiny chapels clinging to rocky hillsides, the people will be working through their own rugged metrical forms. In the lively meetings of the less formal 'Community Church', you may clap hands to songs with phrases lifted freely from the same Bible source. And in their different forms, Psalms introduce weddings ('Praise, my soul, the King of heaven'), are sung at funerals ('The Lord's my shepherd') and accompany national remembrance ('O God, our help in ages past').

These Hebrew songs have become part of a totally international body of praise. They adapt to plainchant; Gregorian, Anglican or Taizé chanting; solemn Genevan paraphrase; exuberant hymns; and the music of flute or guitar, synthesizer or whatever is to come. In the monastic stream, notably among the Benedictines, each of the day's services has its own mood and music, with the rotation of Psalms as a fundamental element of their song.

From the Rule of St Benedict: sixth century

'The Psalmist says, "seven times a day have I praised you". We will fulfil this sacred number of seven if we satisfy our obligations of

Transformation

But from its earliest days Christianity had to repudiate the idea that it was simply a new sect or subdivision of Judaism. In worship as in teaching, the dying and rising again of Jesus the eternal Son of God was central. His coming marked not simply a new direction, but in some ways a total contrast with what had gone before. Continuity and contrast are found in perfect balance in the New Testament Letter to the Hebrews.

The New Testament has nothing like the musical detail, or even the poetry, of the Old. What it does have, apart from encouragements to sing (Ephesians 5:19 and Colossians 3:16), is an apparently random sprinkling across its pages of some of the new songs (e.g. Ephesians 5; Philippians 2; 2 Timothy 2). They sparkle within their prose context mainly by vocabulary and rhythmic structure. The climax of all such writing comes with the sequence of poems in the last book of the Bible (Revelation), which opens the door an inch or so to catch the sound of singing in heaven. In all these songs, the focus is different from the Old Testament Psalms. The centre of praise is now Jesus Christ the Lord: specifically the Lord once crucified, now living and reigning in the glory of the Father.

A singing faith

The pre-eminence of Jesus in the New Testament is matched exactly in one of the earliest pieces of evidence about the Church, from a writer outside its membership – even outside Judaism.

'*On an appointed day*', wrote Pliny the Younger to the Roman Emperor Trajan in about AD 112, the Christians '*had been accustomed to meet before daybreak, and to recite a hymn antiphonally to Christ as to a god …*'.

Having gradually transferred some of the Sabbath (Saturday) traditions to the first day of the week in honour of Christ's resurrection, Christians went on singing this kind of hymn for the next 20 centuries. One of the finest survivors from the Church's youth (probably fourth century) is the Latin *Te Deum Laudamus*: 'We praise thee, O God, we acknowledge thee to be the Lord… Thou art the King of glory, O Christ.'

English-speakers can still enjoy the flavour of the ancient Greek and Latin hymns in the paraphrases of John Mason Neale, a Victorian pioneer in their recovery, and some more recent versions. Medieval Christendom leaned heavily on the Psalm tradition, and Miles Coverdale added 'spiritual songs' to his sixteenth-century translation of the Psalms. After the Reformation, it was the 'Old Version' of paraphrases by Sternhold and Hopkins which held sway in parish churches – true to the Hebrew but harsh to the ear.

Martin Luther, the father of the European Reformation, was a keen singer, a gifted musician, and a strong believer in the power of hymns (not just psalms) in his vernacular German (not just Latin). '*Next to the word of God*', he said, '*music deserves the highest praise*'. Not only Germans but most English-speaking Christians still sing his tunes and themes, e.g. *Ein' feste Burg* (*A safe stronghold our God is still*), as well as much gentler music and the secular melodies he adapted for sacred purposes. John Calvin, by contrast, determined to stick to Psalms in church.

By around 1700, however, there was a new version of the Psalms by Nahum Tate and Nicholas Brady – more poetic and soon popular enough to be bound alongside the Book of Common Prayer (1662). This practice continued for a further hundred years.

Also around 1700, a young Southampton man named Isaac Watts (1674–1748) complained about the version of the Psalms sung in his dissenting chapel. His father challenged him to do better, and the English hymn as we know it was born. Just turned 30 years, Watts wrote with a scholar's discipline, a communicator's clarity, a preacher's passion – and sometimes a patriot's idiosyncrasy. He pioneered original hymns ('*When I survey the wondrous cross*') as well as transforming the Psalter – an alternative name for the Psalms.

A generation later, Charles Wesley (1707–88) greatly extended the range of hymnody. His hymns were enlivened by the direct freshness of his evangelistic travels on horseback, informed by his encyclopedic memory of the Bible, and constructed with amazing speed. His soaring verse still dominates most major hymn books and adorns many literary anthologies as poetry in its own right. Charles was uniquely assisted by his elder brother John, who also wrote hymns and translated others from German, as well as promoting and publishing Charles' hymns. To this day, the Methodist Church is renowned for its hymn singing.

> *When I survey the wondrous cross*
> *On which the Prince of Glory died,*
> *My richest gain I count but loss,*
> *And pour contempt on all my pride.*   Isaac Watts

> *Hark! The herald angels sing*
> *Glory to the new-born King,*
> *Peace on earth, and mercy mild,*
> *God and sinners reconciled ...*   Charles Wesley

Technically, the Wesleys were lifelong Anglicans, and other Church of England writers continued where they left off. From a long list we may select John Newton (1725–1807) – a converted slave-trader – and William Cowper (1731–1800), a poet of the first rank. Distinguished Victorian writers include Catherine Winkworth, Frances Ridley Havergal, and (Mrs) Cecil Frances Alexander. In their hymns we hear a clearer call to worldwide mission. Meanwhile, James Montgomery and Philip Doddridge led the Free Church stream. Reginald Heber, Christina Rossetti and Robert Bridges were genuine poets whose gifts were also used in hymn-writing.

To the present day

The first half of the twentieth century saw some falling-off in writing, and the consolidation of *Hymns Ancient and Modern* (which began in 1861) as *the* archetypal English-speaking hymn book. Its nearest rival was the *English Hymnal* (1906), revised by Ralph Vaughan Williams in 1933.

Recent decades have seen a worldwide explosion of hymnody, still too close for evaluation. Three of today's most popular writers of hymns and songs are Bishop Timothy Dudley-Smith, Christopher Idle and Graham Kendrick. The Taizé and Iona communities (notably John Bell) also produce music which is sung around the world.

With increasing technology and mass communication, Christian songs and hymns have crossed confessional and national boundaries more quickly than ever. American, Afro-Caribbean and Australasian tastes may not be the same, but styles overlap and mingle in recent hymnals and song-books. However, it is possible to move from one church to its next-door neighbour and find an entirely different pool of favourites. These are often sung with the aid of a large screen rather than a book.

SPIRITUALS

The Spiritual, whose mood and rhythms have crossed the Atlantic twice over, has proved to be an enduring art form. Its roots are in black Africa; its main development was among the slaves of the American continent. Its more genteel flowering, adopted by white North Americans and Europeans, has found ready affinities with folk-song and gospel hymns.

Oppressed peoples of many nations still find in them a vehicle for their cries to God for help in this life and the next. But it is not only the persecuted and poor who enjoy and appreciate them, and gospel choirs have never been more popular.

Music versus words

The art of written musical notation was developing around AD 1000. The choir could now sing a tune its members had never heard, simply by reading marks on paper! For the first time, a melody could be fixed and even attached to a composer's name. The art of harmony grew and musical decoration became increasingly complex. Reformers like John Wycliffe in the fourteenth century sounded a warning which was repeated four centuries later by John Wesley and is still heard today. What is the point of lovely music, he asked, if it obscures the sense of the words and is produced by those who neither mean nor believe what they sing?

▶ *In 1519, Erasmus expressed a trenchant criticism of ornate music that obscured the text:*

> **Modern church music is so constructed that the congregation cannot hear one distinct word. The choristers themselves do not understand what they are singing... Words nowadays mean nothing.**

▶ *At the Reformation, the emphasis changed markedly from long, intricate lines and harmonies with Latin words, to simple settings in English, which had to be comprehensible to the listener. Archbishop Holgate's injunction in 1552 to the Dean and Chapter of York Minster reveals this tension:*

> **We will and command that there be none other note sung or used ... saving square note plain, so that every syllable may be plainly and distinctly pronounced, and without any reports of repeating which may induce any obscureness to the hearers.**

▶ *The Council of Trent (1545–63) decreed that liturgical words should be clearly heard, and that music should avoid profane origins and associations. Both of these directives proved something of a losing battle.*

> *In 1550, John Merbecke produced his 'noted' version of the main church services in line with Reformation ideals, and with free rhythms matching the natural flow of the words. His acclaim came much later in the revival of his work, for different reasons, nearer our own times. The work of Thomas Tallis and William Byrd, also in the sixteenth century, and Henry Purcell in the next, retains its power and attraction for many.*

Insight

The tussle between 'keep it plain' and 'let's beautify in praise of God' was joined in the visual arts *and* in Church music. The great Lutheran composer J S Bach added the words *Soli Deo Gloria* (To God alone be glory) to many of his scores.

MAGNIFICENT MUSIC TO WONDERFUL WORDS

The decades from 1600 onwards saw a magnificent flowering of church music, notably in Italy, and the beginnings of oratorio. But it was the Lutheran J S Bach (1685–1750) who emerged as possibly the greatest composer ever produced by Western culture. As an organist he was breathtaking, as a composer, prolific. He set Bible narrative to music as none before or since. His contemporary G F Handel wrote many oratorios, including *Messiah* (1741) – possibly the most popular of all religious compositions. This work retains its wide appeal, and has given rise to many choirs formed to sing it. Haydn's *The Creation* (composed in 1798) is another great work from the oratorio repertoire by a devout Christian.

Applause for popular oratorios like *Messiah* was not universal. Was it right to make the person of Jesus Christ the subject of what looked like, and was promoted as, popular entertainment?

Similar questions have greeted more recent shows and films. Critics argue that shows like *Jesus Christ Superstar* create an entirely new 'Jesus' and wrap him up in the pop music of its day. Others argue that musicals like *Godspell*, plays like Dennis Potter's *Son of Man* and films like *Jesus of Nazareth* contain substantial material from the Gospels. They can and do speak with a fresh voice to those outside the community of faith.

Haydn, Schubert, Verdi and Brahms are among a number of first-rank composers who wrote a Mass (sometimes more than one). This is a musical setting to five lyrical and significant passages from the Latin service. Among the greatest are Mozart's *Requiem Mass* (1791), Bach's *Mass in B Minor* (completed in 1738), and Beethoven's *Mass in D* (1825).

The Passion Narratives, using the words of the New Testament Gospels, have also been a fruitful source of musical inspiration. Two of the greatest examples of this form are the *St Matthew Passion* and *St John Passion* by J S Bach.

Composers continued to be inspired by the Scriptures, the Liturgy and Christian poetry. Still popular with choirs is Stainer's *The Crucifixion* (1887). More recent works of note include Edward Elgar's setting of Cardinal Newman's poem *The Dream of Gerontius* (1900); William Walton's *Belshazzar's Feast* (1931); Benjamin Britten's *Noye's Fludde* (1957), Leonard Bernstein's *Chichester Psalms* (1965) and David Willcocks' many carols. Many of today's composers – such as John Rutter, John Tavener, James MacMillan, Andrew Carter, Malcolm Archer, Philip Moore, Bob Chilcott and Richard Shephard – find inspiration from Christian themes.

Music in the local churches

The above are essentially 'performance' works requiring great skill, talent, and hard work in rehearsal. Back in the English parish church in the nineteenth century, music was again on the move ...

Thomas Hardy's novel *Under the Greenwood Tree* (1872) reflects the sadness of villagers in his father's time, at losing their gallery orchestra and choir as the organ took over. Parish churches began to imitate a style more appropriate to the cathedral; this initiative was driven forward by the spirit of the Oxford Movement (Chapter 18). Less affluent churches opted for harmoniums or even a barrel organ. The chanting of Psalms, in Coverdale's Prayer Book version, came to appear characteristically Anglican. But chanting is losing ground today, except where a strong and older musical tradition is maintained.

In our own day, the pendulum has swung again as other instruments are commonly heard, including drums, guitars and synthesizers. Christian worship continues to inspire creativity. Many local church organists and choir directors, such as Martin Dales and Meurig Watts, compose musical settings. Other musicians write and sing Christian songs in a more popular style – Dave Casswell, Ian White and Sharon Winfield, among many others. Dave Godfrey's songs, based on the Bible, are very popular with children.

TOP OF THE POPS

The Second Vatican Council in the 1960s gave encouragement to Roman Catholic writers and composers alike. New responsorial settings to the Psalms have been one outcome. But the older monastic music continues to be popular – Gregorian chant topped the charts for several weeks in 1995! The Bible is no stranger to the pop scene. In recent years, passages from Scripture heard by millions include Ecclesiastes ('*a time to weep and a time to laugh, a time to mourn and a time to dance … a time to love and time to hate*') and Psalm 137 ('*By the rivers of Babylon we sat and wept when we remembered Zion*').

Some Christian singers are firmly established as popular entertainers (Cliff Richard, Amy Grant, Beth Redman, Natasha Bedingfield). The work of other famous singers (Johnny Cash, Bob Dylan, Van Morrison) has been influenced by the Christian message. Elvis Presley acknowledged his Christian roots and his love of gospel music. The number of Christian bands playing contemporary music (often written by band members) is enormous. The annual Greenbelt Arts Festival gives many of these an opportunity to be heard by the thousands (of mainly young people) who attend. Other art forms flourish too; some examples are poetry (Steve Turner; Mark Halliday), drama (The Riding Lights Theatre Co.), mime (Geoffrey Stevenson), dance ('Springs'), magic (Mark Townsend) and clowning (Roly Bain). This is my personal selection from a wide range of possibilities.

The literature of faith

Insight

The earliest English literature is almost entirely Christian in character. Over the centuries the number of writers – dramatists, poets, novelists – who worked on Christian themes reads like a list of all-time greats. From Caedmon to Shakespeare, Milton to Charles Dickens, and on to the present day.

Caedmon (seventh century) is the earliest known English Christian poet; he is credited with the earliest surviving Christian hymn in the English language. The prose of King Alfred (848–99), like much of the whole corpus of Old and Middle English, clearly comes within the same tradition of faith.

The Mystery Plays of the thirteenth to sixteenth centuries have enjoyed a new lease of life in our own day. Following the Miracle Plays, they probably took their name from the 'mysteries' or trade guilds who performed them. They vividly presented great Bible events from the Creation onwards, developing strong local styles and texts, especially in the north of England.

The most popular survivor of all is the *Nativity Play* accompanied by Christmas carols. The huge number of Christmas carols in use reflects the pre-eminence of this festival in folk-religion, greatly reinforced by Charles Dickens and other Victorians. The Service of *Nine Lessons and Carols* was first sung in Truro Cathedral in 1880. The Service from King's College, Cambridge, was first broadcast by the BBC in 1928 and has become a media event of professional excellence, rather than the boisterous local celebration in which everyone joins. Both ends of this spectrum are valued by many millions around the world.

The writing of Geoffrey Chaucer (c. 1342–1400), together with his near contemporary William Langland and his successors, Spenser, Shakespeare and other Elizabethans, reflect their Christian heritage. Two masters of English prose who paid for their writings with their lives were the liturgical reformer Thomas Cranmer, and the Bible translator William Tyndale (page 200). The former enabled English speakers to pray in their own tongue; the latter made it possible for them to read or hear the Scriptures in English. We have already noted Melvyn Bragg's astonishing statement that Tyndale's work is 'probably the most influential book that's ever been in the history of language – English or any other' (page 97).

The poet George Herbert (1593–1633) and the satirist Jonathan Swift (1667–1745) were clergymen and Samuel Johnson (1709–84) was a devout layman. John Donne, appointed Dean of St Paul's Cathedral in 1621, is remembered for both religious and erotic poetry and for his powerful and original sermons.

> *All mankind is of one author, and is one volume. When one man dies, one chapter is not torn out of the book, but translated into a better language; and every chapter must be so translated ... No man is an island, entire of itself. Every man is a piece of the continent, a part of the main. If a clod be washed away by the sea, Europe is the less, as well as if a promontory were, as well as if a manor of thy friends or of thine own were. Any man's death diminishes me, because I am involved with mankind. And therefore never send to know for whom the bell tolls; it tolls for thee.* (John Donne: *Devotions upon Emergent Occasions*)

Two other Johns, Milton (1608–74) and Bunyan (1628–88), the scholar-statesman and the tinker-preacher, both stand in the Puritan tradition. Each produced several works of enduring worth and one masterpiece; in order, *Paradise Lost* and *Pilgrim's Progress*. Both created unforgettable images in verse and prose respectively, one from his study, the other largely from a prison cell. Each used his powerful imagination to illuminate eternal truth and practical living, from the enticement of temptation in the garden of Eden to the trials and triumphs of Christian pilgrims in this world's Vanity Fair.

Among the more committed, but less predictable authors was William Blake (1757–1827), visionary poet, painter and engraver. His poem 'Jerusalem' has become a popular and rousing hymn. Blake is one of those who would be surprised to find their prophetic verses adopted and domesticated in this way.

Insight

Two of the most significant lines in all English literature come at the end of a sonnet by John Donne (Dean of St Paul's Cathedral from 1621–31) celebrating Christ's Easter victory:

... One short sleep past, we wake eternally,
And death shall be no more. Death, thou shalt die.

To the present day

Many nineteenth-century poets explored questions of religious faith and doubt, including Samuel Taylor Coleridge, William Wordsworth, Robert Browning, Lord Alfred Tennyson and Matthew Arnold. Among twentieth-century Christian poets we note T S Eliot (a key figure in the transformation of poetry), Gerard Manley Hopkins (undiscovered until the twentieth century), Jack Clemo, Norman Nicholson, R S Thomas and W H Auden. David Adam and others have popularized a revived Celtic culture. *The river wanders, varies in pace and depth, but never runs dry.*

'Twenty years ago, I was driving up the M1 to Sheffield on All Souls' night. It was the year after my mother died and the Messiah was playing full blast on the car radio. And just for a moment, I had the certainty of resurrection. Maybe that's what great art does. Maybe art – music, writing, whatever – is a kind of resurrection, a redemption of the past... or, maybe, that's all just part of the illusion.'   (Margaret Drabble, novelist)

The desire to explore and explain the Christian faith has prompted apologetics (the defence of the faith), novels, poetry, essays and drama from twentieth-century believers such as Dorothy L Sayers, C S Lewis, G K Chesterton, J R R Tolkien and Charles Williams. Three Catholic writers – Anthony Burgess, Graham Greene and Evelyn Waugh – were powerful novelists, whose religious background and troubled faith strongly influenced their work. Novels and plays by Christians and unbelievers continue to explore great themes such as the existence and nature of God, suffering, meaning and purpose.

Biblical vocabulary and Christian concepts have become part of our cultural heritage and have found their way into everyday speech:

▶ *'It's the eleventh hour.'*
▶ *'She's the salt of the earth.'*
▶ *'He passed by on the other side.'*
▶ *'I wash my hands of the matter.'*
▶ *'She's a good Samaritan.'*
▶ *'He's a Judas.'*

Words and phrases from the same sources spill over into literature of various kinds, on a range of themes; for example, Aldous Huxley's novel *Eyeless in Gaza* (a phrase based on the story of Samson in the Old Testament), Arthur Miller's play *After the Fall* and P D James' whodunnit *Original Sin*.

In this brief note we have concentrated on English literature, but the Christian legacy is to be found in many languages. Christian writers find inspiration in a short passage originally written in Greek: a passage which reminds us of the power of words – and the significance of 'the Word made flesh'.

> **In the beginning was the Word, and the Word was with God, and the Word was God ... In him was life, and the life was the light of men. The light shines in the darkness, and the darkness has not overcome it ... And the Word became flesh and dwelt among us, full of grace and truth.** (John 1:1, 4–5, 14 RSV)

'Christian truths, Christian images, resonate more widely than the boundaries of Christian belief. Jonathan Miller, for example, who comes from a secular Jewish background, has said that Christian imagery constantly reinforces his sense of human tragedy.

The tragedy of being human, and the idea of the Incarnation is one of the great imaginative inventions of the moral imagination. I would find it very hard to think forcefully and properly without in fact being stocked with such images.

To a Christian, such a positive affirmation of Christian imagery should not be as surprising as at first glance it might appear. For Christian truths are not just beliefs which a select body of believers happen to hold. They are the reality in which the whole universe is grounded. So works of art can awaken faith, or at least the longing for faith. Van Gogh said he could not look at a picture by Rembrandt without believing in God. At the very least art, in all its forms, keeps the possibilities of faith alive. Christian art makes the faith explicit.'

(*Art and the Beauty of God*, Richard Harries)

'For many today, art has replaced God. The answer is not to turn art into Christian propaganda which all too soon passes its sell-by date, but for the church and the Christian community to allow art to speak as it should – to the imagination which, along with the conscience, is the only path for God to break through our shell of self-sufficiency. Art must delight [or shock] us before it can teach us and, if we honestly aim at the first we may well achieve the second; if we try for the second we shall nearly always miss the first.'

(*The Lantern and the Looking Glass*, Nigel Forde)

10 THINGS TO REMEMBER

1 Jesus and his disciples said and sang the same psalms from the Jewish Scriptures (the Old Testament) that Christians still sing today.

2 Martin Luther (1483–1546), Isaac Watts (1674–1748) and Charles Wesley (1707–88) are key names in the history of hymn writing.

3 Since then, Christians have written (and are writing) thousands of hymns and 'worship songs'.

4 Victorian hymn writers included many women – perhaps the best known is (Mrs) Cecil Frances Alexander.

5 'Spirituals' such as Swing Low, Sweet Chariot have become a popular vehicle for worship (and for rugby fans!)

6 Over the centuries there has been tension between ornate church music, and a desire for the words to be heard clearly and easily.

7 Many of the greatest composers wrote church music.

8 Much of the earliest English literature was Christian in content.

9 Phrases from the English Bibles of the sixteenth century have permeated the English language.

10 Melvyn Bragg made the remarkable claim that William Tyndale's Bible translation is 'probably the most influential book that's ever been in the history of language – English or any other'.

21

Modern lives

In this chapter you will learn:
- **that witnesses are the best evidence**
- **that not all Christians are inspiring**
- **that some Christians are very inspiring indeed.**

St Paul described members of the Corinthian Church as '*a letter from Christ ... written not with ink but with the Spirit of the living God*' (2 Corinthians 3:3). In the first letter of St Peter, believers are described as 'living stones' who together make up a 'spiritual house' (1 Peter 2:5).

Important as buildings, works of art and literature are, the greatest heritage bequeathed to us by the Christian centuries are people whose lives have been touched by Christ. It is *people* who believe in, or deny or ignore, the Christian faith. It is *people* who encourage and inspire us to follow Christ – or who put us off.

To end on a personal note – this has certainly been true for me. It was a fellow student who lived the Christian life with sensitivity and integrity, who set me thinking about questions of the Spirit. Questions about:

- ▶ *the existence and nature of God*
- ▶ *whether life has purpose and meaning*
- ▶ *whether Jesus' resurrection from the dead really happened*
- ▶ *whether prayer is valid, or superstitious nonsense.*

Since those early days I have been fortunate to meet a number of stimulating, intelligent Christians who have encouraged me in my discipleship. Of course I have also met bigoted, off-putting believers, too. And I am acutely aware that others may choose to use similar words about me. But I take heart from the fact that the first disciples were a very mixed bunch, too.

I think it was the Jewish writer Martin Buber who suggested that, concerning belief in God, '*there are no evidences, only witnesses*'. As this book has attempted to show, this is an exaggeration (Chapters 1, 3 and 6). But it is a helpful exaggeration. So it will be appropriate to end by glimpsing a few Christians' lives from around the world – people who are living witnesses to Jesus Christ.

Sister Sarah is an Indian Roman Catholic nun. Sisters from her religious order are scattered around the world; the headquarters are in London. For some years Sister Sarah worked in India, where she was born and brought up. She became expert in primary health care in rural areas. Her success in raising standards gave rise to invitations to speak at International Health Conferences. Now she lives and works in rural Peru, where I met her.

Her aim is to show the love of God in practical ways – through health care and feeding programmes. By means of a simple 'come and collect' system, she and her American colleague, Sister Antonia, provide a daily breakfast for 1000 Peruvian farmers – in no more than 30 minutes! The intention is not to make these families dependent; rather, it is to help provide the necessary energy required for long hours of survival-farming in arduous conditions.

Sarah does not usually wear a nun's habit. She wears scruffy trousers and a worn sweater like most of the farmers. Two things remain in my memory from our conversation: her tranquillity and her chuckle.

Jason Robinson had the distinction of playing for England at both rugby league and rugby union. He was a member of the Rugby Union World Cup winning team in 2003, and the team which lost in the World Cup final in 2007. He earned the nickname 'Billy Whizz' for his blistering acceleration and ability to weave and sidestep through defences. In recognition of his 51 rugby union international test caps for England he was awarded the OBE in 2008.

In *Finding my Feet: my autobiography* he describes how his journey into Christian faith helped him overcome problems with alcohol. His story shows the importance of day-to-day Christian witness. Jason came to faith largely as a result of observing the Christian example of rugby league player **Va'aiga Tuigemala**. In turn, Jason has influenced others, including the Scottish international **Euan Murray**, who also speaks of how re-discovering his faith has helped him on and off the field. Another former rugby player who is well known for his faith in Christ is New Zealander **Jonah Lomu**, as this report in the *Independent* shows:

> *As he thunders down the wing his opponents could be forgiven for dropping to their knees in prayer. He would be delighted if that happened. The brightest star of the World Cup may run at the opposition like a charging bull, but off the pitch the All Black is a shy young man and a devout Christian.*

The link between Christianity and sport is strong

▶ The YMCA (Young Men's Christian Association) was founded in London in 1844 and the YWCA in 1855. Both have become international movements and have produced some fine sports teams, especially in the USA.

▶ Some of Britain's famous football (soccer) clubs started as Sunday School or Church teams e.g. Aston Villa in 1874 by members of the Wesleyan Chapel Bible class, and Everton in 1878 by boys from St Domingo's Chapel Bible class. Sir Alex Ferguson, the legendary manager of Manchester United, owes much of his early enthusiasm for football to the Boys' Brigade (129 Glasgow Company).

Dr Veronica Moss is Chief Executive and Chief Medical Officer of the Mildmay Hospital in London's East End. The Mildmay is an independent Christian charity which specializes in HIV/AIDS.

In the early 1980s, there was great fear of this new disease: 'people hurled stones and bottles at our windows'. The Mildmay now plays a key role, not only in Britain (with an estimated 63,500 HIV/AIDS sufferers) but in Africa too (there are some 40 million sufferers worldwide; 90 per cent of them in the developing world). Since Veronica joined the Mildmay in 1986 it has changed from being an AIDS hospice to a rehabilitation centre, as anti-retroviral drugs mean that many HIV/AIDS sufferers now have a long life span.

Asked in 2007 about her hobbies, Veronica replied that she does a lot of reading – both for work and for pleasure. She added, 'I do not have much time for hobbies, but would love to learn to fly properly, as I had some lessons once.'

Gaza is often in the headlines and in 2007 the British press followed closely the kidnapping and ultimate release of the BBC journalist Alan Johnston. Gaza was back in the news following the murder of **Rami Ayyad**. Rami was a Christian who ran the only Christian bookshop in Gaza City. Married with two children, his wife was expecting their third child. Labib Madanat of the Palestinian Bible Society said, 'Rami was the ever-smiling one. He was the face of our Bible shop, always receiving visitors and serving them as Jesus would.'

It was reported that he was unpopular with radical Islamists who accused him of missionary activities. Rami received threats and his shop was bombed. In the face of all this, the 31-year-old continued his work. On 6 October 2007, as he closed the doors of the Bible Society bookshop, he was kidnapped and murdered by an unknown group. His body was found the next morning with bullet and knife wounds.

Eileen is a teacher from England who was forced to take early retirement because she suffers from multiple sclerosis. She continues to lead an active life although her mobility is severely limited. Two particular interests are music and enlisting support for *Save the Children* – which she does very effectively.

Eileen has a quiet faith. She does not feel angry at God for 'allowing' this to happen to her. She recognizes that illness and accidents are facts of life. Instead of asking, 'Why me?' she asks, 'Why not me?' She realizes that suffering is a problem which makes belief in God difficult for some people – but not for her. Eileen feels supported by friendship and by prayer. She retains her sense of humour and her peace of mind, as the following extract from one of her letters makes clear:

> *I've had to give up driving. The fatigue is rotten, but not such a worry now that I've stopped working. The blurred and double/ triple vision is a nuisance, but curiously interesting – for example the Cathedral has had two spires for a couple of years, there are three moons in the sky and an awful lot of eight-legged cats about! I am quite used to it now and it's not a worry. I've made no retirement plans, confident that something will emerge for me, when the time is right.*

These brief sketches make it clear that following the Christian Way involves much more than 'going to church' or belonging to a cultural group. When it is true to itself, Christian faith engages with real life. It brings challenge and inspiration; it gives strength and comfort in trouble.

Being a Christian means ... being a person in whom his (Jesus') life and character and power are manifest and energized ... Christian experience is not so much a matter of imitating a leader as accepting and receiving a new quality of life – a life infinitely more profound and dynamic and meaningful than human life without Christ. (Harry Williams CR: Anglican monk)

Glossary

Abba Father 'Abba' is one of the few Aramaic words found in the New Testament (Aramaic was Jesus' first language). It is an intimate family word – the nearest English equivalent is probably 'Dad' or 'Daddy'. Jesus addressed God the Father in this way – so did the first Christians. The word, and the close relationship to God which it describes, was a gift from Jesus to his disciples.

canon A Greek word meaning *rod* or *rule*, which came to signify a list or catalogue. In Christian usage it denotes the list of books regarded as Holy Scripture (Chapter 4).

creed A definition or summary of Christian belief. The earliest creeds are found in the New Testament, for example Romans 10:9 ('Jesus is Lord') and 1 Corinthians 15:3 (page 54). Later creeds include the *Apostles' Creed* and the *Nicene Creed*.

eternal life A new quality of life to be entered into, by God's grace, through faith in Jesus Christ. It starts in this world and continues beyond death – into eternity. The phrase is found frequently in John's Gospel and first letter.

evangelism Proclaiming or sharing the good news of God's love revealed in Jesus Christ. Roman Catholics tend to use the word *evangelization*. Sometimes this means the same as evangelism; sometimes it refers to the permeation of relationships and cultures with gospel values.

the gospel The good news of God's love revealed supremely in the life, teaching, death and resurrection of Jesus Christ. It means 'Glad tidings of great joy' (Luke 2:10).

William Tyndale wrote: 'Evangelio (that we cal gospel) is a greke word, and signyfyth good, mery, glad and joyfull tidings, that maketh a mannes hert glad, and maketh hym synge, daunce and leepe for joye.'

Gospels, synoptic The term used for the first three accounts of the life of Jesus in the New Testament. The Gospels of Matthew, Mark and Luke each have distinctive features but they share much similar material. The Fourth Gospel (the Gospel according to John) takes a very different approach to the life, teaching, death and resurrection of Jesus (Chapter 4).

high priest A title given to Jesus in the New Testament (especially in the letter to the Hebrews), signifying the fact that he has dealt with human sin. The offering he made was the perfect sacrifice of his own life.

Holy Spirit In the New Testament the Holy Spirit has many titles: the Spirit of God, the Spirit of Christ, the Spirit of Jesus, the Spirit of Truth, the Counsellor… Many of these titles convey the notion of the closeness (the 'immanence') of God, as opposed to the 'transcendence' of God the Father.

Incarnation The Christian belief that in Jesus, God became a human being in order to save the world. (This is quite different from *Reincarnation* – see page 167 and **Trinity**.)

liturgy Literally in Greek, 'the work of the people'. It came to be applied to worship offered in the Temple and, later, to Christian worship – especially the Eucharist.

mission Mission is a wider concept than evangelism, though it includes this. It embraces *all* that God calls his Church to do in the world: care for Creation and the pursuit of justice and peace, as well as praying for the world and spreading the gospel of Jesus Christ. The Swiss theologian Emil Brunner declared that 'the Church exists by mission as a fire exists by burning'.

monotheism Belief in one God. The three great monotheistic faiths are Judaism, Islam and Christianity. Because all three look back to the patriarch, Abraham, they are sometimes called 'the Abrahamic faiths'.

myth In common speech this is usually a 'bad' word, referring to something which is untrue – a fabricated story, perhaps even a lie. In theological language it is usually a 'good' word – referring to something so important and profoundly true that it can only be conveyed in the form of a story (page 64).

New Age 'The fastest growing spiritual movement in the world today' (Margaret Brierly). It is a movement without hierarchy or central organization. It stresses *spirituality*, which in this context means 'doing your own thing' – anything from meditation to hugging trees. '*In one sense the New Age Movement is a religion without being a religion, with its emphasis on self-realization rather than upon God*' (Graham Cray). See **post-modernism**.

polytheism Those religions which, like Hinduism, honour many Gods. Some Hindus believe in One Supreme Being. It is their belief that the 'many Gods' are different manifestations of the One God.

post-modernism 'Modernism' was the child of the Enlightenment (Chapter 18). *Post-modernism* is a 'buzz' word suggesting a time of rapid transition – a new way of viewing the world. '*Post-modernity is a flux of images and fictions … truth is human, socially produced, historically developed, plural and changing*' (Don Cupitt). Truth is viewed as relative not absolute, and insights from various places may be pulled together to form a view of life – a 'pick and mix approach' (see **New Age**).

salvation The activity of God which – supremely in Jesus Christ – brings healing, wholeness and reconciliation with God and one another.

Son of Man The title which, in the Synoptic Gospels, is used by Jesus to refer to himself. Scholars have debated its background and significance, and whether Jesus did in fact use the phrase. Its likely origins can be found in two Old Testament books. Throughout Ezekiel, God addresses the prophet as 'son of man' – i.e. *as a fragile human being*. In Daniel 7:13–14 the phrase refers to an awesome *heavenly* figure.

synagogue A Jewish meeting place for worship. Unlike worship in the Temple, synagogue worship did not (and does not) include animal sacrifice, but is based on prayers and readings from the Hebrew Scriptures. At the time of Jesus, as now, synagogues were established in every town with a Jewish community.

tabernacle A portable sanctuary (an elaborate 'tent') in which God 'dwelt' among the Israelites in the desert. It was the forerunner of the Temple.

Temple The first Temple was built by King Solomon (2 Chronicles 3). At the time of Jesus, the Temple in Jerusalem (built by Herod the Great) was the focus for national worship – including animal sacrifice. Herod's great Temple was destroyed by the Romans in AD 70. The Western Wall (sometimes called 'The Wailing Wall') remains from the original building and is a place for Jewish prayer and pilgrimage.

the Trinity The Christian doctrine that there are three 'Persons' in one God (page 114).

Virgin Birth The belief that Jesus Christ had no human father, but was conceived by Mary through the power of the Holy Spirit (Matthew 1; Luke 2). More properly called 'the virginal conception'.

wish-fulfilment The view of Sigmund Freud and others that Christians believe in God because (unconsciously) they find reassurance in the notion of a 'Father in heaven'. This criticism can be turned against itself. For example, Aldous Huxley admitted that for years he believed that the world was without ultimate meaning and moral purpose, because he wished to be free of irksome moral constraints.

Please refer to the Index for other topics (page 398).

Also by the author...

The Case Against Christ *John Young with David Wilkinson*

ISBN 0 340 90882 3 Completely revised in 2006.

Christianity is on trial. The authors act as Counsel for the Defence in the Case against Christ, then invite you to make your own decision.

Makes a brilliant case for Christ. Robert Warren, co-author of Emmaus

This book does much to set the record straight. Sir Cliff Richard

John Young has a great gift for communicating profound ideas simply and readably. Lord Habgood, former Archbishop of York

Quite first class. Bishop Hugh Montefiore

Essential reading for anyone earnestly questioning the Christian faith. Compelling reading. Mike Pilavachi of Soul Survivor

Addresses many major objections to the Christian faith ... a classic which we often recommend on Alpha. Nicky Gumbel

Taking it further

Many new books on various aspects of Christianity are published every month. It is therefore difficult to compile a list of titles which will not soon be out of date. Some books – including autobiographies – have been mentioned in the text (e.g. pages 86, 103, 104, 162, 165, 186, 210, 381, 385). To help readers who wish to explore further, some useful websites are given below, together with the names of some established authors and their areas of expertise.

Standard texts

Oxford Dictionary of the Christian Church (4th edition) (OUP, 2005)

Oxford Dictionary of Saints (OUP, 2004)

Catechism of the Catholic Church (Geoffrey Chapman, 2000)

Illustrated History of Christianity, (ed) McManners, John (OUP, 2001)

A History of Christianity, Diarmaid MacCulloch (Allen Lane 2009)

Publishers of Christian books

Hodder & Stoughton
www.hodderchristianbooks.co.uk

Bible Reading Fellowship
www.brf.org.uk

Church House Publishing
www.chpublishing.co.uk

Columba Press
www.columba.ie

Continuum
www.continuumbooks.com

DLT
www.darton-longman-todd.co.uk

Lion-Hudson plc
www.lionhudson.com

SCM-Canterbury Press Ltd
www.scmpress.co.uk

SPCK
www.spck.org.uk

York Courses
www.yorkcourses.co.uk

Other useful websites

www.anglicancommunion.org
www.caseresources.org (Catholic)
www.catholic-church.org.uk
www.christianaid.org.uk
www.christianityonline.co.uk
www.christianity.org.uk (Christian Enquiry Agency)
www.cofe.anglican.org
www.damaris.org
www.freshexpressions.org.uk
www.justchurch.info (Church Action on Poverty)

www.thegoodbookstall.org.uk
www.rejesus.co.uk
www.yorkcourses.co.uk (Group study material)

Some established authors

David Adam (Celtic spirituality; prayer)

Richard Bauckham (the Gospels – eyewitnesses and reliability)

Stephen Cottrell (Living the faith; spirituality)

Grace Davie (Sociology of religion)

Eamon Duffy (Church history)

John Drane (Christianity and new age ideas)

David L Edwards (History; Christian commentary on our times)

David Ford (Christian theology; inter-faith relations)

Paula Gooder (New Testament; devotional)

Billy Graham (Famous evangelist)

David Hay (Religious experience)

Joyce Huggett (Prayer)

Gerard Hughes (Jesuit priest – spirituality)

Bob Jackson (Church growth strategy)

Hans Küng (History and Christian commentary on our times)

C S Lewis (Modest-sized paperbacks on apologetics plus *Narnia Chronicles* and Science Fiction)

Martin Luther King (Great American civil rights leader)

Alister McGrath (Scholarly and evangelical, including *The Dawkins Delusion*)

Henri J M Nouwen (Spirituality: Catholic with wide appeal)

Daniel J O'Leary (Catholic spirituality)

Rob Parsons (Family life)

Adrian Plass (Living the Christian faith – a humorous approach)

John Polkinghorne (Science and religion)

John Pollock (Christian biographies)

John Stott (Scholarly evangelical)

Desmond Tutu (Faith in turbulent times)

Keith Ward (Philosophy; Christian commentary on our times)

Rick Warren (Strategy for leadership)

Robert Warren (Church strategy; living the faith)

Rowan Williams (Living and understanding the faith)

Lucy Winkett (Christian life and faith)

Tom (N T) Wright (Popular paperbacks and large academic works)

Philip Yancy (Living the faith – an evangelical perspective).

Index

Abba Father, *29, 118, 155, 164, 166, 167, 388*

Abelard, Peter, *313*

abortion, *262–3, 297*

Abraham, *94, 101*

absolution, *149*

abstract art, *364*

Act of Supremacy (1534), *324*

Act of Uniformity (1662), *328*

Acts of Pilate, *82*

Acts of the Apostles, *74–5*

adoration, prayers of, *120, 123*

Advent, *130, 132*

affusion, *140*

afterlife, *163–9*

agnosticism, *206*

Aidan, Saint, *302*

Aitken, Jonathan, *103*

Akabusi, Kriss, *95*

Albright, W.F., *88*

Alcuin of York, *303*

Alexander VI, Pope, *309*

Alexandria, *293*

Alfred, King, *377*

All Saints' Day, *197*

Alpha, *250*

Amnesty International, *265*

Anabaptists, *323–4*

Anderson, Sir Norman, *53*

Andrewes, Lancelot, *39*

Anglican Church, *227–30*
    and Evangelization, *246–7, 332–4*
    membership, *213*
    transformation of, *335–6*

Anglo-Catholics, *228–9*

Anglo-Roman Catholic International Commission (ARCIC), *146*

Annunciation, *198*

Anointing of the Sick, *149–50*

Anselm, *39, 313*

Anthony of Egypt, *296*

anthropic principle, *185*

Antioch, *293*

apartheid, *268*

apocalyptic writings, *75, 82–3*

Apocrypha, *68–9*

apostasy, *292*

Apostles, *283–7*

Apostles' Creed, *157, 161, 168*

apostolic succession, *294–5*

Aquinas, Saint Thomas, *313*

architecture, *351–7, 359–60, 361–6*

Arius, *293*

Arnold, Matthew, *335*

art, *357–63, 366*

Ascension Day, *132*

asceticism, *295*

Ash Wednesday, *131*

assisted suicide, *274–5*

Athanasius, Saint, *293*

atheism, *206, 230, 260, 342*

atheistic fundamentalism, *244*

Atherton, John, *271*

atonement, 35, 72
    theory of, 37–8
Auden, W.H., 160
Augsberg Confession (1530), 225
Augustine, Archbishop of
    Canterbury, 300–1
Augustine of Hippo, Saint, 103,
    106, 196, 292, 296, 300
Avignon Popes, 309
Ayyad, Rami, 386

Bach, J.S., 374, 375
Baker, Bishop John Austin, 46
Ballard, J.G., 170
Balthasar Hans Urs von, 161
baptism, 6, 31, 137–41, 150–1
Baptist Church, 139, 140–1, 224,
    226–7, 336
Barbour, Ian, 188
Barnabas, Saint, 285, 287
Baroque architecture, 362–3
Barth, Karl, 277, 336–7
Bartlett, David, 193
Base Communities, 241
Basil of Caesarea, 296
basilica, 354, 356
Bauckham, Richard, 16
beatification, 202
Bebbington, D.W., 334
Becket, Saint Thomas, 198
Bede, 168, 301
believers' baptism, 139, 141
Bellamy, David, 187
Benedictines, 361
Benedict XVI, Pope, 155, 223, 241
Bennett, Dennis, 251
Berenson, Peter, 265
Berlin Wall, 267–8

Bernadette, Saint, 356
Bernard of Clairvaux, 310, 361
Bible
    Apocrypha, 68–9
    canonical criticism, 86
    Christian view of, 80–1
    experiences of God in, 101–2
    form criticism, 85
    influence on art, 360
    as inspiration, 91–2
    languages of, 79–80
    in modern world, 61–3
    narrative criticism, 86
    New Testament, 69-76, 81-3
    Old Testament, 63–8
    power of, 95–6
    redaction criticism, 86
    reliability of
        manuscripts, 87–90
    and salvation, 35–7
    sex and violence in, 93–4
    source criticism, 84–5
    textual criticism, 84
    translations of, 96–7, 303–4,
        378
    vocabulary of, 370
    as word of God, 90–1
Bible Sunday, 91
Blake, William, 379
Blandina, 29
Bloom, Anthony, 103–4
Bonhoeffer, Dietrich, 21, 261
Boniface, Saint, 302–3
Boniface VIII, Pope, 309
Book of Revelation, 75–6
Booth, William, 232, 263, 339
born-again Christians, 105–6
Bosch, David, 186

Bourdeaux, Michael, *106–7, 210*
Boyle, Robert, *175*
Breaking of Bread, *141–2, 143, 144–7*
Bridge, Tony, *209*
Britain
 Evangelization, *301–4*
 multicultural society, *276–7*
 see also England
British Association for the Advancement of Science, *174–5*
Buber, Martin, *23–4, 384*
Bunyan, John, *141, 328, 378*
burial, *169–70, 352, 354*
Butler, Bishop Joseph, *331*

Caecilian, Bishop of Carthage, *292*
Caedmon, *377*
Calvin, John, *225–6, 322–3, 361–2*
Camara, Archbishop Helder, *242*
Campion, Edmund, *201*
canon, *388*
canonization, *196–7, 202, 203–4*
Carey, Archbishop George, *207*
Carey, William, *226–7*
Carthusians, *310*
Cassian, John, *296*
catacombs, *352*
Catechism of the Catholic Church, *80–1, 102, 138, 147, 162, 273*
catechumenate, 137
cathedrals, *359–60, 364, 365*
celibacy, *221–2, 256–7, 305*
Celtic missionaries, *301–3, 355*
Chadwick, Owen, *109, 261, 297, 336*
charismatic movement, *213, 251–2*

charismatic worship, *232–3*
Charlemagne, Emperor, *303–4, 306*
Charles V, Emperor, *320*
Chartres Cathedral, *359*
Chaucer, Geoffrey, *378*
Chavasse, Bishop F.J. *152*
child abuse, *269*
child poverty, *343*
China, churches, *218–19, 262*
Christians in Science, *175*
Christian Socialism, *339–40*
Christian Union, *253*
Christmas, *130*
Chrismation, *148*
church attendance, *229–30, 231, 266*
church
 birth of, *283–7*
 as community of hope, *346–7*
churches, *212–36*
 art and architecture, *351–66*
 decoration of, *357–8*
 disharmony in, *234–5*
 shifting centre of gravity, *233–4*
church membership, *213, 341, 345*
Church of England, *126, 127, 227–30*
 creation of, *324–5*
Church of South India, *239*
Church of the Holy Wisdom, Constantinople, *354*
Church of the Sepulchre, Jerusalem, *353–4*
church 'planting', *230*

church statistics, 214–16
circumcision, 285–6
Cistercians, 310, 361
civil rights movement, 267, 268
Clapham Sect, 333–4, 339
Clark, Lord Kenneth, 111, 263–4
Clitherow, Margaret, 201
Cockshut, A.O.J., 338
Columba, Saint, 301–2
Communion of Saints, 197
Conciliar Movement, 309
Conference on Politics,
    Economics and Citizenship
    (1924), 340
confession, prayers of, 121–2, 123
    see also reconciliation
confirmation, 147–8
Constantine, Emperor, 260, 291,
    292, 293, 295, 304, 352, 354
consubstantiation, 145–6
Contarini, Cardinal, 326
contemplation, 123–5
contraception, 273
conversion, 102–6, 285–6
    see also reconciliation
corruption, 308–9, 315
Council of Chalcedon (451),
    293–4
Council of Constantinople
    (381), 293–4
Council of Nicaea (325), 293–4
Council of Trent (1551), 145, 222,
    326–7, 373
Counter-Reformation, 325–7
Coverdale, Miles, 370
Cowper, William, 371
Cranmer, Thomas, 200, 227, 325,
    378

Creation, 177–8, 180, 184–6
Creationism, 244
creed, 388
cremation, 169–70
Cromwell, Thomas, 325
cross, 355, 358
    focus on, 31
crucifixion
    and atonement, 37–8
    and Christian martyrs, 29–30
    final week, 26–8
    power of, 40–1
    and salvation, 31–7
    through the centuries, 38–9
crusades, 308–9
culture
    and Christianity, 290–1
    and worship, 126–9
Cupitt, Don, 249
Cyprian, Bishop of
    Carthage, 294–5
Cyril, Saint, 304

daily life
    early Christianity, 290–1
    experience of God in, 112–13
    Middle Ages, 307–8
Daniel, Walter, 311
Dante, 158
Darling, Lord, 46
Darwin, Charles, 177–8, 336
Davie, Grace, 347
Dawkins, Richard, 179
Dead Sea Scrolls, 83, 88–90
death, 155–6
    and afterlife, 157–69
    end of, 57–8
    funeral rites, 169–70

Deism, *331*
Descartes, René, *330*
Devotio Moderna
movement, *318*
Diet of Worms (1521), *320*
disciples, *283–4*
belief in resurrection, *52–4*
suffering of, *50–2*
discipleship
demands of, *33–4*
experience of God
through, *113–14*
dissent, *267–8*
Divine Will, alignment with,
118–20
divinity of Jesus, *16–20, 292–4*
doctrine, *292–4*
Dodd, C.H., *18*
Doe, Bishop Michael, *228, 241*
Dominical Sacraments, *147,
149–50*
Dominic, Saint, *312*
Donation of Constantine, *304*
Donne, John, *164, 378, 379*
Drabble, Margaret, *379*
Duffy, Eamon, *309, 317–18*
Dunn, James, *48, 53–4*
Dyson, Freeman, *185*

Easter, *50, 131–2, 164*
Eastern Church *see* Orthodox
Church
Eastern Europe, churches
in, *267–8*
Eastern Orthodoxy, *306–7*
ecumenical movement, *225,
237–9, 338*
Edict of Milan (313), *291, 300*

Edict of Nantes (1598), *327*
Edwards, David L., *21, 105*
Edwards, Jonathan, *159, 333*
Einstein, Albert, *24, 182, 187, 188*
Elizabeth I, Queen, *151, 325*
Elizabethan Settlement
(1559), *325*
Elizabeth (Queen Mother), *64*
Elton, G.R., *326*
Emerson, Ralph Waldo, *4*
Emmett, Michael, *250*
England
Evangelization, *301–4*
Reformation, *324–5*
religious toleration, *328*
English Book of Common
Prayer, *227*
Enlightenment, *330*
challenges of, *336–7*
and the Church, *331–4*
Epiphany, *130–1*
Episcopalian Church *see* Anglican
Church
Epistles, *72–4*
Erasmus, Desiderius, *314, 322,
373*
escapism, worship as, *128–9*
eternal life, *71, 388*
ethical dilemmas, *186–8*
Eucharist, *143, 294–5, 322*
euthanasia, *274–5*
Evagrius, *296*
Evangelical Alliance, *238*
Evangelical Revival, *332–4*
Evangelicals, *228–9, 244–5*
evangelism, *388*
Evangelists, *287*
Evangelization, *245–9, 300–4*

Evans, C.F., *57*
Evans, Gillian, *167–8*
evolution, *177–8, 336*
evil, *160*
excommunication, *239*
exile, *67–8*
Exodus, *65, 138*
extemporary prayer, *123–5*

faith, *206–7*
    and facts, *182*
    literature of, *377–9*
Faith in the City (1985), *340–1*
Faraday, Michael, *175*
feminist theology, *242*
First Vatican Council (1869–70),
  222, 335
Ford, David, *73, 88*
forgiveness *see* reconciliation
Fox, George, *232*
Francis of Assisi, Saint, *312*
Fraser, Giles, *206*
Fresh Expressions, *247*
Freud, Sigmund, *178–9*
Fry, Elizabeth, *263, 264*
Fuller, Michael, *182*
fundamentalism, *243–5, 279*
funeral rites, *169–70*

Galileo, *177*
Gallego, Ruben, *210*
Gandhi, Mahatma, *23*
garden tomb, Jerusalem, *355*
gender and language, *253–5*
Geneva Bible, *97*
Gentiles, preaching to, *286–7*
George, Saint, *197–8*
Gilbertines, *310*

Glorious Revolution (1688), *328*
glossary, *388–92*
Gnosticism, *288–9*
God
    and the Bible, *101–2*
    in daily life, *112–13*
    experience of, *101–16*
    the Father, *118*
    grace of, *157–8*
    and Jesus Christ, *15, 36–7*
    love of, *32*
    as mother, *253–4*
    sons and daughters or, *254–5*
Good Friday, *131*
Good Samaritan, *10–11, 71*
gospel, *388–9*
    future of, *344–5*
    witness to, *383–7*
Gospels, *69–72, 287*
    criteria for inclusion in, *81–3*
Gothic architecture, *335,*
  359–60, 363
Graham, Dr Billy, *246*
Graham, Elaine, *266*
Great War, *337*
Gregory I, Pope, *300–1*
Gregory VII, Pope, *305, 308*
grief, *157*
Gryn, Rabbi Hugo, *37*
guidance, *106–8*
guilt, *205*
Guinness, Alec, *104–5*
Gutenberg Bible, *97*

Habitat for Humanity, *264*
Hadrian, *306*
hallucination theory,
  resurrection, *52–3*

Handel, F.G., *374*
Harding, Stephen, *310*
Hardy, Alister, *111*
Harries, Bishop Richard, *40, 381*
Hawking, Stephen, *180*
Hay, David, *111*
heaven, *163–5, 166–9*
Hebrew Scriptures *see* Old Testament
Heidegger, Martin, *156*
hell, *158–60*
 Jesus' descent into, *161*
Henry IV, Emperor, *305*
Henry VIII, King, *201, 310–11, 324–5*
Herbert, George, *378*
heresy, *217, 288–9*
Hick, John, *278*
Hilda of Whitby, Saint, *302*
Hildebrand, *305*
Hinnom, Valley of, *158, 159*
Hitler, Adolf, *260*
HIV/AIDS, *386*
Hobbes, Thomas, *156*
Hodgson, Peter, *174*
Holgate, Archbishop, *373*
Holocaust, *261*
Holy Communion, *31, 141–7, 151–2*
Holy Days, *129–33*
Holy Island, *357*
Holy Spirit, *118, 332, 389*
Holy Trinity, *18, 71–2, 114–15, 118, 126–7, 140, 161, 391*
Holy Week, *26, 131*
homosexuality, *157*
Hooker, Richard, *325*
hope, *207–8, 346–7*

Hospice Movement, *265*
hospices, *291, 297*
Houghton, Sir John, *176, 245*
House Churches, *252*
Huguenots, *327*
human involvement, sacred books, *80–1*
Humanism, *321–3*
humanity of Jesus, *16–20, 292–4*
Hume, Cardinal Basil, *112–13, 165*
Hume, David, *331, 334*
humility, *182–4*
Hus, John, *332*
hymns, *367–72*

icons, *357–8, 361*
Ignatius of Antioch, *294*
Immaculate Conception, *199*
immersion, *140*
Incarnation, *20–1, 41, 71–2, 331, 381, 389*
India, churches, *218–19, 239*
Independent Churches, *233, 235*
 membership, *213*
Industrial Revolution, *339–40*
intellectual challenges, *331–4*
intellectual developments, *312–14*
intercession, prayers of, *122*
inter-faith dialogue, *19, 146, 234–5*
 see also ecumenical movement
International Anglican-Roman Catholic Commission for Unity and Mission (IARCCUM), *146*
Isaac, *94*
Isaiah, *101*

Islam, *17, 81, 279, 299–300, 306*
    crusades against, *308–9*
Islamic fundamentalism, *243*

James, Saint, *194, 287*
Japan, churches, *218–19*
Jardine, Lisa, *187*
Jeeves, Malcolm, *181*
Jeffery, Jon, *95*
Jesuits, *326*
Jesus Christ
    authority of, *13–16*
    baptism of, *6, 136–7*
    Christian view of, *21–4*
    continuing presence of,
      55–6, 58–9
    descent into hell, *161*
    divinity and humanity of,
      16–20, 292–4
    early non-Christian
      references to, *22–4*
    as high priest, *35, 352, 389*
    image of, *20–1*
    impact of, *3–4*
    life of, *4–6*
    as Lord, *54–5*
    as mediator, *30–1*
    as Son of Man, *35, 36, 72,*
      118, 194, 391
    teaching of, *6–13*
    testimony to, *12–13*
    and women, *255–6*
    see also crucifixion;
      resurrection
Jews
    conquest and exile, *65–7*
    and monotheism, *17–18, 54–5*
    judgement and Exodus, *65*

Joad, C.E.M., *180*
John, Gospel of, *71, 82*
John Paul II, Pope, *223, 246*
John, Saint, *285*
John the Baptist, *6, 69, 136–7*
John, XIII, Pope, *222–3, 239*
Johnson, Samuel, *378*
Josephus, *23*
Judaism, *246, 283–7, 351–2*
Judas, Gospel of, *82*
judgement, *157*
    and exile, *65–7*
    and Exodus, *65*
Julian, Emperor, *210, 260*
Julius II, Pope, *309*
Jung, Carl Gustav, *179*
Jursa, Michael, *90*

Keble, John, *335*
Khouds, *119*
King James Bible, *97*
King, Martin Luther, *204*
Kingdom of God, *8–13*
King, Martin Luther, *267, 268*
Kingsley, Charles, *263, 340*
Kitson Clark, G., *41*
Kolbe, Maximilian, *202, 203*
Korea, churches, *218–19, 262*
Kozyrev, Valentin, *210*
Kraemer, Hendrik, *277*
Küng, Hans, *3–4, 21, 87, 255, 307,*
  308

laity, *252–3*
    communal element, *318*
Lambeth Conference, *228, 257*
lamentation, prayers of,
    122–3

language, *79–80, 96–7*
    and gender, *253–5*
Lapide, Rabbi Pinchas, *46–7, 56*
Last Supper, *15, 27, 67–8, 141–2, 143, 166, 260, 367*
Law, Cardinal Bernard, *269*
Law, William (1686–1761), *39*
Lazarus, raising of, *71*
Lent, *131*
Leo I, Pope, *295*
Leo III, Pope, *303, 306*
Leo XIII, Pope, *340*
Lewis, C.S., *113–14, 162–3, 165, 182*
Liberal theology, *228–9*
liberation theology, *240–2*
Lindisfarne Gospels, 302, 357
literature, *377–81*
liturgy, *389*
Locke, John, *331*
Lomu, Jonah, *385*
Longley, Clifford, *185*
Lord's Prayer, *118, 120, 122*
Louis, King, *327*
Lourdes, *356*
love, *208–10*
Loyola, Ignatius, *326*
Luke, Gospel of, *71, 74–5, 78, 82*
Luther, Martin, *67, 145–6, 225, 319–21, 324, 370*
Lutheran Churches, *144, 149, 224, 225*
Luwum, Archbishop Janani, *203*

MacCulloch, Diarmaid, *3, 341*
McGrath, Alister, *82, 166*
Machovec, Milan, *23*
McLeod, George, *33–4*
McMahon, Dorothy, *255*

McManners, John, *153*
Macmurray, John, *173*
Magnusson, Magnus, *89*
Maitland, Sara, *188*
Mandela, Nelson, *265, 268*
Manning, Henry Edward, *335*
Mark, Gospel of, *69–70, 82*
marriage sacrament, *148*
Marshall, Howard, *62*
Martin, David, *133, 234, 242*
Martin of Tours, *301*
martyrs, *29–30*
    early, *194–5*
    Reformation, *200–1*
    veneration of, *195–6*
Marxism, *239, 241, 242, 261–2, 267–8*
Mary Magdalene, *44–5*
Mary, Mother of Jesus, *198–200*
Mass, *143–4*
Matthew, Gospel of, *70, 82*
Maundy Thursday, *131*
Maurice, F.D. *339–40*
mausoleums, *354*
Mayr-Harting, Henry, *303*
mediation, *30–1, 123–5*
medical science, *186*
Melanchthon, Philipp, *326*
Mendel, Gregor, *175*
Merbecke, John, *374*
Merton, Thomas, *128–9, 342–3*
Methodist Church, *127, 230–1, 332–3, 334, 371*
Methodius, Saint, *304*
Middle Ages, *299–312*
Millard, Alan, *89*
Millennium Development
    Goals, *344*

Milton, John, *378*
Mingguxan, Pastor Zhang, *219*
ministry
    ordination of, *148–9*
    structure of, *294–5*
miracles, *9, 71*
mission, *246–7, 277, 389*
missionaries, *218, 226–7, 234, 264–5, 268, 277*
    Middle Ages, *300–4*
missionary movement, expansion of, *337–8*
Mitchell, Basil, *263*
modern architecture, *363–4*
modern lives, *342–5, 383–7*
    Bible in, *61–3*
modern movements, *237–58*
Moltmann, Jürgan, *36*
monasteries, *357*
monasticism, *221, 225, 304, 310–11, 361*
    birth of, *295–6*
    decline in, *318*
    dissolving of, *325*
monotheism, *17–18, 19, 41, 54–5, 94, 390*
Montanus, *289*
Montefiore, Hugh, *104*
More, Sir Thomas, *169, 324*
Mormons, *81*
Morris, Colin, *34–5, 308*
Moses, *65, 101*
mosques, *354*
Moss, Veronica, *386*
Mother Julian of Norwich, *110, 207, 313*
Mother Teresa of Calcutta, *202, 204*

Moule, C.F.D., *57*
M'Pherson, P.K.M., *41*
Muhammad, *299–300*
multicultural society, *276–9*
Münzer, Thomas, *324*
Murray, Euan, *385*
music, *367–77*
    in local churches, *375–7*
    versus words, *373–5*
mysterion, *136*
Mystery Plays, *377*
mysticism, *109–11*
myths, *64, 390*

Nativity Plays, *377*
natural world, *337*
'nature religions', *163–4*
Nazism, *261*
Neal, John Mason, *370*
near death experiences, *170*
Neill, Stephen, *203*
neo-classical architecture, *363*
Nero, Emperor, *194–5*
New Age, *342, 390*
New Testament
    Acts of the Apostles, *74–5*
    Book of Revelation, *75–6*
    Gospels, *69–72, 81–3*
    Letters, *72–4*
Newman, Cardinal, *169*
Newton, Isaac (1642–1727), *175*
Newton, John, *371*
Newman, John Henry, *335*
Nicene Creed, *16–17, 212, 293, 306–7*
Nicodemus, Gospel of, *82*
Niemöller, Martin, *61–2, 261*
Night Stop, *344*

Niles, D.T., *248*
Nine Lessons and Carols, *377*
Ninety-five Theses, *319–20*
Noah, *65*
non-Christian faiths, *19*
  Christianity's relations
    with, *19*
non-governmental
  organisations, *264–6, 344*
Northern Ireland, troubles
  in, *269*
novelists, *379–80*

Obama, Barack, *207*
Olave, Saint, *197*
Old Testament, *63–8*
One God, belief in, *54–5, 114–15*
open air religious sites, *351, 355–6*
Order of the Knights
  Templar, *354*
ordination, *148–9*
  of women, *228, 255*
Oriental Orthodoxy, *217*
Origin of the Species (Darwin),
  177–8
ornamentation, reaction
  against, *361–2*
Orthodox Churches
  Church buildings, *354*
  membership, *213*
  sacraments, *140, 147, 148*
  separation from Catholic
    Church, *220, 306–7*
Our Lady of the Angels, Los
  Angeles, *364*
Oxford Movement, *229, 335, 375*

Pachomius, *296*
Palm Sunday, *27*

papacy, *220, 222–3, 304–5, 308–9*
papal infallibility, *222, 335*
parables, *9–13*
Paradise Lost (Milton), *378*
parish churches, music in, *375–7*
Pascal, Blaise (1623–1662), *110*
Passover, *27, 65, 141*
Pasteur, Louis, *188*
Patrick, Saint, *301*
Paul II, Pope, *202*
Paul IV, Pope, *327*
Paul, Epistles of, *73–4, 82*
Paulinus, Bishop, *58*
Paul, Saint, *40–1, 54, 74, 102, 106,
  219, 285–7, 383*
Peace of Westphalia (1648),
  327
Peacocke, Arthur, *167*
penance *see* reconciliation
Pentecost, *50, 74, 132, 284*
Pentecostal Church, *139, 140–1,
  231–2*
  membership, *213, 234*
persecution
  early church, *285–6, 291–2*
  and power, *260–2*
Peter, Gospel of, *82*
Peter, Saint, *219, 284, 285, 287*
petition, prayers of, *122, 123*
Philip, Saint, *285*
Pietistic movement, *332–3*
pilgrimage, *355–6*
Pilgrim Fathers, *325*
Pilgrim's Progress (Bunyan),
  378
Pio, Saint, *356*
Pius IX, Pope, *334, 335*
Pius XII, Pope, *261*
places of worship, *351–66*

Planck, Max, 187
Pliny the Younger, 22, 370
pluralism, 278–9
politics and religion, 239–42
Polkinghorne, John, 31, 56, 183, 185
Polycarp of Smyrna, Bishop, 195, 196
polytheism, 390
post-modernism, 342, 390
poverty, 240–2, 343–4
praise, prayers of, 120
prayer, 108–9, 117–25
    aspects of, 120–3
    experience of God
      through, 108–9
    place and posture of, 123
    significance of, 125–9
    through saints, 197–8
Presbyterian Church, 126, 224, 225–6
Pridmore, John, 70
priesthood and celibacy, 221–2, 256–7, 305
Priestland, Gerald, 109
Prodigal Son, 10–11, 71
protection, 108–9
Protestant Church, 139, 146, 162, 199, 223–5
    membership, 213
Psalms, 368, 370–1
purgatory, 161–3
Puritans, 325
Pusey, E.B., 335

Quakers, 126, 127, 150, 231–2

radicalism, 323–4
Rahner, Karl, 278

Ramsey, Archbishop Michael, 20, 129
ransom, 35
Rationalists, 323–4
Ratushinskaya, Irina, 108–9
reassurance, 108–9
reconciliation, 35
redemption, 165
Redhead, Brian, 62
reductionism, 180–1
Rees-Mogg, Lord, 210
Reformation, 223–4, 317–29, 361–2
    Catholic response to, 325–7
Reformation martyrs, 20–1
Reformers, 145–6
reincarnation, 167
relics, 195–6
religion
    exclusive approach, 277
    inclusive approach, 278
    pluralist approach, 278–9
religious leader, Jesus as, 49–50
religious movements, 314, 237–58
Renaissance, 313–14
repentance, 160
Requiem Mass, 170
Rerum Novarum, 340
resurrection, 163
    centrality of, 45–6
    evidence for, 46–57
    implications of, 57–9
    of the body, 168–9
    transforming power of, 56–7
revelation, 115
Rieu, E.V., 72
Rievaulx Abbey, 310
Robinson, Bishop John, 15, 53, 86, 87

Robinson, Jason, 384–5
Roman Catholic Cathedral,
    Liverpool, 364
Roman Catholic Church
        and child abuse, 269
        and Counter-Reformation,
        325–7
        and ecumenical
        movement, 239
        English split with, 324–5
        and liberal theology, 241
        Mass, 143–4
        membership, 213
        and Nazism, 261
        papacy, 220, 222–3, 304–5,
        308–9
        priesthood, 148–9
        reform of, 305
        revival in Europe, 334–5
        saint-making, 202–4
        and sexual issues, 221–2,
        256–7, 272–3
Roman Empire
        Church under, 291–2
        collapse of, 295, 296–7
Romanesque architecture, 359
Romanticism, 334
Romero, Archbishop Oscar, 203,
    241
Rossetti, Christina, 39
Rousseau, Jean-Jacques, 334
Royal Society, 174
Ruether, Rosemary Radford, 242
Russian Orthodox Church, 152,
    218, 235, 238–9, 261–2

Sabbath, 14
Sacks, Rabbi Jonathan, 276

Sacraments, 125, 135–54
Sagrada Familia, Barcelona, 364
Saint Paul's Cathedral, 365
saints
        early, 196–8
        Mary as, 198–200
        Modern, 202–4
        praying through, 197–8
sacrificial system, 35, 94, 158
Salisbury Cathedral, 359
Salvation Army, 150, 231–2, 339
salvation, 205–6, 391
        and the Bible, 35–7
        and crucifixion, 31–4
        and Lutherans, 319–21
Samaritans, 264
Sanders, E.P., 23
Sarah, Sister, 384
Saunders, Dame Cicely, 15
Schillebeeckx, Edward, 146, 162
schisms, 220, 289, 292, 306–7,
    309, 319–27
schools, 266, 311
Schweitzer, Albert, 58–9
science
        challenges of the
        Enlightenment, 336–7
        conflict with Christianity,
        176–82
        ethical dilemmas, 186–8,
        274–5
        and humility, 182–4
        and intelligent design, 184–5
        origins of, 173–6
scrolls, 79, 88–90
Sea of Faith movement, 249–50
Second Vatican Council (1962–5),
    144, 149, 220–1, 222, 239, 345, 376

secular society, *342, 347*
    church role in, *271*
Sermon on the Mount, *7–8, 14, 70*
sexuality, *255–7*
Shackleton, Ernest, *106*
Shaftesbury, Lord, *263–4, 333–4*
Shelter, *264*
Sheppard, Bishop David, *147*
shrines, *195–6, 355–6*
Shrove Tuesday, *131*
signs, *153*
Sikhism, *17*
Simeon, Charles, *333–4*
simony, *305*
sin, *32, 157–8, 204–6*
    confession of, *121*
    and God's grace, *157–8*
    and hell, *158–60*
    and redemption, *165*
Sixtus IV, Pope, *309*
slavery, *339*
Smart, Ninian, *67*
social problems, *342–5*
social reformers, *263–7*
society and church, *259–80,
339–41*
    current issues, *270–5*
    failure of church, *268–9*
Society for Ordained
Scientists, *175*
Society of Friends *see* Quakers
Society of Jesus *see* Jesuits
Solzhenitsyn, Alexander, *108, 111,
218*
South Africa, churches in, *268*
South America, liberation
theology, *240–2*
Southern, R.W., *310, 312*

Specola Vaticana, *172*
Spe Salvi (Benedict XVI), *155*
spiritualism, *167*
spirituals, *372*
Spurgeon, C.H., *336*
Stephen, Saint, *157, 194, 285–6*
Stott, John, *40, 245, 346*
street pastors, *267, 344*
Studdert Kennedy, G.A., *39–40*
Suenens, Cardinal, *252*
suffering, *36–7*
Swift, Jonathan, *378*
'swoon theory', *51–2*
symbols, *153*
symbolism, *364*
synagogue, *391*
Synod of Whitby, *302*
Synoptic Gospels, *69, 389*

tabernacle, *35, 92, 391*
Tacitus, *22*
Taizé, *355*
TALMUD, *23*
Taylor, Bishop Humphrey, *128*
teachings of Jesus, *6–16*
Temple, *35, 92, 391*
Temple, Archbishop William, *107,
340*
Temple, Jerusalem, *14, 32, 351*
Tertullian, *194, 289*
thanksgiving prayers, *120–1, 123*
Theodore, Saint, *306*
Thirty Nine Articles, *227*
Thomas à Kempis, *318*
Thomas, Infancy Gospel of, *82–3*
tomb veneration, *48–9*
Toynbee, Arnold, *188*
Tractarian Movement, *335*

translation, Bible, *96–7, 303–4,*
378
trans-signification, *146*
transubstantiation, *144–7*
Trinity *see* Holy Trinity
Trinity Sunday, *132*
Tuigemala, Va'aiga, *385*
Tutu, Archbishop Desmond,
10–11, 242, 268
Tyndale Bible, *97*
Tyndale, William, *200–1, 378*

Uganda, martyrdom, *203*
Ultramontanism, *335*
uncertainty, *345*
Unitarianism, *332*
universe, design of, *184–6*
universities, *311, 312*
Urban II, Pope, *308*
US, religious culture, *341*

Vanier, Jean, *33*
Varah, Chad, *264*
Vaughan Williams, Ralph, *372*
Vermes, Geza, *24, 56, 89*
vestments, *357*
Vikings, *299–300, 304*
Virgin Birth, *5, 199, 392*
virtues, *206–10*
Voltaire, *331*
Vulgate, *97, 136, 322*

Wallis, Jim, *245*
war, challenges of, *337*
wars of religion, *327–8*
water, significance of, *137–8*
Watson, Richard, *332*
Watts, Isaac, *370–1*
Webb, Pauline, *256*

Weisskopf, Vicky, *183*
Wells, H.G., *24*
Wesley, Charles, *231, 371*
Wesley, John, *110–11, 231, 332–3,*
371, 373
Whitefield, George, *39, 333, 334*
Whitsun *see* Pentecost
Wilberforce, William, *263–4,*
333–4, 339
Williams, Archbishop Rowan, *61,*
161, 247, 257, 275, 279
Williams, Harry, *387*
wish-fulfilment, *179, 392*
withdrawal, *128–9*
Wolfendale, Arnold, *175*
women
and Jesus, *255–6*
ordination of, *228, 255*
words versus music, *373–5*
Wordsworth, William, *334*
World Council of Churches, *146,*
215, 238–9, 340
Worlock, Archbishop Derek, *164*
worship
focal points for, *356–7, 362*
places of, *351–66*
significance of, *125–9*
Worsley, Malcolm, *103, 106*
Wren, Christopher, *362*
Wycliffe, John, *373*

Yadin, Yigael, *89*
York Minster, *359, 360, 365*
Young, Frances, *107–8*
Young Men's Christian
Association (YMCA), *385*
Young Simpson, James, *175*

Zinzendorf, Count, *332*

Credits

Notes

Notes

Notes